# THE ECONOMICS OF THE EUROPEAN UNION

## Policy and Analysis

Edited by

MIKE ARTIS AND NORMAN LEE

OXFORD UNIVERSITY PRESS

Oxford University Press, Walton Street, Oxford OX2 6DP

Oxford New York

Athens Auckland Bangkok Bombay
Calcutta Cape Town Dar es Salaam Delhi
Florence Hong Kong Istanbul Karachi
Kuala Lumpur Madras Madrid Melbourne
Mexico City Nairobi Paris Singapore
Taipei Tokyo Toronto
and associated companies in
Berlin Ibadan

Oxford is a trade mark of Oxford University Press

Published in the United States
by Oxford University Press Inc., New York

First published in 1994
Hardback and paperback editions reprinted 1995

British Library Cataloguing in Publication Data
Data available

Library of Congress Cataloging in Publication Data  .
The economics of the European union: policy and analysis/edited by
Mike Artis and Norman Lee.
Includes bibliographical references.
1. European Economic Community.  2. European Economioc Community
countries—Economic policy.  I. Artis, Michael J.  II. Lee, Norman.
1936–
HC241.2.E297  1994  94–19773
337.1'42dc20
ISBN 0–19–877372–2
ISBN 0–19–877373–0 (Pbk)

Printed in Great Britain
on acid-free paper by
Biddles Ltd., Guildford and Kings Lynn

# CONTENTS

# ABBREVIATIONS

| | |
|---|---|
| AASM | Association of African States and Madagascar |
| ACP | African, Caribbean, and Pacific |
| ACARD | Advisory Council for Applied Research and Development |
| ACOST | Advisory Council on Science and Technology |
| AMS | Aggregate measure of support |
| BMFT | Federal Ministry for Research and Technology (Germany) |
| BTG | British Technology Group |
| CAP | Common Agricultural Policy |
| CCIR | International Radio Consultative Committee |
| CEC | Commission of the European Communities |
| CEEC | Central and East European Country |
| CEPR | Centre for Economic Policy Research |
| CET | common external tariff |
| CFSP | Common Foreign and Security Policy |
| CI | Community Initiative |
| c.i.f. | cost insurance, and freight |
| CMEA | Council for Mutual Economic Assistance |
| CQS | Community Quota System |
| CREST | Scientific and Technical Research Committee |
| CSF | Community Support Framework |
| CTP | Common Transport Policy |
| DAC | Development Assistance Committee |
| DFG | German Research Association |
| DG | Directorate-general |
| DoT | Department of Transport |
| DRS | domestic rate of substitution |
| DRT | domestic rate of transformation |
| EAGGF | European Agricultural Guidance and Guarantee Fund |
| EC | European Community |
| ECB | European Central Bank |
| ECE | Economic Commission for Europe |
| ECJ | European Court of Justice |

| | |
|---|---|
| ECSC | European Coal and Steel Community |
| Ecofin | Council of Economics and Finance Ministers |
| Ecu | European Currency Unit |
| EDC | European Defence Community |
| EDF | European Development Fund |
| EEA | European Economic Area |
| EEC | European Economic Community |
| EFTA | European Free Trade Association |
| EIB | European Investment Bank |
| ELDO | European Launcher Development Organization |
| EMCF | European Monetary Co-operation Fund |
| EMI | European Monetary Institute |
| EMS | European Monetary System |
| EMU | European Monetary Union |
| EP | European Parliament |
| EPO | European Patent Office |
| EPU | European Payments Union |
| ERDF | European Regional Development Fund |
| ERP | European Recovery Programme |
| ESCB | European System of Central Banks |
| ESF | European Social Fund |
| ESPRIT | European Strategic Programme for Research and Development in Information Technology |
| ESRO | European Space Research Organization |
| ESA | European Space Agency |
| ETUC | European Trade Union Confederation |
| EU | European Union |
| Euratom | European Atomic Energy Community |
| EUREKA | European Research Co-ordination Agency |
| FAST | Forecasting and Assessment Science and Technology Programme |
| f.o.b. | free on board |
| FRT | Foreign Rate of Transformation |
| FTA | free trade area |
| GATT | General Agreement on Tariffs and Trade |
| GDP | Gross Domestic Product |

| | |
|---|---|
| GNP | Gross National Product |
| GSP | Generalized System of Preferences |
| HDTV | high-definition television |
| IATA | International Air Transport Association |
| ICP | International Comparison Project |
| IGC | intergovernmental conference |
| IICA | inter-institutional collaborative agreements |
| IMF | International Monetary Fund |
| IPRs | Intellectual Property Rights |
| IT | information technology |
| JHA | Justice and Home Affairs |
| JIT | just-in-time |
| JRC | Joint Research Centre |
| JRNC | Joint Nuclear Research Centre |
| LAC | long run average cost |
| LTA | Long Term Arrangement |
| MCA | Monetary Compensatory Amount |
| MDS | Maximum Divergence Spread |
| METS | minimum efficient technical scale |
| MFA | Multi-Fibre Arrangement |
| m.f.n. | most favoured nation |
| MIP | minimum import price |
| MITI | Ministry of International Trade and Industry, Japan |
| MMC | Monopolies and Mergers Commission |
| MPTC | marginal pollution treatment cost |
| MRD | marginal reduction in damage |
| MSC | marginal social cost |
| NAFTA | North American Free Trade Agreement |
| NGO | non-governmental organization |
| NATO | North American Treaty Organization |
| NRDC | National Research Development Corporation |
| NSI | National Systems of Innovation |
| NTB | non-tariff barrier |
| OCTS | Overseas Countries and Territories |
| ODA | Official Development Assistance |

| | |
|---|---|
| OECD | Organization for Economic Co-operation and Development |
| OEEC | Organization for European Economic Co-operation |
| OFT | Office of Fair Trading |
| OP | Operational Programme |
| OPT | outward processing traffic |
| PAC | Pollution Abatement and Control |
| PEG | Production Entitlement Guarantee |
| PPP | purchasing power parity |
| PPS | Purchasing Power Standards |
| PSE | Producer Subsidy Equivalent |
| R&D | research and development |
| SDI | Strategic Defense Initiative |
| SEA | Single European Act |
| SEM | Single European Market |
| SMU | Support Measurement Unit |
| Stabex | System for the Stabilization of Export Earnings |
| Sysmin | System for safeguarding and developing mineral production |
| TEU | Treaty on European Union |
| TIP | Technology Integration Projects |
| UNDP | United Nations Development Programme |
| UNICE | Union of the Industries of the European Community |
| VER | Voluntary Export Restraint |
| VHSIC | Very High Speed Integrated Circuits |
| VIL | variable import levy |
| VSTF | Very Short Term Financing |

# LIST OF CONTRIBUTORS

HARVEY ARMSTRONG   Senior Lecturer in Economics Lancaster University

MIKE ARTIS   Professor of Economics University of Manchester

ROBIN BLADEN-HOVELL   Senior Lecturer in Economics University of Manchester

SIMON BULMER   Reader in Government University of Manchester

DAVID COLMAN   Professor in Agricultural Economics University of Manchester

PAT DEVINE   Senior Lecturer in Economics University of Manchester

NORMAN LEE   Senior Lecturer in Economics University of Manchester

STAN METCALFE   Professor of Economics University of Manchester

LYNDEN MOORE   Lecturer in Economics University of Manchester

FREDERICK NIXSON   Reader in Economics University of Manchester

DAVID PURDY   Lecturer in Economics University of Manchester

DEBORAH ROBERTS   Lecturer in Agricultural Economics University of Manchester

PAULO SAVIOTTI   Lecturer in Economics University of Manchester

PETER STUBBS   Professor of Economics University of Manchester

ELIZABETH SYMONS   Lecturer in Economics University of Keele

JIM TAYLOR   Professor of Economics University of Lancaster

NICK WEAVER   Research Assistant in Economics University of Manchester

ALLAN WILLIAMS   Senior Lecturer in Geography University of Exeter

DAVID YOUNG   Lecturer in Economics University of Manchester

# Introduction

MIKE ARTIS AND NORMAN LEE

The momentum towards 'ever closer union' in Europe—despite the set-backs associated with the upheavals in the currency markets in 1992 and 1993—has been little short of impressive. The development of the EC6 to the EC12, the adoption of the 1992 Single European Market programme, and the inauguration of the European Union (EU) in November 1993 are markers of that progress. As the economic significance and scope of policies decided at the level of the EU have increased and as the integration of the economies of the EU members has proceeded, so the need for sustained study of the development and impact of those policies has grown.

The basic aim of the book is to provide, for the intermediate-level student of economics, a comprehensive account of the economics of the EU. It contains a blend of theory, analysis, and application relating both to the EU as a whole and to a number of its constituent Member States. It is, therefore, intended to be of relevance and interest to university students in other continental countries as well as to those in the United Kingdom.

The political context of the subject under study is of great importance to its economic understanding and for this reason the first chapter in the book is devoted to a political analysis and history of the EU. Chapter 2 contains key statistical information relating to the economies of the EU and its Member States, together with comparative data for Japan and the United States to provide the broader economic context. The theory of customs unions and preferential trading areas—which is essential to the economic analysis of the European experiment—is set out in Chapter 3. This chapter not only covers classical theory but also takes a critical look at some more recent developments, notably the imperfect competition-based approach used by the Commission to evaluate the benefits of the Single Market programme.

Chapter 4 deals with the best-known and, in terms of money spent, much the largest economic policy area of the EU: the Common Agricultural Policy (CAP). It evaluates each of the main agricultural policy instruments which has been used, the need for reform, and the future prospects for the CAP. Competition policy within the EU is reviewed in Chapter 5. It commences by examining the rationale for competition, then analyses the competition policies applied in three Member States, (the United

Kingdom, Germany, and France) and, finally, reviews the development of a Union-level competition policy.

Chapter 6 contains an analysis of science and technology policy within the EU. First, it examines the case for government support of science and technology, then it considers national policies for science and technology in Germany, France, and the United Kingdom, and, finally, it describes and evaluates the development of a Science and Technology Policy within the EU.

Regional Policy is the subject-matter of Chapter 7. It analyses the regional economic disparities within the EU, the case for regional policy at national and Community levels, the policies pursued in different Member States (Netherlands, Germany, the United Kingdom, France, Italy, and Spain), and the operation of Union-level regional policies.

Chapter 8 deals with the Common Transport Policy (CTP). It examines the structure and growth of the Union and Member State transport sectors, the development of the CTP and its application to the major constituents of the transport sector (road transport, rail and inland waterways, maritime and air transport, and transport infrastructure) and concludes with an overall policy evaluation.

The environmental policy of the EU is reviewed in Chapter 9. It covers the evolution of a Union environmental policy, the economic character of the EU's environmental problems, to which it has to respond, the role of economic and regulatory instruments in dealing with these problems, and possible future developments in policy.

Chapter 10 is concerned with the role of social policy within the EU. To this end a typology of social-policy regimes is presented and explained (traditional–rudimentary, liberal–individualist, conservative–corporatist, and social democratic), which is then used to explain the development of EU social policy and the forces which have constrained its scope.

The commercial policies of the EU *vis-a-vis* third countries are studied in Chapter 11. The analysis highlights the use of non-tariff barriers such as Voluntary Export Restraints (VERs) to limit competition from third countries in certain product areas. There is a detailed examination of the most important of these, ranging from steel and textiles to cars and electronic products.

Prior to the speculative crises of 1992–3, the development of the European Monetary System (EMS) had been accounted without reservation as one of the most successful aspects of the European experiment. The nature of that achievement and the reasons for the collapse of the EMS are analysed in Chapter 12. The success of the EMS had been great enough to foster the conception of European Monetary Union (EMU), which is analysed in Chapter 13. This chapter reviews the analytics of monetary union within a cost-benefit framework and goes on to discuss the criteria set out in the Maastricht Treaty for progression to EMU and the provisions made in that Treaty for a European Central Bank.

Chapter 14 discusses the evolution of the EU budget, the development and refinement of the 'own-resources' principle for funding the budget, and the resolution of the problem of budgetary imbalance as it affected the United Kingdom and Germany. The possibility of introducing a stabilization role for the budget is also examined.

Chapter 15 examines the foreign aid and external assistance afforded by the Member States of the EU and the development of policy at the Union level through the Lomé Conventions.

A list of discussion questions, arranged by chapter, appears at the end of the book.

It is clearly important that a book such as this should be as up to date as possible and for this reason we plan to issue revised editions every two years. In this edition we have endeavoured to ensure that the analysis and description are as accurate as possible as of the end of 1993. However, the ambition to be up to date can be only imperfectly realized in relation to the European Union, where events can move quickly. Indeed, the reader cannot fail to note that, while the chapters in this book mainly refer to EC experience, the title of the book refers to the European Union. The signature of the Treaty on European Union (the 'Maastricht Treaty') in 1992 and its final ratification in November 1993 led to the change of name to 'European Union' as reflected in the title. (The background to this is fully explained in Chapter 1.) However, the references to the EC in the individual chapters have been retained, as this was the institutional title under which most of the experience which is described took place. No doubt, 'EU' will progressively replace 'EC' in subsequent editions.

# 1

# History and Institutions of the European Union

SIMON BULMER

## 1.1. INTRODUCTION

On 1 November 1993, after final ratification of the Treaty on European Union (TEU or, colloquially, the Maastricht Treaty), the European Union (EU) came into existence. No great transformation occurred at midnight on 31 October 1993; rather, a further step was taken in the lengthy evolution of post-war European integration. However, an important formal development did occur: the economic activities of the twelve Member States in the European Community (EC) were subsumed within the wider political context of the EU. This formal change is particularly relevant to explaining the relationship between this chapter and the rest of the book. Over the years, the spotlight has been on the economic activities of the EC. But, increasingly since 1970, other joint activities have been developing, hidden away from public attention—for instance, activities on foreign policy and combating terrorism. The EU brings all the different activities together and places the economic activities of the EC in a wider context. The book is concerned with the economic activities. However, this chapter aims to show how a knowledge of the wider context—historical, political, and institutional—is essential to an understanding of the economic activities.

The peaceful integration of the European national economies has been a development specific to the post-1945 era. The integration of Europe was proposed as early as the fourteenth century, but it was not until the period of economic, political, and military reconstruction following the Second World War that it was put into practice. The form taken by integration was strongly influenced by the historical experiences of its founding fathers. Hence they sought to avoid the excesses of nationalism and of the nation-state system that had been demonstrated by the German Nazi regime. They also sought to open up the national economies as a means of avoiding the protectionism that had characterized inter-war Europe. Poor economic performance was widely perceived to have provided a climate of political instability conducive to the growth of Fascism in Europe.

Economic integration has also been rooted in a particular European geography. This, too, has a historical explanation, namely in the division of Europe through the Cold War. Thus the history of economic integration in the EC, until the 1990s at least, is *West* European history. Only with the collapse of Communism in Eastern and Central Europe at the end of the 1980s did the EC need substantively to develop economic relations with the other half of the Continent.

If the division of Europe has major contextual importance to economic integration, so in particular does the division of one state, Germany. After the Second World War France was concerned that the revival of the German coal and steel industries might trigger expansionism. The principal objective of the European Coal and Steel Community (ECSC) was to allay fears of a 'military–industrial complex' fuelling renascent German nationalism. The roots of economic integration through what we may call the 'Community method' (see below) thus lay in the need to find a political solution to the turbulent past of Franco-German relations.

There are many other ways in which historical circumstance has shaped the pattern of economic integration. In particular, it can explain the tortuous way in which the United Kingdom has come to grips with the integration process, as a reluctant participant seeking to come to terms with its 'descent from power'. Similarly, the persistence of non-democratic forms of government in Greece and on the Iberian peninsula isolated those states from the EC until their domestic political transformation permitted membership, as part of a second wave of enlargement in the 1980s.

Thus history has conditioned the process of economic integration. But what of the politics and institutional framework of economic integration? These, too, are important.

Economic integration has not evolved as the result of some functional logic. Nor has it developed as the result of some 'natural' economic law enforced by Adam Smith's 'invisible hand'. Functional and economic determinism fail to explain both the setbacks to integration and the relaunches; economic integration has not been a smooth process following some scientific logic. Rather, it has been dependent upon political and institutional dynamics.

At the level of the major integration developments—from the Schuman Plan creating the ECSC to the signature of the TEU in 1992—the need to create a package deal satisfying the participants' national interests has been paramount. Without satisfying all Member States, no deal can be achieved. However, where the agreement amounts to a new treaty or a treaty amendment, even consensus between the member governments may be insufficient. The French National Assembly's actions in August 1954 led to rejection of the European Defence Community Treaty and the collapse of that initiative. More recently, the Single European Act (SEA) was subject to referenda in both Denmark and the Irish Republic before it could be implemented from July 1987. The need to satisfy domestic political concerns was demonstrated most dramatically with the Maastricht Treaty—the TEU. The Danes' need to hold a second referendum following the Treaty's initial rejection by a narrow margin of voters in June 1992; the successful referenda in the Irish Republic and in France; and the tortuous ratification process during 1992–3 in the UK House of Commons: these all demonstrated the contingency of treaty amendments on domestic politics. Thus major integrative developments require not only agreement between the member governments but an ability on the part of the latter to ensure domestic approval.

On a more routine level, integration may be less publicly politicized. However, the political dynamics of policy-making are no less important. The EU is not like the many international organizations on the world stage. Uniquely amongst European and international organizations, it has supranational characteristics. These are concentrated overwhelmingly in the institutional arrangements concerning the economic pillar of activity, the EC. It has its own body of law which has direct effect in the Member States, and takes precedence over national law. It has institutions with autonomy from the Member States. The most prominent of these are: the European Commission, which serves as an executive civil service; a parliamentary assembly which has been directly elected since 1979; a European Court of Justice which makes rulings on matters of law. Balanced against these three are two powerful institutions representing the interests of the member governments, namely the Council of Ministers and the European Council. The former is comprised of national ministers; the latter of heads of government or state. The EC is not like other international economic organizations, and this is reflected in the way that economic integration has been a continuing process of evolving goals from the first steps undertaken with the ECSC to the TEU and beyond.

Above all, however, it must be remembered that economic integration has never been an end in itself. It has always served as a means towards the end of political integration. The ECSC involved the integration of the coal and steel sectors as a means towards Franco-German reconciliation and towards creating a new system of post-war European relations. Similarly, an important motivating factor for some states, in particular France, in negotiating the TEU was to strengthen integration in the context of German unification in 1990. The French government feared that a more powerful Germany might become less predictable in European politics; it sought to pre-empt this through closer integration. These political objectives have set the path towards the EU apart from the paths of more modest organizations, such as the European Free Trade Association (EFTA).

In reviewing the history of the EU, we explain the key developments summarized in Table 1.1. To do so, we need to commence with the situation in 1945, at the end of the Second World War.

TABLE **1.1.** *Key stages in the development of the European Union*

| Year | Key developments |
|---|---|
| 1951 | Treaty of Paris is signed, bringing the European Coal and Steel Community into effect from 23 July 1952. Membership comprised Belgium, the Federal Republic of Germany, France, Italy, Luxemburg, and the Netherlands. |
| 1957 | Treaty of Rome is signed, bringing into effect the European Economic Community and the European Atomic Energy Community from 1 January 1958. |
| 1965 | Merger Treaty is signed, with the effect of merging the principal institutions of the three communities from 1967. Henceforth the three communities are known collectively as the EC. |
| 1973 | Denmark, the Irish Republic, and the United Kingdom join the EC on 1 January. |
| 1981 | Greece joins the EC on 1 January. |
| 1986 | Spain and Portugal join the EC on 1 January. The Single European Act is signed, coming into effect on 1 July 1987, and introduces the first systematic revisions to the founding treaties. |
| 1992 | Treaty on European Union is signed (following broad agreement in December 1991 at a meeting in Maastricht in the Netherlands). It entails systematic revisions to, and extension of, the existing treaties. Following ratification, the TEU comes into effect on 1 November 1993. Within the European Union, the EC represents one 'pillar' of activities: the others relate to foreign and security policy; and justice and home affairs. |

## 1.2. ECONOMIC INTEGRATION IN HISTORICAL AND POLITICAL PERSPECTIVE

### *Why European Co-operation and Integration?*

Although European integration was not an idea new to the post-1945 era, it was propelled initially by a distinctive 'mix' of circumstances and impulses. These comprised:

- the defeat of Nazi Germany and of the Axis powers;
- the wish to avoid a repeat of the excesses of nationalism and of the nation-state system by creating a new system of European international relations;
- the economic dislocation caused by wartime destruction;
- the emergence of two global superpowers with competing political and economic ideologies;
- the division of Europe and the wish in the West for security from the Soviet threat;
- the need to base Western security and defence on economic reconstruction and well-being; and

● the desire for Franco-German reconciliation as the bedrock of stability within Western Europe.

In short, European integration was motivated by political, economic, and security considerations.

The protagonists of co-operation and integration were by no means of one view on how to address these issues. *Federalists* placed primary emphasis on the superseding of the nation state with a larger democratic structure. Their roots were frequently in the European resistance movements, and, in 1944, at a meeting in Geneva, they had already drawn up a plan for a federal European order based on a written constitution.

A second category of protagonists may be termed *functionalists*. Like the federalists, they were strongest in continental Europe, but they lacked the federalists' organization. They shared the federalists' objective of a united Europe but adopted a more pragmatic approach to its realization. They saw the need for economic co-operation as a starting-point for achieving their political goals. The Frenchman Jean Monnet was the most prominent figure in this camp. Other political figures, especially from the Low Countries, shared this approach. By 1944 the exiled governments had already agreed on the establishment of Benelux, a customs union to comprise Belgium, the Netherlands, and Luxemburg.

A third category may be termed the *nationalists*. Although they did not display nationalism in its negative sense, these figures did not see any need to participate in a new political order. The nationalists were strongest in those Member States which had either escaped invasion during the Second World War or had remained neutral, and fiercely retained national political traditions. Hence they were strongest in the United Kingdom, Scandinavia, the Irish Republic, and Switzerland.

For the United Kingdom, the allied victory was seen as the source of heightened pride in national institutions; it had, moreover, galvanized relations with the United States. The resultant 'special relationship', together with the Commonwealth, represented powerful alternative poles of attraction for post-war UK foreign policy. Both the main parties in the United Kingdom opposed participation in any integration schemes which would jeopardize national sovereignty.[1] Winston Churchill, regarded in continental Europe as one of the protagonists of a federal Europe, was most supportive of integration when out of power. Moreover, he saw the United Kingdom's relations with the strongest protagonists as 'with them but not of them'. The nationalists were prepared to participate in a number of European organizations, but these were characterized by co-operation between sovereign nation states. It was not until the 1960s that the position began to change, as nationalists came to realize that this approach offered very limited opportunities for joint policy action.

A final set of protagonists—and one which must not be forgotten—was comprised of *external actors*. Essentially this was the political élite of the United States. The US position was to support co-operation and integration, both through exhortation and through financial and political assistance. The European Recovery Programme (ERP), popularly known as the Marshall Plan, played a major role in facilitating economic reconstruction. US leadership within the North American Treaty Organization (NATO) provided the security framework within which economic integration could flourish.

By the early 1950s a small group of six Member States had emerged that had shared objectives and a willingness to sacrifice national sovereignty to achieve them. These were the states which launched the process of supranational integration (see Table 1.1). A wider group—which also included these six—was willing to co-operate on various economic, political, or security-policy goals. However, states in this group were unwilling to go further. It was the different response to post-war circumstances on the part of the six which led them to favour *supranational integration*, whereas the wider group was unwilling to go beyond *intergovernmental co-operation* between sovereign states. Accordingly, the European organizations established in the post-war period tended either to be limited to co-operation or to entail the formal transfer of sovereignty that characterizes supranational integration.

### The International Organization of the Western European Economies

The first attempt to organize the European economies in the post-war period was made with the establishment in 1947 of the Economic Commission for Europe (ECE), created under the auspices of the United Nations. However, its pan-European nature was to be its undoing, for the emergence of the Cold War rendered it unworkable as a body aimed at facilitating the reconstruction of Europe as a whole. From this point onwards we are concerned with Western European integration. The Eastern European economies were brought together in the Soviet-led Council for Mutual Economic Assistance (CMEA), which was set up in 1949.

The emergence of the Cold War overshadowed co-operation and integration at the end of the 1940s. In consequence, this was a period where the United States showed leadership in promoting West European developments. The scene was set when President Truman pledged US support for 'free peoples who are resisting attempted subjugation by armed minorities or by outside pressures'. The specific trigger for the 'Truman Doctrine' had been Communist destabilization in Greece, but the declaration was a broader commitment to contain Communism.

The Marshall Plan was announced in June 1947. The US Administration recognized that the objectives of the Truman Doctrine could best be attained if Europe's democracies were based on sound economies. Hence the initiative made by Secretary of State George Marshall was a response to the continued economic dislocation and food-rationing in Western Europe. Although notionally offered to all European states, Marshall aid was in fact accepted only by those in the West.

In defence policy the counterpart to the Marshall Plan was the signature, in April 1949, of the Atlantic Charter which created NATO as the principal organization for the defence of Western Europe. The United States was to play the leading role in NATO.

US leadership was not confined to the European arena. The principles of *international* monetary co-operation had already been established at the Bretton Woods conference of 1944 which led to the establishment of the International Monetary Fund and the World Bank. In October 1947 the General Agreement on Tariffs and Trade (GATT) was created, providing the guiding principles of liberalization in the trade arena, namely through tariff reductions. The economic principles embodied in these organizations were to have an important impact on economic co-operation within Western Europe.

The first step towards economic integration came at the start of 1948 with the creation of the Benelux customs union, complete with the introduction of a common customs tariff. Benelux was to serve as a precursor to the European Economic Community (EEC).

Of wider geographical significance was the foundation, in April 1948, of the Organization for European Economic Co-operation (OEEC). This was the organization entrusted with implementing the Marshall Plan. Disbursement of US aid was very much a matter to be organized by the European states themselves through the OEEC and its key governing body, the Council of Ministers. The OEEC was essentially an intergovernmental organization, characterized by co-operation between states. It ensured fulfilment of the US condition that reconstruction should be co-ordinated, and that tariff reductions should be implemented. Its activities were concentrated on facilitating the reconstruction of the national economies, and reducing quotas on interstate trade and tariffs. Under its umbrella were established other, more specialized, bodies and arrangements such as the European Payments Union (EPU). Established in 1950, the EPU was designed to facilitate a multilateral system of payments for trade until initial liquidity problems were alleviated.

The OEEC, having overseen the task of reconstruction, was succeeded in 1961 by the Organization for Economic Co-operation and Development (OECD), an agency no longer confined to the West European economies. The OEEC and Marshall aid had facilitated the construction of an economic platform, upon which supranational integration could be founded.

For some states the OEEC was not enough. It neither took on ambitious tasks nor had any political component. The May 1950 Schuman Plan was an attempt by France to seize the reins of integration and take a different direction. Conceived as a Franco-German scheme, it was nevertheless open to other states to join. However, there was a condition: the principle of supranationalism, i.e. of relinquishing national power, had to be accepted. This pre-condition (and other factors) had the effect of ensuring that the United Kingdom did not participate in the negotiations.

The Schuman Plan, named after the French foreign minister, had in fact been elaborated by Jean Monnet. Its principal concern was with ensuring that reconstruction in the western part of Germany should not endanger peace. The heavy industries of the Ruhr had been under allied control, but this could not continue indefinitely. The proposed arrangements were also welcomed from the German side, for they offered a route to its regaining control over its key industrial sectors, as well as to international rehabilitation.

Thus the Schuman Plan was an explicitly political proposal; it offered a breakthrough into supranationalism; and it followed a functional approach of sectoral integration but with wider objectives in view. These features have come to characterize the 'Community method' of integration. The plan was favourably received in Belgium, the Netherlands, Luxemburg, and Italy as well as in France and West Germany. These six states were to form the sole participants in the Community method until 1973 (see Table 1.1).

Before the ink was dry on the April 1951 Treaty of Paris, which established the ECSC, proposals had already been made for further integration in the shape of a European Defence Community (EDC). Conceived at the height of the Cold War, and with an eye upon the hostilities in Korea, the EDC proposal was designed to facilitate the rearmament of Germany through supranational control, since a German contribution was seen as indispensable to West European security. The French National Assembly's failure, in August 1954, to ratify the Treaty represented the first setback to supranational integration. German rearmament was achieved in May 1955, when the intergovernmental Western European Union commenced operations.

Those favouring further supranational integration were undeterred by this setback. The reasons for French non-ratification were varied but did not represent a rejection of supranationalism. Rather, there was a feeling that a supranational defence community was proceeding too far too fast. The death of Stalin and the end of the Korean War had also reduced the urgent need for the EDC. By 1955 new ideas were being floated for developing integration beyond the coal and steel sectors. Milward (1992: 120) points out that these proposals were not an attempt to relaunch integration *after* the failure of the EDC. Moves for a wider European customs union had already been mooted.

The forum for initial discussions on the proposals, which were advanced in particular by the Benelux countries, was to be the Messina conference of

June 1955. This was attended by the foreign ministers of the EC6. The proposed areas for further integration comprised the creation of a common market (i.e. beyond the coal and steel sectors), a common transport policy, and integration in the energy sector. These ideas received broad support, and, in consequence, a committee of governmental representatives was set up, chaired by the Belgian Paul-Henri Spaak.

The United Kingdom was invited to participate in the negotiations; it accepted the invitation but then withdrew from the Spaak Committee, once again because of outright opposition to the proposed supranational form of integration. Negotiations between the EC6 were quite protracted, because of several thorny issues, and some matters were barely resolved by the time the EEC Treaty was finalized. Hence the Treaty contains quite limited indications as to the direction to be taken in the integration of agricultural policy and social policy. Nevertheless, negotiations during 1956 and early 1957 led to the two Treaties of Rome: the EEC Treaty and the Treaty establishing the European Atomic Energy Community (Euratom). They were signed on 25 March 1957. Following ratification, they came into effect from the start of 1958.

One further development must be referred to before examining the three European Communities in more detail. Having withdrawn from the Spaak Committee, the UK government began to reappraise its policy. Following a UK initiative, a committee was set up in the framework of the OEEC to examine the creation of a European free trade area. Although the resultant report deemed such a development feasible, there was considerable suspicion on the part of the EC6 that the UK initiative was designed to undermine their much more ambitious plans of a common market and a supranational political system to supervise it. It was only once the Treaties of Rome had come into effect, and the EC6 had gone their own way, that the negotiations on a free trade area gained momentum. They culminated in the signing, on 4 January 1960, of the Stockholm Convention creating the European Free Trade Association (EFTA). The founding members were the United Kingdom, Norway, Denmark, Sweden, Austria, Portugal, and Switzerland.

EFTA was a classic intergovernmental forum for economic co-operation. There was no threat to national sovereignty. As such, it suited the instincts of UK politicians. EFTA was centred around trade in industrial goods; agriculture was largely excluded. As a free trade area, each Member State was free to set its own external tariff. This enabled the United Kingdom to continue its trading relations with the Commonwealth countries.

Until the 1970s the EC6 and the 'EFTAns' comprised two distinct camps within Western Europe. With the first EC enlargement of 1973, it was agreed to reduce tariff barriers on industrial trade between the two groupings. By the late 1980s a much closer relationship was proposed: the European Economic Area (see below).

The two camps corresponded quite neatly to the two different political approaches to integration that were identified earlier. The EC6 comprised those states which were prepared to transcend the nation state by means of supranational integration. By contrast, EFTA was composed of those states which preferred more limited arrangements and the maintenance of national sovereignty. How, then, did integration through the Community method shape the form of integration pursued by the EC6?

## Integration through the Community Method

### The ECSC

The ECSC, which commenced operations in July 1952, was the starting-point of the Community method of supranational integration. Its provisions were set out in the Treaty of Paris, which runs to 100 articles. The ECSC had three key features.

First, it proposed a degree of economic integration that went beyond anything developed in the other existing European organizations. It was not concerned with the lowest level of economic integration (a free trade area) but with the higher goal of a common market, albeit confined to the coal, steel, and related sectors. Nevertheless, given that these sectors were then regarded as the 'commanding heights' of the economy, the ECSC was concerned with core activities of the EC6. The ECSC's chief aims were to ensure security of supplies through the removal of quotas and customs duties over a five-year transitional period; the rational expansion and modernization of the industries; and the provision of mechanisms for managing serious shortages or gluts. The ECSC sought to restrict Member States' use of discriminatory state subsidies and it provided a common external commercial policy relating to the two sectors.

It is worth pointing out that the economic philosophy behind the Treaty of Paris was more interventionist than that behind the later EEC Treaty. This *dirigisme* owed much to the influence of the French; it was no coincidence that the author of the Schuman Plan, Jean Monnet, was head of the French Commission for Economic Planning. Moreover, the Treaty of Paris spelt out most of the detailed arrangements, thus reducing the need for secondary legislation. The ECSC's activities were financed by levies on coal and steel production.

The second key feature was that these detailed arrangements were subservient to the political goal of providing a framework for Franco-German reconciliation. One indicator of the success of this was the relatively smooth reintegration of the Saar into (West) Germany in 1956, after some ten years effectively under French control.

The third key feature, and central to the Community method, was the set of strong, supranational central institutions associated with the ECSC.

These provided a model which was later employed for the EEC and Euratom.

The ECSC comprised five institutions:

- the executive, known as the High Authority (equivalent to the European Commission of today);
- the Council of Ministers, comprising representatives of the member governments;
- the Consultative Committee, consisting of representatives of employers/industry, trade unions, and consumers concerned with the ECSC's activities;
- the Assembly, composed of a total of sixty-eight delegates from the six national parliaments;
- the European Court of Justice (ECJ).

These institutions were all located in Luxemburg, thus explaining why some services of the institutions of the merged Communities, the EC, are located there.

The High Authority had a considerable degree of autonomy in carrying out the tasks entrusted to the ECSC. It was headed by nine members who were appointed from the Member States but were to act independently in carrying out their duties. Fittingly, the first president of the High Authority was Jean Monnet. Beneath the 'members'—equivalent to present-day EC commissioners—the High Authority was staffed by an independent civil service. The independence of the High Authority and its staff from the national governments was a characteristic of the supranational approach to integration.

A Council of Ministers was created to allay the concerns of the Benelux countries. They were worried that the ECSC might be dominated by French and German interests. They were also concerned that the High Authority might pursue an excessively *dirigiste* form of economic policy. The Council of Ministers was thus a check against the realization of these worries. Although a check on supranationalism, the Council could not be compared with similar bodies in, for example, the OEEC. This was because the ECSC Council was able, under specified circumstances, to take decisions by qualified majority voting and simple majority, as well as by the conventional method of unanimity.[2]

The Consultative Committee and the Assembly were much less important institutions, confined to advisory roles. The ECJ, however, had a more important function. It was responsible for adjudicating on disputes relating to the ECSC's activities.

In operation, the ECSC was regarded initially as successful. Production and interstate trade in coal and steel increased markedly, although how much of this could be attributed to the ECSC's existence is open to question. The initial success was followed by a period of less progress.

The coal crisis towards the end of the 1950s was caused by falling demand owing to cheap oil imports. The High Authority's attempt in 1959 to declare a 'manifest crisis' in the coal industry, so as to obtain powers of intervention in the market, failed because it could not obtain the necessary majority in the Council of Ministers. The ECSC was regarded as having failed its first real test. This was the first of numerous challenges by national interests to the supranational principles of the Community method. It indicated that the ECSC was not so supranational in practice as it was designed to be.

The ECSC retained its separate existence until implementation of the Merger Treaty in 1967. This resulted in the High Authority's absorption into the EC Commission. The Assembly and the ECJ had already been shared with the other Communities from 1958. The Consultative Committee continues to retain its separate identity.

Following the creation of the EEC and the merger of the three European Communities, activities based on the ECSC Treaty have tended to be overshadowed. In the coal sector activities have concentrated on combating the effects of declining demand. A more effective role has been hampered by the absence of clear provision for an EC energy policy. There has been greater prominence in the management of surplus capacity in the steel sector, where severe problems emerged in the 1980s.

*Euratom*
The Treaties of Rome expanded the area of joint activity considerably. Of the two, the Euratom Treaty was of much less significance. It was largely the product of French pressure. France had begun to develop a civilian nuclear programme and saw Euratom as a way of obtaining financial support for its extension and of developing a market for French technology.

In fact, Euratom was rather a failure. Differences between the Member States resulted in Euratom having little control over the development of the nuclear sector. Measures have been undertaken on health and safety in the nuclear industry, to promote joint research, and so on, but the core activities of civilian nuclear power have remained in the hands of the Member States.

*The EEC*
The establishment of the EEC was a most significant development in supranational integration. The ECSC's model of identifying functional bases for joint policy was continued. European integration retained a political objective, although no longer centrally concerned with fears of renascent German power; and the EEC Treaty followed the supranational model already established, albeit in a moderated form.

The activities and arrangements covered by the EEC Treaty can be seen from a summary of its structure (see Table 1.2). The EEC's policies are

Putting the customs union into operation was achieved early, as already noted. The institutions were put into practice, although the (enlarged) Assembly and the ECJ were shared from 1958 with the ECSC and Euratom. The first president of the EEC Commission, Walter Hallstein, was a forceful individual and gave that institution activist leadership. In 1965 the first constitutional amendment was agreed: the Merger Treaty, which came into effect in 1967.[3] This merged the three Communities, with the creation of a single Commission being the principal result. The Treaties were not merged, however, and a few features remained distinct, such as the separate budgetary provisions for the ECSC.

A number of important legal developments occurred during the 1960s, also with a consolidating effect. These emerged in judgments on specific cases brought before the ECJ but that had wide-ranging implications and strengthened the EC's supranational character. Two cases were of particular importance. In its 1963 judgment on the *Van Gend en Loos* case, the ECJ established the principle of direct effect, i.e. that EC law confers both rights and duties on individuals that national courts must enforce. The effect of this was to make it possible for private individuals or companies to use the national courts to oblige governments to implement treaty provisions. Had this principle not been established, in what was an expansionist judgment on the part of the ECJ, progress towards the common market would have been much more difficult. The ECJ has made a number of major judgments facilitating the creation of the internal market. However, it cannot make these judgments until a case is referred. And private parties have proven to be more effective at policing the common market than the member governments.

A second important legal principle, that of the primacy of EC law over national law, was also established in the 1960s: a feature which had not been specified in the Treaty. This principle was enunciated in *Costa* v. *ENEL* (case 6/64) and in other ECJ judgments. The effect was to reinforce the supranationalism of the EEC. Added to the earlier case establishing the principle of direct effect, this facilitated a process of integration through law. So, whilst the 1960s are often characterized as a period of resurgence in national interests, as demonstrated by the 1965 crisis (see below), important legal developments were under way which had the opposite effect. They have also been of major importance in the realization of the economic objectives set out in the treaties.

Consolidation was also achieved through the translation of treaty objectives into secondary legislation. This was particularly necessary in the agricultural sector, for the whole regulatory structure of the CAP had to be introduced. Given the level of French interest in this policy area, it is not surprising that this was one of the principal battlefields for de Gaulle's assault on supranationalism.

De Gaulle's policy was based on a nation-state-centred view of world

*History and Institutions of the EU*

19

politics, and his particular wish was to strengthen French grandeur. His policy generated three specific flashpoints regarding the development of integration. The first resulted from his proposal for a 'Political Union'. Far from being an attempt to advance supranational integration, this was to be organized along traditional intergovernmental lines. The other Member States regarded it as a threat to the successful supranational Community method. His proposal failed. The second occurred as a result of a reconsideration by the United Kingdom of the merits of membership. The Conservative government of Harold Macmillan had already applied for membership in 1961. Applications were later made by Ireland, Denmark, and Norway. However, in a dramatic move, de Gaulle unilaterally rejected the UK application (and by extension the others) at a press conference in January 1963. De Gaulle clearly did not want competition from the United Kingdom for the leadership of the EEC. His actions irritated the other five governments both procedurally and substantively. In 1967 he vetoed the second UK application, this time made by the Labour government of Harold Wilson.

The third and most dramatic clash came with the 1965 crisis. Its immediate cause was the creation of the system for financing the CAP. Hallstein sought to link this provision with the creation of a self-financing, or 'own-resources', EEC budget. For de Gaulle, Hallstein was becoming too much like a government head. In addition, a step towards budgetary autonomy for the EC was a further (for de Gaulle, undesired) reinforcement of supranationalism. In the background, but at least as important, was the projected 1966 introduction of qualified majority voting in the EEC Council of Ministers. This was also regarded by de Gaulle as a major threat to national sovereignty, for that would mean that French interests could be overridden in the Council. The result was that in June 1965 France withdrew from the workings of the Council of Ministers. It was not until January 1966 that a solution was found in the so-called Luxemburg Compromise. Whilst this has no status in EC law, it established the convention that, on matters of 'vital national interest' to one or more Member States, discussions would continue until consensus had been reached. The Luxemburg Compromise was important in practice, for it led to integration being dictated by the pace of the most reluctant Member State.

The result of the Luxemburg Compromise was a slowing-down of decision-making in the Council of Ministers. The need to satisfy all national interests contrasted with what was supposed to happen, namely decisions being taken by qualified majority vote. The Commission became less ambitious and the Community's supranationalism was in decline. This situation was not really reversed until the 1980s and the SEA. The exact status of the Luxemburg Compromise is unclear. It has not been invoked since the SEA, although in December 1992 the French government *threa-*

*tened* to use it in conjunction with GATT negotiations on the Uruguay Round.

## Revival through Summitry

It was not until de Gaulle's resignation that the political will of the EC could be revived. Even so, Gaullist ideas continued to influence the policies of his successor as president, Georges Pompidou. Pompidou initiated a meeting with the heads of government of the other five states. Designed to give the EC new momentum, the summit initiated a number of developments:

- the opening of negotiations for enlargement of the EC;
- re-examination of the financing of the budget;
- the creation of a system of foreign-policy co-operation; and
- the drafting of proposals for an Economic and Monetary Union (EMU).

The enlargement negotiations were successful and, on 1 January 1973, the United Kingdom, the Irish Republic, and Denmark joined the EC. Norway, which had negotiated its terms of entry, rejected membership in a referendum held in September 1972. An 'own-resources' system was introduced for the EC budget through two treaty amendments (1970 and 1975). The new system was fully operational from 1980. A foreign-policy co-operation procedure was set up in 1970 and has developed considerably over the intervening period. Finally, the EMU initiative was launched as a response to currency instability in the EC at the end of the 1960s. The proposals failed because of the collapse of the Bretton Woods international monetary system and the impact of the 1973 oil crisis.

Subsequent summits in 1972 and 1974 were less successful, although providing some initiatives. The 1972 Paris summit, for instance, placed environmental policy on the EC's agenda. The 1974 summit, again held in Paris, was more noteworthy. On the institutional front there were two key achievements. The first of these was agreement to the principle of holding direct elections to the European Parliament (EP). This distinctly supranational step, aimed at giving European parliamentarians their own source of democratic legitimacy, was first put into practice with elections in 1979. The second was the agreement to hold regular summit meetings, known as the European Council, at least twice each year. In the period since 1975 'most of the major political decisions in the EC have been taken in the European Council' (Bulmer and Wessels 1987: 2). The main policy decision was agreement on the establishment of the European Regional Development Fund.

With two former finance ministers at the heart of the European Council— Chancellor Schmidt of Germany and President Giscard d'Estaing of

France—it was scarcely surprising that international monetary affairs should feature strongly at its meetings. Thus in 1978 Schmidt launched the initiative for the European Monetary System (EMS) at the Copenhagen European Council. After elaboration of its operation by a group of three experts, it came into effect in March 1979. It was to be one of the main achievements of this period.

The period from 1979 to 1984 was dominated by the UK budgetary problem. Mrs Thatcher's Conservative government was intent upon achieving a lasting solution to what it perceived as an inequitable system. It had been anticipated from the outset of membership that the EC's own resources budget would not favour the United Kingdom (see Scott 1992). However, the economic recession induced by the oil crisis resulted in few of the predicted trade benefits of membership accruing to the United Kingdom. It was only after protracted negotiations that a settlement was reached at the Fontainebleau European Council in 1984.

This agreement was part of a typical 'package deal' of EC negotiations. Not only did the meeting provide a solution to the UK budgetary crisis, increase the size of the budget, and provide for limited CAP reform, it also decided to look at the institutional structure of the EC, the start of the process leading to the SEA. A further part of the package was to give approval in principle to Spanish and Portuguese enlargement. The two states joined on 1 January 1986; Greece had joined from the start of 1981. The southern enlargements were motivated essentially by political considerations—namely, the wish to strengthen these new democracies, for the three states' economies were at a relatively low level of development.

## The SEA and Renewed Dynamism

The SEA was signed in February 1986 and came into effect on 1 July 1987. It had been negotiated within an intergovernmental conference (IGC) under the supervision of the European Council. The SEA's significance was that it amounted to the first comprehensive revision of the treaties. The motivations for it included:

- a recognition of the need to overcome the 'Eurosclerosis' that had characterized the EC economy compared with its global competitors;
- a wish to provide a stimulus to the European economy by means of the liberalization associated with completion of the internal market;
- a wish to bring the treaties into line with actual practice in the EC;
- a wish to relaunch supranational integration because of a realization that decisional weakness had impeded the collective interest; and
- a recognition of the need to make the EC more politically responsive if the Iberian enlargement were not to create political sclerosis.

The content of the SEA can be divided into two—namely, the policy and the institutional provisions. The policy developments took two broad forms. Some of the treaty revisions were largely concerned with formalizing the EC's competence—for example, in environmental policy, 'monetary capacity', and research and technology policy. In these cases the treaty revisions gave clearer competence for EC action. The codification of foreign-policy co-operation, including enhanced institutional provision, had a similar effect, but this development was contained in a separate part of the SEA. The SEA's measures relating to the single market, however, were rather different. This was not a new policy area; rather, the SEA drew up a changed route map to the destination. It had three features:

- a relatively small legislative programme (282 items) aimed at setting the essential requirements, by the end of 1992, for completion of the internal market, and with the SEA including new provision for increased use of qualified majority voting in the Council of Ministers, thereby reducing earlier obstructionism under the unanimity rule;
- reliance on the principle of mutual recognition of standards as established in ECJ landmark decisions, such as the 1979 *Cassis de Dijon* case; and
- the 'new approach' of devolving decisions on European standards from the Council to standard-setting agencies.

The institutional changes comprised increased provision for qualified majority voting, increased powers for the EP, and the creation of the Court of First Instance as a means of alleviating the backlog of work facing the ECJ. Initially regarded as rather modest in nature, the SEA succeeded in developing renewed momentum for integration, not least by the establishment of the 'end-1992' deadline for completion of the SEM.

In the aftermath of the SEA, the European Council became concerned with various 'flanking measures', especially relating to economic and social cohesion. The first of these became important in the negotiations surrounding the 'Delors package'—a set of measures designed to help the less-developed EC economies, and those regions suffering from industrial decline, to contend with the competitive challenges posed by the single market. Agreement was finally reached at the 1988 Brussels summit to provide the finance for such measures, including through new restrictions on CAP spending. The wish to avoid the SEM being developed at the cost of declining social provision lay behind the so-called Social Charter. This whole area remains highly contested, as symbolized by the UK government's refusal to sign the charter at the December 1989 European Council in Strasburg. Subsequently, in the negotiations leading to signature of the TEU in 1992, the United Kingdom secured an opt-out of the Social Protocol, an arrangement designed to put the Social Charter into practice.

The momentum for integration was maintained by a revival of interest in EMU, culminating in the June 1988 decision of the European Council to establish a committee under the chairmanship of Jacques Delors to report on its feasibility. The subsequent Delors Report, and the broad support to take discussion of EMU further (a position not shared by the UK government), contributed to the wish to engage in a further round of constitutional reform which culminated in the Maastricht negotations and the Treaty on European Union (TEU).[4]

## The TEU

Whilst the initial momentum for reform was largely attributable to EMU, this was rapidly joined by other major political impulses. These derived from the collapse of Communism in Eastern Europe and the new role expected of the EC in international relations after the Cold War. There was also a recognition that the number of applications for EC membership would consequently increase, and that work should commence on reforming the institutions to facilitate an effective political process within a Community of some twenty members. German unification in October 1990—creating the EC's first enlargement without formal accession—reawakened strong concerns about German power. For some states, especially France, the solution lay in containing this power through the deepening of European integration. Hence the support of its government and of President Mitterrand for the goal of EMU. Finally, there was a wish, as with the SEA, to tidy up constitutional provisions and make substantive policy changes beyond EMU.

The resultant Treaty, which was finalized at the Maastricht European Council in December 1991, had been prepared by two parallel IGCs. The structure of the Treaty is usually described as resembling a temple. Hence the 'roof' sets out various broad objectives in the so-called 'common provisions'. The roof is located on three pillars. The first pillar consists of the EC activities, i.e. comprising the three Communities as further enhanced by the TEU itself. The second pillar provides a stronger footing for what is to be called a Common Foreign and Security Policy (CFSP). The third pillar covers Justice and Home Affairs (JHA), i.e. police co-operation, combating drug-trafficking and fraud, regulating immigration from third countries, and similar matters. The policies contained in the last two pillars are given greater prominence than before, and are strengthened but retain an intergovernmental basis under the TEU. Finally, there is the plinth of the 'temple', detailing relationships with existing EC treaties, ratification arrangements, and so on. There are also eighteen protocols (e.g. the UK 'opt-outs' on EMU and the new social-policy provisions) and over thirty declarations.

It is the first of these pillars which is of principal importance to economic integration. Once again the new provisions can be divided into policy provision and institutional provision. The most prominent policy development concerned the conditions and timetable set for achieving EMU by the end of the 1990s. In return for agreement to this, the economically weaker Member States insisted on the creation of a Cohesion Fund to enable resource transfers to their economies; this was also provided for. The EC12 had sought to give a treaty base to the substance of the Social Charter, but the situation was clouded by the UK opt-out. There are numerous other policy developments—for instance, on the EC's infrastructure, consumer protection, and industrial policy.

In order to put the institutional aspects of the TEU into context, attention is now turned to policy-making in the EC pillar.

## 1.3. ECONOMIC INTEGRATION AND ITS POLICY-MAKING CONTEXT

Economic integration is heavily dependent on legislation. Legislation takes one of two forms. Regulations are used chiefly to legislate on quite technical matters. They have direct effect in the Member States. *Directives* are used where there are different national traditions and it is felt more appropriate just to legislate on the objectives of policy. National legislation must then be enacted in order to translate these goals into national law. A third legal instrument is the *decision*. This is not so much a method of legislating as of taking administrative decisions, such as on competition policy cases. A decision of this kind may be no less significant, especially if it imposes a substantial fine on a company in breach of EC competition law. Resort to *recommendations* is another option, but these do not have binding effect; they are not part of EC law.

To explain how legislation is developed, attention is first of all paid to the various EC institutions. Then brief attention is turned to other policy actors.

The EC's structure comprises three supranational institutions which are independent of the national governments, namely the Commission, the EP, and the ECJ. As a counter-balance there are two powerful institutions comprising representatives of the national governments: the European Council and the Council of Ministers.

The *Commission* consists of seventeen members (commissioners), with specific portfolios. The commissioners are appointed by the national governments but are then expected to detach themselves from national loyalty. Each commissioner has a group of political advisers to act as his or her 'eyes and ears'; they constitute the commissioner's 'cabinet'. One commissioner is appointed president and there are two vice-presidents. These have renewable terms of two years, but a minimum four-year term is the norm. The five larger Member States (France, the United Kingdom, Germany, Spain, and Italy) have two commissioners. The Commission is divided into directorates-general (DGs), which deal with specific policy areas. There are twenty-three DGs at present as well as specific services, such as the legal and translation services. The overall staffing of the Commission exceeds 16,000, but only about 10,000 fulfil executive and policy functions, once translation and scientific research centre staff are discounted.

The functions of the Commission are:

- the proposal of legislation;
- mediating between governments to achieve agreement on legislation;
- management of technical details of policy;
- representing the EC, particularly in commercial policy negotiations (for instance, within GATT);
- acting as the defender of collective EC interests;
- acting as guardian of the Treaties by ensuring that EC law is upheld.

The Commission's strength has varied over the years but had achieved particular prestige by the end of the 1980s. Its influence is threatened most when national interests are in the ascendent. President Delors has served since 1985 and was appointed for a further two years from 1993. Under the terms of the TEU, the Commission team from 1995 will be subject to the approval of the EP. From 1995 the commissioners will have five-year terms coinciding with the electoral periods of the EP. A reduction in the number of commissioners is under consideration as well as restructuring of the DGs.

The EP, originally known as the Assembly, consists of members (MEPs) who, since 1979, have been directly elected by Member States on five-year mandates. The 1989–94 parliament comprises 518 MEPs, but after the June 1994 elections this is to be increased to 567 in a re-balancing exercise taking account of German unification in 1990. The EP plenary sessions currently meet in Strasburg for twelve week-long sessions each year. Meetings of its committees, which generally 'shadow' one or more of the Commission's DGs, are held in Brussels..

The EP has ways of calling to account the Commission and, to a much lesser degree, the Council of Ministers. It has the power to dismiss the Commission but has never done so. Its chief contribution to EC policies is through the legislative process. However, its influence is dependent on the policy area, for the latter determines the extent of its procedural rights.

- Under the consultation procedure, which originally applied to all legislation, the EP merely gave its opinion and had no effective sanction over the real decision-making agency, the Council of Ministers.
- Under the 1970 and 1975 budget treaties the EP gained important

. powers in this policy area, including the power to reject the budget outright.

- Under the SEA the assent of the EP is needed in respect of the accession of new Member States and for Association Agreements with third countries. The TEU extended this procedure.
- The SEA also introduced the co-operation procedure as a result of which certain legislation undergoes two readings in the EP. This allows the EP to propose amendments or even reject legislation, but such decisions may be overruled by the Council of Ministers under specified circumstances. Ten treaty articles, including Article 100a relating to the SEM, afforded the EP these powers. Under the TEU this procedure now covers eighteen articles.
- Under the TEU (Article 189*b*) the EP gained a new co-decision procedure. This is similar to the co-operation procedure, except that, ultimately, rejection by the EP can kill legislation taking this route. It applies to fifteen areas but some of these—e.g. the internal market—were formerly subject to the co-operation procedure.

The picture, as will be gathered, is highly complex but reflects a gradual extension to the EP of new powers, which that institution uses to full effect (see Jacobs, Corbett, and Shackleton 1992). Turn-out for EP elections remains low by comparison with national elections; how far these new powers will affect this remains to be seen.

The ECJ consists of thirteen judges and six advocates-general. The ECJ does not formulate policy but, in line with provisions in the treaties for referral, the ECJ's judgments on matters relating to the interpretation and application of EC law are cumulatively of great importance to the operation of the EC. The ECJ is assisted by a Court of First Instance.

The *Council of Ministers* consists of ministers of the Member States. It meets about 100 times per annum but in different guises according to the subject-matter. Hence the Council of Agriculture Ministers deals with the CAP, the Council of Economics and Finance Ministers (Ecofin) with matters such as the EMS, and so on. These two Councils, along with the Council of Foreign Ministers, meet most frequently. Meetings are chaired by one of the Member States, which holds the 'presidency' of the Council for a six-month period. The United Kingdom last held this post July–December 1992. The presidency has become an important office facilitating the EC's operation. Meetings of the Council are prepared by the Committee of Permanent Representatives and an associated committee system. These meetings are attended by national civil servants and aim to pave the way for political agreement by the Council.

The Council is empowered to take decisions by qualified majority rather than unanimous vote in a number of policy areas. This was the case according to the original EEC Treaty but majority voting was rarely practised because of the Luxemburg Compromise. The *practice* of majority voting increased first from the 1970s, following treaty changes relating to the budget, then following the SEA. The TEU has extended provisions still further. The dynamism of the Council of Ministers determines the effectiveness of the EC. The increased practice of majority voting has assisted the EC's decision-making speed, particularly to meet the 1992 deadline for the SEM. However, this is achieved by each Member State recognizing that it will on occasion be in the minority, with a negative effect on its national sovereignty. The Council of Ministers is no longer a classic intergovernmental body because of the departure from unanimous voting.

The *European Council* has, since its establishment in 1974, become a very powerful body. Comprised of the French president and the eleven government heads, twelve foreign ministers, the Commission president, and a vice-president, it has had a hand in all the major EC decisions in the intervening period. The European Council meets at least twice a year. Its decisions are political; transposition into EC law is left to the Council of Ministers. The European Council is important to the strategic development of the EC and of other joint activities (i.e. the other two 'pillars' of the TEU). It is the principal institution of the EU, being common to all three pillars of activity. It has become a major 'media event', however, which can detract from its efficiency.

A number of additional institutions also exist. The Economic and Social Committee, a kind of parliament of interest groups, is consulted on most EC legislation but is overshadowed by the EP. The TEU provided for the creation of a Committee of the Regions. Its role is designed to reflect the increased involvement of sub-national government in EC activities, most notably in regional policy. The Commission has sought to allay concerns that it is a centralizing agency by promoting links with regional authorities, some of which have important powers in their domestic context.

Surrounding the EC institutions are numerous lobby groups. There are thought to be some 500 such groups, which chiefly focus their activities on the Commission. The Commission is comparatively open to such lobbying, not least because it has no field agencies in the Member States; hence it needs information. Thus lobbies are an important part of the decision-making framework.

The result of all this is that policy-making consists of a dense network of contacts. The nature of the contacts depends on the precise form that policy-making takes in the area concerned (e.g. which procedure in the EP; what type of voting in the Council?), as well as on the efficiency of lobby groups (and there may be several in competition with each other). The increasing complexity of policy-making led to calls during the ratification of the TEU for greater openness and more decentralization of power following the so-called subsidiarity principle.[5] Some developments in this direction seem inevitable unless the EC is to lose touch with the European public.

Two characteristics of the EC's institutional structure unify the complex structure. First, the EC's predominant style of policy-making is a regulatory one: it provides a *framework* for economic and political action that is largely left to the Member States themselves to enact and administer. The lack of large-scale supranational budgetary resources reinforces this regulatory approach at the expense of macroeconomic or redistributive activities. A characteristic of regulatory politics is the conduct of policy-making in relatively closed groups of policy specialists. Thus, if decision-making at the more routine level has a relatively low profile, this does not mean that the political dynamic is absent; rather, it is present in discussions between specialist national civil servants, Commission officials, interest group representatives, and committee members of the EP.

Secondly, national interests still loom large in these technical discussions. Thus, behind an apparently technical debate about standardizing axle weights for heavy goods vehicles may stand national motor industries with different interests, governmental authorities faced with divergent financial implications for road improvement programmes, and so on. However, at the technical level national interests are often challenged. The increased utilization of qualified majority voting can mean that decisions can be reached against the wishes of a minority of governments, and enforced by EC law, which takes precedence over national law. What is important here, then, is that there are *supra*national interests challenging national ones. The supranational institutions—the Commission, the ECJ, and the EP—have their own power resources and these often come into play at the technical level.

### 1.4. THE EC IN THE 1990s

The EC has an extensive agenda for the 1990s. This agenda is largely concerned with issues of widening and deepening the Community.

The deepening of integration is a major task. A lot of the SEM programme has to be transposed into EC law during the middle of the 1990s. On top of this there is the programme agreed in the TEU. However, speculative attacks against the EMS in 1992 and 1993 raised serious questions about attaining the goal of EMU. The ratification process relating to the TEU also revealed serious problems in several Member States. One common strand to this was a perceived remoteness of the EC, engendered as a result of the essentially élite-drive route that integration has taken.

Just as in the period leading to the 1973 enlargement, deepening has been linked to widening.[6] At the Edinburgh European Council in December

1992 the EC12 decided to press ahead with enlargement negotiations. At the front of the queue were a number of EFTA members, including Austria, Finland, Norway, and Sweden, with a new round of enlargement anticipated for 1995. Other countries which have made formal, but more problematic, applications are Turkey, Malta, and Cyprus.

The EFTA members are also pursuing their links through the European Economic Area (EEA) Treaty, which was signed in Portugal in May 1992. This was motivated by the EFTA states' fear of losing out from being outside the EC single market, and aimed to provide a half-way house as an alternative to membership (see Michalski and Wallace 1992).

A third category of states waiting in the wings are the Central European countries: Poland, Hungary, and the Czech and Slovak Republics. With the collapse of Communist regimes and the dissolution of the Soviet-dominated CMEA in 1991, these states are orienting themselves towards the goal of EC membership. For the time being they have been given close links with the EC through what are called Europe Agreements. These were signed between the EC and Hungary, Poland, and (the then) Czechoslovakia in December 1991. They are designed to align the states with the EC's economic and legal practice. It remains to be seen how the states fare in economic restructuring (including with EC aid) and in developing a secure liberal-democratic underpinning. The European Bank for Reconstruction and Development, which the EC helped initiate, is active as a post-Cold War, pan-European agency assisting the economic transformation of Central and Eastern Europe.

The agenda of the 1990s thus provides the European Union, and its EC pillar, with a full work-load. European integration has certainly not reached 'the end of history'. Many economic issues wait to be addressed. But the effectiveness of the Member States in developing supranational economic policies will remain dependent on the constellation of political forces at the national level and in the EU.

# NOTES

1. The history of the United Kingdom's relationship to integration cannot be dealt with in detail here. For an account, see George (1990). For an interpretation, see Bulmer (1992).
2. Qualified majority voting is a system whereby the importance of larger countries is increased in relation to smaller ones in voting through the assignment of a weighting. This system continues to operate: see the chapter on the Council of Ministers in Nugent (forthcoming).

3. It is from this date onwards that one can refer to 'the EC', i.e. referring to the three Communities. However, where reference is made to the specific treaty provisions, it is necessary to refer to the community concerned.
4. For consideration of various aspects of the treaties, see Artis (1992), Corbett (1992), and Nugent (1992).
5. The subsidiarity principle calls for collective solutions within the EC/EU only where the national level cannot provide them. However, some see subsidiarity as a call for power at the regional, sub-national level.
6. On the issue of enlargement, see Michalski and Wallace (1992).

# REFERENCES

Artis, M. (1992), 'The Maastricht Road to Monetary Union', *Journal of Common Market Studies*, 30/3: 299–309.

Bulmer, S. (1992), 'Britain and European Integration: Of Sovereignty, Slow Adaptation and Semi-Detachment', in S. George (ed.), *Britain and the European Community* (Oxford: Oxford University Press), 1–29.

—— and Scott, A. (1994) (eds.), *Economic and Political Integration in Europe: Internal Dynamics and Global Context* (Oxford: Blackwell).

—— and Wessels, W. (1987), *The European Council: Decision-Making in European Politics* (Basingstoke: Macmillan).

Corbett, R. (1992), 'The Intergovernmental Conference on Political Union', *Journal of Common Market Studies*, 30/3: 271–98.

George, S. (1990), *An Awkward Partner: Britain in the European Community* (Oxford: Oxford University Press).

—— (1991), *Politics and Policy in the European Community* (Oxford: Oxford University Press).

Jacobs, F., Corbett, R., and Shackleton, M. (1992), *The European Parliament*, 2nd edn. (Harlow: Longman).

Keohane, R., and Hoffmann, S. (1991) (eds.), *The New European Community: Decisionmaking and Institutional Change* (Boulder, Colo.: Westview Press).

Laffan, B. (1992), *Integration and Cooperation in Europe* (London: Routledge).

Michalski, A., and Wallace, H. (1992), *The European Community and the Challenge of Enlargement*, 2nd edn. (London: Royal Institute of International Affairs).

Milward, A. (1992), *The European Rescue of the Nation-State* (London: Routledge).

Nugent, N. (1992), 'The Deepening and Widening of the European Community', *Journal of Common Market Studies*, 30/3: 311–28.

—— (forthcoming), *The Government and Politics of the European Union* (Basingstoke: Macmillan).

Pryce, R. (1987) (ed.), *The Dynamics of European Union* (Beckenham: Croom Helm).

Sbragia, A. (1992) (ed.), *Euro-Politics: Institutions and Policymaking in the 'New' European Community* (Washington DC: The Brookings Institution).

Scott, A. (1992), 'Fiscal Policy', in S. Bulmer, S. George, and A. Scott (eds.), *The United Kingdom and EC Membership Evaluated* (London: Pinter), 45–56.

Urwin, D. (1991), *The Community of Europe* (Harlow: Longman).

Wallace, W. (1990), *The Transformation of Western Europe* (London: Pinter/Royal Institute of International Affairs).

# 2

# The European Economy

MIKE ARTIS AND NICK WEAVER

## 2.1. INTRODUCTION

The primary purpose of this chapter is to provide the reader with a statistical illustration of the basic economic features of the European Community (EC) and its constituent members. Some comparison between the EC as a whole and the United States and Japan and a brief examination of some possible future entrants to the EC are also made.

Whilst such a statistical picture of the European economy is useful, some discussion of economic policy is essential. Whatever problems there have been with the Treaty on European Union (the 'Maastricht Treaty')—the 'No' vote in the Danish referendum, the refusal of the UK negotiators to accept the Social Chapter, and the substantial difficulties facing the Exchange Rate Mechanism (ERM)—the authors think it likely that the approach adopted there will continue to dominate the European policy-making agenda over the next few years. To this end a discussion of the convergence criteria advanced in the Treaty on European Union (TEU) is presented in the final part of this chapter.

Often statistics, such as those presented in the first part of this chapter, are simply reproduced on the assumption that their meaning is unambiguous. This assumption is not always safe. An effort is, therefore, made to explain something about the nature of the statistics themselves, as well as the information they convey about the world.

In producing a statistical picture, it is always difficult to decide what to include and how it should be presented. Presenting data relating to all of the variables, for all the countries, for all the years, could easily result in an information overload. The approach taken here is to present figures and tables illustrating the major economic indicators in the most recent year for which a complete and consistent data set is available and to look at the behaviour of some of the variables over a longer period.

A problem particular to discussions of the EC is that it has grown over time, the most recent additions being Spain and Portugal. In this chapter figures for the EC refer to all the EC12 not the EC9 or EC6 of the time. The more recent addition of the eastern *Länder* to Germany is statistically a more difficult problem. No allowance has yet been made for these territories in historical statistics, but figures for the most recent year are given, where possible, for a unified Germany and for the EC12 including this addition. In most cases, however, data are available only for West Germany. These distinctions are indicated using the convention that Ger.+ (and, correspondingly, EC+) refer to measures including the eastern *Länder* of Germany, whilst Ger. (and EC) refer to measures that do not.

## 2.2. POPULATION

The populations of the EC12 and of the United States and Japan for 1993 are shown in Fig. 2.1. The population of the EC at 348 million is greater than both the other major economies; the United States' population is 259 million and Japan's is only 125 million. The situation is, however, not static. Several European countries are currently negotiating admittance to the EC, and the United States is currently negotiating the North American Free Trade Agreement (NAFTA), which seeks to establish a free-trade block with Canada and Mexico.

In terms of population, the most notable feature of the EC's constituent members is that most of the population lives in just a few big countries. Roughly 85 per cent of the total live in just five countries: Germany,

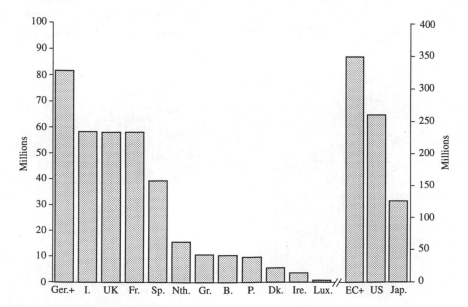

**FIG. 2.1.** Population 1993
*Source*: Derived from Eurostat (1993*a*).

France, Italy, the United Kingdom, and Spain. The seven smallest countries—the Netherlands, Greece, Portugal, Denmark, the Irish Republic, and
Luxemburg—together account for only around 15 per cent.

It is difficult to make any broad statements about population densities,
but it is possible to discern a London–Milan axis around which are areas of
relatively high density (more than 100 inhabitants per square kilometre). In
contrast, much of Spain, south and central France, the Irish Republic,
Denmark and Greece, outside the major urban centres, is relatively
sparsely populated (less than 100 inhabitants per square kilometre).

## 2.3. NATIONAL INCOME AND EXPENDITURE

There are various ways of measuring the size of an economy, Gross
Domestic Product (GDP) being the most commonly quoted. The GDP
measure includes all goods and services for final consumption which are
produced by the economic activity of producer units resident in an economy. It is a territorial measure. The other measure that is often used is
Gross National Product (GNP). This measures the income earned by
domestic citizens regardless of whether they earn their income at home
or abroad. GNP equals GDP plus net property income from abroad. Fig. 2.2
shows both GDP and GNP and illustrates the fact that there is a difference
of less than 1 per cent between GDP and GNP for most of the Twelve and
for both the United States and Japan. The three exceptions are: Denmark,
where GDP is 4 per cent greater than GNP; Ireland, where the GDP is 10

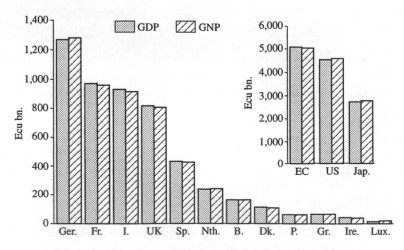

FIG. 2.2. GDP and GNP at current market prices and current exchange rates 1991
*Source*: Eurostat (1993*a*).

per cent greater than GNP, and Luxemburg, where GNP is 36 per cent greater than GDP.

A note of warning needs to be sounded about the use of either GDP or GNP as unqualified indicators of the size of an economy. Even in countries with advanced statistical services, a large part of economic activity goes unrecorded, whilst some important corrections cannot be made. Accounting techniques are not available to measure the value of unmarketed production (such as housework and DIY activities), nor to provide estimates of the costs of pollution and environmental destruction. Tax evasion and moonlighting give rise to a substantial unrecorded 'black economy'. In 1987 Italy, in response to evidence of the massive extent of under-reporting of economic activity, raised its estimate of GDP by 18 per cent. Despite the fact that the absence of broader measures has for a long time been recognized as a serious problem, progress in this area is only slowly being made and as yet there is no widely available alternative to GDP and GNP that is consistently reported.

In order to make international comparisons, GDP, which is initially calculated in terms of domestic currency, needs to be re-expressed in terms of some common or *numeraire* currency. Internationally this is usually done in terms of the US dollar, although any currency can be used. Increasingly within the EC the European Currency Unit (Ecu) is being used. The Ecu is based on a weighted basket of all the EC's currencies (see Chapter 12 for more details).

However, the use of market exchange rates when making international comparisons has been criticized on the grounds that it gives rise to a systematic bias (Gilbert and Kravis 1954). Market exchange rates do not necessarily reflect the amount of goods that can be bought with a currency— that is, the purchasing power of a currency in terms of a volume of goods. This is because the market exchange rate is the result of a whole variety of factors, including not only the supply and demand for foreign exchange required to match the flows of real goods and services but also the speculative activities of foreign-exchange dealers, capital flows, and so on. To the extent that these factors do not influence the purchasing power of the currency in a country, the market exchange rate will not be a good measure of the purchasing power of a currency in a country.

Various ways have been proposed to get around this problem. One simple method, proposed by *The Economist*, is the use of the 'Big Mac' index. This uses the relative prices of Big Macs in two countries to construct a new exchange rate. Big Macs are used because they are a standardized commodity whose price is widely known. However, price-level differences between countries vary for different commodities, and a more sophisticated measure using a similar principle to the Big Mac index but taking into account a larger basket of goods is required. Purchasing power parity (PPP) estimates attempt to do just this, their aim being to try to get rid of the difference in price levels to enable a comparison of the quantities or volumes that can be purchased.

The measures of PPP used in this chapter, Purchasing Power Standards (PPS), are produced by Eurostat (the EC's statistical office) which calculates them using methods established by the International Comparison Project (ICP) of the United Nations. They are calculated on the basis of a list of products chosen because of their representativeness and comparability. For each product a price ratio is established and a weighted average across all the products in the list can then be formed for each country. These weighted average price parities give an alternative (PPP) set of exchange rates which can be applied to the original national currency estimates of GDP to give PPP estimates of GDP. A scaling procedure ensures that the EC's total GDP in PPS is the same as in Ecus.

From Fig. 2.3 it can be clearly seen that a comparison of the relative sizes of the EC, the United States, and Japan is influenced, to some extent, by whether market exchange rates or PPS measures are used. At market exchange rates, the United States is around 10 per cent smaller than the EC and Japan is just over 50 per cent of the EC. At PPS the United States is 3 per cent bigger than the EC and Japan is around 44 per cent of the EC.

In terms of GDP(PPS), the dominance of the five biggest EC economies—Germany, France, Italy, the United Kingdom, and Spain—is again clear. Together they account for over 87 per cent of the total GDP of the EC12.

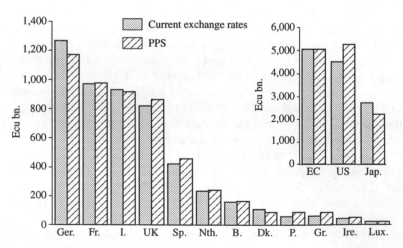

**F IG. 2.3.** GDP at current market prices, evaluated at current exchange rates or in PPSs 1991
*Source*: Eurostat (1993*a*).

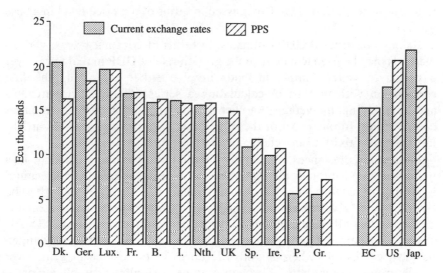

**FIG. 2.4.** GDP per capita, evaluated at current exchange rates or in PPSs 1991
*Source*: Eurostat (1993*a*).

## Per capita GDP

Scaling GDP by population gives us a measure of GDP per capita. Fig. 2.4 shows GDP per capita in both PPS and Ecus. Here the effect of adjusting the GDP figures for PPS is clear. All the countries having a below EC average per capita income (the United Kingdom, Spain, the Irish Republic, Portugal, and Greece) are, in real terms, richer than would appear to be the case if market exchange rates instead of some measure of PPP were used. This is the systematic bias that Gilbert and Kravis noted. The spread is still considerable, with the GDP(PPS) per capita in the richest country—Luxemburg—being more than twice that in the poorest—Greece. In terms of the more populous countries, Germany, France, and Italy are above the EC average and the United Kingdom and Spain below it.

## Economic Growth

In addition to looking at the static picture that the statistics discussed above provide, it is interesting to look at how the economies have grown. To study the change over time it is again necessary to adjust the GDP estimates for price changes so that comparisons in terms of volumes can be made. The most appropriate measure of changes in the level of prices in this context is based upon a weighted basket of the prices of *all* products (not just those purchased by households). This measure of inflation, the GDP deflator, enables nominal GDP, which is expressed in current terms, to be converted into real GDP expressed in terms of the price level in a base year.

Having constructed GDP estimates, in terms of constant prices, various methods may be used to calculate the growth rate of GDP in real terms over a period of years. Simple methods involve either comparing the first observation with the last or calculating a series of annual growth rates and then finding an average. Another popular method uses the continuous compounding formula. All of these methods have drawbacks—in particular, their sensitivity to the choice of the period chosen.

In some circumstances a preferable method will be to find the slope of a trend line fitted through the data. This is done by regressing the natural logarithm of GDP on time and an intercept; i.e. $Lngdp_t = \alpha + \beta t$. The coefficient, $\beta$, gives the trend annual growth rate. The advantage of this method is that all the data are used in the calculation of the trend. This is important when comparing countries which may have differently timed business cycles and where slight differences in the choice of years over which to measure the rate of growth may have significant implications.

Fig. 2.5 shows GDP and GDP per capita annual growth, measured using the regression method, over the period 1970–91. It is noticeable that the four EC countries with the lowest GDP per capita (see Fig. 2.4)—Greece, Portugal, the Irish Republic, and Spain—all grew faster in terms of their real GDP than the EC average. Luxemburg, the richest, also grew fast—a factor directly attributable to the growth of the EC's institutions located there.

Since population growth in the EC countries has not been uniform,

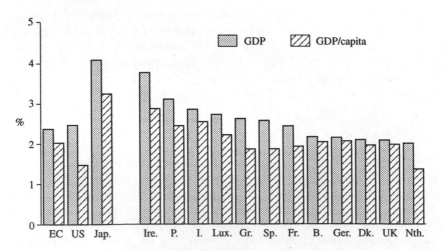

**FIG. 2.5.** Real GDP PPS and per capita growth rates 1970–91
*Source*: Eurostat (1993a).

growth of GDP per capita tells a different story from GDP growth *per se*. Many of the faster growing economies have also been countries with faster growing populations. For example, Greece, which has had the fifth fastest growth rate in total GDP, has also had the second lowest growth rate in GDP per capita.

Figures such as these enable us to examine the extent to which the GDP per capita of the EC economies are converging. Here we must be aware that convergence of levels requires divergence in growth rates. Thus for GDP per capita to converge across the economies of the EC, the poorest countries must grow faster than the richer ones.

The differences in growth performance have led to changing positions in terms of the league table expressed in real per capita income terms, the most notable features being 'il sorpasso', when Italy overtook the United Kingdom in the mid-1980s and the relative decline in the Dutch economy.

## Regional GDP

In addition to the considerable differences in GDP per capita between Member States, there are even greater differences at the regional level both within individual countries and between regions in different EC countries. The existence of these marked differences have led to calls from groups within some regions for the EC to become a 'Europe of regions' rather than of nations.

Regional level estimates of GDP per capita are produced by Eurostat. They are based on estimates of the gross value added in the region (in PPS) divided by the estimated residential population. This leads, for example, to the very high per capita GDP estimates for Hamburg with its large number of non-residents working there, but much lower per capita GDP estimates for adjoining regions with relatively large 'dormitory' populations. An additional complication is that figures are based on national purchasing powers rather than regional ones. Higher prices in wealthier areas will tend to generate an upwards bias and lower prices in poorer areas will tend to generate a downwards bias.

The richest regions, when measured in terms of GDP(PPS) per capita, include Hamburg, Ile de France (including Paris), Brussels, Darmstadt, Greater London, Bremen, Oberbayem, Stuttgart, Groningen, and Lombardia. As can be seen from Fig. 2.6, the poorest regions are the regions of Greece, Portugal, the *Mezzogiorno* in Italy, and the Irish Republic. These are mainly agricultural areas, far from the London–Milan axis. The decline in 'traditional' industries like coal, steel, and shipbuilding has led to the relative decline of other regions. Regional data are not at the time of writing available for the new *Länder* (the former East Germany) and it is more than likely that some regions there, as a result of the loss of most of the industrial base, would fall in to the bottom ten. It needs to be noted that within regions

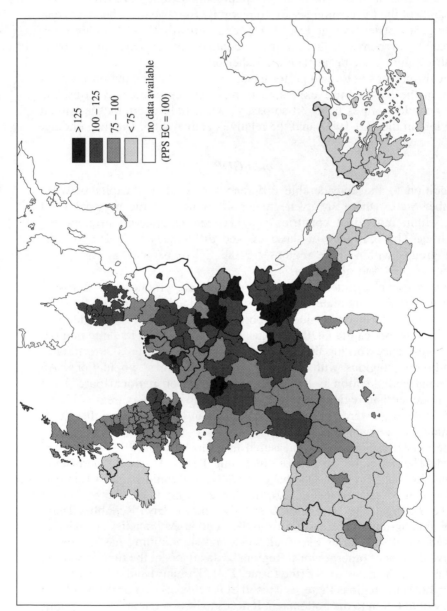

**Fig. 2.6.** Regional GDP per capita 1990
*Source:* Eurostat (1993*b*).

themselves there are considerable disparities. Greater London, for example, the richest region in the United Kingdom and one of the richest regions in the EC, has within it areas where the level of poverty is as bad as anywhere in the EC.

## 2.4. DISAGGREGATION OF GDP

GDP can, in principle, be found as the sum of expenditures, the sum of sectoral value added, or the sum of factor incomes in the economy. Correspondingly, there are three possible disaggregations of GDP. Figures are shown for a recent year illustrating each of these.

### The Disaggregation of GDP by Expenditure

Total expenditure in an economy can be found by summing private consumption $(C)$, government consumption $(G)$, investment $(I)$, changes in stocks held by businesses $(\Delta S)$ and the balance of trade $(X - M)$.

$$\text{GDP}_{\text{expenditure}} = C + I + \Delta S + G + (X - M).$$

Private consumption is made up of household expenditure on food, clothing, housing services, household goods, transport, and health. Government consumption consists of expenditure on health, education, defence, and social security payments. Investment includes expenditure on machinery, transport equipment, and building construction. Exports of goods and services minus imports give the balance of trade. Fig. 2.7 shows GDP disaggregated by expenditure for 1991.

As might be expected, private consumption shares of GDP in most of the countries are close to the EC average. The noteworthy exceptions are Greece, Portugal, and the United Kingdom, where private consumption is considerably higher, and Denmark and the Irish Republic, where it is lower than average.

Government expenditure as a share of GDP is high in Denmark, the United Kingdom, and Greece and relatively low in Germany, Holland, and Belgium. Differences in the shares between private and government consumption are an indicator not only of what might be termed 'real' differences in the structure of the economy (for instance, how much is actually spent on health) but also of institutional differences (for instance, health services may be almost entirely government run—as is the case in Denmark—and classified as government consumption, or there might be substantial private provision, in which case it would be classified in part as private consumption).

Investment expenditure, as a share of GDP, is relatively high in

*Mike Artis and Nick Weaver*

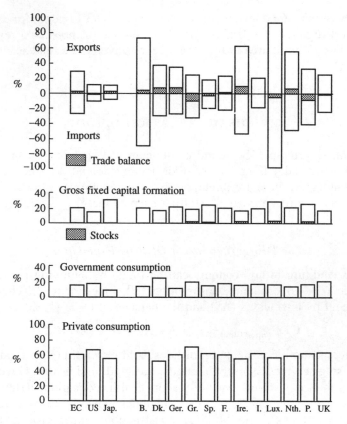

**Fig. 2.7.** Percentage of GDP by expenditure 1991
*Source*: Eurostat (1993*a*: 52–3).

Luxemburg, Portugal, and Spain and low in the United Kingdom, Denmark, and the Irish Republic.

Exports plus imports are a good measure of the extent to which an economy is open to the rest of the world. By this measure the most open economies are those of Luxemburg, Belgium, the Irish Republic, and the Netherlands, all of whose exports plus imports are greater than 100 per cent of GDP. Spain and Italy are both relatively closed.

### The Disaggregation of GDP by Sectoral Value Added

The total value added in an economy may be found by the summation of the value added by each economic sector (or, at a more disaggregated level, by summation for each 'industry' within each sector).

$$\text{GDP}_{\text{value added}} = \text{VA Services} + \text{VA Industry} + \text{VA Agriculture.}$$

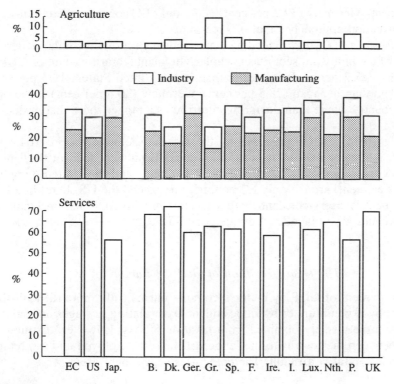

FIG. 2.8. Percentage of GDP by sectoral value added
*Note*: Data are for various years 1987–90.
*Source*: *OECD* (1993*a*).

Value added by the industrial sector is often subdivided into value added by manufacturing and value added by production industries.

Again, there are definitional problems with all the categories. The value added by cleaners of factories may well be added to service sector value added if outside contractors are hired or might be allocated to industrial sector value added if the cleaners work for the factory directly. Fig. 2.8 shows GDP disaggregated by sectoral value added. Consistent data are again hard to come by. The OECD data used are for various years between 1987 and 1990.

Agriculture provides a slightly higher percentage of GDP in the EC (2.9 per cent) than in either the United States (2.0 per cent) or Japan (2.5 per cent). For most of the Twelve, agriculture's share is less than 5 per cent. Only in the EC's three poorest countries (Greece 13.8 per cent, the Irish Republic 9.6 per cent, and Portugal 6.2 per cent) is it greater than this.

The share of GDP provided by industry in the EC (32.7 per cent) is greater than in the United States (29.2 per cent) but less than in Japan (41.8

per cent). Germany (39.2 per cent) is the only EC country where industry's contribution approaches that of Japan.

The share of GDP provided by manufacturing follows a similar pattern to that of the industrial sector as a whole. The manufacturing share of GDP in the EC (23.3 per cent) is greater than in the United States (19.3 per cent) but less than in Japan (28.5 per cent). Germany (30.8 per cent) is the only EC country where manufacturing contributes a bigger share than it does in Japan.

The share of GDP provided by the service sector in the EC (64.4 per cent) is greater than in Japan (55.7 per cent) but less than in the United States (68.8 per cent). Denmark (71.7 per cent) and the United Kingdom (69.2 per cent) are the only EC countries to exceed the US share. In all the EC countries, services contribute a greater share to GDP than in Japan and they could all be labelled 'service economies'.

## The Disaggregation of GDP by Factor Income

Measurement of GDP by factor income is intrinsically more difficult than either by expenditure or by value added. Data relating to wages and salaries are relatively easily obtained from taxation offices. However, distinguishing between the returns to the labour of the self-employed and the returns to their capital is difficult. The categories shown here are:

1. compensation of employees (which includes wages and salaries);
2. net operating surplus of the economy (which can be viewed as an aggregate of profits, rent, and some return to the labour of the self-employed);
3. depreciation of the capital stock; and
4. net taxes (direct taxes less subsidies).

$$\text{GDP}_{\text{factor incomes}} = \text{compensation of employees} + \text{net operating surplus of the economy} + \text{depreciation of capital} + \text{net taxes.}$$

Fig. 2.9 shows GDP disaggregated by factor income for 1991 in percentage terms. Despite its theoretical appeal—particularly for political economists—the disaggregation of national income by factors that is available is not very revealing. Little can be said by way of intra-country comparison about compensation of employees, net operating surplus, or consumption of capital, since variations in the figures are as much a reflection of institutional differences as they are of real differences. This, too, is an area of accounting that needs more work.

The one statement of any importance that we might make is that both subsidies and taxes are a higher share of GDP in all EC countries than in either the United States or Japan.

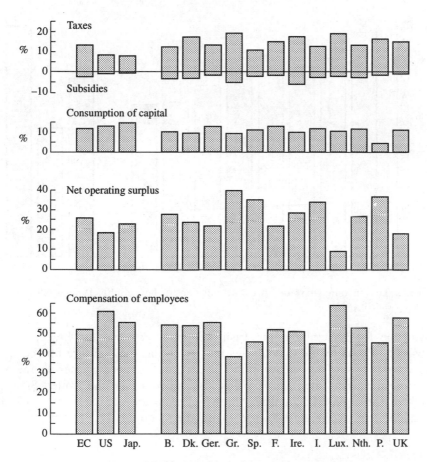

**FIG. 2.9.** Percentage of GDP by factor income 1991
*Source*: Eurostat (1993*a*).


## 2.5. INCOME INEQUALITY

In addition to disaggregating income by factors of production, it is desirable to analyse what is generally referred to as income inequality. The normal 'ideal' procedure is to rank households in terms of income received, no matter what the source, and plot a Lorenz curve showing the cumulative percentage of national income received by the households. Ideally such a curve would be plotted for each country. Data availability and space again preclude this. Rather, Fig. 2.10 shows simple statistics produced by the United Nations Development Programme (UNDP) which aim to provide a summary measure of income inequality: the income share of the lowest 40 per cent of households. Even for a measure as simple as this, data are not

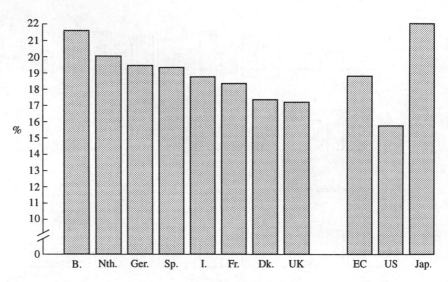

**Fig. 2.10.** Income share of lowest 40 per cent of households 1985–1989
*Source*: UNDP (1993).

available for Luxemburg, the Irish Republic, Portugal, or Greece. The absence of data for these countries may well bias the measure for the EC as a whole. Using this measure, the EC as a whole has a greater degree of income inequality than Japan but is less unequal than the United States, and, of the eight EC countries for which data are available, the United Kingdom has the greatest degree of income inequality.

## 2.6. LABOUR MARKET

The standard procedure when analysing the basic features of the labour market involves distinguishing the population of working age from the total population. The population of working age is then divided into three mutually exclusive and all-encompassing categories: persons in employment, the unemployed, and the inactive. The unemployed plus the employed together make up the labour force. From these categories various measures such as employment/population ratios (employment as a percentage of the population of working age), activity rates (the labour force as a percentage of the population of working age), and unemployment rates (the number of unemployed as a percentage of the labour force) can be calculated. International comparability is again difficult because countries' statistical services tailor their own data to their national requirements and the political significance of the statistics renders them particularly vulnerable to interference. Eurostat, by adjusting national measures with

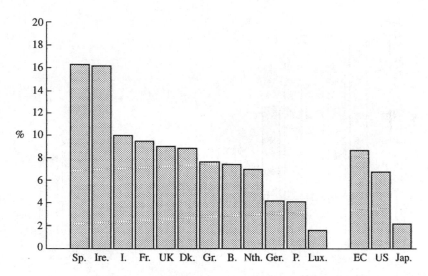

**FIG. 2.11.** Standardized unemployment rates 1991
*Source*: Eurostat (1993*a*).

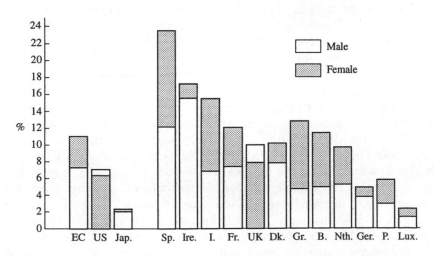

**FIG. 2.12.** Male and female standardized unemployment rates 1991
*Source*: Eurostat (1993*a*).

the help of the EC-wide Labour Force Survey, aims to produce comparable standardized statistics.

The most commonly quoted of the above measures is the unemployment rate. Fig. 2.11 shows that the standardized annual unemployment rate in

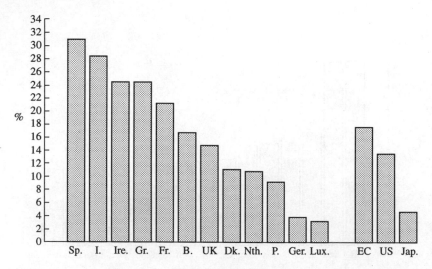

**FIG. 2.13.** Youth (<25) standardized unemployment rates 1991
*Source*: Eurostat (1993*a*).

1991 in the EC (8.7 per cent) was higher than either in the United States (6.7 per cent) or in Japan (2.1 per cent). Unemployment rates varied widely between the EC countries in 1991. Spain (16.3 per cent) and the Irish Republic (16.2 per cent) had the highest rates. Only Luxemburg with 1.6 per cent had a rate lower than Japan.

Different sections of society are more or less vulnerable to unemployment. Fig. 2.12 shows unemployment, disaggregated by gender. The 1991 unemployment rate for females was 50 per cent higher than for males in the EC, 10 per cent higher than for males in Japan, and was 10 per cent less for females in the United States. Again there were wide differences across countries. The differences are greatest in Greece, Italy, Portugal, and Belgium, where the female rate was more than 100 per cent greater than the male rate. The United Kingdom is the only EC country where the unemployment rate for females is less than for males.

Fig. 2.13 shows that unemployment has particularly affected the young in the EC countries. Youth unemployment rates in 1991 were generally far higher than the average. In Spain, Italy, Greece, and the Irish Republic one in four of those aged less than 25 was unemployed. Only in Germany, with its exceptional training policy, was youth unemployment less than the national average. Comparable data for ethnic minorities could not be found.

As a supplement to the picture of the sectoral structure of the economies shown in Fig. 2.8 the sectoral structure of employment is shown in Fig. 2.14. The two illustrate the same structure, with the differences between them being due to differences in sectoral productivities.

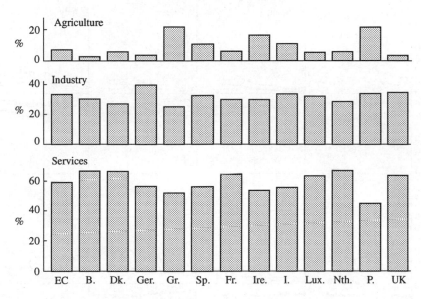

**FIG. 2.14.** Share of employment by sector
*Source*: CEC (1993*b*: 49, 51).

## 2.7. TRADE

A major economic justification for the establishment and growth of the EC arises from the expansion of opportunities to exploit competitive advantages that result from the removal of barriers to trade. The beneficial effects of the removal of such barriers in theory are that high-cost sources of supply are replaced by lower-cost sources. Such a process is referred to as *trade creation*. Undoubtedly, the establishment of the EC has led to substantial trade creation. There are, however, other less beneficial effects associated

**TABLE 2.1.** *EC exports and imports of goods and services by source and destination as a percentage of total*

| Source or destination | 1958 Exports | Imports | 1991 Exports | Imports |
|---|---|---|---|---|
| Intra EC | 37.2 | 35.2 | 61.6 | 58.6 |
| Other OECD Europe | 13.7 | 10.1 | 11.4 | 10.4 |
| USA and Canada | 10.2 | 15.0 | 7.2 | 8.5 |
| Japan | 0.6 | 0.7 | 2.0 | 4.3 |
| Rest of world | 38.3 | 39.0 | 17.8 | 18.2 |
| Total extra EC | 62.8 | 64.8 | 38.4 | 41.4 |

*Source*: Eurostat (1993*a*).

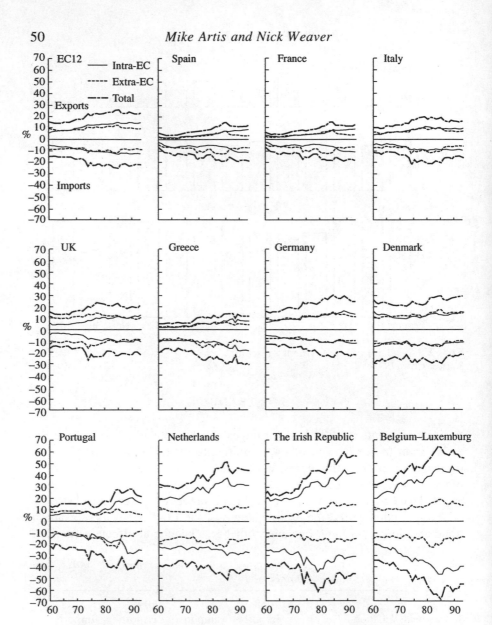

**Fig. 2.15.** Intra, extra, and total EC goods trade as a percentage of GDP 1960–1993

*Note*: Figures for 1992 and 1993 are, respectively, estimates and forecasts.
*Source*: CEC (1993*a*: 219–23).

with those aspects of the EC commercial policy which have led to high-cost sources of supply supplanting lower costs, a process referred to as *trade diversion*. (Chapter 3 provides a thorough analysis of these concepts.)

Fig. 2.15 shows total, intra-EC and extra-EC trade in goods for the EC12 and for the EC in total from 1960 to 1993. The trend over the whole period has been towards an increase in openness when measured as the total of goods trade as a percentage of GDP. This process has been driven for the most part by the expansion of intra-EC trade.

The relatively higher growth of intra-EC trade has led to a substantial change in the direction of trade, particularly with the rest of the world, as is shown in Table 2.1.

### 2.8. POSSIBLE FUTURE ENTRANTS TO THE EC

The number of countries in the EC has grown considerably since its foundation and many more over recent years have expressed interest in joining.

At the close of 1993 most non-EC European countries were viewed as possible future entrants. They are often divided into three distinct groups on the basis of institutional and economic characteristics: the European

TABLE 2.2 *Some major economic indicators of the possible future entrants to the EC 1990*

| Country | Population (m.) | GDP/capita (US$000) | Share of work-force in agriculture (%) | CEPR estimated net contribution to EC budget (Ecu m.) |
| --- | --- | --- | --- | --- |
| Austria | 7.7 | 21,000 | 9 | 661 |
| Finland | 5.0 | 28,000 | 10 | 261 |
| Iceland | 0.3 | 22,000 | 10 | n.a. |
| Norway | 4.2 | 25,000 | 7 | 668 |
| Sweden | 8.6 | 26,000 | 4 | 1,067 |
| Switzerland | 6.7 | 34,000 | 6 | 855 |
| Bulgaria | 8.8 | 2,300 | 20 | −1,458 |
| Czechoslavakia | 15.7 | 3,400 | 12 | −1,189 |
| Hungary | 10.0 | 2,600 | 19 | −1,458 |
| Poland | 38.2 | 1,900 | 27 | −5,192 |
| Romania | 23.2 | 1,400 | 28 | −3,603 |
| Cyprus[a] | 0.7 | 8,020 | 26 | n.a. |
| Malta[a] | 0.3 | 6,610 | 5 | n.a. |
| Turkey | 58.0 | 1,640 | 58 | −8,368 |

*Note*: n.a. = not available.

[a] Data for 1991.

*Source*: CEPR (1993), World Bank (1993).

Free Trade Association (EFTA) countries, the Central and East European Countries (CEECs), and some Mediterranean countries. Table 2.2 sets out some pertinent data in relation to those possible future entrants to the EC.

The EFTA countries—Sweden, Norway, Finland, Iceland, Austria, Switzerland, and Liechtenstein—are all relatively rich stable countries with economies. Austria, Finland, Sweden, and Switzerland have all applied for full EC membership, and, were the nordic countries to join, it is hard to imagine Norway failing to follow them. Only Iceland, because of fear for its fishing interests, and Liechtenstein are unlikely to apply.

However, the EFTA countries already have most of the benefits of access to the EC's market through their membership of the European Economic Area (EEA). The EEA's stated aim is to reduce frontier barriers and to allow the free movement of goods, services, capital, and workers. Agriculture is, however, a notable exception.

Because of their small size, there is little for the EC to gain from bringing the EFTA countries into the single market of the EEA. On the other hand, the EC would gain in terms of its budget if EFTA countries were to become full members. The Centre for Economic Policy Research (CEPR 1993) estimated that EFTA countries, were they all to join, might be expected to contribute an additional 14 per cent to the EC's budget. Because their GDP per capita is something like 35 per cent higher than the EC average, they could hardly expect to receive substantial sums from the structural funds.

As far as the EFTA countries themselves are concerned, membership of the EC could affect them in a variety of ways. Their heavy dependence on the EC for trade means that there are potentially large gains to be made from participating in the single market.

The CEPR report estimated that increased competition would reduce costs and boost productivity, raising EFTA's GDP by up to 5 per cent. Full membership would entail adoption of the EC's Common Agricultural Policy (CAP) by the EFTA countries. This could cause problems for the EFTA countries, because their agriculture is even more heavily subsidized than the EC's (EC subsidies are roughly equal to 49 per cent of the value of farm output. EFTA countries' subsidies average 68 per cent of farm output and Swiss subsidies as much as 80 per cent).

Within the EEA, the EC's competition policy must be applied to cross-border trade in manufactured goods. Full membership requires competition policy to be applied to a much wider range of domestic activities. This would restrict much of the state aid to industry and restrictive business practices which are common in the EFTA countries.

The CEECs—Hungary, the Czech and Slovak Republics, Poland, Bulgaria, and Romania—are all former Communist countries and, as such, have had weak institutional links with the EC. Hungary, Czechoslovakia (prior to its partition), and Poland all signed bilateral EC association agreements and between themselves established the Visegrad grouping with the expressed aim of co-ordinating their joining of the EC.

Relative to the EC, the CEECs are all fairly poor. The 1991 figures of GDP per head (in market prices) of Bulgaria, Czechoslovakia, Hungary, Poland, and Romania amount to only 13 per cent of the EC average. They are all fairly large countries in terms of population, and agriculture employs a relatively high proportion of the work-force. All these factors would make the CEECs eligible for large grants from both the structural fund and the CAP were they to become members. The CEPR study estimates that net annual transfers to the five economies could amount to 13 billion ecus.

The Mediterranean applicants Turkey, Cyprus, and Malta have for a long time had close links with the EC but for a variety of reasons have not yet come close to membership. The EC–Turkey association agreement of 1963 specifically mentioned the possibility of Turkey's eventual accession to the EC after a twenty-two-year transitional period.

As things stand, both the EFTA countries and the CEECs seem to have pushed into the queue ahead of Turkey.

## 2.9. ECONOMIC POLICY

The associated problems of low economic growth rates and high unemployment have not been addressed directly by any of the EC12 over the recent past. Rather, the approach that has dominated their economic policy-making has been that of reducing inflation and, in the context of the TEU, ensuring sufficient economic convergence to create the conditions for European Monetary Union (see Chapter 13). The crisis in the European currency markets in 1992 and 1993 severely, if not finally, set back the hopes of its proponents for a progression to monetary union. But the objective of convergence on sustainable low inflation enshrined in the Treaty continues to provide a significant input into economic policy-making. Thus it is important to set out the precise provisions of the Treaty in some detail. The Treaty sets out criteria in relation to fiscal stance (budget deficits and debt burdens), inflation performance, interest rates, and exchange-rate stability. Except in the case of the exchange-rate criterion, which is discussed fully in Chapter 13, the exact criteria are set out below, together with some relevant statistical information. It is important to note that the notion of economic convergence associated with these criteria refers essentially to 'nominal convergence', which should be distinguished from what might be referred to as 'real economic convergence'. Real economic convergence is the process of equalization of national/regional GDP per capita and the convergence of economic structures and institutions.

## Budget Deficits and Debt Burdens

Budget deficits are the difference between government expenditure (including interest payments on debt) and receipts. Such deficits are financed either by borrowing, which is usually done by selling bonds, or by selling foreign-exchange reserves or other nationally owned assets including the privatization of publicly owned enterprises.

Controlling the size of government has been the thrust of much policy. This has meant that, rather than just controlling deficits, policy has been aimed at trying to reduce government expenditure because it has been thought that political expediency rules out increased taxation.

The protocol on convergence criteria in the TEU (Council of Ministers 1992) requires that 'at the time of the examination the Member State is not the subject of a Council decision under Article 104c(6) of this treaty that an excessive deficit exists'. More specifically, an excessive deficit would be deemed to exist if the ratio of planned or actual government deficit to gross domestic product exceeds a reference value, unless either the ratio has declined substantially and continuously and reached a level that comes close to the reference value; or, alternatively, the excess over the reference value is only exceptional and temporary and the ratio remains close to the reference value (p. 27), where the reference value for the ratio of planned or actual government deficit to gross domestic product at market prices is 3 per cent.

Asset-selling can only be a temporary measure and continuous budget deficits lead to the accumulation of debt. Accumulated debt becomes a problem in so far as government expenditure must be diverted towards paying interest on the debt.

As far as government debt is concerned, the convergence criterion is 'whether the ratio of government debt to gross domestic product exceeds a reference value, unless the ratio is sufficiently diminishing or approaching the reference value at a satisfactory pace' (p. 27), where the reference value for the ratio of government debt to gross domestic product at market prices is 60 per cent.

Article 104c(6) together with the further protocols indicates that the fiscal criteria are subject to a degree of discretion. In particular, whilst minimum targets are specified by the reference values—a general government deficit of no more than 3 per cent of GDP and a gross government debt of no more than 60 per cent of GDP are set out for the general government deficit and gross government debt—caveats are provided. In respect of the deficit it appears that an excess can be 'forgiven' if 'the ratio has declined substantially and continuously and reached a level that comes close to the reference value . . . or, alternatively, the excess over the reference value is only exceptional and temporary and the ratio remains close to the reference value' (p. 27). In respect of the debt ratio, it appears that an excess can be forgiven if 'the ratio is sufficiently diminishing or approaching the reference value at a satisfactory pace' (p. 27).

Should a Member State fail under one of these criteria, then the Commission would prepare a report which 'shall also take into account whether the government deficit exceeds the government investment expenditure and take into account all other relevant factors, including the medium term economic and budgetary position of the Member State' (p. 27).

The intellectual rationale for these fiscal convergence criteria, whilst not spelt out in the Treaty, is to be found in the argument that excessive debt is a temptation to governments to manipulate a surprise inflation as a means of wiping out its real value. The analysis of Sargent and Wallace (1981) was responsible for suggesting that, at some point, a large enough ratio of debt to GDP implies monetization and inflation.

Neither Sargent and Wallace nor the architects of the TEU are able to indicate critical magnitudes for this ratio, and the reference values quoted in the Treaty have been heavily criticized (see, particularly, Buiter and Kletzer (1992) and Buiter, Corsetti, and Roubini (1992) for their apparent arbitrariness).

There is an additional point that must be borne in mind, however, which is the critical need for fiscal flexibility. With already large outstanding debts, governments will feel constrained in their resort to fiscal policy.

Leslie (1993) makes the point that there is no likelihood that pressures on government expenditure are going to diminish. Simplifying the argument—since government expenditure is concentrated on the provision of services and service-sector productivity is likely to grow less rapidly than productivity more generally—then, in order merely to go on providing the same level of services, governments will need to spend a growing proportion of income.

Fig. 2.16 plots the ratio of gross public debt to GDP against the ratio of the budget deficit to GDP for each country for the years 1990–4. The shaded area in the bottom left-hand corner of the figure is formed by the TEU criteria for these rates (respectively 60 and 3 per cent). As can be seen, the recessionary conditions of the early 1990s have worsened the countries' positions considerably. None is predicted to be in the box in 1994 (the predictions are by the OECD); every country is expected to have worsened its position in respect of at least one of the criteria between 1990 and 1994.

## Inflation

Low inflation has been one of the major policy targets pursued by all of the governments of the EC12 during the 1980s and early 1990s. The reaction to the experience of the first oil shock of 1973/4 was to induce caution in dealing with the second one in 1979/80. The doctrine of 'inflation first'

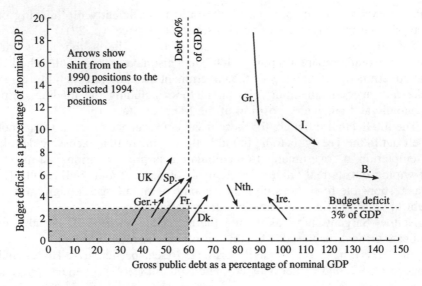

**FIG. 2.16.** Fiscal convergence criteria
*Source*: OECD (1993*b*: tables 1, 46).

placed priority on the control of inflation, even to the point of implying that the control of inflation was an essential condition for economic growth. Echoing many who have questioned this proposition, we might note that Stanners (1993), in a study which includes all the major OECD countries, finds little evidence to support the notion that a low rate of inflation has been associated with improved growth rates.

Fig. 2.17 shows inflation in consumer prices since the 1960s, where the impact of the 1973/4 oil price shock and the smaller 1979/80 shock clearly stand out.

As far as inflation is concerned the TEU argues:

The criterion on price stability referred to in the first indent of Article 109*j*(1) of this treaty shall mean that a Member State has a price performance that is sustainable and an average rate of inflation, observed over a period of one year before the examination, that does not exceed by more than 1½ percentage points that of, at most, the three best performing Member States in terms of price stability. Inflation shall be measured by means of the consumer price index on a comparable basis, taking into account differences in national definitions. (p. 185)

Following Englander and Egebo (1992), we interpret the criterion as implying that a country is convergent in this respect if its consumer price inflation is no more than 1½ points above the average of the three best performing countries. Table 2.3, which incorporates International Monetary Fund (IMF) estimated and forecast data for 1993 and 1994, shows the

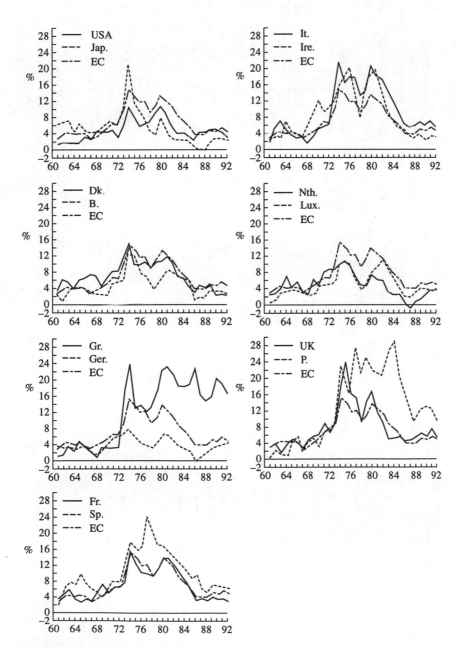

**FIG. 2.17.** Inflation: Private consumption deflators 1960–92
*Source*: Eurostat (1993*a*).

TABLE 2.3. *Inflation rate convergence criterion: Private consumption deflators (%)*

| Country | 1990 | | 1991 | | 1992 | | 1993 | | 1994 | |
|---|---|---|---|---|---|---|---|---|---|---|
| | Actual | Cut required | Actual | Cut required | Actual | Cut required | Estimated | Cut required | Forecast | Cut required |
| Greece | 19.8 | 16.1 | 18.4 | 14.2 | 15.5 | 11.8 | 13.8 | 10.4 | 10.7 | 7.1 |
| Portugal | 12.6 | 8.9 | 12.0 | 7.8 | 9.4 | 5.7 | 7.4 | 4.0 | 6.2 | 2.6 |
| Italy | 6.2 | 2.5 | 6.8 | 2.6 | 5.4 | 1.7 | 5.7 | 2.3 | 5.1 | 1.5 |
| Spain | 6.4 | 2.7 | 6.2 | 2.0 | 6.2 | 2.5 | 4.9 | 1.5 | 4.1 | 0.5 |
| UK | 5.3 | 1.6 | 7.1 | 2.9 | 5.0 | 1.3 | 3.4 | n.a. | 3.8 | 0.2 |
| Germany | 2.6 | n.a. | 3.8 | n.a. | 4.7 | 1.0 | 4.3 | 0.9 | 3.1 | n.a. |
| Luxemburg | 3.6 | n.a. | 2.9 | n.a. | 3.4 | n.a. | 4.1 | 0.7 | 3.1 | n.a. |
| Irish Republic | 1.7 | n.a. | 3.2 | n.a. | 3.0 | n.a. | 3.3 | n.a. | 3.1 | n.a. |
| Netherlands | 2.3 | n.a. | 3.3 | n.a. | 3.2 | n.a. | 2.3 | n.a. | 2.4 | n.a. |
| Belgium | 2.9 | n.a. | 2.7 | n.a. | 2.4 | n.a. | 2.5 | n.a. | 2.4 | n.a. |
| France | 2.9 | n.a. | 3.0 | n.a. | 2.4 | n.a. | 2.4 | n.a. | 2.0 | n.a. |
| Denmark | 2.6 | n.a. | 2.5 | n.a. | 1.9 | n.a. | 0.9 | n.a. | 1.9 | n.a. |
| Average of three lowest | 2.2 | n.a. | 2.7 | n.a. | 2.2 | n.a. | 1.9 | n.a. | 2.1 | n.a. |
| Convergence Limit | 3.7 | n.a. | 4.2 | n.a. | 3.7 | n.a. | 3.4 | n.a. | 3.6 | n.a. |

*Note*: n.a. = not applicable.
*Source*: IMF (1993).

actual rate of inflation for each of the countries and the cut required to meet this criterion.

### Interest Rates

One of the major ways of financing a budget deficit is by the selling of government bonds. These bonds are one of the most secure forms of investment, and in most EC countries the market for them is one of the largest sectors of the capital market. Other 'private' rates will tend to be higher, indicating the greater risks. Different governments sell different forms of bonds, and comparison is again complicated; the rather loose description 'nominal long-term interest rates' covers a whole range of different bond prices.

The criterion on the convergence of interest rates referred to in the fourth indent of Article 109*j*(1) of this Treaty shall mean that, observed over a period of one year before the examination, a Member state has had an average long-term interest rate that does not exceed by more than two percentage points that of, at most, the three best performing States in price stability. Interest rates shall be measured on the basis of long-term government bonds or comparable securities, taking into account differences in national definitions. (p. 186)

According to the convergence criteria, long-term interest rates must be

TABLE **2.4.** *Nominal long-term interest rate* (%)

| Country | 1990 | | 1991 | | 1992 | | 1993 | | 1994 | |
|---|---|---|---|---|---|---|---|---|---|---|
| Greece | | | | | | | | | | |
| Portugal | 16.8 | 5.1 | 17.1 | 5.9 | 15.0 | 3.9 | 16.1 | 5.1 | 10.5 | 2.1 |
| Italy | 13.4 | 1.7 | 13.0 | 1.8 | 13.7 | 2.6 | 13.1 | 2.1 | 10.3 | 1.9 |
| Spain | 14.7 | 3.0 | 12.4 | 1.2 | 12.2 | 1.1 | 12.6 | 1.6 | 9.2 | 0.8 |
| UK | 11.1 | n.a. | 9.9 | n.a. | 9.1 | n.a. | 9.1 | n.a. | 7.0 | n.a. |
| Germany | 8.9 | n.a. | 8.6 | n.a. | 8.0 | n.a. | 7.9 | n.a. | 6.4 | n.a. |
| Luxemburg | 8.6 | n.a. | 8.2 | n.a. | 7.9 | n.a. | 7.9 | n.a. | 6.8 | n.a. |
| Irish | | | | | | | | | | |
| Republic | 10.1 | n.a. | 9.2 | n.a. | 9.1 | n.a. | 9.4 | n.a. | 7.6 | n.a. |
| Netherlands | 9.0 | n.a. | 8.9 | n.a. | 8.1 | n.a. | 8.1 | n.a. | 6.2 | n.a. |
| Belgium | 10.1 | n.a. | 9.3 | n.a. | 8.6 | n.a. | 8.6 | n.a. | 7.1 | n.a. |
| France | 9.9 | n.a. | 9.0 | n.a. | 8.6 | n.a. | 8.6 | n.a. | 6.4 | n.a. |
| Denmark | 11.0 | n.a. | 10.1 | n.a. | 10.1 | n.a. | 9.8 | n.a. | 6.7 | n.a. |
| Average | 9.8 | n.a. | 9.2 | n.a. | 9.1 | n.a. | 9.0 | n.a. | 6.4 | n.a. |
| Convergence | | | | | | | | | | |
| Limit | 11.8 | n.a. | 11.2 | n.a. | 11.1 | n.a. | 11.0 | n.a. | 8.4 | n.a. |

*Note*: n.a. = not applicable; figures in the first column under each year are actual; figures in the second column indicate the cut required by the convergence criterion.
*Source*: IMF (1993).

within two percentage points of the average of the three lowest inflation rate states.

Table 2.4 shows long-term interest rates in the Member States from 1990 to 1993 (1994 figures are forecasted), indicating the cuts required in order to meet the criterion in the protocol. More precisely, the convergence limit is the unweighted average of the interest rate in the three countries with the lowest inflation rate plus 2 per cent. In terms of inflation performance the three best performers in the successive years were as follows:

1990: Irish Republic (1.7%), Netherlands (2.3%), and Germany and Denmark (2.6%),
1991: Denmark (2.5%), Belgium (2.7%), and Luxemburg (2.9%),
1992: Denmark (1.9%), and Belgium and France (2.4%),
1993: Denmark (0.9%), Netherlands (2.3%), and France (2.4%).

These are, it must be emphasized, not necessarily the countries with the lowest interest rates and this is a problem to the extent that, if the interest rates are being consulted as an index of sustainable inflation performance, it might seem more appropriate to base the convergence limit on the countries' best interest rate performance. The upshot of the table is clear: Italy, Spain, and Portugal fail the interest-rate criterion in all the years.

# REFERENCES

Anderson, V. (1991), *Alternative Economic Indicators* (London: Routledge).

Barrell, R. (1992) (ed.), *Economic Convergence and Monetary Union in Europe* (Association for the Monetary Union of Europe and the National Institute of Economic and Social Research; London: Sage).

Buiter, W., and Kletzer, K. (1992), 'Reflections on the Fiscal Implications of a Common Currency', in A. Goivannini and C. Mayer (eds.), *European Financial Integration* (Cambridge: Cambridge University Press), 221–56.

———, Corsetti, G., and Roubini, N. (1992), *Excessive Deficits: Sense and Nonsense in the Treaty of Maastricht* (Discussion Paper No. 750; London: Centre for Economic Policy and Research).

CEPR (1993): Centre for Economic Policy Research, *Is Bigger Better? The Economics of EC Enlargement* (Monitoring European Integration 3, Annual Report, 1992; London: CEPR).

CEC (1993*a*): Commission of the European Communities, *European Economy*, 54.

——— (1993*b*), *Employment in Europe* (Luxemburg: CEC).

Council of Ministers (1992), *Treaty on European Union* (Luxemburg: Commission of the European Communities).

Englander, A., and Egebo, T. (1992), 'Institutional Commitments and Policy Credibility: A Critical Survey and Empirical Evidence from the ERM', in Organization for Economic Co-operation and Development, *Economic Studies* (18) (Spring), 45–84.

Eurostat (1985), *Purchasing Power Parities and Gross Domestic Product in Real Terms* (Results, 2 C; Luxemburg: Commission of the European Communities).

—— (1988), *Labour Force Survey* (Methods and Definitions, 3 E; Luxemburg: Commission of the European Communities).

—— (1989), *Labour Force Survey* (Results 3 C; Luxemburg: Commission of the European Communities).

—— (1992), *Europe in Figures* (Luxemburg: Commission of the European Communities).

—— (1993*a*), Appendix to *European Economy*, 54.

—— (1993*b*), *Rapid Reports, Regions*, 1 (Luxemburg: Commission of the European Communities).

Gilbert, M., and Kravis, I. B. (1954), *An International Comparison of National Products and the Purchasing Power of Currencies: A Study of the United States, the United Kingdom, France, Germany and Italy* (Paris: Organization for European Economic Co-operation).

IMF (1993): International Monetary Fund, *World Economic Outlook* (Washington DC: IMF).

Leslie, D. (1993), *Advanced Macroeconomics: Beyond IS/LM* (London: McGraw-Hill).

OECD (1993*a*): Organization for Economic Co-operation and Development, *Economic Outlook, Historical Statistics 1960–1990* (Paris, OECD).

—— (1993*b*), *Economic Outlook*, 53 (June).

Sargent, T., and Wallace, N. (1981), 'Some Unpleasant Monetarist Arithmetic', *Federal Reserve Bank of Minneapolis Quarterly Review*, 5 (Fall), 1–17.

Stanners, W. (1993), 'Is Low Inflation an Important Condition for High Growth?', *Cambridge Journal of Economics*, 17: 79–107.

UN and CEC (1986): United Nations and Commission of the European Communities, *World Comparisons of Purchasing Powers and Real Product for 1980; Phase IV of the International Comparison Project: Part I: Summary Results for 60 Countries* (New York: UN).

UNDP (1993): United Nations Development Programme, *Human Development Report* (New York: UN).

World Bank (1993), *World Tables Database*.

# 3

# The Economic Analysis of Preferential Trading Areas

LYNDEN MOORE

## 3.1. INTRODUCTION

The European Community (EC) was established in 1957 as a *customs union*; all tariffs and quotas were abolished in stages on trade between member countries, and a common external tariff (CET) was imposed on imports from outside. With the establishment of the Single European Market (SEM) at the end of 1992, other non-tariff barriers with respect to standardization and public procurement, which enable governments to discriminate in favour of their own nationals, should have been removed.

In 1973 the EC also formed a *free trade area* (FTA) in manufactures with the remaining members of the European Free Trade Area (EFTA). This involved the removal of all barriers to trade in manufactures between member countries, but the EFTA members retained their own level of tariffs on imports from third countries (that is, those outside the EC and EFTA). In order to avoid imports into a FTA coming through the member country with the lowest external tariff, a FTA agreement limits free trade status to member countries' products. These are specified by its rules of origin.

In addition, the Lomé developing countries generally have free access to the EC market for their products. Other developing countries can export their manufactures to the EC under the generalized system of preference by which they are allowed in tariff free, but this is hedged in by limits and exceptions. The EC also has association agreements with Mediterranean countries, and in 1992 it negotiated the removal of tariffs, phased over ten years, on imports from Poland, Hungary, the Czech Republic, and Slovakia (with exceptions made for steel, textiles, and agricultural products) (Woolcock 1993).

Thus, although the EC originated as a customs union, a much more complex system of preferential trading has gradually been built up over time.

In this chapter we will begin by considering an economic analysis of the effects of such preferential trading areas, and calculations as to their magnitude. First, we consider the effect of the imposition of a tariff, and then examine the situation in which the tariff is removed on imports from the partner country. We will assume that the market for the product is small enough for us not to have to consider the effect of changes in consumption and production on the total economy. Thus we will be able to use supply and demand curves in a partial equilibrium analysis.

### 3.2. PARTIAL EQUILIBRIUM ANALYSIS OF TARIFFS

The effect of a tariff on imports can be seen in Fig. 3.1. The country is assumed to be 'small' and therefore faces an infinitely elastic supply schedule from the rest of the world $S_W$. The domestic supply schedule is shown as the upward-sloping supply line $S_H$ and the demand schedule as the downward-sloping line $D_H$. Under free trade the price on the domestic market is the world price, $P_W$. Domestic consumption is $Q_1$ and domestic production is $Q_2$ with imports of $Q_1Q_2$. If a tariff is imposed on imports of $t$ in percentage terms or $d$ in absolute terms with

$$t = P_WP'_W/OP_W \qquad \text{and} \quad d = P_WP'_W$$

it appears to domestic consumers and producers that foreigners are now only willing to supply the domestic market at $P'_W$—that is, it looks as if the foreign supply schedule has shifted upwards to $S'_W$. Domestic consumers and producers respond by reducing consumption to $Q_3$ and increasing production to $Q_4$ respectively. Imports fall to $Q_3Q_4$, *both* because produc-

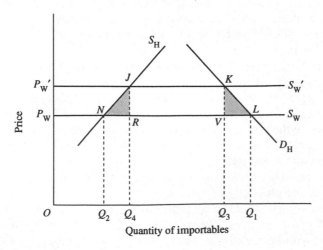

FIG. 3.1. Partial equilibrium analysis of a tariff

tion has increased by $Q_2Q_4$ *and* because consumption has fallen by $Q_1Q_3$. This involves a loss in consumer surplus of $P_WP'_WKL$. However, part of this represents a redistribution in favour of producers: there is a gain in producer surplus of $P_WP'_WJN$; and another part takes the form of a gain in tariff revenue (which could in principle be redistributed to consumers) of $JKVR$. The net result is an efficiency loss of the two triangles $JRN$, which is the additional cost of obtaining the extra output $Q_2Q_4$ from domestic sources instead of from the international market, and $KLV$, which is the consumer surplus lost on the reduction in consumption $Q_1Q_3$.

## Preferential Trade Agreements: Partial Equilibrium Analysis

The formation of a customs union or FTA was initially regarded as a movement towards free trade. But Viner (1950) pointed out that it also included an element of greater discrimination between member countries and non-member countries. He distinguished two aspects of the situation, one in which production is transferred from a higher-cost to a lower-cost source of production, say from the home country to the partner country, because tariffs have been removed from the latter country's products, which he termed *trade creation*. The other occurs when production is transferred from a low-cost source to a higher-cost source of production—say, from a third country to a partner country because tariffs are no longer imposed on products from the latter; this he termed *trade diversion*. Trade creation he regarded as always beneficial, and trade diversion as detrimental (Viner 1950).

This is to look at benefits and costs entirely from the production point of view—Viner assumed that the commodities were always consumed in the same proportion. It was left to Lipsey to point out that there was also a consumption angle. Indeed, the consumer benefits occurred in both cases and might even outweigh the losses in the case of trade diversion (Lipsey 1957).

To illustrate the effect on the market for a particular importable of a country becoming a member of a free trade area or customs union we may consult a figure which was first employed by Kindleberger (1973) (Fig. 3.2). The partner's supply schedule is also assumed infinitely elastic at $S_P$, but to lie above the rest of the world's supply schedule $S_W$; with a tariff, the partner's supply schedule is above $S'_W$ and is not shown. The domestic supply schedule $S_H$ is assumed to be upward sloping. The domestic demand schedule is $D_H$. Consumers are assumed not to differentiate according to the origin of the product.

Before the formation of the customs union, all imports come from the rest of the world as they appear cheapest. The price on the domestic market is equal to the world price $P_1$ plus the tariff $P_1P_2$ and is thus $OP_2$. Consumers purchase a quantity $OQ_3$ and the output of domestic producers is $OQ_4$. $Q_4Q_3$

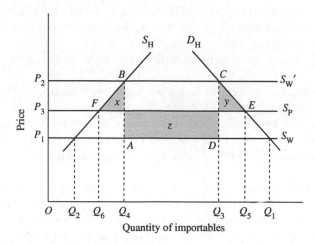

**Quantity of importables**

**Fig. 3.2.** Trade creation and trade diversion

is imported from the rest of the world, requiring a foreign-exchange expenditure of $ADQ_3Q_4$ and providing a tariff revenue of $BCDA$.

If a customs union or free trade area is formed, the tariff is removed on the partner's goods but not on those from the rest of the world and thus goods from the partner country appear cheaper at $OP_3$. If $P_3$ is less than $P_2$, prices on the domestic market fall. All imports are then acquired from the partner country and are greater in quantity at $Q_6Q_5$. There is, therefore, a diversion in the purchase of imports of $Q_4Q_3$ from non-members to the partner country. There is also trade creation of $Q_6Q_4$ which is now supplied by the partner country instead of domestic producers. In addition there is an increase in consumption of $Q_3Q_5$, which is supplied by the partner country. There is a gain in consumers' surplus of $P_2CEP_3$ and a loss in producers' surplus of $P_2BFP_3$ due to the lower price, and also a loss in tariff revenue of $ABCD$. In total this is equal to a net gain of $x + y - z$. $z$ can be regarded as the cost of trade diversion—that is, of transferring purchases from a low-cost producer $W$ to a higher-cost producer $P$. $x$ and $y$ are the familiar efficiency gains obtained from the reduction in tariffs.

Cooper and Massell (1965) challenged the assumptions underlying this particular argument. The comparison was being made between the pre- and post-customs unions position in order to assess whether it was beneficial. They argued that a comparison should be made between a discriminatory reduction of tariffs as in the formation of a customs union or free-trade area, and a non-discriminatory removal of tariffs. A non-discriminatory removal of tariffs would always be superior and would avoid any trade diversion.

Nevertheless, most economists carrying out applied work have continued to use the original framework and have compared the situation of the country before and after it joined the preferential trading area. This then is a theory of 'second best'.

From this theory some general principles can be deduced:

1. The benefits are likely to be greater the higher the original level of the tariff—the larger will be $x$ and $y$.
2. Losses due to trade diversion are likely to be lower, the smaller the differences in costs of production between the partner countries and third countries—in Fig. 3.2 the smaller $P_3P_1$ and therefore the smaller $z$.
3. A general principle not demonstrable from Fig. 3.2 concerns the relative merits of unions between competitive and complementary economies. Two economies are complementary when they produce a different range of products. Initially a union between complementary economies was regarded as the most beneficial. But it provides the least scope for trade creation and the most for trade diversion. Competitive economies produce the same range of products, and therefore there is scope for the low-cost producers to oust the higher-cost producers when barriers to trade are removed—that is, trade creation. So a union of the United Kingdom with Germany, which has almost the same industrial structure, provides considerable scope for trade creation. The actual benefits from this trade creation depend on the differences in cost.

*Customs Unions and Free Trade Areas with Upward-Sloping Partner Supply Schedules*

Let us now drop some of the assumptions made in the previous theoretical analysis in a bid for greater realism. First, let us drop the assumption of an infinitely elastic supply schedule of the partner country. Secondly, let us drop the implicit assumption in the previous analysis that the CET of the customs union is imposed at the same rate as the previous tariff.

Let us analyse the situation for a preferential agreement between two countries, $H$ for home, and $P$ for partner. Let us assume that the marginal costs of production are greater in the home than in the partner country owing to the higher level of protection in the former. Thus the initial price $T_H$ in country H is greater than that of the partner country $T_P$. Let us also make Robson's simplifying assumption that at the initial level of protection in the partner country it is just self-sufficient (Robson 1984). We will follow Robson's analysis and consider the final price and equilibrium that is established, the changes in welfare, and the effect on trade with the rest of the world (Robson 1984).

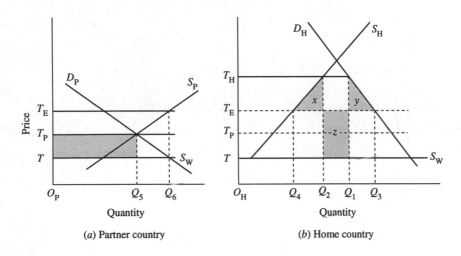

(*a*) Partner country                     (*b*) Home country

FIG. 3.3. Free trade area

*Free Trade Area*
Each member country can retain its previous tariff on imports from outside
the area. However, it is now possible for the high-priced home country $H$
with a price level initially at $OT_H$ (see Fig. 3.3$b$) to import goods duty free
from the lower-priced partner country $P$ with an initial price level $O_PT_P$
(see Fig. 3.3$a$). The maximum that the home country can import from the
partner country will be the whole of the latter's *production*. The price in the
country will come down to the world price plus the tariff in the partner
country $OT_P$ if the latter can supply all the home country's requirement at
that price. This involves what is termed *trade deflection*. The partner
exports its own output to the home country, and imports from the rest of
the world to supply its own consumers.

The overall effect depends on the relationship between the supply
schedule of the partner country $S_P$ and the import schedule (demand minus
supply) of the home country. If equilibrium can be achieved only at a price
above that initially existing in the partner country such as $T_E$, then the
partner producers will expand output from $O_PQ_5$ to $O_PQ_6$ and will gain
from extra profits, and the partner country consumers will continue to
purchase $O_PQ_5$ as before because they can import any amount at the world
price plus tariff $O_PT_P$. Tariff revenue will be earned in the amount indicated by the shaded area owing to the switching of consumption from
domestic to third-country sources.

The net effect in the home country is that it obtains the efficiency
gains of $x$ and $y$ due to the trade creation and consumption effects
respectively, but with the loss of $z$ due to the trade diversion effect of

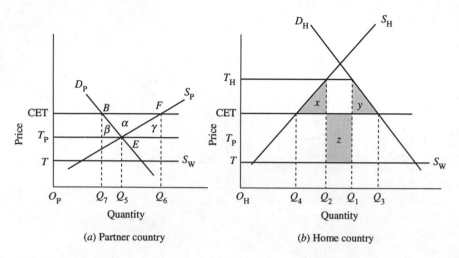

**Fig. 3.4.** Customs union

obtaining $Q_2Q_1$ imports from the partner country rather than from the rest of the world.

As the partner country now imports $O_PQ_5$, the imports of the free trade area as a whole from the rest of the world have increased by $O_PQ_5 - Q_2Q_1$. There has been trade creation through the intermediation of the partner country.

### Customs Unions

To comply with the rules of the General Agreement on Tariffs and Trade (GATT), the level of protection in a customs union should be no greater than before. Thus, the EEC decided to set its CET at the arithmetic average of the previous tariffs of member countries. This, therefore, raised the level of protection against third countries in those members with liberal trade regimes and lowered it in the more protectionist ones.

Let us return to the analysis of two countries, assuming the CET is the average of previously existing tariffs with the resulting tariff-distorted price denoted by CET in Fig. 3.4. The ceiling price becomes that at which imports can enter—that is, the CET price throughout the union.

In the home country shown in Fig. 3.4$b$, the reduction in apparent price of imports from $OT_H$ to the CET level will lead to an increase in imports from $Q_2Q_1$ to $Q_4Q_3$ and to the familiar trade creation gain of $x$ and consumption gain of $y$. There will also be the welfare cost $z$ of diverting $Q_2Q_1$ imports from the rest of the world to the higher-cost partner country.

In the partner country (see Fig. 3.4$a$), prices will rise owing to increased protection. Thus, there will be a reduction in consumer surplus of $CETBET_P$, and a gain in producer surplus of $CETFET_P$ leading to a gain of $\alpha$. This the partner country gains from her exports to the home country, which also compensates her for the marginal consumer loss $\beta$ and producer loss $\gamma$. The ruling price will be at the ceiling if the partner country cannot supply, or can only just supply, the amount required by the home country, $Q_6Q_7 = Q_4Q_3$.

In the former case, there will be fewer imports from the rest of the world and in the latter none. However, the equilibrium price may be below the ceiling, with the partner country supplying all the imports of the home country and cutting out all imports from the rest of the world.

This analysis suggests that a customs union is inherently more likely to reduce trade with third countries than a free trade area. This is because of our assumption about the CET, which, though it reduces protection in one country, raises it in another; by contrast, in a free trade area the trade deflection effect lowers the price in the highly protected market *without* increasing the prices to consumers in the other.

## 3.3. APPLICATIONS OF THE THEORY

The above theoretical analysis identifies the effects that would be expected from the formation of a customs union, assuming everything else remained constant. However, to work out the effect of the formation of the EC in practice, allowance must be made for changes in other economic variables; for instance, demand and supply schedules may be expected to shift with changes in incomes and productivity. Herein lies the problem in calculating the economic effect of any institutional change—namely, that, in order to do so, an assumption has to be made about what would have happened in its absence. There are several approaches to that problem reflected in econometric exercises carried out to quantify the effect of the formation of the EEC and EFTA.

Balassa, in his investigation of the effect of the original EC6 (France, Germany, Italy, Belgium, Netherlands, and Luxemburg), assumed that the income elasticity of demand for imports would have remained the same in the absence of its formation (Balassa 1974). By income elasticity, he meant the ratio of the annual rate of change of imports to that of GNP, measured at constant prices. Thus, the effect of integration was assumed to be the residual. He thus calculated this income elasticity of imports for the period 1953–9 before any tariff cuts were instituted and compared it with periods afterwards, 1959–65 and 1959–70, for total imports of the EEC, intra-area imports, and extra-area imports (see Table 3.1).

A rise in the income elasticity of demand from the earlier to the later periods for intra-area imports would indicate gross trade creation (due to substitution for either domestic or third-country sources of supply). A rise in the import elasticity from all sources would indicate true trade creation.

**TABLE 3.1.** *Ex-post income elasticities of import demand in the EC6*

| Import Categories | | Ex-post income elasticity of import demand | | |
|---|---|---|---|---|
| | | 1953–9 | 1959–65 | 1959–70 |
| Total imports | | | | |
| 0+1−07 | Non-tropical food, beverages, tobacco | 1.7 | 1.6 | 1.5 |
| 2+4 | Raw materials | 1.1 | 1.1 | 1.1 |
| 3 | Fuels | 1.6 | 2.3 | 2.0 |
| 5 | Chemicals | 3.0 | 3.3 | 3.2 |
| 71+72 | Machinery | 1.5 | 2.8 | 2.6 |
| 73 | Transport equipment | 2.6 | 3.4 | 3.2 |
| 6+8 | Other manufactured goods | 2.6 | 2.5 | 2.5 |
| 0 to 8−07 | Total of above | 1.8 | 2.1 | 2.0 |
| Intra-area imports | | | | |
| 0+1−07 | Non-tropical food, beverages, tobacco | 2.5 | 2.4 | 2.5 |
| 2+4 | Raw materials | 1.9 | 1.9 | 1.8 |
| 3 | Fuels | 1.1 | 1.3 | 1.6 |
| 5 | Chemicals | 3.0 | 4.0 | 3.7 |
| 71+72 | Machinery | 2.1 | 3.1 | 2.8 |
| 73 | Transport equipment | 2.9 | 3.8 | 3.5 |
| 6+8 | Other manufactured goods | 2.8 | 2.9 | 2.7 |
| 0 to 8−07 | Total of above | 2.4 | 2.8 | 2.7 |
| Extra-area imports | | | | |
| 0+1−07 | Non-tropical food, beverages, tobacco | 1.4 | 1.2 | 1.0 |
| 2+4 | Raw materials | 1.0 | 0.9 | 1.0 |
| 3 | Fuels | 1.8 | 2.5 | 2.1 |
| 5 | Chemicals | 3.0 | 2.7 | 2.6 |
| 71+72 | Machinery | 0.9 | 2.5 | 2.4 |
| 73 | Transport equipment | 2.2 | 2.4 | 2.5 |
| 6+8 | Other manufactured goods | 2.5 | 1.9 | 2.1 |
| 0 to 8−07 | Total of above | 1.6 | 1.7 | 1.6 |

*Source*: Balassa (1974: 97).

A fall in the import elasticity from third countries would indicate trade diversion. Comparing the period 1953–9 with 1959–70, Balassa calculated that the overall income elasticity of demand for imports from all countries had increased from 1.8 to 2.1—this suggests trade creation proper. The import elasticity of demand from non-member countries had stayed the same, suggesting no trade diversion.

However, the results for the individual categories of goods were very different. The union appeared to have had no appreciable effect on trade in raw materials. This was not surprising, as the initial tariffs on raw materials were zero or very low. There was a considerable amount of trade diversion in food, beverages, and tobacco. This was due to the Common Agricultural Policy (CAP). In fuels there was an increase in the import elasticity of demand from all sources. This was partly the result of the operation of the European Coal and Steel Community (ECSC) in the closing-down of high-cost coalmines and substitution of oil for coal. There was also an increase in the import elasticities of demand for machinery, and transport equipment, from all sources, in particular from non-members, which rose by respectively 1.5 and 0.3 from the earlier to the later period.

The reduction in the income elasticity of imports from non-member countries after 1953–9 in chemicals and other manufactured goods (clothing, travel goods, scientific instruments, etc.) indicated trade diversion.

Balassa at the time recognized that one of the problems with his approach was that some categories of goods were inputs into others. If, for instance, there was trade diversion in clothing (included in other manufactures) away from third countries, this would increase the relative demands for inputs into it, leading to trade creation in those categories. However, any approach through input–output tables appeared very complex.

He was also criticized by Winters for assuming that integration would lead to a change in an elasticity rather than a single (parametric) shift in trade between member countries (Winters 1984: app. 2).

## EFTA

These problems were avoided by the EFTA Secretariat in its study of the effects of the formation of EFTA (EFTA 1969). In this case, imports were related to apparent consumption. The average annual change in the share of imports from 1954 to 1959 was extrapolated to the post-integration period 1959–65 and compared with the actual share of imports in apparent consumption, i.e output minus exports plus imports. This comparison was carried out for imports from all areas, imports from other EFTA countries, and imports from non-EFTA countries.

In so far as imports from non-EFTA countries were lower than estimated by extrapolation from 1954 to 1959, this was regarded as trade diversion, and in so far as imports from EFTA countries were higher than the extrapolated estimate, this was regarded as trade creation. The results were that by 1965 the value of trade creation amounting to US$373 million was less than the value of trade diverted of US$457 million (EFTA 1969). This could be partly explained by the more complementary nature of the EFTA economies.

In both the Balassa and EFTA studies the whole of the difference between the estimate of what would otherwise have happened (the 'anti-monde') and what actually occurred is attributed to economic integration and thus is termed one of 'residual imputation'. This is generally regarded as producing rather high values.

### Recent Studies of the Effect on the United Kingdom of its Entry

The EFTA approach using shares in an export or import market has been used in assessing the effect on the United Kingdom of its entry into the EC, although some economists have just used total exports or imports. Most of these studies are of aggregate trade in manufactures. Winters (1987) criticizes those that used the residual imputation method and endeavoured to model the situation more directly by including dummy variables for the effect of UK entry in regression estimates.

The situation is complex because, while the United Kingdom by its entry gained free access to the EC market for its exports, it lost its preferential position in the markets of EFTA countries, the Irish Republic, and the Commonwealth. These countries also lost their preferential position in the UK home market, as imports from the other members of the EC could then enter freely. But, in addition, the EC's CET was lower for certain products than the United Kingdom's previous most-favoured-nation (m.f.n.) tariff.

The author has calculated that from 1970 to 1987 the real value of trade with the Commonwealth, that is exports and imports, fell. Trade with EFTA increased, but that with the EC increased at a much faster rate, exports increasing by 172 per cent and imports by 250 per cent. For manufactures there was a fivefold increase in imports from the EC (Moore 1989).

How much of this was due to integration? Winters investigates UK trade in manufactures with each of the main industrial countries (Winters 1987). He concludes that accession boosted exports to the EC by £4.5 billion but curtailed those elsewhere by £1.7 billion. More striking was the massive decline of £12 billion of sales by UK producers to their home market, i.e trade creation. He qualifies this estimate by then saying that £4 billion of this reduction might reflect a long-term secular decline. This still leaves a reduction in home sales of £8 billion, which is only balanced by an increase in exports of £3 billion, leaving an increased manufacturing deficit of £5 billion. Even when modified to £3 billion, this still represents about 1.5 per cent of GNP. There is an increase in consumer surplus to set against this; the question is whether it is large enough to offset it.

Both in these exercises and in subsequent ones the implicit assumption is that an appropriate means of assessing any economic integration is to compare what would happen if there had been no reduction in tariffs with the effect of reducing trade barriers in the partner country. There is no comparison with the most efficient system of free trade.

Our exposition of the theory has been of the markets for individual products. The econometric work we have surveyed has made a similar approach, although the categories considered have been very much larger. Clearly, on joining a preferential trading area, the different markets within a country would be affected differently. If the resulting changes in trade do not balance out, some adjustment of the exchange rate has to take place. The overall effect on resource allocation has been considered in terms of whether trade creation outweighs trade diversion. The effects on consumer and producer surplus were also considered.

However, from the point of view of the individual country entering a customs union, there is also the effect on the rate at which exports are exchanged for imports—that is, its 'terms of trade'. An improvement in a country's terms of trade may balance out negative efficiency effects. For an individual product this is illustrated in Fig. 3.4*a*. However, to allow for the interconnection between markets we must employ a general equilibrium analysis.

## 3.4. A SIMPLIED EXPOSITION OF THE GENERAL EQUILIBRIUM THEORY OF CUSTOMS UNIONS

Let us now consider the general equilibrium approach to customs unions. Let us assume that there are only two products, manufactures and food. Perfect competition is assumed and increasing costs. Thus the country is operating on the outer boundary of its production possibilities, the production possibility curve (see Fig. 3.5). The slope of this curve at any point represents the domestic rate of transformation (DRT) between the two products—that is, the amount of food that would have to be given up at the margin in order to produce one more unit of manufactures. Equilibrium in production will be reached at the point where:

$$DRT = \frac{\text{price of manufactures.}}{\text{price of food}}$$

Demand is introduced into the picture by the use of community indifference curves. These are aggregates of the individuals' indifference curves and thus represent the contour lines of utility for the country as a whole. Here they are taken both to show the response of consumers to changes in price, and as levels of welfare; they are therefore assumed not to cross, and problems of the effects of the distribution of income on welfare are ignored.

If the country is closed to trade, the maximum welfare attainable will be where the production possibility curve just touches the highest possible community indifference curve with domestic prices indicated by their slope at this point.

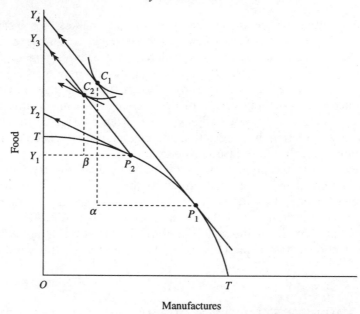

**FIG. 3.5.** Consumption and production with free trade and tariffs

If the world price of manufactures in terms of food is greater than the domestic one (the price line is steeper), then, when the country is opened to trade, producers will have an incentive to increase their output of manufactures and reduce that of food. This will continue until the DRT is just equal to the international price as at point $P_1$, where the international price is given by the slope of $Y_4P_1$ equal to that of $Y_3P_2$ (see Fig. 3.5). On the other hand, the higher relative price of manufactures will induce consumers to switch purchases from them to food. However, the increase in real incomes resulting from the trade will tend to increase the consumption of both goods, assuming neither of them is inferior. The net result of changes in relative prices and incomes will be a change in consumption to point $C_1$, where the rate at which consumers are willing to substitute food for manufactures is just equal to the relative price of manufactures in relation to that of food, as indicated by the international price line.

Trade is the difference between production and consumption. The trade triangle $C_1 \alpha P_1$ indicates that, at an international price given by the slope of $Y_4P_1$, the country would export $\alpha P_1$ of manufactures in exchange for $C_1 \alpha$ of food. If the price of manufactures had been higher, the degree of specialization in manufactures would have been greater still—that is, more manufactures and less food would have been produced.

An 'offer curve' showing the trade a country is willing to undertake at each relative price can be obtained by a plotting of the trade triangles, as in Fig. 3.6. *OR* represents a country's offer of manufactures for food. International equilibrium is reached when the country's offer curve intersects the offer curve of the rest of the world, assumed here to be infinitely elastic. At that equilibrium price $OK$, the country wants to export $OX_1$ of manufactures in exchange for $OY_1$ of food.

Tariffs and subsidies destroy the equality between domestic and international prices: see Fig. 3.5 again. If tariffs are imposed on imports of food, both consumers and producers face a higher price of food indicated by the slope of $Y_2P_2$. This induces an increase in the output of food at the expense of manufactures, and production shifts from $P_1$ to $P_2$. This reduction in efficiency lowers real income. But the country as a whole can still trade at the ruling international prices, and thus its consumption possibilities are along $Y_3P_2$. Consumers will equate their marginal rate of substitution indicated by the slope of their community indifference curve to the domestic tariff distorted price; this would suggest consumption along $Y_2P_2$. But if the tariff revenue is redistributed back to them, they will be able to consume along $P_2Y_3$ say, at $C_2$. $C_2\beta$ food will be imported, $\beta P_2$ of manufactures exported. The overall effect has been a contraction of trade, even though international prices remain the same.

Thus, a tariff has the effect of moving the offer curve depicted in Fig. 3.6 inwards to $OR'$. If, as we have assumed, the country is small, the international price, equivalent to the rest of the world's offer curve, remains the same. Thus the effect of the tariff is a clear efficiency loss in a general equilibrium, as in our previous partial equilibrium analysis.

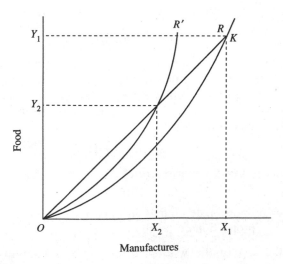

**FIG. 3.6.** Offer curve of a country exporting manufactures

However, a large country is by definition one with some monopoly power in world trade. With free trade

$$DRS = DRT = \text{international price}$$

but, unlike the situation of a small country, this is not equal to the *marginal* rate at which the large country can exchange manufactures for food on the world market, its foreign rate of transformation (FRT). A large country will face a less than infinitely elastic curve on the part of the rest of the world and will be able to improve its terms of trade by a tariff which leads to an inwards shift in its offer curve. The welfare of a country is always assumed to increase with an improvement in its terms of trade—that is, a rise in the price of its exports in relation to the price of its imports. Therefore, a large country can set the gain in its terms of trade against its efficiency loss.

### Trade Indifference Curves

In order to consider the optimum tariff a large country can impose, it is necessary to introduce the concept of trade indifference curves, each one representing the combination of exports and imports between which the country would be indifferent. Each trade indifference curve of a country is uniquely associated with a community indifference curve, but the former includes the net result of changes in consumption and production on imports as relative price changes. At any point, the slope of a trade indifference curve is identical to that at the equivalent point on a community indifference curve.

### Optimum Tariff

The optimum tariff a large country can impose is one where at the margin the terms-of-trade gains just equal the efficiency losses. This is where the large country's trade indifference curve is tangential to the rest of the world's offer curve. At this point the tariff is inversely related to the elasticity of the other country's offer curve.

$$t^* = 1/(e_W - 1)$$

where $e_W$ is the rest of the world's price elasticity of demand for imports, i.e.

$$e_W = \frac{\text{proportionate change in import volume demanded}}{\text{proportionate decrease in real price of imports}}$$

Thus, when the rest of the world's offer curve is infinitely elastic, the optimum tariff is zero.

## Customs Unions

Now let us turn to the analysis of the formation of a customs union.

Let us simplify the analysis by assuming that there are three regions: $A$, the existing customs union or the country with whom membership is planned; $B$, the country whose interests we are considering; and $W$, the rest of the world. World efficiency will be maximized by free trade.

Calculations of the effect of the customs union will depend on the alternative scenario envisaged, i.e. the anti-monde. Are we, for instance, comparing the country in a customs union with its position under free trade, or with a tariff, maybe an optimum tariff? Given this point of comparison, the question is then whether membership of the customs union improves a country's terms of trade and who gains the tariff revenue; both will determine whether its consumers end up on a higher indifference curve than before.

Generally, it is assumed that both $B$ and $A$ specialize in the same products; in so far as the United Kingdom and the EC are taken as examples, let us assume that they both export manufactures in exchange for food. The situation is depicted in Fig. 3.7. $OW$ is the rest of the world's offer curve, and $OA+B$ is the offer curve of $A+B$ with free trade. They can both be obtained by radial summation—that is, by adding the amount each country in the group would export and import at any given terms of trade.

### Free Trade

If $A$ and $B$ were to pursue a free-trade policy, the equilibrium position would be $T_1$ and the terms of trade $OT_1$. $A$'s trade position would be at $a_1$ and $B$'s would be at $b_1$. Exports of manufactures by $A$ and $B$ would be $OM_2$ and $OM_3$ respectively, summing to $OM_1$. Imports of food would be $a_1M_2$ and $b_1M_3$ respectively, summing to $T_1M_1$. Thus:

International price = domestic price = slope of $OT_1$.
Exports of $A + B = OM_2 + OM_3 = OM_1$.
Imports of $A + B = a_1M_2 + b_1M_3 = M_1T_1$.

### Tariff Imposed by A

If $A$, say the EC, then decided to impose a tariff on imports of food such that its internal domestic price is shown by the slope of $Qa_2$, this would induce a shift in its production from manufactures to food, and a substitution of food for manufactures in consumption. The offer curve of $A$ would shift to $A'$ and the overall offer curve of $A$ and $B$ would shift to $OA'+B$. This would increase the relative price of manufactures to food on the world market. Both would thus benefit from an improvement in their terms of trade. But $B$ would be able to take advantage from it by expanding its trade, in particular increasing its exports from $M_3$ to $M_5$. To summarize:

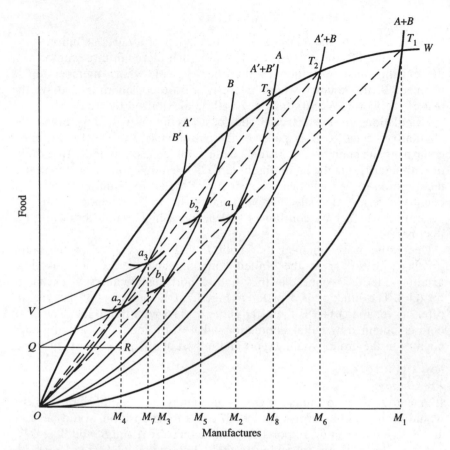

**Fig. 3.7.** General equilibrium theory of customs unions

The offer curve becomes $A' + B$.

International Price = domestic price of $B$ = slope of $OT_2 = \dfrac{a_2 M_4}{OM_4}$.

Domestic price in $A$ equals slope of $Qa_2$.

The proportionate tariff $t$ is placed on imports of food.

$\therefore$ The price of food on $A$'s domestic market is equal to $(1+t) \times$ international price of food.

$$\frac{QR}{a_2 R} = \frac{OM_4}{a_2 R} = (1+t)\ \frac{OM_4}{a_2 M_4}$$

$$t = \frac{a_2 M_4 - a_2 R}{a_2 R} = \frac{RM_4}{a_2 R}.$$

Imports of $A$ fall from $a_1 M_2$ to $a_2 M_4$.

Exports of $A$ fall from $OM_2$ to $OM_4$.
Imports of $B$ increase from $M_3b_1$ to $M_5b_2$.
Exports of $B$ increase from $OM_3$ to $OM_5$.

Thus from Fig. 3.7 it appears that although the imposition of a tariff by $A$ has improved its terms of trade, its overall level of welfare may have fallen rather than increased, that is $a_2$ may be on a lower trade indifference curve than $a_1$. Whereas there has been a clear welfare gain by $B$: $b_2$ is higher than $b_1$.


### B *Enters a Customs Union with* A

Let us apply this argument by analogy to the position of the United Kingdom in relation to the original EC6. The very high protection of agriculture within the EC6 improved its terms of trade but constricted its exports of manufactures abroad. The United Kingdom, outside the EC, benefited not only from the improvement in its terms of trade but also from being able to expand its exports of manufactures.

Clearly it is in the interests of the EC6 for the United Kingdom to join them and impose the same tariff on imports. Let us assume that the combined group maintains the same internal relative price of food to manufactures. Let us also assume for the sake of diagrammatic simplicity that the new offer curve for $B$, $B'$, coincides with $A'$. Their overall offer curve shifts to $OA'+B'$ (assumed for diagrammatic simplicity to coincide with the previous offer curve $OA$). The relative price of manufactures on the world market rises still further to the slope of $OT_3$. Thus, we can see from Fig. 3.7 that:

The international price becomes $OT_3$.
The domestic price in $A$ and $B$ is assumed to be the same as $A$'s previous price, i.e. $Va_3$ is parallel to $Qa_2$.
Both $A$ and $B$ are assumed to export $OM_7$ $\therefore$ $2\ OM_7 = OM_8$.
Both $A$ and $B$ are assumed to import $a_3M_7$ $\therefore$ $2\ a_3M_7 = T_3M_8$.

$a_3$ now represents the trade indifference point of both $A$ and $B$; it is clearly higher than $a_2$ and may also be higher than $a_1$—if it is not higher than $a_1$, $A$ has not been pursuing an optimum policy.

On the other hand, $B$ may or may not be worse off, depending on the relative size of $B$ in relation to $A$ and the world market. Furthermore, the assumption so far made that the tariff revenue is redistributed back to the consumers of the country concerned does not apply to the EC where it is transferred to the Commission. (Thus, in Fig. 3.5, instead of reaching consumption point $C_2$, the country would be operating on the budget line $Y_2P_2$. Under these circumstances consumers are always worse off. The actual change in the offer curve also depends on how the Commission spends the revenue.)

There are clear limitations to this type of analysis. One is that both *A* and *B* are assumed to purchase all their imports of food from the world market.

However, Ghosh (1974) has considered customs unions of complementary economies. He evaluates the effect of union with respect to the prior tariff-ridden state of the constituent economies. He assumes that, with a union between two countries, one of them, described as passive, trades exclusively with the other. The active member trades its surplus with the rest of the world. The member that ends up with the more favourable terms of trade will gain and the other will lose. This situation most aptly reflects the entry of the smaller agricultural exporting countries into the EC, such as the Irish Republic, Portugal, and maybe Denmark, which have benefited greatly from an improvement in their terms of trade due to the CAP.

Thus, both partial and general equilibrium comparative static analyses show that entry to a customs union is not necessarily an improvement on a country's previous position. Furthermore, in both cases, from the point of view of the world as a whole, it is an inferior position to a non-discriminatory reduction of tariffs or the optimum of free trade. This applies also to a free-trade area, except, as explained, because the prices to consumers are not raised, the cost of trade diversion is less.

This is why so much emphasis is placed on the other benefits that are alleged to arise from preferential trading areas, in particular, benefits arising from the greater exploitation of economies of scale, which it is claimed that such arrangements encourage.

### 3.5. THE CONCEPT OF ECONOMIES OF SCALE

The concept of economies of scale has been carefully analysed by Silberston (1972), and discussed by Pelkmans (1984), whilst statistical evidence on the size of scale economies has been provided by Pratten and Dean (1965) and Pratten (1971). Scale economies exist if average costs fall when a firm increases its output by investing in greater productive capacity—that is, by increasing its scale of operations. It is shown by a fall in the long-run average cost curve, which is the envelope of the short-run average cost curves. Technological knowledge and the prices of factors of production, which include the rate of interest, are assumed constant for any given long-run average cost curve.

The economies are partly associated with the size of plant—that is, production at any given geographical location. They may occur because capital costs do not increase proportionally with output—machines producing twice as fast may not cost twice as much. There may also be a spreading of indivisibilities associated with operating at any particular location in the form of secretarial and administrative services. These will be called plant economies. The actual shape of the long-run average cost curve of a plant will depend on the relative factor prices of factors of production, and the way they are combined. For instance, with a given plant, a doubling of the number of hours it is worked per year with the same manning levels, say from 4,000 to 8,000, would halve the capital costs per unit of output. The minimum efficient technical size of a plant with these longer hours would be different from one in which the increase in output had been obtained by continuing to work 4,000 hours but building a larger size of plant. Thus, what are called 'engineering' estimates of economies of scale must include some assumption about the number of hours a plant is worked.

There may also be economies associated with the length of production run. Each time the specifications of a product are changed, turnround time is required for resetting machines. In so far as the production of a particular specification is carried out in only one plant, these are often regarded as contributing to plant economies.

However, the economies of scale may also be associated with the size of firm—that is, the unit of control and decision-making. In particular, for the high-technology industries, an increase in the total output of a product reduces the research-and-development (R&D) expenditure per unit.

These are all internal economies, the benefits of which may be appropriated by a firm. There are also external economies associated with the expansion of an industry which lead to the cost curves of firms within the industry falling as total output is increased. These may be due to the development of specialized services and the improvement in marketing facilities which may result from the expansion of industrial output.

The general approach in the theory is to assume that the firm discussed has only one plant and is the sole domestic producer of the product. Implicitly, the economies of both plant and firm are being considered.

Let us now consider how the formation of a customs union may lead to the greater exploitation of economies of scale, and the benefits and losses that will accrue to the member countries. We will first consider this within a comparative static framework which is a development and extension of work by Mead (1968) and Corden (1972); this will be called Model T (for traditional). Then we will consider the imperfect competition model, termed Model M, which has been devised by Smith and Venables (1988a, 1988b).

### Traditional Analysis: Model T

In the traditional Model T, the product of the home industry is taken as indistinguishable from that of the foreign partner firms or the rest of the world. If the home producer is the sole seller in the domestic market, it might find it difficult to reach a profit-maximizing position, because, as the long-run marginal cost is below the long-run average cost curve, equating marginal cost with marginal revenue may lead to a firm making a loss unless the demand curve is relatively inelastic (although less than $-1$). A profit-maximizing firm would then either refrain from producing or produce the minimum possible. In order to avoid this, the government often regulates the price. The presumption in much theoretical work is that a policy of average cost pricing is pursued. This we will call assumption (i), which is assumed to be a possibility even with trade.

However, if the economy is open, the firm is faced with two exogenous prices—on the one hand, the world price, at which it can export the product, on the other hand, the tariff-distorted price, at which products can enter the market from abroad. These represent its minimum and maximum price respectively.

The general argument is that, if the country's cost curve is relatively low compared with that of the world as a whole, then it will expand production and export and will not need a preferential system to exploit economies of scale. No further mention will be made of this situation.

However, if the cost curve is high in comparison with the world price, it may be assumed (as in Corden 1972) that a firm will maximize its profits by charging the maximum price—that is, the price at which the product from abroad will just enter. If it can cover costs at this price, it will produce; otherwise it will not. This is taken as assumption (ii).

Therefore, in considering the outcome of a customs union formed between two countries whose long-run average cost curves exhibit economies of scale but lie above the world price, the important features are the pricing policies pursued, and whether the countries produce before and after the union.

For the sake of simplicity, we will assume that the level of protection existing in the members of the customs union prior to entry was the same level as the CET. To focus on the issues involved, the production function is assumed to be the same in the home and partner country, and is implicitly assumed to be that of an industry, maybe consisting of only one firm, maybe consisting of only one plant.

Three situations can be distinguished, as shown in Fig. 3.8.

*(a) No production prior to entry in either country* (see Fig. 3.8a)
Prior to entry, imports will provide for all consumption in both countries, $OQ_1$ in $H$ and $OQ_2$ in $P$. Home market prices will be $P_W'$ and the tariff revenue will be $P_W P_W' \times OQ_1$ in $H$ and $P_W P_W' \times OQ_2$ in $P$.

After entry, if one country supplies the whole of the market, it can now produce at a lower average cost (LAC) along LAC than $P_W'$. Let us assume that production is now carried out by $H$. There are two possibilities.

(i) If prices are equated with average cost, no producer surplus will be earned. The price within the customs union will fall to $P_U$ with output $OQ_3$. There will be a gain in consumer surplus in both countries and a loss in tariff revenue. The net gain in each country will be the consumption

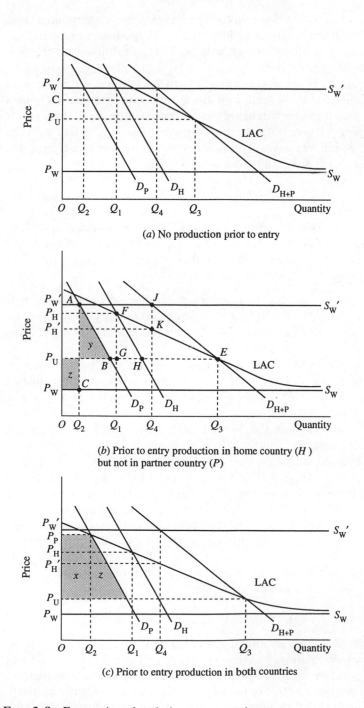

(a) No production prior to entry

(b) Prior to entry production in home country (H)
but not in partner country (P)

(c) Prior to entry production in both countries

FIG. 3.8. Economies of scale in customs unions

effect—that is, the consumer surplus on the increase in consumption, minus the cost of trade diversion from the low-cost world producers to the higher-cost home-country producer, which will be $P_UP_W$ multiplied by the previous quantity of imports.

(ii) However, if prices remain at $P_W'$, there will be no benefits to consumers. One country, assumed to be $H$, can now produce $OQ_4$ at a lower cost $C$ than it can be purchased from third countries with the CET. If the partner country $P$ now obtains all its supplies from $H$ it suffers a loss of tariff revenue which represents its welfare loss; $H$ also loses tariff revenue, but set against this it has profits of $P_W'C \times OQ_4$.

*(b) Prior to entry production in home country* H *but not in partner country* P see *(Fig. 3.8b)*

Prior to entry, the partner country will import all its supplies $OQ_2$ from third countries at a foreign-exchange price $P_W'$, which with its tariff will appear as a price $P_W'$. Tariff revenue will be $P_WP_W'$ $AC$. Again there are two possibilities.

(i) If average cost pricing is assumed prior to entry, country $H$ will produce all its requirements $OQ_1$ at a price $OP_H$. On entry $H$ will expand its output to $OQ_3$ at a price $P_U$—i.e. its costs of production will have fallen from $P_H$ to $P_U$.

There will be a gain to consumers in both countries. The partner country will gain consumer surplus of $P_W'ABP_U$. This must be set against its loss of tariff revenue of $P_W'ACP_W$. Thus it shows a consumption gain of $y$ and trade diversion loss of $z$.

The home country gains the benefit of a *cost reduction* due to the expansion of its industry. Thus, $OQ_1$ is now obtained at a lower cost—that is, $P_U$ compared with a previous $P_H$—and the whole of this benefit is passed on to consumers. In addition, consumers gain a surplus of $FHG$ on the expansion in their consumption. Thus, the home consumers have a clear gain and there are no trade diversion losses to set against them.

(ii) If prices remain at $P_W'$ there are no benefits to consumers. If the partner country $P$ transfers its purchases $OQ_2$ to the home country, it sustains a loss of tariff revenue and welfare of $P_W'ACP_W$. Country $H$ will expand production to $OQ_4$. Its cost of production will now be $P_H'$ and producers will make profits of $P_W'JKP_H'$.

*(c) Prior to entry production in both countries* (see Fig. 3.8c)

(i) If the prices in both countries are equal to their LAC, then prior to entry the price in the partner country will be $P_P$ and quantity produced and purchased $Q_2$, and in the home country the price will be $P_H$ and quantity produced and consumed $Q_1$. There will be no imports into either country.

With the formation of the union, assuming that it is the firm in $H$ which expands to supply the customs-union market, the price will fall to $P_U$. Country $H$ will produce $Q_3$. Consumers in $H$ will benefit from the *cost-reduction* effect $P_H P_U \times OQ_1$ on the amount $H$ was originally supplying plus the additional consumer surplus on the increase in consumption that takes place because of the fall in price.

The industry of the partner country $P$ completely disappears because of the expansion of it in $H$. There appears to be an efficiency gain due to trade creation equal to the shaded area $x$, and a gain in surplus on additional consumption $z$. Thus, country $P$ appears to show gains without any losses.

(ii) If the prices charged are equal to $P_W'$, then the initial production in both countries would be lower and so would the production after entry at $OQ_4$. The final cost of production would be $P_H'$ and the difference between this and the price, $P_W' P_H' \times OQ_1$, represents profit which would go entirely to the producers in country $H$.

## Conclusions

Consumers benefit only if prices are equated with average costs, or if such an extreme assumption is modified, if they face lower prices which means that possibility (ii) examined above for the three cases does not hold.

If a country is initially importing from third countries, entry into the customs union will always involve it in making a loss due to trade diversion. Thus, the only circumstances in which trade-diversion costs are not incurred is when both countries are initially dependent on home production. In that case, expansion of production in one country leads to the disappearance of the industry in the other. This is not regarded as a loss in this type of marginal welfare analysis. But clearly, if this involved a number of industries in $P$ or was important to country $P$'s economy, some adjustment to exchange rates would be required.

Because of the assumption that the LAC curves are the same in both countries, the direction of trade is inherently indeterminate, although the country that can produce in the larger market will appear to have lower costs of production.

In all cases shown, the countries would be better off if they imported from the rest of the world.

## Imperfect Competition: Model M

The Emerson Report on the benefits the EC would obtain by removing their non-tariff barriers to trade by the end of 1992 approached the problem in an entirely different way (CEC: 1988) using an imperfect competition model, Model M, developed and applied by Smith and Venables (1988*a*, 1988*b*).

In the Smith and Venables model each EC firm is assumed to produce in only one EC country, and, as in the previous analysis, implicitly in one plant. Each firm may produce several varieties of product, but the varieties are peculiar to it and cannot be produced by any other firm. The products of different firms within the same industry are imperfect substitutes.

Each firm can produce for its home market or can export its product; it will receive the consumer price in the former, but only $(1-t)$ multiplied by the consumer price in the latter, where $t$ represents the selling costs associated with exporting. It is assumed that because of the selling cost the firms will account for a smaller proportion of their export than home markets. A reduction in the selling costs, such as those associated with the removal of non-tariff barriers to intra-EC trade, will lead to greater exports and thus induce greater competition and lower prices in all markets. This will expand consumption and allow firms further to exploit their economies of scale.

The empirical basis of this Emerson Report was a series of studies, in particular Pratten (1988). Much of the data referred to the 1960s. Pratten identified various factors which contributed to economies of scale and then listed the 'engineering' estimates. Most of these were associated with the size of plant or production runs, but some were also attributed to the spreading of R&D expenditure over more units. The minimum efficient technical scale (METS) of plant is defined where costs cease to fall rapidly. The measurement of economies of scale is the percentage increase in costs at half or a third of the METS.

Smith and Venables initially propose a cost function with an initial fixed cost and a constant marginal cost. This then becomes modified by averaging it with another function with a declining marginal cost. They regard this as approximating Pratten's empirical findings on economies of scale.

Each producer is assumed to maximize profits by equating marginal cost with marginal revenue. This is achievable because there are a number of producers which each individually face an elasticity very much greater than the elasticity of demand for the product itself. Smith and Venables considered the firms to be making either the 'Cournot' assumption, in which each firm regards the sales of other firms as fixed, or the 'Bertrand' assumption, in which each firm regards the prices of other firms as fixed. In both cases, the elasticity of demand that the firm faces in its export market is assumed to be greater than that in the home market and therefore marginal revenue is a greater proportion of price in the former.

As sales expand, so does output, and therefore there is a greater exploitation of economies of scale. If the less efficient firms are forced out by the increased competition, this will enable those remaining to exploit their economies of scale still further.

Smith and Venables take production and consumption data for ten industries as follows:

242  cement, lime, and plaster
257  pharmaceutical products

260 artificial and synthetic fibres
322 machine tools
330 office machinery
342 electrical motors, generators, transformers
346 electrical household appliances
351 motor vehicles and engines
438 carpets, carpeting, oilcloth, linoleum
451 footwear

In some cases these industries were divided up into a number of equal-sized sub-industries—for instance, office machinery was broken down into two sub-industries, electric motors into three, and domestic electrical appliances and pharmaceuticals each into five. Each of these industries or sub-industries is treated as one market.

In order to apply this model, Smith and Venables divided the world into six 'countries'—France, Germany, Italy, the United Kingdom, the rest of the EC, and the rest of the world. For each industry a matrix of production and consumption for the six 'countries' was obtained for 1982. The elasticities of demand for the products of the industries were available, but, in order to obtain the elasticities of demand facing the individual firms, information on concentration was required. This was constructed from the Eurostat data on the size distribution of firms using the Herfindahl index of concentration from which was 'calculated the number of "representative" firms in each country. This is the number of equal-sized firms which would give rise to the same effective degree of market concentration as the observed distribution of unequal-sized firms . . . The minimum efficient scale [was] taken to be the size of the average "representative" firm in the EC' (Smith and Venables 1988*a*: 5.9).

The removal of non-tariff barriers was regarded as being equal to a tariff equivalent reduction of between 2.5 and 13.5 per cent. This was then regarded as a reduction in the selling cost of exporting to other EC countries.

Using these calculations, the Emerson Report shows the percentage reduction in cost from exploiting economies of scale and from restructuring—that is, the disappearance of the less efficient firms. The greatest welfare gains were expected from the chemical industry (Ecu 7.7 billion), electrical goods (Ecu 5.4 billion), motor vehicles (Ecu 4.7 billion), and mechanical engineering (Ecu 4.6 billion) (CEC 1988: table A.7).

## Comparison of Model M *and* Model T

Clearly, the assumptions underlying the two analyses of economies of scale, Model T and Model M, are entirely different. In Model T one industry or firm is assumed for each country, the production functions for different firms are the same (although this assumption could be modified), and the benefits and costs from the formation of a customs union depend on the reduction in the average cost obtained, and the pricing policy pursued. The absolute height of the tariff (or tariff equivalent of non-tariff barriers) determines the maximum exploitation of economies of scale that can occur because of the customs union, because at the tariff-distorted world price imports could enter and at the world price the country could export.

However, in Model M, because of the heterogeneity of product, there is no 'world price'. Model M allows for several firms in each country and for differentiation of products. But these advantages of approximation to reality are thrown away by substituting a number of representative firms for the actual number and size distribution of firms. There is also a very limited concept of differentiation.

From the point of view of trade, the question is whether in the long run the initial advantages of a country or firm are sufficient to determine trade flows. Thus although, in Model T, $H$ is assumed to have the lowest average cost and therefore to increase its output, in the very long run $P$ would be just as cheap a location. The direction of trade flows is therefore indeterminate. In Model M, where individual firms appear to have advantages specific to themselves, if these are specific to the firm as distinct from the country, it is not clear why the firm should not relocate its production to the cheapest location within the EC or maybe abroad. This is precisely what worries trade unionists in the countries with higher wages and higher social-security contributions.

Another aspect of the situation is the identification of the economies of scale. The implicit assumption in both models appears to be that a one-plant firm is being considered; in particular, the Emerson Report is perpetually slithering from a discussion of the METS and economies of scale of plant to that of a firm without distinguishing the two. However, Smith and Venables discount economies of scale assocated with plant size by assuming that their representative firms are at the METS; it is not clear whether their cost function, which appears to allow for the further spreading of fixed cost, which they discuss in terms of R&D, is therefore only an economy of scale of a firm. If it is specific to the firm, then the argument in the previous paragraph applies.

The greatest contrast between these models is in their treatment of trade with the external world. In Model T it is assumed that, if by exploiting its economies of scale, a firm could produce at the world price that it would have already expanded sufficiently to export. However, in the Emerson Report, one of the advantages that is said to accrue from further exploitation of economies of scale is that, as costs fall, European firms will become more competitive and their exports to the outside world will increase. But in this case the argument used in Model T—that they will already be exporting—appears just as applicable to imperfect competition. Furthermore, there are considerable exports to non-member countries of all the products considered by Smith and Venables. This suggests that economies of scale of the most efficient firms are already being exploited.

Both models assume that the removal of barriers to trade between members of preferential-trading-area countries is likely to lead to trade diversion from non-member countries.

Neither of the models allows for the multinational nature of the firms operating in the industry. In so far as these producers straddle national boundaries the assumptions about the bases of the competing firms do not hold. For instance, the choice is not so much whether the French and Germans buy French or German cars, but where the Germans wish to produce their cars. The concept of differentiation being associated with a firm producing in a particular country which then determines trade collapses. The location of production becomes determined by costs. Clearly, the fewer the barriers to trade, the easier it is to locate production cheaply. That is why multinationals are always in favour of reductions in barriers to trade.

### 3.6. CONCLUSION

The traditional analysis of the exploitation of economies of scale in a customs union has been in terms of a homogeneous product. In this case, a firm may benefit and expand its output if its potential long-run average cost of production lies somewhere between the international price at which it could export and the tariff-distorted price at which imports can enter the union. The actual distribution of costs and benefits depends on which firms produce before and after the formation of the union, and the price policy being pursued.

The imperfect competition approach pursued by Smith and Venables for the Emerson Report eschews all consideration of the level of protection. It is solely concerned with firms within the customs union. Each is assumed to be based in its home country producing and exporting from it. In the Emerson Report the economies of scale of plant are not distinguished from those of the firm. The more efficient firms are regarded as expanding at the expense of the less efficient.

However, both models exclude the possibility of firms choosing to shift production to lower-cost locations, which has occurred. The great incentive to inward direct investment which is provided by high levels of protection is also ignored.

# REFERENCES

Balassa, B. (1974), 'Trade Creation and Trade Diversion in the European Common Market', *Manchester School*, 62/2: 93–135.

CEC (1988): Commission of the European Communities, 'The Economics of 1992: An Assessment of the Potential Economic Effects of Completing the Internal Market of the European Community' (the Emerson Report), *European Economy*, 35 (Mar.).

Cooper, C. A., and Massell, B. F. (1965), 'A New Look at Customs Union Theory', *Economic Journal*, 75: 742–7.

Corden, W. M. (1972), 'Economics of Scale and Customs Union Theory', *Journal of Political Economy*, 80: 465–75.

EFTA (1969): European Free Trade Association, *The Effects of EFTA on the Economies of Member States* (Geneva: EFTA).

Ghosh, S. K. (1974), 'Towards a Theory of Multiple Customs Unions', *American Economic Review*, 64/1: 91–101.

Kindleberger, C. P. (1973), *International Economics*, 5th edn. (Homewood, Ill.: Richard D. Irwin).

Krugman, Paul R. (1979), 'Increasing Returns, Monopolistic Competition, and International Trade', *Journal of International Economics*, 9: 469–79.

Lipsey, R. G. (1957), 'The Theory of Customs Unions: Trade Diversion and Welfare', *Economica*, 24: 40–6.

Mead, D. C. (1968), 'The Distribution of Gains in Customs Unions between Developing Countries', *Kyklos,* 21: 713–34; repr. in P. Robson (ed.), *International Economic Integration* (Harmondsworth: Penguin, 1972), 278–303.

Moore, L. (1989), 'Changes in British Trade analyzed in a Pure Trade Theory Framework', in D. Cobham, R. Harrington, and G. Zis, (eds.), *Money, Trade and Payments: Essays in Honour of D. J. Coppock* (Manchester: Manchester University Press), 153–75.

Pelkmans, J. (1984), *Market Integration in the European Community* (The Hague: Martinus Nijhoff).

Pratten, C. (1971), *Economies of Scale in Manufacturing Industry* (Department of Applied Economics, Occasional Papers, No. 28; (Cambridge: Cambridge University Press).

—— (1988), 'A Survey of the Economies of Scale', in Commission of the European Communities, *Research on the ' Cost of Non-Europe'—Basic Findings, ii. Studies on the Economics of Integration* (Luxemburg: Office for Official Publications of the European Communities).

—— and Dean, R. M. (1965), *The Economies of Large-Scale Production in British Industry* (Department of Applied Economics, Occasional Papers, No. 3 (Cambridge: Cambridge University Press).

Robson, P. (1984), *The Economics of International Integration*, 2nd edn. (London: Allen & Unwin).

Silberston, A. (1972), 'Economies of Scale in Theory and Practice', *Economic Journal*, 82: 369–91.

Smith, A., and Venables, A. J. (1988a), 'The Costs of Non-Europe: An Assessment

Based on a Formal Model of Imperfect Competition and Economies of Scale', Commission of the European Communities, *Research on the Cost of Non-Europe'—Basic Findings, ii. Studies on the Economics of Integration* (Luxemburg: Office for Official Publications of the European Communities).

—— —— (1988b), 'Completing the Internal Market in the European Community', *European Economic Review*, 32: 1501–25.

—— —— (1991), 'Economic Integration and Market Access', *European Economic Review*, 35.

Viner, J. (1950), *The Customs Union Issue* (Carnegie Endowment for International Peace), 41–55.

Winters, L. Alan (1984), 'British Imports of Manufactures and the Common Market', *Oxford Economic Papers*, 36: 103–18.

—— (1987), 'Britain in Europe: A Survey of Quantitative Trade Studies', *Journal of Common Market Studies*, 25/4: 315–35.

Woolcock, Stephen (1993), 'The European *acquis* and Multilateral Trade Rules: Are they Compatible?', *Journal of Common Market Studies*, 31/4: 539–58.

# 4

# ommon Agricultural Policy

D COLMAN AND DEBORAH ROBERTS

## 4.1. INTRODUCTION

The Common Agricultural Policy (CAP) of the European Community (EC) is a remarkably complex assembly of instruments and regulations covering trade controls, price support measures, income transfers, production subsidies, investment grants, conservation policies, health regulations, labelling standards, etc. It has its own monetary unit—the 'green Ecu' (European Currency Unit)—and a huge bureaucracy to manage and oversee its operations. Additional complexity continually emerges as the policy as a whole (if it can be rightly considered as a whole) battles with the quadruple pressures of (1) budgetary and consumer costs, (2) anguished responses by non-Member States whose trade interests are damaged, (3) concerns for the environmental change caused by modern farming methods, and (4) protests about falling farm incomes despite the high costs of the policy.

In response to these pressures, the CAP underwent a major change in structure in 1992–3 which added to its complexity. This involved a large reduction (phased until 1995–6) in the commodity price support levels, and the introduction of a system of partial compensation for the price cuts for those farmers prepared to reduce and limit input use (essentially in respect to area planted and number of livestock). In the wake of these changes, it is now necessary to explain both elements of this system, the 'old' system of price support, which continues but with diminished importance, and the 'new' system of compensation or income support which has been grafted on.

There is no doubt that the 1992–3 reform was greatly influenced by the negotiations in the Uruguay Round of the General Agreement on Trade and Tariffs (GATT) which took place from 1986 until the signing of the GATT Agreement on 15 April 1994 in Marakesh.[1] It may be that further changes in the CAP will be required if the agricultural reforms already enacted by the EC are to meet the obligations of this Agreement. In the process of trying to resolve issues, in November 1992 Agricultural Commissioner Ray MacSharry negotiated a bilateral agreement with the United States, the so-called Blair House accord, which he claimed could be honoured without any further adjustment of the 1992–3 CAP reforms undertaken by the EC. Some EC member countries, particularly France, dispute this and believe that further reductions in EC agricultural support will be needed if the terms agreed with the United States and signed in Marakesh are not to be violated. Since further diminution of support is unacceptable in France, the EC may encounter problems in marrying the reformed CAP to the 1994 GATT Agreement.

In reflection of the situation sketched above, the chapter continues by exploring the economics of the main agricultural policy instruments which have endured since the founding of the EC in 1963. This is followed in Section 4.3 by a brief review of the pressures which have helped to bring about the reform of the CAP. Section 4.4 deals with the reforms themselves, starting first with reforms prior to 1992 and then proceeding to examine the 'MacSharry reforms package'. This is followed by a brief concluding section.

## 4.2. THE ORIGINAL SYSTEM OF CAP

The establishment of an integrated common market for agriculture by its original six Member States was a pivotal task in the formation of the EC, and is the one which has persistently made the largest demands on its budgetary resources. Article 39 of the Treaty of Rome set out a number of objectives, including ensuring supplies to consumers at reasonable prices, but the consistent emphasis of the CAP until the mid-1980s was 'to increase agricultural productivity by promoting technical progress' and 'to ensure a fair standard of living for the agricultural community'.

In the post-war period, when the memory of food shortages was relatively fresh, the productivist emphasis of the founding Member States was understandable. The dominant method of agricultural support had been import tariffs, which were effective means of raising agricultural prices, since, in the early 1960s, the six Member States were net importers of cereals and oilseeds and only just self-sufficient in livestock products. With this background of external protection, the movement to a common external tariff (CET) for agriculture, as required by the Treaty of Rome, was a politically acceptable step towards the creation of a common market when accompanied by the abolition of customs duties on internal trade within the ring-fence of the CET. For agriculture, instead of fixed tariffs, the EC adopted a variable import tariff system. This entailed setting minimum import prices (MIPs) with variable import levies (VILs) equal to the difference between the MIP and the *lowest* c.i.f. price offered by importers at the EC borders. In the case of cereals, the MIP is called the *threshold price*; for beef it is the *guide price*.

Because the MIP for all major products has (with minor exceptions in

1974 and 1978) been consistently maintained above the c.i.f. international prices ($P_m$), at which imports were available, EC market prices of imported commodities have been forced upwards. Fig. 4.1 shows the theoretical effects of this. EC supply is increased from $S_m$ to $S$ and demand is depressed from $D_m$ to $D$. Thus the imported quantity falls from ($D_m$ − $S_m$) to ($D$ − $S$). This trade-distorting feature of the policy is, however, exacerbated from the standpoint of agricultural exporting countries by two attendant facts. One is that import demand ($D$ − $S$) is completely inelastic to changes in world prices. As $P_m$ falls, the VIL increases to ensure that no imports enter the EC at below the MIP; the EC market is completely insulated from all movements in international prices unless they rise above the MIP. The second is that international market prices are forced downwards; they would rise if EC price support and trade distortion were reduced.

The increase in internal EC prices causes *producer surplus to rise* by the value of area $A$, as shown in Fig. 4.1. *Budgetary revenues* equal in value to $C$ accrue to the EC from import levies and may be counted as a gain (less some cost for collection). These gains are, however, more than offset by the *loss in consumer surplus* equivalent to areas $A + B + C + D$.[2] In fact, using this neo-classical economic calculus shows an overall *economic welfare loss* to the EC from the policy of $B + D$, reflecting a basic result of comparative static economic theory that free trade is optimal and that trade interventions result in a loss of economic welfare.

This last result can be confirmed by a dual calculation based on Fig. 4.1. *Extra resource costs* of $B + E$ are stimulated by the price support to generate output which could be *imported at a cost* of $E$, thus registering a *welfare loss B*. Consumers have also reduced consumption which they value at $F + D$, but which cost them only $F$ before the imposition of the

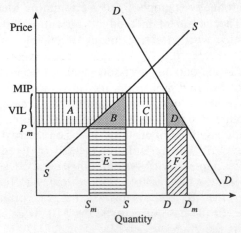

**F**ɪɢ **4.1.** Basic system of external protection for imported commodities

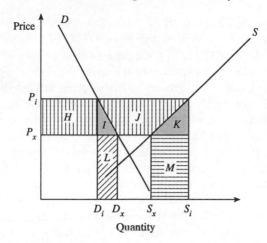

**F**IG **4.2.** Basic system of internal protection for commodities in surplus

MIP, resulting in an additional *welfare loss* of $D$ for the total economic welfare or ' *deadweight loss*' of $B + D$.

Because of rapid technical change in agriculture, further stimulated by prices supported above international levels, agricultural supply growth in the EC has continuously exceeded demand growth and resulted in the emergence of excess supply in cereals, beef, dairy products, wine, and some fruits. This has meant that the internal price support mechanism of *intervention buying* (Fig. 4.2) played an increasing role as production of more commodities in the EC moved into surplus. This internal support system operates through the process whereby national authorities operating the EC policy offer to buy produce of minimum standard quality at certain times of the year at the intervention price $P_i$. The latter is set in Ecus at the Community-level annual price-fixing round and is the basis of common pricing throughout the EC. In effect, $P_i$ acts as a floor price in the market,[3] and it has been consistently set above the f.o.b. export price, $P_x$, which could be obtained by exporting the surplus. This form of price support has not been applied to all commodities covered by the CAP, but applies to wheat, barley, butter, skimmed milk powder, beef, and wine after distillation. In a modified form it applies to certain fruits and vegetables and fish, surpluses of which cannot be stored but have to be destroyed.

The effects of the internal price support policy are broadly as shown in Fig. 4.2. The higher price and additional output stimulated (from $S_x$ to $S_i$) results in *increased* producer surplus of $H + I + J$. *Consumer surplus* is reduced by $H + I$ as demand is cut from $D_x$ to $D_i$. The amount by which supply exceeds commercial demand, $S_i - D_i$, is purchased into intervention stores, where it develops into the beef and butter mountains and wine lakes, as they are often referred to in the media. It is conventional to explain the *budgetary costs* which arise from these intervention surpluses as being equivalent to areas $I + J + K$ in the figure. This is the cost which would arise if all the surplus $(S_i - D_i)$ is disposed of as exports with the aid of a variable export refund, or export subsidy, equal to $P_i - P_x$; alternatively it is the loss made by the intervention authority from buying the surplus at $P_i$ and selling at $P_x$. In reality $I + J + K$ underestimates the budgetary cost of surplus management, since it does not allow for the storage costs or for the deterioration and wastage of product while stored. If, however, we accept this measure of budgetary cost and add the consumer surplus loss of $H + I$, it transpires that the producer surplus gain of $H + I + J$ only partially offsets it, and leaves an economic welfare loss of $I + K$. The same result is obtained by setting the increased export revenue $(L + M)$ against the resource cost $(K + M)$ plus the reduction in consumption value $(I + L)$.

A point which should be emphasized is that the system of intervention buying (Fig. 4.2) cannot be operated without a MIP policy (as in Fig. 4.1) if $P_i$ exceeds $P_m$, which is how the CAP has been operated. For, without a MIP in excess of $P_i$, it would be profitable to import at price $P_m$ in order to sell into intervention, which would be a completely unstable and untenable state of affairs. Thus, even though in the 1980s and early 1990s the primary instrument of agricultural price support has been intervention buying, the VIL/MIP system has been necessary to protect its operation.[4]

## The Agrimonetary System

The MIPs, intervention prices, import levies, and export refunds described above are all fixed in terms of Ecus and converted into each of the Member States' national currencies using so-called 'green rates' of exchange. If, as was originally intended, these green rates of exchange were exactly equivalent to each Member State's market exchange rate with the Ecu, then the level of institutional prices, import levies, and refunds would be the same in real terms in each country. However, in the late 1960s and early 1970s fluctuations in the world currency markets, combined with differing national priorities and a desire to keep farm prices relatively stable, led to governments allowing their green and market rates of exchange to diverge. This, in turn, led to differing real support and thus food prices within the EC.

In the absence of any countervailing action, such a situation would have been unsustainable. Exports of farm commodities from countries whose green rate of exchange was overvalued (and thus had support prices 'too low' in their own currency) would have flooded into countries whose green rate of exchange was undervalued relative to the market rate of exchange (and thus had support prices for agricultural commodities too high). Similarly, in order to attract lower levies, imports from third countries would have been channelled through countries with overvalued green rates of exchange whilst exports would be channelled through countries with undervalued green rates of exchange so as to collect the maximum export refund. To counteract such trade distortions, a complex system of border taxes and subsidies on intra-Community trade was introduced so as to bridge the difference between market and green exchange rates or the 'monetary gap'[5] and thus allow commodities to be traded between countries *as though* common prices prevailed. Further, these border taxes and subsidies, known as Monetary Compensatory Amounts (MCAs) were used to adjust the import levies and export refunds applying to third-country trade as and when necessary. The existence of MCAs undermined the principle of common pricing on which the CAP was intended to operate and distorted the relative competitiveness of each Member State's agricultural sector.

In 1984 a radical reform to the agrimonetary system took place which involved the introduction of the so-called 'switchover mechanism'. Amongst other things, the switchover mechanism changed the manner in which MCAs were calculated. From 1984 onwards, in the event of realignments in European currency markets, common support price levels were tied to the strongest currency in the EC. Henceforth, monetary gaps were calculated as the difference between a country's green rate of exchange and a new hypothetical green ecu rather than the real Ecu, where the green ecu was set at such a level so as to eliminate the possible creation of new positive monetary gaps. This method of calculation thus removed the need for any government to revalue its green rate to bring it in line with its market rate of exchange, thereby inflicting a support price reduction for domestic farmers. The cost of avoiding such positive monetary gaps was the creation of larger negative monetary gaps for all but the country with the strongest currency, namely Germany. Under the rules of the new agrimonetary system, such negative monetary gaps had to be removed (by green-rate devaluations) within a certain time period, thus building into the system increases in CAP support prices as expressed in national currencies for all farmers except those in the country with the strongest currency. The overall level of CAP support was, therefore, increased, as was the complexity of the policy.

The problems that were eventually to develop as a result of the switchover mechanism were not immediately apparent, since the Exchange Rate Mechanism (ERM) in the mid- to late 1980s was relatively stable. However, under the rules of the switchover, the gap between the value of the real Ecu and green Ecu could increase but never decrease, and, as a result of exchange-rate fluctuations, by December 1992 the difference had risen to 19.5 per cent—an indication of the inflationary bias of the system. Moreover, at that time, the Commission faced an even more significant problem. How could a system requiring border taxes and levies continue to operate following the removal of internal frontiers as required under the Single European Act?

The success of the reforms to the agrimonetary system that came into force on 1 January 1993 has proved short-lived. Given that MCAs can no longer be collected or distributed, a system was agreed whereby the Commission was given the responsibility of fixing and adjusting green rates of exchange so as to avoid significant monetary gaps over any length of time. Importantly, the switchover mechanism was maintained, meaning that countries within the narrow band of the ERM were, initially, protected from support price reductions, although such price reductions (via green-rate revaluations) were not ruled out for Member States with floating currencies. Further, the retention of the switchover mechanism allowed the difference between real and green Ecus to continue to be ratcheted up with currency fluctuations, increasing the gap to 20.75 per cent by the end of July 1993.

The widening of the bands of the ERM to ±15 per cent in August 1993, whilst having no direct effect on the agrimonetary system, seems to have dealt the most recent agrimonetary system a fatal blow. Under such wide bands of fluctuation, all currencies are effectively floating and therefore vulnerable to support price cuts as well as increases. Green-rate changes for all countries became more frequent as the Commission strove to apply the new rules of the system within an environment that could scarcely have been predicted at the start of 1993. At the time of writing, political pressure has led to the current suspension of the agrimonetary system, with green rates frozen at September 1993 values.

What will replace the system has yet to be resolved, but any changes will obviously have to be compatible with the 1992 MacSharry reforms to the CAP. On the one hand, the weakening of the basic price-support mechanism under the reform package should mean that price-support differentials between Member States will, in future, be less important. However, this is to some extent counterbalanced by the increased use of direct compensation payments to farmers, which will have to be converted under some formula from Ecus to national currencies.


### 4.3. THE PRESSURES FOR CAP REFORM


#### *Budgetary Pressure*

The budgetary costs of the CAP have proved to be a persistent political thorn for the EC, and contributed significantly to the need to increase the total tax transfer from 0.77 per cent of the GDP of the nine Member States in 1980 to 1.03 per cent of the GDP of the Twelve in 1989. This has

TABLE 4.1. *EAGGF expenditure on the CAP, selected years (Ecu m.)*

| Year | Guarantee Section expenditure | | | Guidance Section expenditure |
|------|------------------------------|---|---|-----------------------------|
|      | Export restitutions | Other[a] | Total |  |
| *EC6* | | | | |
| 1971 | 879 | 1,129 | 2,008 | n.a. |
| 1972 | 1,186 | 1,514 | 2,700 | 376 |
| *EC9* | | | | |
| 1973 | 1,026 | 2,807 | 3,833 | 182 |
| 1975 | 925 | 3,411 | 4,336 | 262 |
| 1977 | 2,191 | 4,794 | 6,585 | 157 |
| 1979 | 4,704 | 5,713 | 10,417 | 274 |
| 1980 | 5,441 | 5,850 | 11,291 | 479 |
| *EC10* | | | | |
| 1982 | 4,739 | 7,632 | 12,371 | 563 |
| 1984 | 6,202 | 12,128 | 18,330 | 702 |
| 1985 | 6,587 | 13,141 | 19,728 | 243 |
| *EC12* | | | | |
| 1987 | 9,14 | 13,802 | 22,950 | 895 |
| 1988 | 9,786 | 16,614 | 26,400 | 1,142 |
| 1989 | 9,708 | 16,164 | 25,872 | 1,348 |
| 1990 | 7,722 | 18,731 | 26,453 | 1,648 |
| 1991 | 10,029 | 22,306 | 32,385 | 2,128 |
| 1992[b] | 9,348 | 23,586 | 32,934 | 2,895 |

*Note*: n.a. = not available.
[a] Includes storage, withdrawals from the market, price subsidies (including aids to producers, processors, and marketeers), and guidance premiums.
[b] Budgeted amounts.
*Source*: CEC, *Official Journal* (various issues).

permitted some expansion of spending on regional and social policy, and has allowed the percentage of total EC budgetary expenditure on the CAP to drop from 73 per cent in 1980 to 66 per cent in 1989. This modest change was only achieved by a combination of a stream of patching, *ad hoc* measures, as described in Section 4.4 below, to contain agricultural spending, and by the periodic effects of a weaker US dollar, which reduced the subsidy cost of exporting EC surpluses.

It is the costs of agricultural surplus management which dominate the budgetary expenditure of the European Agricultural Guidance and Guarantee Fund (EAGGF).[6] This is apparent from Table 4.1, which shows export restitution costs alone regularly accounting for over 30 per cent of total EAGGF, and with the bulk of the 'other expenditure' being on costs for surplus storage and subsidized market disposal within the EC. As can be seen, Guidance Section expenditure on improving the farm structure of agriculture has remained small, with the vast bulk of budgetary resource diverted to market support.

Some of the patching measures to contain budgetary costs and surpluses prior to the 1992 reform package were quite significant, such as the quotas and co-responsibility levies which are discussed below. These measures failed to halt the relentless rise in the budget required for CAP. It is pertinent to reflect on why they failed, and why there was not the political will to do more.

It must be recognized that budgetary costs are *transfers*. Funds are paid as taxes by certain groups in society and paid out or transferred to others. In economic-welfare terms, such transfers are not a complete loss of resource, which is consistent with the analysis based on Figs. 4.1 and 4.2, where the triangular areas of deadweight loss are much smaller than the budgetary and consumer cost transfers. In the case of the budgetary transfers, revenue is raised as a VAT levy at the country level, through direct national budgetary contributions and through import and sugar-production levies, and these are transferred to the EC in support of the principle of common financing of the EC's costs. These revenues are then largely used to finance storage and subsidized disposal of surplus products. It follows that countries which import more agricultural products tend to contribute more and that there is a net transfer to countries with greater surpluses to store and export. Thus Germany, the United Kingdom, and Italy find themselves making large net transfers to Denmark, Holland, the Irish Republic, and France. Inevitably it has been the case that some countries have pressed for budgetary reform of the CAP with less enthusiasm than others, and that those which have pushed, such as the United Kingdom, have sometimes been accused of lacking 'Community spirit'.

### Consumer Pressure

All the estimates of the costs of the original CAP system have demonstrated (unsurprisingly given the assumption that any change in agricultural prices in the EC would be fully transmitted to food consumers[7]) that the estimated transfer costs from consumers exceed the budgetary or taxpayer transfer by a significant margin. This is shown in the estimates for the EC by Roningen and Dixit (1989) in Table 4.2.[8]

Various estimates have been made of the average cost imposed on EC non-farm families through higher prices and taxes to support the CAP. For 1984 the Department of Primary Industry (DPI)—Australia (1986: 1) estimated this at US$900 per family per year. This estimate of £600 (at

TABLE **4.2.** *Benefits and costs of agricultural support, 1986/7*

| Countries | Producer benefits (US $bn.) | Consumer costs (US $bn.) | Taxpayer costs (US $bn.) | Net Economic costs[a] (US $bn.) | Transfer ratio[b] |
|---|---|---|---|---|---|
| USA | 26.3 | 6.0 | 30.0 | 9.2 | 1.4 |
| EC | 33.3 | 32.6 | 15.6 | 14.9 | 1.5 |
| Japan | 22.6 | 27.7 | 5.7 | 8.6 | 1.5 |

[a] Consumer costs + taxpayer costs − producer benefits.
[b] (Taxpayer + consumer costs)/producer benefits.
*Source*: Roningen and Dixit (1989).

an exchange rate of US$1.5 : £1), or £11.54 per week per family, compares with other estimates which range up to £16 per week per family of four depending upon the year considered. Since even non-taxpayers, the poorest members of society, may have to bear perhaps 60 per cent of this cost, and since larger farms and generally wealthier farmers benefit most, the CAP can be legitimately criticized for transferring funds from the poorest members of society (since all must eat) to some who are relatively well off—there are also many poor farmers in the EC. While this fact has been well recognized, the political lobby for consumers' interests has not developed the same weight of influence as the farm and agro-industry lobbies, which have a specified central place in agricultural-policy negotiations. Thus it has been largely left to academics, and particularly economists, to argue for CAP reform on the grounds of excessive cost to non-farm families as consumers and taxpayers (e.g. BAE (1985: ch. 6); Brown (1989); Josling and Hamway (1972)).

### External Pressure—The Uruguay Round of GATT

The CAP gave rise to progressive increases in trade distortion up to 1990. This was not even disguised by the expansion of the EC to incorporate new Member States, which, by a process of trade diversion, switched a significant proportion of their agricultural imports from non-member to Member States. (This was particularly true of the accession to the EC of the Irish Republic, the United Kingdom, Spain, and Portugal). Table 4.3 confirms this general picture, showing, for several major commodities, either a substantial increase in EC net exports between 1973 and 1990 or, even more strikingly, a switch from being a net importer to a major net exporter. From the standpoint of non-member exporters of temperate-zone

TABLE **4.3.** *EC net external trade in selected agricultural products, selected years*

| Year | Product | | | | | |
|------|---------|---|---|---|---|---|
| | Wheat (million tonnes) | Other cereals (excl. rice) (million tonnes) | Sugar (million tonnes) | Butter (thousand tonnes) | Cheese (thousand tonnes) | Beef and veal[a] (thousand tonnes) |
| *EC9* | | | | | | |
| 1973 | — | −10.8 | −1.1 | +204 | +41 | −913 |
| 1977 | +0.9 | −20.8 | +0.1 | +140 | +84 | −210 |
| *EC10* | | | | | | |
| 1981 | +10.7 | −3.4 | +3.3 | +373 | +213 | +389 |
| 1983 | +11.5 | +0.5 | +2.6 | +250 | +292 | +165 |
| 1986 | +11.9 | +5.5 | +2.6 | +220 | +269 | +714 |
| 1988 | +13.8 | +4.9 | +3.2 | +565 | +289 | +335 |
| 1989 | +18.3 | +7.6 | +3.3 | +332 | +324 | +589 |
| 1990 | +18.5 | +6.5 | +3.6 | +146 | +343 | +383 |
| 1991 | n.a. | n.a. | +3.6 | +275.2 | +374.2 | +804.0 |

*Notes*: Net imports are denoted by a minus (−) sign and net exports by a plus (+) sign.
n.a. = not available.
Dash = negligible.
[a] Estimated; includes the carcass-weight equivalent of trade in live animals.
*Sources*: CEC, *Agricultural Situation in the Community*; *Official Journal of the European Communities* (various issues).

TABLE **4.4.** *Export volume indices of agricultural products 1980–6 (1980 = 100)*

| Countries | 1980 | 1981 | 1982 | 1983 | 1984 | 1985 | 1986 |
|-----------|------|------|------|------|------|------|------|
| EC10 | 100 | 109 | 109 | 116 | 124 | 132 | 136 |
| USA | 100 | 100 | 93 | 89 | 90 | 73 | 67 |
| Other developed countries | 100 | 110 | 108 | 106 | 111 | 113 | 119 |

*Source*: GATT (1988: i, app., table III).

agricultural products, not only have they suffered a severe contraction of their EC market as a consequence of the principle of Community preference, but they have had to face intensified competition in other markets from the EC's subsidized exports. Australia and New Zealand were particularly badly affected when the United Kingdom joined the EC, and the United States as the world's largest agricultural exporter suffered particularly in the early 1980s prior to the inauguration of the Uruguay Round of negotiations on GATT in 1986. As an indication of this, Table 4.4 displays the dramatic changes in EC and US agricultural export volume in this period.

The United States' concern about the CAP, and about protective policies in Japan and elsewhere, can be gauged from the fact that, although it was at the United States' insistence that agricultural policy was excluded from earliest rounds of GATT negotiations and agreements, it was made the centre-piece of the Uruguay Round. Although agriculture is only one of fifteen negotiating heads,[9] the United States has stated that without a satisfactory solution on agriculture it will not sign an agreement. In seeking drastically to reduce agricultural support policies, the United States has been backed by the so-called Cairns Group of agricultural exporting countries, which includes Australia and New Zealand.

In order to explain how the GATT negotiations have influenced the 1992 reform of the CAP, it is helpful to give a simplified account of the negotiating position of the United States and the EC. (These and the positions of other groups are more fully summarized in Rayner, Ingersent, and Hine (1993).) At the outset, in 1987–8 the United States demanded (i) elimination of all trade-distorting subsidies within ten years, (ii) elimination of all import barriers, including all health and non-health non-tariff barriers, (iii) changes to policies for individual commodities to permit the agreed phasing-out of government support, and (iv) use of an aggregate measure of support (AMS), to establish initial levels of protection and to monitor progress with their elimination.

The importance of the last condition is apparent. In order to obtain multinational agreement covering many commodities on reforming agricultural policy, there has first to be agreement using a common measure as to what is the distortion to be reduced or eliminated, and what is its size for each commodity and each country. Then it is possible to negotiate timetables for reducing this distortion. The United States proposed a version of a measure called a Producer Subsidy Equivalent (PSE).

From the outset the EC has accepted the need for an AMS but has championed its own version, the Support Measurement Unit (SMU), which could reflect the impact of supply and support control measures taken in the second half of the 1980s. The EC, however, did not accept the objective of eliminating all agricultural support, proposing instead the notion of a short-term agreement on international market-sharing and prices, with a long-term strategy of achieving more balanced support through reciprocal agreements.

In the process of negotiation which has ensued, some key ideas have emerged, two of which, *tariffication* and *decoupling*, should be mentioned here. Instruments of EC policy which are particularly abhorrent to other exporting countries are the variable import levies and variable export subsidies, since (as noted above) these insulate the EC market almost completely from short-term fluctuations in world prices. The proposal for tariffication which has been generally accepted is that, at a base date, all protection, including non-tariff barriers, should be expressed as a tariff which is fixed and that this fixed tariff should become the only measure of external protection and should be reduced according to the negotiated schedule. In this way the dismantling of protection can be monitored.

Given that the central issue is trade distortion, it can reasonably be argued that there is no fundamental cause for international dispute if a country chooses to support its farmers in ways which do not cause supply to exceed competitive free-trade levels ($S_m$ and $S_x$ in Figs. 4.1 and 4.2). Such payments might be said to be decoupled from supply response and not to be trade-distorting. Academically the hunt has been on to identify forms of support which might be classed as decoupled. One proposal (Blandford, de Gorter and Harvey 1989) was for the introduction of Production Entitlement Guarantees (PEGs), whereby, for each commodity, farmers would be eligible for fixed payments on a quantity of output less than $S_m$ and $S_x$ in Figs. 4.1 and 4.2. In that way, it can be argued, supply at the margin would be influenced only by the free-market price and would not be affected by the support payment offered.

In the end, rather than these decoupled payments, the United States agreed to accept that certain types of support, modelled very much on its own policy, are sufficiently decoupled to be exempt from the reductions in support levels required by GATT. These are support payments, for which farmers can qualify only by adopting certain supply-restricting measures, such as *setting aside* (taking out of production) a proportion of previously farmed arable land. The acceptance of these and other environmentally related support payments has proved critical in bridging the gap between the US position and that of the EC and led, in November 1992, to the signing of the so-called Blair House accord, a bilateral agreement between the two negotiating parties.

The Blair House accord contains four critical elements to be phased in over the period 1993–9. First, a commitment to *tariffy* all existing border measures and reduce tariff levels by 36 per cent (although an element of Community preference has been maintained by the EC via the so-called 'special-safeguard clause'); secondly, an agreement to reduce internal support measures by 20 per cent from 1986–8 levels (with new MacSharry compensation payments exempt for the reasons outlined above); thirdly, a commitment to reduce the value of export subsidies by 36 per cent and subsidized export volume by 21 per cent; and, finally, the acceptance of a 'Peace Clause' which effectively limits either the EC or the United States from taking unilateral trade action against each other's farm policies in the future.

Although initially met with much enthusiasm and even touted as the prototype solution to the agricultural negotiations under GATT, some Member States of the EC, in particular France, have raised strong objections to the accord, arguing that, because of an underestimation of future supply growth of farm commodities within the EC, it is not compatible with the MacSharry reform package outlined below and thus would require the reform of the CAP to go yet further. The accord did not become operational until a new GATT agreement was signed.

### Environmental Pressure

As agricultural production has intensified since 1960, particularly in the northern EC countries, concern about its adverse environmental impacts has grown. Increased use of inorganic fertilizer has resulted in high nitrate and phosphate levels in rivers and lakes, with consequent problems of eutrophication. Field sizes have been increased by eliminating hedgerows and removing small woodlands and trees, with a consequent loss of wildlife. Wildlife has also been adversely affected by the use of pesticides and herbicides, some of which cause a damaging build-up of toxic compounds in the food chain. Draining of wetlands and improvement of permanent pasture have caused serious habitat loss to birds, plants, insects, and amphibians. While these changes have occurred in areas of higher agricultural potential, more remote disadvantaged areas have been struggling to maintain farming systems held to have high landscape value. There, the underlying problems are agricultural neglect and depopulation of some areas.

To the extent that most of the environmental concerns are the consequence of intensification of production, itself stimulated by EC price support, diverse strong environmental pressure groups have emerged arguing for agricultural-policy reform. Among measures introduced since 1987 are payments in certain environmentally sensitive and special areas; the payments compensate for profitability loss as a result of agreeing to de-intensify production and take measures to conserve traditional methods, features, and habitats. Further, controls of the disposal of livestock and other assets are being introduced in several Member States to assist agriculture in disadvantaged regions.

### 4.4. THE START OF THE REFORM PROCESS: THE INTRODUCTION OF SUPPLY CONTROL MECHANISMS

Throughout the existence of the CAP, its policy instruments and regulations have been adapted to meet the changing economic and political circumstances of the EC. For example, during the 1970s, in response to the growing surpluses of some commodities, the EC introduced several *new* measures to the CAP designed to encourage domestic consumption, including subsidies to certain categories of final consumers, subsidies to industrial users of food products, and even 'denaturing premiums' to encourage the use of grain in livestock feed. Alternatively, the EC attempted to decrease the budgetary cost of an existing policy instrument, intervention buying, by manipulating its rules of operation. For many commodities supported by this policy instrument, the period of availability of intervention buying has been shortened and the quality standards for acceptance have been raised, whilst the price received for sales to intervention has been reduced to a so-called 'buying-in price', set some percentage points below the relevant intervention price. However, most, if not all, of these 'patching' measures did little to alleviate the mounting pressures for more radical reform of the CAP.

It was not until the early 1980s that more significant changes to the CAP were initiated with the introduction of three new supply control mechanisms—marketing quotas, co-responsibility levies, and budgetary stabilizers. The introduction of these supply control mechanisms essentially marked the end of unlimited price guarantees, with each incorporating what has become known as the 'fourth principle' of the CAP: *producer co-responsibility* for surplus production. For commodities covered by such policy instruments, if production exceeded a certain fixed level (known as the guarantee threshold), action was triggered which ensured that at least part of the cost of the additional surplus disposal was born by producers. The discussion below focuses on one mechanism which was retained in the May 1992 CAP reform package—marketing quotas.

## The Economics of Marketing Quotas

Marketing quotas were first imposed on EC dairy producers in spring 1984 against a background of long-term structural surpluses of dairy products, an extremely depressed world market, and escalating budgetary costs of milk support. Throughout the 1970s and early 1980s the milk regime accounted for the largest proportion of total guarantee expenditure of the CAP. Indeed, it is still the most expensive commodity regime, although its proportion of total EAGGF expenditure has fallen from 29.7 per cent in 1984 to 18.2 per cent in 1992.

Prior to the introduction of quotas, in 1981 the EC had introduced a system of maximum guaranteed thresholds intended to operate in such a way that, should milk deliveries in any year exceed the (pre-fixed) quantitative threshold, action would be triggered to offset the additional costs of the regime caused by the excess production. As early as 1983 the guarantee threshold was exceeded by 6.5 per cent. The reduction in intervention price for dairy products which should have been triggered by this surplus was estimated by the Commission to have been in the order of 12 per cent—too large to be politically feasible. Instead, the EC chose to maintain the level of price support at its existing level and adopt a system of marketing quotas made effective by charging a very high tax, or super-levy, on excess deliveries beyond the quota.

Initially, each Member State was allocated a national quota or 'reference quantity' set equal to their 1981 milk delivery levels plus 1 per cent (apart from Italy and the Irish Republic, whose initial reference quantities were based on the quantity of milk delivered during 1983). Quotas were then allocated to individual farmers, again on the basis of their historical production levels.

The welfare implications of quotas as compared to those arising from a straight price-support reduction for dairy products are shown in Fig. 4.3. Importantly, both sets of welfare effects are measured relative to a base scenario of surplus production and of the EC maintaining a support price at a level significantly above the world price for dairy products. In other words, the base scenario is intended to reflect the situation in the EC dairy industry at the beginning of the 1980s.

A straight reduction in the level of intervention price for dairy products from $P_i$ to $P_i'$, it is shown, would cause EC consumers to increase their consumption from $D_i$ to $D_i'$ and farmers to decrease their production from $S_i$ to $S_i'$ by moving down the supply function $SS$. Consequently, the level of surplus production decreases from $(S_i - D_i)$ to $(S_i' - D_i')$ and the

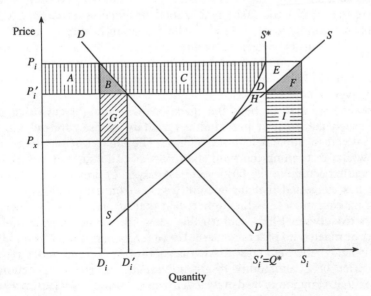

FIG. 4.3. Comparison of welfare effects of quotas and support price reductions

budgetary cost of disposing of the surplus through variable export refunds falls. A cut in the level of price support would *increase consumer surplus* by area $A + B$, *reduce producer surplus* by the area $A + B + C + D + E$ and *reduce the budgetary cost* of support by $B + C + D + E + F + G + I$, causing overall a net welfare gain relative to the base scenario of $B + G + F + I$.

In comparison, the imposition of a total quota at $Q^*$ (which, for ease of comparison, is set equal to $S_i'$) shifts the supply curve to $SS^*$. At output level $Q^*$, the supply curve is perfectly inelastic, implying that the penalty for surplus production is severe enough to discourage any farmers from exceeding the production threshold and thus incurring the super–levy. Consumers are unaffected by the implementation of the new policy instrument—they continue to purchase the same level of output, $D_i$, at prices significantly above the world price of the commodity, $P_x$; thus the change in *consumer surplus* is zero. The figure suggests that farmers lose producer surplus equal to area $E + D + H$. Whilst area $E$ is an unavoidable loss of surplus because of the output-restricting nature of the policy instrument, area $D + H$ is lost because of the manner in which quotas are allocated between individual producers. Distributing quotas purely on the basis of historical production levels rather than efficiency criteria means that some low-cost, efficient production is lost from the industry whilst some high-cost, inefficient production is maintained. If, following the initial allocation, sale of quota is permitted, then it can be shown that low-cost producers would be willing to purchase or lease quota from high-cost producers and the area of surplus $D + H$ is removed (Burrell 1989). Assuming that such trade takes place, total *producer surplus loss* to the dairy industry can be reduced to $E$.[10] The reduction in surplus production by $(S_i - Q^*)$ results in *budgetary savings* relative to the base scenario of $E + F + I$. Thus, overall, Fig. 4.3 suggests the implementation of quotas results in a net welfare gain of only $F + I$ which is less than that of a price cut to $P_i$ by $B + G$.

The preceding analysis begs the question: if a straight cut in support prices offered the greatest potential net welfare gains, why did the EC choose instead to implement milk quotas? The answer seems to be that quotas, whilst restraining the budgetary cost of milk support, minimized the dislocation caused to the farm sector. Analysis of previous CAP policy changes has suggested that the weight given to farmers' interests in the decision-making process is far higher than that afforded to consumers or taxpayers (MacLaren 1992), and, in this sense, the choice of milk quotas simply conformed with past precedent. However, quotas also helped nullify a widely held belief amongst CAP decision-makers—that reducing the support price of a commodity might not rapidly lead to a reduction in output of that commodity and may even cause output levels to increase. Whilst little empirical evidence has been found to support this idea of 'perverse' supply response, it is interesting to contrast the two alternative policy options from a producer's perspective. A straight reduction in price support levels keeps the marginal revenue and average revenue of output perfectly elastic at the new (lower) price and retains the open-ended nature of support. Thus, it can be argued that it offers individual producers an incentive to reduce costs per unit output but not necessarily their total output level. Surplus production has long been considered by the Commission as the central problem of the CAP, and it was consequently keen to introduce a policy instrument which gave it direct control over aggregate output levels.

The total EC quota for milk has been periodically reduced from 103.7 million tonnes in 1984 to 96 million tonnes in 1991/2 for the EC10, although, with the inclusion of Spain, Portugal, and East Germany, the total has increased to 109.6 million tonnes. The system, as noted above, has been fairly successful at reducing the budgetary cost of the milk regime, but its success has been possible only because of the system of milk-marketing. Virtually all milk is sold from farms to a relatively small number of processing plants. This bottleneck in the marketing chain allows the output of each producer to be monitored and, if necessary, permits enforcement of the quota by charging appropriate individuals the super-levy on excess production. The same policy instrument would be ineffective if applied to the cereals regime, because no equivalent bottle-neck in the marketing chain of cereals exists. Instead, during the 1980s, the EC adopted the other two types of supply control methods mentioned above—*co-responsibility levies* and *budgetary stabilizers*—to control the output level and budgetary cost of the cereals regime. Whilst both these mechanisms share the basic characteristics of quotas in that they penalize production in excess of some threshold quantity by imposing some kind of pricing penalty, they offer far less of an incentive to an individual producer to reduce output levels. As explained by Burrell (1987: 5), a rational individual producer will respond to a quantitative threshold on output only if that threshold has been imposed directly on his own production levels: 'Otherwise he is a price-taker, and in spite of the threshold for aggregate output, he perceives the demand for his own output as perfectly elastic at the going price.'

The introduction and gradual increased reliance on supply control mechanisms in the 1980s failed to stifle the calls for yet more fundamental reform of the CAP. Instead, in May 1992 the CAP entered into a second stage of reform marked by the Council of Ministers' acceptance of the MacSharry reform package.

### 4.5. THE MACSHARRY REFORM PACKAGE

The nature of the MacSharry reform package owes much to the ongoing multinational trade negotiations and the pressure from agricultural trading

TABLE 4.5. *Summary of the MacSharry CAP reforms*

| Commodity regimes | Cuts in support | Compensation and other gains | Production control |
|---|---|---|---|
| Cereals | • Target price cut by 29% from 1991/2 buying-in price<br>• Price reduction phased in over three years from 1993/4. | • Per hectare compensation payments available provided set-aside is implemented<br>• Compensation payments based on historical yield levels for regions of the EC<br>• Co-responsibility levy abolished from 1992/3 | • Annual set-aside required for producers to be eligible for compensation payments<br>• Minimum set-aside area 15% of total arable hectarage<br>• Set-aside area to be rotated (the same land can be idled only once every six years) |
| Oilseeds and pulses | • No price support 1993/4 onwards | • Per hectare payments are available but cut from 1992/3 levels | • Controlled by same set-aside scheme as cereal production |
| Sheep | • Payment of ewe premium restricted by producer quota<br>• Producer quotas based on number of ewe premiums paid in 1991 | • Capital value of sheep quota<br>• Lower feed grain costs | • Full payment of ewe premium set at maximum of 500 ewes in lowlands, 1,000 ewes in less favoured areas<br>• 50% of premium paid for ewes above these limits up to producer quota |
| Beef | • Intervention price cut by 15% from 1993/4<br>• 350,000t. limit set on intervention purchases by 1997 | • Beef and suckler cow premium increased but made contingent on stocking levels<br>• An extra extensification premium available if stocking rates below minimum level<br>• Capital value of suckler cow quota<br>• Lower feed grain costs | • Beef premium limited by regional ceiling equal to number of premiums paid in 1991; if exceeded, producer payments reduced per rata<br>• Suckler cow premiums restricted by producer quota |
| Dairy | • 5% cut in butter intervention price by 1994/5 | • Possible future quota cuts compensated by redeemable bond<br>• Co-responsibility levy abolished from 1992/3 | • Quotas to be cut by proposed 2% by 1994/5 |

partners to reduce the level of trade distortion caused by the CAP. Whilst the basic price support mechanisms described in Section 4.2 are to be retained, reductions in the level of support prices will significantly weaken their effectiveness. The impact of such price cuts for commodities in surplus can be ascertained by referring back to Fig. 4.2—consumers should benefit (assuming that reductions in the support price of cereals are passed on in the form of lower cereal-based food products), the budgetary cost of disposing of any remaining surplus production should decrease, and the farm sector, in the absence of any countervailing policy action, should suffer a loss in producer surplus. However, to compensate farmers for their potential loss in income, the EC has decided to give direct income payments to farmers provided they adhere to certain restraints on input use. For livestock producers, compensation payments will be limited to a fixed number of animals based on historical herd sizes and will be contingent upon a maximum stocking density; whilst for arable producers, compensation will be paid only if a farmer agrees to set aside (take out of production) at least 15 per cent of his total arable area on a rotational basis.

By partly replacing price support with direct income payments, the correlation between the amount of support received and the amount of output produced has been weakened. In the jargon of the GATT negotiations, the MacSharry reform package marks a move towards 'decoupled' farm income support.[11] The main changes to the commodity regimes of the CAP following the reform agreement are summarized in Table 4.5.

## The Economics of the New Arable Regime

The changes to the arable regime of the CAP are particularly significant, not just because of the introduction of a set-aside,[12] but because of the importance of cereals within the agricultural industry. In future, each cereal farmer in the EC faces a decision of whether (a) to use the whole of his arable acreage, and receive the new (lower) market price for cereal output, or (b) to comply with the set-aside requirements and thus be eligible for compensation payments in addition to his market returns for output from land remaining in production.

For those who adopt the latter strategy and opt into the set-aside scheme, two types of compensation payments can be distinguished—price compensation and set-aside compensation. The level of both payments over the transitionary period are shown in Table 4.6. The level of price compensation is shown to increase gradually throughout the transitionary period as the gap between the old buying-in price and new target price widens. Importantly, price compensation is converted from a tonnage to area basis by applying a fixed yield factor. The yield factor has been calculated from historical data and varies between regions of the community. The table shows that for England, it has been set at 5.93 tonnes per hectare, thus

TABLE **4.6.** *Compensatory payments for the reformed CAP cereals regime*

|  |  | Marketing year | | |
|---|---|---|---|---|
|  |  | 1993/4 | 1994/5 | 1995/6 |
| A. | 1991/2 Buying-in price (ecu/t.) | 155 | 155 | 155 |
| B. | Target price (ecu/t.) | 130 | 120 | 110 |
| C. | Price compensation [A − B] (ecu/t.) | 25 | 35 | 45 |
| D. | Yield factor (England) (t./hectare) | 5.93 | 5.93 | 5.93 |
| E. | Price compensation per hectare (England) [C × D] (ecu/hectare) | 148.25 | 207.55 | 266.85 |
| F. | Set-aside compensation (England) (ecu/hectare) | 266.85 | 266.85 | 266.85 |

implying that, by the end of the three-year period, every farmer who chooses to participate in the set-aside scheme will receive a payment of Ecu 267 for each hectare remaining in production. In addition, participating farmers will receive a compensation payment for land left idle. The level of this set-aside compensation does not vary during the transitionary period and has been set equal to the level of price compensation in 1995/6. Thus, when the scheme is fully implemented, participating farmers will receive exactly the same direct income payment for every hectare of their total (original) arable area.

The decision whether or not to participate in the new set-aside scheme will depend on the market price of cereals. In particular, the decision will depend on the value of compensation payments relative to the revenue from planting the extra 15 per cent of arable area. When cereal prices are high, the opportunity cost of leaving land to stand idle is also high, and a farmer is not likely to participate in the scheme. As the market price for cereals falls, the opportunity cost of idling land also falls. At some point, the value of the compensation payments from participating in set-aside will exactly equal the profit that could be earned from planting the additional set-aside area. The price of cereals which gives rise to this equivalence can be called the 'indifference price', since at this price the farmer is indifferent as to whether he opts out of production and into set-aside—either way his total profit level is the same. If the market price of cereals exceeds the indifference price, a rational producer would choose to plant his full area. Alternatively, if the market price for cereals is less than the indifference price, a rational producer would participate in the set-aside scheme in order to be eligible for the compensation payments.

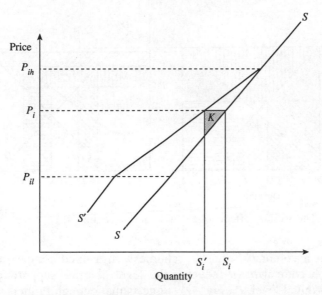

**Fig. 4.4.** Cereal supply curve under voluntary set-aside

Because farms are not identical, indifference prices will vary between cereal producers. One would expect inefficient, high-cost producers to have a low opportunity cost of idling land and thus a relatively high indifference price. Conversely, one would expect efficient, low-cost producers to have a high opportunity cost of leaving land fallow and thus a relatively low indifference price. Taking such variability into account and aggregating across all producers in the industry, the supply curve for cereals under the new voluntary set-aside scheme would shift from its original competitive level, $SS$, to the kinked curve $S'S$, as shown in Fig. 4.4.

In Fig. 4.4, $P_{ih}$ and $P_{il}$ represent the highest and lowest indifference price in the industry respectively. At any price above $P_{ih}$, the market return for cereals is sufficient to deter *any* farmer from participating in set-aside. Therefore, the total arable area would be utilized and the supply curve would coincide with the competitive supply curve, $SS$. However, once the price of cereals falls below $P_{ih}$, the least efficient, high-cost producers would chose to opt out of full production and into set-aside, idling at least 15 per cent of their land and thus causing the supply curve to rotate to the left. As the price falls further, more and more farmers opt into set-aside and more and more land is withdrawn from production. Once the price has fallen to $P_{il}$, *all* farmers choose to idle the necessary portion of their land in order to be eligible for compensation payments.

The shift in supply curve shown in Fig. 4.4 allows us to identify the minimum value of set-aside compensation payments necessary to induce a certain reduction of cereal output. For example, if the EC had decided to

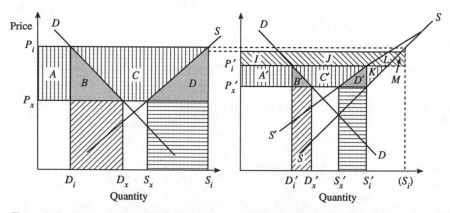

**FIG. 4.5.** The welfare effects of the new arable regime

implement a voluntary set-aside scheme with a fixed compensation payment per hectare *without* reducing the level of price support for cereals from its original level, $P_i$, Fig. 4.4 suggests that enough farmers would opt into the scheme to cause output levels to fall from $S_i$ to $S_i'$. By deduction, since the scheme is voluntary, this would occur only if there is no overall reduction in producer surplus. In other words, the value of set-aside compensation payments must be at least equal to area $K$ in the figure, which represents the amount of surplus lost from production.

The new supply curve with set-aside, $S'S$, is replicated in Fig. 4.5, where the changes in welfare and transfer effects between the old and new cereals regimes are investigated. Analysis focuses on the situation when the new cereals regime is fully implemented.

From an initial buying-in price of $P_i$, the support price for cereals once the scheme is fully implemented falls to $P_i'$. Additionally, by the time the full reduction of 29 per cent in support price has been phased in, the world market price for cereals is shown to have increased from $P_x$ to $P_x'$, because of the reduction in volume of subsidized exports from the Community. These changes in prices suggest that, relative to the free-trade scenario, the *change in consumer surplus loss* is given by $(A + B) - (A' + B')$, implying that in principle EC consumers should benefit from the change in the CAP.

The welfare effect for producers is less clear-cut. From a starting position of producer surplus gain of $(A + B + C)$ under the old regime, their surplus from cereal production is reduced to $(A' + B' + C')$. However, in addition they receive direct compensation payments. Since, as drawn, the new (lower) support price $P_i'$ corresponds to the lowest indifference price of the industry, we can assume that every cereal producer is participating in the set-aside scheme.[13] Since the per hectare value of both set-aside and price compensation payments are equal and based on historical output levels, the total value of compensation is shown in the figure as area

$I + J + L + M$. In other words, one can convert the area payments to an output equivalent using the fact that the fixed reference yield has been derived on the basis of the historical output level, $S_i$, and the total arable area. Thus the *change in producer surplus gain* is given by $(A + B + C)$-$(A' + B' + C' + I + J + L + M)$. Whether or not this is positive or negative depends on whether the value of compensation payments is larger or smaller than the loss in producer surplus from reducing output level to $S_i'$.

The impact of the new regime on the budgetary cost of cereal support is also not easily predicted. Whether or not the total budgetary cost of supporting cereal farmers decreases or increases depends upon whether the saving in terms of the disposal of surplus production $(B + C + D) - (B' + C' + D')$ is larger or smaller than the value of compensation payments $I + J + L + M$. As drawn, the figure suggests a fall in the budgetary cost of support. However, in practice this will depend upon the change in the world price for cereals and the extent of participation in the set-aside scheme. The reduction in net welfare loss caused by the policy reform is less ambiguous. Taking into account the preceding analysis, the reduction in net welfare loss is represented by area $(B + D)$ less $(B' + D')$. Importantly, as drawn, the MacSharry reforms reduce but do not eliminate the trade distortion caused by CAP support for cereal producers with the level of exports falling from $(S_i - D_i)$ to $(S_i'$-$D_i')$.

Whilst useful as an indication of the general welfare effects of the new CAP arable regime, the preceding analysis has ignored the more detailed aspects of the regime which will be critical in governing its effectiveness. For instance, no mention has been made of the problem of *slippage*, which is associated with any policy requiring that farmers set aside land. Slippage can be most easily described as the phenomenon whereby a certain reduction in cereal area does not necessarily lead to the same percentage reduction in cereal output. In terms of Figs. 4.4 and 4.5, slippage would result in a smaller rotation in the supply curve for cereals to the left. There are many different reasons for slippage, including farmers using inputs more intensively on the land remaining in production, the setting-aside of less productive land, and land increasing in fertility as a result of being left to stand fallow, which would result in increased yields once that land is brought back into production; alternatively, slippage may occur simply because of ineffective policing of set-aside, allowing farmers to plant more hectares than intended under the rules of the new regime. The analysis has also ignored the fact that the rules of the regime are such that the base arable area of each individual farmer is defined to include ground previously sown with oilseeds and protein crops as well as cereals. Thus there will not even be a direct correspondence between the change in cereal area and the area of land removed from production under set-aside, even before considering the complications of slippage. Again, the rotation in cereal supply curve shown in Figs. 4.4 and 4.5 may be less pronounced than initially implied.[14]

Currently, the Commission is proposing certain modifications to the arable regime, as described in Table 4.5. As well as adjusting the proportion of arable land to be set aside and hence the value of compensation payments, it is also proposing to make the scheme more flexible, in particular by allowing farmers to mix rotational and non-rotational set-aside. With such modifications looking set to continue, it is clear that the period of reliance of the CAP primarily on market price support is well and truly over.

## 4.6. SUMMARY AND OUTLOOK

The 1992 CAP reform package represents an uneasy compromise between continuing the traditional policies of protecting agriculture through price supports and income aids and the various pressures for reform discussed in Section 4.3. The decision to scale down EC price support for agriculture and the switch to direct income aids for farmers can be seen to reflect proposals discussed in the Uruguay Round and the pressure of the United States in particular. That the scale of support reduction measured by the SMU is planned, under the Blair House accord, to be limited to 30 per cent until 1996 reflects political reluctance to move rapidly to free trade and to abandon well-established policies.

By compensating for commodity price reductions by the introduction of compensation payments to farmers, the reform has allowed a transfer of some of the cost of support from food consumers to taxpayers, which is socially progressive in reducing food costs to poor non-taxpayers. It also means that the costs of the CAP will be increasingly transparent, being revealed in budgetary accounts rather than being hidden away in the mass of consumer spending. Nevertheless, by retaining some price support and adding the new compensation payments, the operation of the CAP has been made even more complex. This is because the compensation payments are conditional upon compliance with a variety of qualifying actions, all of which have to be checked before payment is authorized. Inevitably, this raises administrative costs and increases the size of the bureaucracy, while at the same time increasing the incentives and possibilities for fraud which are already a well-established feature of the CAP.

Adding new supply controls in the form of arable land set aside and animal stocking rates to the existing marketing quotas for milk and sugar has been necessary to achieve an approximation to the decoupling of agricultural support and to help control budgetary costs. However, these actions reflect continued unwillingness to subject EC agriculture to the rigours of free trade and open competition. A solution of managed markets is still politically preferred, with the levels of support prices and restrictions fairly clearly established until 1996. This will reduce the amount of time used in the annual negotiations on price and policy determination which in the past have been lengthy and argumentative, and it will enable energies to be focused on the form of the CAP after 1996. There are clearly many possibilities: to muddle on with the current compromise, to reduce price support further and to increase or maintain direct payments, or to link farm income support more distinctly to environmentally sensitive management or to regional disadvantage.

# NOTES

1. For a review of these negotiations and their substance, readers are referred to Rayner, Ingersent, and Hine (1993).
2. This assumes that all increases in the price of agricultural commodities such as wheat are passed through to the retail prices of bread, cakes, flour, etc.
3. For a whole series of reasons (Colman 1985), the floor is not as rigid as portrayed in Fig. 4.2, but it is an acceptable approximation for much analysis.
4. It may be noted that the position is more complex than this. For example, although the EC is a large exporter of soft wheat, it still has to import hard wheats for bread-making. VILs calculated with respect to soft wheats result in hard wheats entering the EC at prices very much higher than the MIP.
5. A monetary gap is defined as the difference between a currency's agricultural conversion rate (green rate) and its representative market rate, expressed as a percentage of its agricultural conversion rate.
6. This is also known by its French initials FEOGA.
7. The standard approach to calculating the effects of the price support which exists is to estimate what would happen if price support were reduced. The current position, with support, is known; the question is, what would the position be if it was reduced or eliminated?
8. The numbers in this table are generated by a computable model, and reflect estimates of the *reductions in cost* which would arise if agricultural policy was reformed in a specific way. This explains why the estimated EC taxpayer cost of US$15.6 bn. is less than actual EC budgetary expenditure of around Ecus 22.5 bn. in 1986/7.
9. The fifteen negotiating groups are listed by Greenaway (1991: 372, table 5). Among the more important groups (in addition to agriculture) are textiles and clothing, services, and trade-related intellectual property rights.
10. This assumes that there are no inefficiencies in the quota market.
11. Under 'truly' decoupled income support, a farmer's production decisions would be based on the free-price equivalents of commodities. Since, under the new CAP arable regime, the decision of whether or not to set aside land depends on the relative size of compensation payments *vis-à-vis* the new *support* price for cereals, the move towards decoupled farm income support is far from complete.

12. The option allowing EC farmers voluntarily to set aside arable land in return for compensation strictly dates from 1988. However, the impact of the initial set-aside scheme was extremely limited, with very low uptake levels in almost all Member States.

13. If this was not the case, it would be impossible to show the value of compensation payments in price/output space as in Fig. 4.5.

14. Yet another complication to measuring the effects of the new arable regime has been caused by farmers planting set-aside land with crops intended for industrial usage (e.g. linseed) or, alternatively, choosing to plant set-aside area with forage crops, which has implications for other commodity regimes.

# REFERENCES

BAE (1985): Bureau of Agricultural Economics, *Agricultural Policies in the European Community* (Policy Monograph No. 2; Canberra, Australia: Bureau of Agricultural Economics).

Blandford, D., de Gorter, H., and Harvey, D. R. (1989), 'Farm Income Support with Minimal Trade Distortions', *Food Policy* (Aug.), 268–73.

Brown, C. (1989), *Distribution of CAP Price Support* (Report 45; Copenhagen: Statens Jordbrugsokonomiske Institut).

Burrell, A. (1987), 'EC Agricultural Surpluses and Budget Control', *Journal of Agricultural Economics*, 38/1: 1–14.

——— (1989), 'The Microeconomics of Quota Transfer', in A. Burrell (ed.), *Milk Quotas in the European Community* (Wallingford: CAB International), 100–18.

Colman, D. (1985), 'Imperfect Transmission of Policy Prices', *European Review of Agricultural Economics*, 12/3: 171–86.

DPI–Australia (1986): Department of Primary Industry—Australia, *The Political Economy of Agricultural Policy Reform* (Canberra, Australia: DPI).

GATT (1988): General Agreement on Tariffs and Trade, *GATT International Trade 87–88* (Geneva: GATT).

Greenaway, D. (1991), 'The Uruguay Round of Multilateral Trade Negotiations: Last Chance for GATT?', *Journal of Agricultural Economics*, 42/3: 365-79.

Josling, T.E., and Hamway, D. (1972), *Burdens and Benefits of Farm Support Policies* (London: Trade Policy Research Centre).

MacLaren, D. (1992), 'The Political Economy of Agricultural Policy Reform in the European Community and Australia', *Journal of Agricultural Economics*, 43/3: 424–39.

Rayner, A. J., Ingersent, K. A., and Hine, R. C. (1993), 'Agricultural Trade and the GATT', in A. J. Rayner and D. Colman (eds.), *Current Issues in Agricultural Economics* (Basingstoke: Macmillan), 62–95.

Roningen, V. O., and Dixit, P.M. (1989), *How Level is the Playing Field: An Economic Analysis of Agricultural Policy Reforms in Industrial Market Economies* (United States Department of Agriculture, ERS, FAE Report 239; Washington DC).

# 5

# Competition Policy

DAVID YOUNG AND STAN METCALFE

## 5.1. THE THEORETICAL BASIS OF COMPETITION POLICY

### The Rationale for Competition Policy

Competition policy is concerned with maintaining competition between firms in all sections of the economy in an attempt to promote the efficient working of the market. The fundamental rationale for such policy is that the market does not, by itself, function perfectly or that there are certain necessary conditions for the proper functioning of markets which the state can attempt to create. Competitive markets are normally viewed as having a number of inherent advantages, such as the efficient allocation of resources, the maintenance of consumer choice, and the autonomy of industrial enterprises, which it is believed are important for long-run economic progress. Mainstream economics has long emphasized the possible imperfections which may arise from monopoly power, public goods, externalities, and such like, and these may provide grounds for a degree of state intervention via public policy in order to attempt to alleviate such problems.

It is not surprising, therefore, that individual countries within the European Community (EC) have long pursued some type of competition policy. Similarly it is a matter of considerable importance for the development of the Community. A report of the Commission (CEC 1992) emphasized the increasing importance of competition policy within the context of the internal market. The need for 'improved monitoring of Member States' anti-competitive behaviour' (CEC 1992: 9) was noted as a crucial aspect of the move towards a single internal European market. There is, however, a variety of opinions as to the exact nature of competition and the extent to which it requires state intervention. Moreover, it is also the case that any view as to the desirability of any type of competition policy is founded on a particular view of the nature of the competitive process and the workings of a market economy.

## The Nature of the Competitive Process

In order to develop effective competition policy, it is necessary to have a clear view of the meaning of competition. Competition policy is often seen as being necessary or helpful in aiding the competitive process and in correcting any inadequacies or distortions existing in product (or less often factor) markets. But this view is based on a specific notion of the competitive process. Although there is a dominant theory of competition in economics, there are in fact a number of different theories or views of the nature of competition, and the dominant view sometimes draws on ideas from these alternative approaches. Before we can discuss and evaluate competition policy, we must explore the meaning of competition itself.

The mainstream view of competition is founded on the neo-classical notion of perfect competition. Although there are many dissenters from the application of such a strict condition, perfect competition still forms the theoretical basis of modern mainstream analysis of competition and hence competition policy. Perfect competition provides a bench-mark against which all and any actual form of competition may be judged. It defines a position of equilibrium which represents an optimal allocation of resources. This specifies a situation involving zero super-normal profits and free entry and exit. A deviation from this state is definitionally sub-optional (although there may be dynamic gains which offset such static inefficiencies). Firms which possess a degree of market power, that are able to influence the market price, are regarded as distorting the allocation of resources from the socially optimal position. The conception of monopoly/market power as a distortion or imperfection is particularly important and is associated with the view that the market process is basically competitive but that at any time there may be a number of reasons why this is not so. The role of competition policy, therefore, is to correct these distortions and restore the market process to its correct competitive path.

However, some economists have been dissatisfied with such an abstract and static notion of the welfare bench-mark and in response have tried to develop a more suitable description of a baseline from which actual competition may be judged. In particular the idea of 'workable' competition has been proposed. This does not involve any fundamentally different conception of what competition is, but rather is concerned with defining a state which relates more clearly to 'real-world' competitive conditions. It involves a neo-classical view of competition but eschews perfect competition as a realistic objective. Unfortunately, there are a number of different views and definitions of what workable competition actually is (see e.g. Devine *et al.* (1985)). All, however, may be regarded as an attempt to describe a market which has an 'acceptable' set of competitive conditions from a policy perspective. Indeed, it is from a policy, rather than a theoretical, perspective that workable competition has been mainly thought to be a useful notion. Early attempts to define the term have focused on conditions where there are large numbers of sellers of similar products who do not collude, and where entry is not seriously restricted.

More radically different views of the nature of competition are offered by alternative schools of economic thought, such as the Austrian school, which emphasizes the 'process' character of competition. This view has enjoyed something of a revival in recent years (see e.g. Reid (1987)) and has arguably been influential in determining recent changes in government policy on monopolies. The essence of the Austrian view is that competition is an ongoing *process* and that the neo-classical conception of competition, being essentially static, does not provide an appropriate basis for assessing actual markets. Competition, according to this view, is a continual process of entrepreneurial rivalry. Entrepreneurs are alert to profit opportunities, and it is their purposeful pursuit of profit which is the driving force of the economy. This Austrian view, therefore, regards profit as necessary for motivating agents and also forms the basis of co-ordination and market order in the economy. Given that it is argued that perfect competition is not an appropriate baseline, this argument applies to profits generally and may include profits which neo-classical analysis would regard as super-normal profits. Therefore, the argument that super-normal profits necessarily result from firms' monopoly power and that this should be a concern of state competition policy is denied. Rather, in the Austrian view, profits reflect superior firm-specific competence. Another significant dimension of the Austrian approach is the emphasis it places on innovation. This is particularly so in Schumpeterian theories which develop the idea that the efficiency gains from innovations over time may outweigh any short-term inefficiencies resulting from market imperfections. For example, a degree of monopoly power may result in an inefficient use of resources at a particular time, but, if the profits generated by such market power generate greater innovation, then there will be offsetting advantages in the longer term.

Another important alternative view of competition is propounded by radical or Marxian theorists. Though these views have had less impact on mainstream economics in general and competition policy in particular, some of the policy implications to which these approaches give rise represent important alternative perspectives on policy options. There are, in fact, two lines of thought (at least) in radical views on competition. One is based on the notion that market structure has an important influence on market performance, which is clearly similar in certain respects to the neo-classical view; the other is based on a radically different conception of competition as involving competing 'blocks' of capital. According to this latter view, the process of accumulation which drives the economic system involves each block of capital attempting to expand into, and therefore to invade, the domain of other blocks of capital; and it is this process of different capitals expanding and competing with each other which describes the nature of the competitive process. The alternative view accepts the concept of market structure proposed by neo-classical theory, but argues that the market system has a natural tendency towards monopoly. The process of competition involves the gradual monopolization of product markets by large corporations. Oligopoly and market power are seen as the norm. This contrasts with the standard neo-classical view of market power as an imperfection or deviation from a competitive state. Rather, competition is fundamentally about market power and more generally the exercise of economic and political power.

## Impediments to Competition

Having outlined the different views of competition, we are now able to consider the principal sources of departure from a competitive state which might provide the basis for the main issues of concern in competition policy. It should be emphasized at the outset that posing the problem in terms of a departure from an optimal state does in itself form the question in a neo-classical/mainstream way. But, given that it is the most familiar and influential approach, this seems acceptable in the present context.

The most obvious obstacle to competitive behaviour in a market is the presence of monopoly. The standard theoretical approach to monopoly defines it as a situation in which there is a single seller of a given product, where there are no close substitutes for this product and where entry into the market is blocked. It is normally further assumed that the firm's (industry) demand curve is downward sloping.

The profit-maximizing firm, as always, equates marginal cost with marginal revenue, and, under perfect competition, this implies producing where $MC = P(= AR)$. The difference between the equilibrium price and output positions, in monopoly and perfect competition, can therefore be compared (see Fig. 5.1).

Under perfect competition, consumer surplus is given by the total area $DP_cB$. After the monopolization of the industry (assuming demand and cost conditions remain unchanged), this is reduced to area $DP_mA$. Part of the difference between consumer surplus under perfect competition and under monopoly now becomes producer surplus—namely, the area $P_m P_c CA$. The remainder is the area $ACB$. This is the 'cost' due to the contraction in output from $Q_c$ to $Q_m$; and hence the triangle $ABC$ represents the 'deadweight' loss to society.

There have been numerous attempts to estimate the social costs of monopoly power. Obviously some idea of the magnitude of welfare losses is of great importance in as much as this can provide some basis for assessing the need for a competition policy. (It might also be noted that it may also be important in assessing the competing claims regarding the

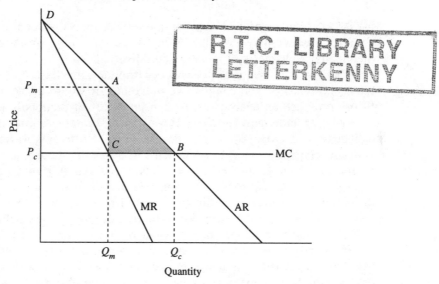

FIG. 5.1. Monopoly welfare loss

inherent tendency of the system towards competition or monopoly.) Early estimates, produced for the United States (e.g. Harberger (1954)) tended to suggest that welfare losses were very low, leading to a 'conventional' view that the social costs of monopoly are in fact rather trivial. However, since the early 1970s there have been a number of studies which have produced quite different estimates, suggesting that the cost of monopoly, associated with the reduction in gross output, is quite significant. For example, Cowling and Mueller (1978) and Sawyer (1980) have published estimates for the United Kingdom which suggest that welfare losses might be as high as 9 per cent of gross output. Similarly, significant 'high' estimates have been produced for France by Jenny and Weber (1983). There are a variety of reasons for the differences between these estimates, but the principal factors which have led to the higher estimates include attempts to include the costs of attempting to acquire and maintain monopoly positions (by including advertising expenditures in some form) and different assumptions regarding demand elasticities.

Other assessments of the magnitude of social costs arising from monopoly power have produced an even more diverse set of estimates. Littlechild (1981), in criticizing the Cowling and Mueller (1978) estimates, adopted an Austrian position, arguing that welfare losses were considerably smaller than Cowling and Mueller suggested. This was due, in his view, to the positive role of profits as the reward for risk-taking and the necessity of profits for encouraging innovation, as well as to a number of other factors, such as alleged aggregation bias and price discrimination. At the other end of the spectrum, Baran and Sweezy (1966) report estimates of surplus value for the US economy which suggest that more than 50 per cent of total US national product may take the form of surplus value produced by the monopolistic character of modern capitalism.

Although basic monopoly theory does provide some basis for identifying the social costs of non-competitive outcomes, it would be helpful if this theory provided an analysis of the consequences of monopoly power and not only of monopoly pricing. However, at present, a full theoretical explanation of monopoly power does not exist. Attempts to remedy this situation may arise out of developments in oligopoly theory, which is now firmly based on game-theoretic models. Although it is not possible or appropriate to discuss these developments here, it is important to consider the principal dimensions of oligopoly as they relate to the state of industrial competitiveness and therefore the formation of competition policy.

A particularly important factor is the notion of dominance. This is of specific concern from a policy perspective, because much legislative action has been concerned with dominant positions. The theoretical basis for this begins with the idea that a particular firm, or group of firms, may, by virtue of its relatively high share of industry/market output, be in a position to exert a degree of dominance over that market. The basic theoretical model which attempts to represent such a situation is referred to as the dominant firm or dominant firm-price leadership model (see e.g. Hay and Morris (1991)). Such a model embodies the assumption that the dominant firm or dominant group acts as the price leader by setting the price for the market in accordance with maximizing its own profits subject to a demand constraint. This demand constraint (i.e. the dominant firm's demand curve) is obtained by deducting the total supply of all other producers in the industry from total industry demand, which is exogenously given. The other producers in the industry are assumed to be a competitive 'fringe', each firm being a price-taker. All of these firms take the dominant firm's (group's) price as given and produce the output which maximizes their profit, given this price. This model has been criticized for a number of reasons, including its essentially static nature, its assumption that the dominant firm knows the supply of the 'fringe', and the narrow conception of dominance involved. In particular, the fact that the 'fringe' treats prices parametically but is important in determining the residual demand curve facing the dominant firm limits the nature of the leading firm's dominance.

A broader view of dominance often involves the idea that a firm can restrict other firms' choices via strategic behaviour. (See, for example, Geroski's and Jacquemin's (1984) discussion of the persistence of dominant firms.) There are potentially many aspects to such behaviour, such as a firm's attempt to secure market share through advertising and attempts to establish a 'reputation' with regard to pricing or output strategies. Another crucial dimension of the interaction between firms which is particularly important is the degree of collusion. Overt collusion is normally the direct concern of competition policy and in many countries is effectively out-lawed. There are various forms which collusion may take, but the main examples may be categorized as either some form of price-setting or some type of explicit agreement concerning outputs. (This is often analysed in terms of cartel behaviour. A cartel is the most formal and explicit form of collusion and normally involves a common price structure and some agreement over the output of the firms within the cartel.)

Although there is a wide variety of issues which must be evaluated when considering a firm's dominance, it should be noted that its relative size in terms of market share is still seen as a singularly important indicator of its potential dominance. This is clearly reflected in a number of previous European competition policy decisions. For example, the well-known *Continental Can* case in the early 1970s invoked the company's substantial market share in establishing its abuse of a dominant position. (For a discussion of this and other cases, see Jacquemin and de Jong (1977).) Further, examples of the importance of market share are provided by various competition policies throughout the EC which we shall discuss later.

Another source of restriction on competition is merger activity. Mergers are normally categorized under three main types: horizontal, vertical, and conglomerate. Each, at least potentially, has welfare implications arising from a variety of effects on the degree of competition. Perhaps the simplest case is that of horizontal merger, which at certain times in the past, such as the famous merger boom of the late 1960s, has been the dominant type of merger. Definitionally, horizontal mergers involve the merging of firms at the same stage of the production process. This can result in direct changes in the level of concentration in a given industry, and this may result in increased market power and higher price-cost margins. For example, two firms merging within a particular industry will clearly reduce the number of firms and increase size inequalities between firms, hence leading to an increase in concentration (as measured by, for instance, the Herfindahl index). The newly-formed firm (resulting from the merger) will have a higher market share and greater market power than either of the previous firms. This market power might be used to increase profit margins, leading to decreases in the level of consumer surplus.

Cases involving vertical mergers—i.e. mergers between firms at different stages of the production process—also have welfare implications. Usually, the principal concern here is the restrictions placed on the suppliers of the vertical outlets for the particular products concerned. For example, if a firm at an intermediate stage of the production process merges with a firm at a later stage (retail), then there might be some welfare concern with regard to the restriction of supplies to other retail outlets supplied by the old intermediate firm, now part of the 'new' merged firm.

Conglomerate mergers have in recent years become the most important type of merger and their welfare implications are potentially very significant. These involve firms merging across different markets (i.e. mergers in which there are no vertical or horizontal relations). The analysis of the effects of mergers of this type, however, is the most complex, as by their very nature they involve activities in a number of different markets, and therefore it is impossible to assess their effects in terms of changes in concentration or vertical constraints. However, the overall effect on the economy may be indicated by changes in aggregate concentration and specific pricing, and/or output effects may be identified. The case of conglomerate merger also raises broader aspects concerning firms' 'power', and this may be of great importance from a policy perspective. For example, Jacquemin and de Jong (1977) have stated that the eventual goals of competition policy in Europe should include 'the diffusion of economic power' and the protection of the 'economic freedom of market participants'. However, these are much more difficult aspects of economic life to regulate, partly because there are quite different interpretations of what constitutes 'economic freedom' and 'economic power'. An important point to note, however, is that consideration of such policy issues broadens our conception of competition to include the Austrian and radical viewpoints outlined previously. For example, Austrians might argue that maintaining the freedom of economic agents is of primary importance, whilst a radical approach might suggest that competition policy should take greater steps to contain the economic (and political) power attained by large corporations.

## 5.2. COMPETITION POLICY IN DIFFERENT EC COUNTRIES

In order to illustrate how the principles of competition policy are applied in practice and to describe the different interpretations and methods of application which exist, it is useful to consider some examples of competition policy in some of the Member States of the EC. In particular, we shall consider the basic legislation and policy measures which have been developed in the United Kingdom, Germany, and France, before proceeding to discuss policy at the EC level, which is our main concern. It is important, however, to consider briefly individual countries' policies, not only to illustrate the different approaches to competition policy but also as an illustration of issues which may arise at the interface between domestic and European competition policy.

### The United Kingdom

The main piece of legislation underpinning much of modern competition policy in the United Kingdom is the 1973 Fair Trading Act. This extended previous legislation concerning monopolies and mergers and established the Office of Fair Trading (OFT), which has the task of monitoring competition. The OFT is under the headship of the Director-General of Fair Trading, who has the legal power to refer any cases of anti-competitive behaviour to the Monopolies and Mergers Commission (MMC). Such anti-competitive behaviour concerns cases which involve the exploitation of a 'monopoly situation' which exists in relation to the acquisition or supply of goods within the United Kingdom. The definition of monopoly was amended in the 1973 Act to apply to a firm holding a 25 per cent market share or more (the previous definition specified one-third market share); a 'complex monopoly', where two or more firms account for at least a 25 per cent share of the market and are deemed to act in such a way as to restrict competition, may also be referred. The definition of the relevant market is, of course, crucial in making such definitions meaningful. This is decided on the basis of a specific range of products and is determined by the Secretary of State for Trade on the advice of the Director-General.

Once a reference has been made, it is then incumbent upon the MMC to decide whether a monopoly situation exists (in accordance with the Act) and whether or not it operates against the 'public interest'. What is or is not against the public interest involves a balancing of the possible efficiency gains (such as scale economies) against the restriction of competition (as caused by the abuse of market power), and this has normally been considered on a case-by-case basis. The criteria used to decide this include the maintenance of effective competition for supply within the United Kingdom; promoting competition through cost reduction by the use of new techniques and products, and facilitating entry into existing markets; maintaining/promoting a balanced distribution of industry and employment throughout the United Kingdom; and the maintenance of competitive activities outside the United Kingdom by UK suppliers and producers. If a firm (or firms) is found to be acting against the public interest, then it will normally be required by law to agree to refrain from the activities identified by the MMC as anti-competitive and harmful to the public interest. The decision on this rests with the Secretary of State.

Two other pieces of legislation of significance for contemporary policy are the Resale Prices Act 1976 and the Restrictive Trade Practices Act 1976. These build on previous Acts in 1964 and 1956 respectively. The 1976 Restrictive Trade Practices Act broadened the information which firms are required to register, which was established in the 1956 Act and requires the Director-General to act against agreements which significantly restrict competition. This usually attempts to prohibit collusion and price-fixing agreements.

Much of the legislative basis of competition policy was altered in the Competition Act of 1980, which widened the investigating power of the Director-General. It also provided for the recommendation that firm's activities were against the public interest on the grounds of only one outstanding effect (such as higher future prices) rather than having to weigh all possible pros and cons. Associated with this principle was the introduction of the concept of an 'anti-competitive practice', which has been interpreted to include refusal to supply 'tie-ins' and discounts, predatory pricing, and forcing retailers to stock a whole range of products ('full-line forcing').

The 1980 Act also provided for the investigation, by the MMC, of public enterprise 'monopolies', which was strongly associated with the government's drive towards privatization and was perhaps inspired in part by the Austrian notion that most (if not all) impediments to competition have their origins in state intervention.

*Germany*

German competition policy is based on the 1957 Act against Restraints on Competition. This Act prohibits actions/agreements to restrain competition, production, or market conditions with regard to trade in goods and commercial services. This includes any form of cartel arrangement, price-fixing, resale price maintenance, exclusive deals, and 'buying' arrangements. The distinguishing feature of German competition policy embodied in this Act is the emphasis on market dominance by large corporations. The Act has been amended several times since its inception, specifically in 1965, 1973, 1976, 1980, and 1989. The 1973 amendments established merger controls and notification requirements for proposed mergers, expanded the legal definition of market dominance, and extended the exemptions of small firms, which was the main amendment introduced by the previous alteration in 1965. The 1980 amendments were particularly significant in clarifying the definitions of abuse of dominant positions by illustrating the principle characteristics of dominant firms, and in specifying the criteria for control of vertical and conglomerate mergers.

The most recent amendment, in 1989, extended the dominance issue to 'powerful' buyers (in addition to sellers) and to situations involving smaller trading partners rather than the hitherto exclusive concern with large firms. This introduced a new dimension to German anti-trust policy, which has, generally speaking, always been primarily concerned with the abuse of dominant market positions, typically by large single suppliers. The system of law supporting this, which is in contradistinction to US legislation, has been adopted by a number of other anti-trust systems, including those in Japan and the EC itself, which we shall discuss later. The actual size of firm is crucial, in that the law is formulated to protect the interest of small firms against the exercise of market power/dominant positions by large firms. Activities of small firms are allowed which would be illegal if they were carried out by large firms, who are regarded as having a natural market advantage. This allows small firms, for example, to attempt to exploit economies of scale without fear of contravening competition policy. This exemption clause is important in simplifying the enforcement of anti-trust law, which, in comparison with the United Kingdom (and also the United States), is generally simpler, as it does not require the balancing of anti-competitive behaviour with efficiency. Under German law conduct which is found severely to restrict competition is generally illegal. Efficiency is treated under grounds for exception rather than by the case-by-case evaluation typified by the United Kingdom, as discussed in the previous section.

### France

Modern competition policy in France also has its legislative roots in the early post-Second World War years. Anti-trust policies of some type, however, are significantly older and represent one of the oldest systems of anti-monopoly legislation in the world. Most current legislation and policy is based on the post-war system, which was substantially revised in 1977. This included a much tougher policy on mergers, which in the 1950s and 1960s had been broadly encouraged in an attempt to strengthen domestic companies in order to make them better able to compete with foreign/international rivals. (This was also an important view prevailing in the United Kingdom during this time, and was, in part, responsible for the merger boom of the late 1960s.) The new policy on mergers required post-merger notice, and provided for the prohibition of mergers including firms with large (domestic) market shares. This Act also established the Commission de la Concurrence, which is empowered to investigate anti-trust violations and to recommend corrective measures. These changes, though altering the underlying laws very little, significantly expanded the means of enforcing anti-trust legislation.

Further changes in 1985 and 1986 strengthened merger policy by subjecting more mergers to the controls established in 1977, and the applicability of competition and anti-trust norms was broadened. This seems to have resulted in a significant increase in enforcement activity in France. The 1986 amendment also replaced the Commission by the Conseil de la Concurrence, which, unlike the Commission, is independent from the Ministry of Economics. Most significantly, this coincided with the separation of the administration from the interpretation and enforcement of anti-trust law. The interpretation of the law became the responsibility of the judiciary. This was an important change, which essentially shifted the onus of anti-trust enforcement from political discretion to judicial assessment. This is in contradistinction to the United Kingdom, where control of implementation rests with the Secretary of State, as noted previously. Merger control, on the other hand, has remained the subject of political review, and in this area recommendations by the Conseil require the authorization of the Minister of Economics.

Finally, it should be noted that these recent amendments (particularly the 1986 amendment) have drawn heavily on Articles 85 and 86 of the EC's Treaty of Rome in formulating a view on competition. This illustrates, as do other national policies, the increasing influence and importance of EC competition policy, to which we may now turn.

## 5.3. EC COMPETITION POLICY

### The Development of Competition Policy

An essential element in the concept of a common market is the unfettered mobility of goods, services, and factors of production so as to ensure the greatest efficiency in resource allocation. This has been an essential theme throughout the development of the Community, culminating in the establishment of the Single European Market (SEM) in 1992. Naturally, the first concern of the founders of the EC was the free mobility of goods, and, since it would be pointless to eliminate national tariff barriers to trade if private firms could construct their own countervailing barriers, the whole question of competition policy has been central to the EC's progress. As with so many areas of EC activity, competition policy has evolved steadily from the founding guidelines established in the Treaty of Rome. The advent of the single market is bound to result in further developments as the experience of trading in different markets identifies new areas of anti-competitive practice previously sheltering in national backwaters. The production of services is one likely focus of attention, as are the enduring questions of subsidiarity and the respective domains of national and EC competition authorities. Among the factors shaping the evolution of policy, in addition to the guidance provided by economic theory, are the diverse traditions of different countries, the extension of the EC to include the European Free Trade Association (EFTA) nations, and the changing role of public monopoly in the Member States. Of some relevance here are the differing Anglo-Saxon and continental approaches to competition. The Anglo-Saxon viewpoint is best exemplified by the US anti-trust practice, of which the UK legislation is a loose imitation based on a case-by-case approach. In the United States, firms are subject to stringent scrutiny and fierce compliance regulations, including provision for triple damages to be awarded to injured third parties. In contrast, the continental view has always been more relaxed, accepting social dimensions to competition, close links between suppliers and customers, and the establishment of group interests to the detriment of outsiders. Agreements not to compete have traditionally been part of a European business mentality. It is not surprising, therefore, that, from the outset, the Commission has faced difficulties in imposing a competition policy on the Member States. At one extreme were Germany, and subsequently the United Kingdom, with well-developed frameworks for dealing with monopoly and restrictive practices, and at the other, states such as Italy and Belgium where a competition-policy tradition scarcely existed. Out of this diversity a clear European dimension has emerged, and our purpose now is to sketch its main features in the light of the previous discussion of economic principle.

## Some History

The central feature of EC policy is the belief in the static and dynamic benefits of competition, and the origins of this view can be traced back to the Treaty of Paris in 1951 and the subsequent establishment of the European Coal and Steel Community (ECSC) in May 1953. Given its concern with these strategic commodities, it is not surprising that the Treaty identified certain business practices and state aids as being incompatible with the foundation of an integrated market in coal and steel. Thus the High Authority of the ECSC was empowered to identify and rule on cases of anti-competitive behaviour. From this foundation, the next step was the Messina conference of May 1955 and the subsequent Spaak Report, which laid the foundations for the Treaty of Rome. By then it was well recognized, within the Commission and more generally, that static considerations relating to the abuse of market power had to be weighed in the balance against the more dynamic considerations relating to technological and organizational innovation. The Treaty of Rome established the Commission as the authority in all matters of competition policy, with DG IV being established as the appropriate branch of the Commission. To this branch fell the complex task of turning the guidelines of the Treaty into a workable policy. The relevant Articles of the Treaty are 85, which deals with anti-competitive practices, and 86, which deals with dominant market practices and their abuse. In addition we should note that Articles 37 and 90 cover the conduct of public enterprises and Article 91 covers dumping of goods across national boundaries. However, our prime concern here is with Articles 85 and 86. The former has certainly been the more actively used of the two. Between 1964 and 1990 a total of 284 formal Commission decisions were made with respect to Article 85 and only twenty-one with respect to Article 86. Indeed, the first referral under the latter did not occur until 1971, an index of the jealousy with which national governments viewed this matter.

## Article 85

This Article sets out the practices deemed to be incompatible with a common market: all agreements between undertakings which may affect trade between Member States and have as their object or effect the prevention, reduction, or distortion of competition within the common market. It covers horizontal and vertical distortions of all kinds, price-fixing, price discrimination, agreements to predetermine market shares, and any controls on production, investment, or technical development. All such practices are declared void and unenforceable. However, it is also recognized that such agreements may, in clearly specified circumstances, be in the public interest and on these grounds exempt from the provisions of this Article. The general rule here permits agreements if they promote efficiency in production and distribution, promote technical progress, and provide consumers with a fair share of the benefits. Provided an agreement is essential to the provision of these beneficial effects, it could be approved. The immediate consequence of these negative (85/1) and positive sides (85/3) to Article 85 is that each situation has to be treated on its own merits, and so DG IV's principal task has been to build the appropriate body of case law. To assist in this process, regulations have had to be drafted which translate the general principles of Article 85 into clear-cut practice.

We should first note that the Commission has very substantial powers of investigation, supported by the relevant national authorities (in the UK case, the OFT) and bolstered by a system of fines for failure to co-operate with an investigation. Investigations can be prompted by the Commission or by the complaints of third parties. These matters are codified in Regulation 17/62, which was the practical response to the experience of the early years gained in DG IV. This regulation empowered the Commission to enforce the rules of competition on a uniform basis throughout the Community and to exempt small firms with less than a 5 per cent market share from the provisions of Article 85, and instituted a system of fines for breaches of the competition rules. In principle, the fine could amount to up to 10 per cent of a company's world-wide turnover. Pressure of work on the Commission soon led to further regulations defining a category of group exemptions to Article 85—that is, a class of practices which by their generic nature are considered not to have anti-competition effects. Thus Regulation 19/65 proposed exemption for resale agreements within the EC and restriction on the acquisition and use of industrial property rights. Group exemptions of this nature are typically granted for a period of ten-to-fifteen years. Not only do they limit the Commission's workload; they also save firms legal and other costs incurred in seeking an individual exemption. In the light of the Schumpeterian conflict between the static and dynamic aspects of innovation-based competition, it is particularly interesting to note the group exemptions which have been developed to accommodate firms' arrangements jointly to develop new technology. Thus, Council Regulation 2821/71 established that Article 85(1) does not apply to agreements between undertakings which have as their objective, the application of standards or the joint undertaking of a research-and-development (R&D) programme up to the stage of industrial exploitation, provided the results are shared between the partners in relation to their contributions. The increasing importance of high-technology competition to the perceived success of the EC *vis-à-vis* the rest of the world led, in the 1980s, to further refinements. Commission Regulation 418/85 extended the group exemptions to cover the joint exploitation of a joint R&D programme. In this context, joint exploitation covers production and marketing, the assignment of licences and other intellectual property, and the commercial know-how required for manufacture. One could hardly find a better example of the continually evolving nature of the Commission's competition policy.

Once a case has been dealt with by the Commission, a number of outcomes are possible. At one extreme is a negative clearance: that is, a declaration that the practice does not violate the conditions of Article 85(1). At the other extreme, a violation is found and fines may be imposed. The policy on fines has grown bolder with the acquisition of experience. The first case occurred in 1969, when a quinine cartel involving Dutch, German, and French firms was decreed in violation of 85(1), and was duly fined by the Commission. Relatively small beer one might think, but large firms in major sectors have not been exempt. Then a market-sharing agreement between ICI and Solvay for the production of soda ash was considered a violation in 1990 and fines of Ecu 17 million and Ecu 30 million were imposed on the respective companies. Nor are non-EC companies exempt: in 1991 Toshiba was fined Ecu 2 million for illegal arrangements with its European distribution companies. In between these extremes are the many cases where the partners involved voluntarily abandon their restrictive agreement or agree to modify it in a way in which the Commission considers is compatible with Article 85(3).

Some examples of the grounds on which the Commission has granted negative clearance may prove helpful at this stage. An early example was provided in 1965 concerning a German manufacturer of mechanical cultivators (Hummel) and its Belgian distribution company (Isbecque). The exclusive nature of the agreement was considered to bring it within the scope of Article 85(1), but, none the less, negative clearance was granted on the grounds that the arrangement led to superior customer services without any adverse pricing effects. Two more recent examples indicate the complexities of a case-by-case approach. In 1988 an arrangement between AEI and Reyroll Parsons to set up a joint manufacturing company (Vacuum Interrupters Limited) was granted exemption in spite of being the sole European supplier, entirely on the grounds that the associated product innovations would benefit consumers. An even more recent example of the Commission's attitude to the dynamics of the competitive process is provided by the decision in 1990 to exempt a joint venture to develop and produce electronic components for satellites (Alcatel Esaci/ANT Nachrichten technik). Notwithstanding the fact that this agreement was judged adversely to affect competition within the EC, it was allowed on the grounds that it strengthened European industry relative to the foreign competition.

## Article 86

Article 86 prohibits the abuse by one or more undertakings of a dominant position within the EC or a substantial part of it, but only in so far as the abuse may affect trade between Member States. It would cover, for example, restrictions on supply or technical development and unfair pricing. Unlike Article 85 there is no provision for granting an exemption, but like that Article the system of fines is used to penalize abuses of dominance. One example is the heavy fine imposed on Tetrapak (a Swiss company): this was fined Ecu 75 million in 1991 for engaging in discriminatory pricing and other practices, including unfair charges for early termination of contracts by its customers. As with decisions reached under Article 85, the European Court of Justice (ECJ) stands as the court of appeal in all cases.

We have already pointed to the relatively infrequent use of Article 86, in part due to the hostility of national authorities. More telling though is the failure of this Article to provide clear guidance on the treatment of mergers and acquisitions within the EC. At best it gives grounds for a decision *ex post* once a merger has been carried out and is judged to lead to adverse dominant behaviour. What it does not do is to provide guidance *ex ante* as to whether a merger is permissible. Equally, it becomes clear that mergers created a loophole in Article 85 in that two independent parties to an anti-competitive arrangement could merge and thereby avoid scrutiny—the Commission having no jurisdiction over internal practices of companies.

The merger boom of the 1980s created very real concerns that a policy on mergers consistent with the principles of the Treaty of Rome was conspicuously absent. The outcome of this debate has been the European Commission Merger Regulation, introduced in 1990.

## The European Commission Merger Regulation

To understand the current position some history is useful again. In 1971 the Commission deployed Article 86 to judge a take-over by the Continental Can Company of New York of a German and a Dutch company. It found against Continental Can on the grounds that its acquisitions had created a monopoly position for metal cans and bottle tops within the Community. The case went to appeal and the ECJ overturned the Commission's judgment. However, in its judgment it ruled that Articles 85 and 86, while they did not mention mergers, possessed a unity of purpose to protect competition and that, on these grounds, Article 86 applied on principle to merger situations. The period of drafting and consultation which followed led finally to Regulation 4064/89, the merger regulation which came into force in September 1990. This outlines the procedure for assessing whether cross-Member State mergers create a dominant position which may have abusive effects, and it may also be applied to mergers between EC and non-EC companies.

Authority to judge is again vested in DG IV, which has established a Merger Task Force to handle these cases. The essence of the EC position is that a merger falls within the regulation's scope if it leads to concentration and passes three tests. First, the aggregate world-wide turnover of all the undertakings involved (including parent companies of merging subsidiaries) must exceed Ecu 5 billion. Secondly, the aggregate EC turnover of each of at least two of the firms involved must exceed Ecu 250 million. Finally, the regulation does not apply if each of the firms involved has two-thirds of its EC-wide turnover within one Member State. In these calculations, turnover is to be calculated net of all sales taxes. It is apparent that the identification of turnover will be a crucial and contentious aspect of the application of this regulation, although it is not obviously the most relevant measure of market dominance. It remains the responsibility of the merging parties to notify the Commission of their intention to merge, and the relevant national authorities lose jurisdiction whenever a merger has the identified EC dimension. We should also note that the merger provisions also apply to co-operative agreements between firms if that agreement is judged to be concentrative rather than co-operative—that is, creates a lasting economic unit to produce a product or develop a technology. The latter remains subject to the provisions of Articles 85 and 86.

As to its procedures, the Merger Task Force has one month from notification to decide whether to proceed with a case, and a further four months to reach a final decision. Once the appropriate market has been defined, the emphasis of the investigation is on the maintenance of competitive conditions. Perhaps the most pressing issues concerning the merger regulation relate to the relationship between the Commission and national authorities. National authorities are kept informed of the progress of an investigation, and they can, under Article 9 of the Regulation, request the referral of the merger back to themselves—a procedure which has happened only once, in response to a UK request. The Commission has proposed a reduction of the aggregate turnover threshold to Ecu 2 billion, and this is certain to meet with opposition from those members with well-established merger policies (the United Kingdom, Germany, and France). Not surprisingly, this has become entangled with post-Maastricht Treaty sensitivities about subsidiarity and the relative roles of national and European-level authorities. Finally, we note that some commentators are in favour of a European Central Office as the focus for merger policy at EC level.

## Overview

It will be apparent from the above that competition policy at the European level has evolved considerably since 1958 and must continue to evolve as the EC grows in membership and the internal market develops. Central to this development will be its relationship with competition policies at national level within the EC and increasingly outside the EC as global competition plays an increasing role in EC thinking.

The extent to which national governments will be willing to forgo the adjudication of monopoly, merger, and anti-competitive practices remains the great practical conundrum for the future of EC policy. But deeper issues are also at work, reflecting the contrasting perspectives on competition outlined in the opening section of this chapter. Broadly speaking, these views may be typified in terms of competition as a state of equilibrium versus competition as a process of change. According to the first view, a firm is more competitive to the extent that it has less power to charge a price in excess of marginal costs (itself a vague concept depending on whether a short-run or long-run view is taken) and to control entry into its specific markets. According to the second view, a firm is more competitive to the extent that it has cost and product advantages relative to its rivals and can turn these advantages into gains in market share. Thus competition implies change in the relative market position of the different rivals, a situation of stable market shares indicating a neutral balance of competitive forces. Whichever view one takes of these contrasting positions, the openness of markets to entry by new firms, new products, and new methods of production is a central feature of a competitive environment. Thus policy to limit entry barriers, deregulate markets, and stimulate innovation through technology policy are immediately recognizable as pro-competitive policies. Whenever entry entails the outlay of irrevocably sunk costs, it is clear that competition cannot be too fierce: as Downie (1956) pointed out, the effective operation of competition requires a modicum of grit in the market mechanism. The obvious example here is when entry is premised on product or process innovations, which require a firm to sink outlays in research, design, and development programmes. If imitation is too easy or the market too competitive, the incentive to undertake those innovation expenditures can be undermined, to the detriment of the dynamics of competition. Within the EC, an obvious case is provided by the regulation of the pharmaceutical industry, which will be one important test bed for competitive policy. Pressure to cut health-service costs and open markets to generic producers will have to be weighed carefully against the need for sufficient profitability to fund the science-and-technology base of the major drug companies. An important policy issue here relates to the question of the optimum length of life of a patent under European law, and the associated regulatory limitations placed on drug developers. In short, firms have to be given sufficient monopoly power to induce the development of beneficial pharmaceutical products, the dynamic gains from product improvement taking precedence over any static losses from granting these companies an element of patent-protected market power.

While open-entry conditions are common to all views of competition, the interpretation of market power and the profits so generated is not. In all practical cases, it is very difficult to decide the extent to which reported profits are the result of market power or the result of the superior competence of the firm in generating lower costs or better service to consumers. The great danger always lies in penalizing the successful for their very success and thus constraining the long-run development of the economic system. None of this, of course, is a recipe for turning a blind eye to anticompetitive practices intended to rig markets and offset the dynamic effects of customers' choice on the relative position of competing firms. Rather, it is a case for careful treatment of each situation on its merits, and an awareness that the competitive process generates losers as well as winners. As with so much in economic theory, the powerful general insights which it provides must always be qualified by the details of the specific circumstances of the individual case. Since these circumstances transcend national boundaries, it is clear that much will be learnt (and needs to be learnt) by the practitioners of competition policy at both EC and national level.

# REFERENCES

Baran, P., and Sweezy, P. (1966), *Monopoly Capital* (New York: Monthly Review Press).

CEC (1992): Commission of the European Communities, *Seventh Report of the Commission to the Council and the European Parliament*, COM (92) 383 final (Brussels: CEC).

Cowling, K., and Mueller, D. (1978), 'The Social Costs of Monopoly Power', *Economic Journal*, 88/4: 727–48.

Devine, P. J., Lee, N., Jones, R. M., and Tyson, W. J. (1985), *An Introduction to Industrial Economics*, 4th edn. (London: Unwin Hyman).

Downie, J. (1956), 'How should We Control Monopoly?', *Economic Journal*, 66: 2, 573–7.

Geroski, P., and Jacquemin, A. (1984), 'Dominant Firms and their Alleged Decline', *International Journal of Industrial Organisation*, 2/1: 1–27.

Harberger, A. (1954), 'Monopoly and Resource Allocation', *American Economic Review Proceedings*, 44/2: 77–87.

Hay, D., and Morris, D. (1991), *Industrial Economics and Organisation: Theory and Evidence* (Oxford: Oxford University Press).

—————— and Vickers, J. (1988), 'The Reform of UK Competition Policy', *National Institute Economic Review* (Aug.), 56–67.

Jacquemin, A., and de Jong, H. (1977), *European Industrial Organisation* (London: Macmillan).

—————— and Sapir, A. (1989) (eds.), *The European Internal Market: Trade and Competition* (Oxford: Oxford University Press).

Jenny, F., and Weber, A. P. (1983), 'Aggregate Welfare Loss due to Monopoly Power in the French Economy', *Journal of Industrial Economics*, 32/2: 113–30.

Littlechild, S. (1981), 'Misleading Calculations of the Social Costs of Monopoly Power', *Economic Journal*, 91/2: 348–63.

Reid, G. (1987), *Theories of Industrial Organisation* (Oxford: Blackwell).

Sapir, A., Buigues, P., and Jacquemin, A. (1992), 'European Competitive Policy in Manufacturing and Services: A Two Speed Approach', *Oxford Review of Economic Policy*, 9: 113–32.

Sawyer, M. (1980), 'Monopoly Welfare Losses in the U.K.', *Manchester School*, 48/4: 331–54.

Schumpeter, J. (1944), *Capitalism, Socialism and Democracy* (London: Allen and Urwin).

# 6

# Science and Technology Policy

PETER STUBBS AND PAOLO SAVIOTTI

## 6.1. INTRODUCTION

The first and most fundamental issue to address in considering the science and technology policy of the European Community (EC) is why nation states and collectivities of nation states should have a science and technology policy at all. Could we not leave the production and distribution of scientific and technological knowledge to the market mechanism, which, after all, ranges from the humblest individual worker to the largest international firm?

Not surprisingly, scientists and technologists tend to oppose such a proposition. Since Bernard Shaw vilified all professions as conspiracies against the laity, we might suspect self-interest in that opposition; governmental support means more jobs, more prestige, and more money for scientists and technologists. Yet even hard-headed economists have argued that, objectively, the scientists have a tenable and intellectually respectable case. The most powerful economic support was offered by Kenneth Arrow (1962), who was to become a Nobel laureate in economics in 1972. He observed that there are three categories of economic problems which make it inadvisable to leave the allocation of resources for invention (and, by implication, technological progress) to the market mechanism. They are uncertainty, indivisibility, and inappropriability, and they require some elaboration.

## 6.2. REASONS FOR THE SUPPORT OF SCIENCE AND TECHNOLOGY

Arrow advocated government financial support for basic research. Basic research is the bedrock of technological progress: its accepted definition is provided by the 'Frascati Manual' as 'experimental or theoretical work undertaken primarily to acquire new knowledge of the underlying foundations of phenomena and observable facts, without any particular application or use in view' (OECD 1981: 19). Clearly, work of this sort is likely to be far removed from the market-place, yet it has the potential to yield immensely important advances such as the microchip or genetic engineering. For most private investors, including even large corporations, the uncertainty of such research disqualifies it as an acceptable pursuit of financial gain. The risks of failure are high, both because the research might lead to a dead end and because there is a risk that, even if it were fruitful, a speedier rival might beat them to the harvest. It also takes many years to recoup the investment, because basic scientific advances usually take much time and money to translate into saleable products or processes. Applying a typical commercial discount rate to compute a net present value for the speculative benefits of long-term basic research tends to disadvantage it when compared with less radical development work with a quicker pay-off.

Governments can pool these risks, since they are bigger than their national companies and may be able to consider longer-term benefits from the social rather than the private point of view: it does not matter to the government whether company *A* or company *Z* exploits the research findings, as long as they are exploited; but, if *A* contemplated doing the research itself, any prospect that *Z*, or *B*, or *C* could exploit it at the expense of *A* would be a disincentive. Notwithstanding, even nation states can find basic research risky; but the funding of much basic research in most countries is a government responsibility.

There is a further benefit from public funding of basic research. Where a private research body would want to maintain its property rights—that is, 'keep hold' of its research results to cover its costs and make private profits—the public source can be more open. Basic research findings may be more likely to be translated into useful innovations if they can 'spill over' and be adopted and developed by a wide range of innovators. The prevailing ethic among basic researchers is for wide publication and circulation of their findings among their peer group, and this is most likely to be realized where there is no corporate restraint due to secrecy.

Indivisibilities present problems. Where markets are indivisible, there are problems both in assessing demand and securing payment. A public-health research programme, analogous to a public-health investment such as urban drainage, can benefit a whole community, but, given the choice of whether to contribute to its costs, some people could become free riders, enjoying the benefits without making any contribution to the costs. In this case it is better to fund and operate the project at community level.

There may also be indivisibilities in the process of research itself. Where an industry is atomistic, with many small producers, no single member may be able to afford a worthwhile research-and-development (R&D) facility. In agriculture a multitude of competing farmers is most unlikely to do systematic R&D; individually they lack the assets, the expertise, and the incentive. Centralized R&D, supported by a levy on users, can overcome this problem; this solution can be applied to specific industrial processes or other small-scale industries by establishing research associations. Governments have subsidized these bodies permanently, or temporarily as a pump-priming exercise, until they becoming self-financing.

Inappropriability is a problem, because the originator of the invention or technology may be unable to gain due reward, unless he or she can appropriate the returns to the effort. Ideas are easily stolen. If much of the originator's benefit is dissipated through copying and illicit application by others, there is no immediate social loss—indeed there may seemingly be social gain if the innovation is diffused more widely and more cheaply, as happens notoriously in the case of pirated computer software, which has been estimated to cost the industry £400m. a year in the United Kingdom alone (*The Times*, 22 Oct. 1993, p. 33). But, quite apart from the issue of legality, the loss to the innovator may prove a serious disincentive to the inspiration and hard work which R&D entails: short-run opportunistic gains would then compromise long-run technological progress. Most nation states, therefore, protect the intellectual property of inventors through patents and copyrights granted upon original works.

A related issue concerns the benefits which accrue to users, as distinct from the innovator. Support for innovation may be given by governments on the grounds that there are social benefits from innovation beyond the private benefits which accrue through payments to the innovator. Empirical studies of specific innovations by Mansfield *et al.*(1976) show that the social rate of return to innovation is usually higher than the private rate, sometimes helped by the spill-over effect noted above. The argument can be pressed further, in suggesting that there are second-order effects in enhancing industrial development and national competitiveness. If so, and the support improves dynamic resource allocation and the responsiveness of the economy, the effects can be subtle, profound, and long lasting. However, it is very problematic to verify these effects in ways rigorous enough to persuade national treasuries to provide funding in the face of other less speculative and more populist claims for finance.

Beyond these central issues of uncertainty, indivisibility, and inappropriability, there are other motives for government support of technology. It is often asserted that imperfect private capital markets restrict the funds available for R&D, that bankers are unappreciative of the full value of technological opportunities. In response to this view, governments have from time to time established mechanisms targeted at the provision of funds for technology, such as the National Research Development Corporation (NRDC) and its eventual successor, the British Technology Group (BTG), which was later privatized.

Government may also act as a disseminator of scientific and technological information, and provide arbitration where there are conflicts arising from the use of new technology. Many governments have given support for communications technology in recent years, and there are well-known cases where they have funded inquiries into technological matters of public concern, such as the Sizewell B nuclear power station in the United Kingdom.

Finally, the view may be expressed that economic objectives alone should not rule the allocation of funds for science (in particular) and technology. This view rests on the belief that scientific investigation is a manifestation of advanced civilization with a justifiable ethic of its own, rendering it just as eligible for state support as the arts are—this latter support perhaps being more generously provided in certain other EC states than in the United Kingdom. In this context, the allocation of resources to science is not simply to be regarded as an investment decision but also involves elements of desirable consumption. Indeed, some of the allocations to basic research face such high degrees of uncertainty and long gestation that it is difficult to apply to them any risk criteria, where risk is understood in Frank Knight's sense of 'measurable uncertainty' (Knight 1921). However, even if this viewpoint is given some credit, there are problems of adjudicating between open-ended claims from the science lobby, and of deciding on the total allocation to the science sector.

### 6.3. NATIONAL POLICIES FOR SCIENCE AND TECHNOLOGY

Before the advent of the EC, national policies for science and technology were inevitably separate. Though they shared a common focus of correcting market failures and enhancing scientific and technological performance in the search for improved economic performance and enhanced scientific prestige, there were evident differences among the nations of the EC in their priorities and methods of support. Since the doctrine of subsidiarity applies today and still admits a wide degree of independence to national policies, it is relevant in both a historic and a contemporary context to examine very briefly the evolution and scope of some of these national policies. Shortage of space precludes treatment of all of them, and we simply select the three biggest spenders, all of which have had different policies and experiences. National expenditures on science and technology in the EC dwarf the levels of EC expenditure. The distribution of some national technological expenditures is tabulated at the end of this section.

*Germany*

German industry grew alongside a strong tradition of education and scientific research. From the first decade of the century to the mid-1960s, Germany led the world in the cumulative number of Nobel prizewinners in physics and chemistry (Nelson and Wright 1992: 1941). This scientific base provided strength for successful industries, particularly in chemical and engineering products, where German export performance in the competitive US market was better than that of its EC partners in the 1970s (Pavitt and Soete 1980) and the 1980s (Saunders, Matthews, and Patel 1991).

Responsibility for research funding is divided between the federal government and the state governments, or *Länder*. The importance of the federal government tended to grow across the 1970s, so that by 1977 it contributed DM13,250 million to R&D compared with DM5,950 million by the state governments. The state contributions were mainly directed to research in universities, whereas the federal support went mainly to business and private non-profit research institutions, such as the German Research Association (DFG), the Max Planck Institute, and the Fraunhofer Association, which are supra-regional in scope. In the mid-1980s the three biggest slices of federal support for research went to energy research and technology, space research, and basic physical and chemical research. Subsidies were granted for external contract research and co-operative R&D, and grants were available for investment in R&D assets. The Federal Ministry for Research and Technology (BMFT) has operated a wide range of government support and promotion programmes in high-risk, long-term project areas (which would accord with Arrow's criteria discussed earlier) such as aerospace and nuclear energy. It has supported work in areas of public concern such as health and environmental protection. It has singled out for support key technologies such as biotechnology and informatics. And it has also supported co-operative industrial R&D in small and medium-sized enterprises, including help in the 1970s and 1980s to establish and underwrite institutions to provide risk capital for technological development. Small and medium-sized enterprises have been observed by Porter (1990: 374) to play a very important role in German international success.

However, though government support has been extensive, it has not been heavy-handed, and direct control has seldom been exercised in either industrial or technology policies. But, as Porter noted (1990: 379–80), Germany has been more successful in building on its early strengths based on chemistry, mechanical engineering, and physics than it has in establishing leading positions in new industries, where the Japanese have performed so well; this point was confirmed by the newly appointed Minister for Science and Technology in 1993. At the end of the 1980s, the prospects for German technology were bullish: expenditure on R&D as a percentage of GNP had overtaken the United States' level, with the proportion of industry's share of R&D spending rising over a decade from 54 to 64 per cent; relatively little expenditure was diverted into defence research, and the scientific community maintained high morale by regularly gaining Nobel prizes (*The Economist*, 11 Nov. 1989, 145–52). However, the costs of unification have since put a strain on research budgets, such that R&D expenditure fell from 2.88 per cent of GDP in 1989 to 2.66 per cent in 1991, while very high labour costs present a further embarrassing burden.

*France*

The French government has been consistently more *dirigiste* than the German or the UK governments across the post-war period, in the sense that the French government, when compared with the other two, has sought a much closer direction of industrial policy. Government financial support for industry was widespread in the post-war period of reconstruction and beyond; as Sharp and Holmes note (1989: 3), the stock market was of negligible importance until the 1980s. From the latter 1960s the French government, like the UK, promoted mergers to encourage the emergence of firms which, supposedly, might compete with leading foreign rivals, of which the United States was perceived to be the most powerful and dangerous. In the absence of a large and sophisticated capital market, the government in a series of national plans sought to identify and foster national champions in industries which were obviously or potentially important. France's élitist bureaucracy and business have often been characterized as being closer than in the United Kingdom, and the state has used its equipment-procurement policies to encourage selected industries such as telecommunications manufacturing and computers. However, Sharp and Holmes (1989: 9–11) suggest that the French state apparatus is more fragmented than the UK, displaying more interdepartmental animosity, and that its civil servants are no more industrially or technologically expert than their UK counterparts.

Many of the *Grands Projets* of the 1970s were technical successes, such as the TGV high-speed train, nuclear-power generation, and telecommunications, though achieved without close regard to cost. High-technology priorities were set for strategic industries such as electronic office equipment, consumer electronics, energy-saving equipment, biotechnology, robotics, and undersea technology. Following the election of a Socialist administration in 1981, eight leading French firms were nationalized, with the intention of expanding employment and implementing new technology; in the event, these ambitious attempts at state-sanctioned plans were thwarted by recession and the commercial imperatives of rationalization and profit. Heads of telecommunications companies reorganized their manufacturing without consulting their bureaucrats, and, as the 1980s progressed, the French bureaucracy seemed to retreat from confident *dirigisme*. French technology policy emphasized the need for continuity of funding, including that for basic research, and the importance of developing co-operation between public laboratories and industry, enhancing the mobility of scientists between public laboratories and industry, and maintaining balance between small and big technology programmes. International commercial reality could not be ignored, and continued state attempts to promote national champions often failed; symptomatic is the state support for the French computer firm Bull which could not prevent

Bull from sustaining huge losses in the 1990s and being targeted in 1993 for eventual privatization. In this context, the observations of Sharp and Holmes (1989: 220–1) are apposite:

The degree to which a nation state can seek to carve out for itself an area of 'industrial space' which it can dominate is now minimal. The growing interdependence of the economic and industrial systems of the nations of Western Europe means that actions pursued in one country spill over rapidly into others . . . the degree of autonomy available to the individual nation state for the pursuit of industrial objectives is severely constrained. . . . It is technology as much as political dogma that has put paid to the era of national champions.

## The United Kingdom

In the United Kingdom technology policy has been less consistent than in France. Centralized industrial policy enjoyed a much shorter vogue than in France. The attempt, partly inspired by French experience, at a national economic plan by the Labour government in 1965 was dashed within a year by a sterling crisis. The Ministry of Technology, established in 1964 with a remit to 'guide and stimulate a major national effort to bring advanced technology and new products into industry', gradually acquired a mixed portfolio of responsibilities for old industries (textiles, shipbuilding) and newer ones (aviation, defence electronics) which constituted a virtual ministry of industry (Gummett 1980: 46). Government also set up the Industrial Reorganization Corporation to foster the assembly through the merger of large companies which supposedly would have enough total resources to become full players in the R&D league of leading international firms. In practice, their near-monopoly status in the domestic market removed a competitive stimulus which Porter (1990) considers to be a general condition for competitive efficiency, and creations such as ICL and an enlarged GEC failed to establish their intended technological eminence.

After the Conservative Party under Heath was elected in 1970, the Ministry of Technology was dismembered and its functions parcelled out to other Ministries. A report by Lord Rothschild in 1971 introduced the 'customer–contractor principle', which proposed a policy for government-funded applied research whereby 'the customer says what he wants; the contractor does it (if he can); and the customer pays'. Across the 1970s, the Conservative government under Heath, and Labour governments under Wilson and Callaghan, sought variously, and generally without success, to improve industrial and technological performance by interventionist policies, but, by the advent of the Thatcher administration in 1979, the civil service had lost any confidence that it might have had to 'pick winners'—that is, to direct closely through chosen companies the strategic development of the nation's industrial technology. The Thatcher government phased out many industrial subsidies and established different priorities, notably a more competitive managerial environment; a reduction of government expenditure on 'near-market' R&D, which it considered best left to firms to fund and conduct; an emphasis on collaborative company programmes and longer-term research; and an emphasis on key generic technologies such as microelectronics and robotics which might be applied across wide ranges of industry rather than picking companies as

TABLE 6.1. *Statistics of national science and technology performance 1991*

| R&D category | Expenditure on R&D as percentage of GDP | | | | | |
|---|---|---|---|---|---|---|
| | USA | Japan | UK | Germany | France | Italy |
| Gross R&D | 2.78 | 2.86 | 2.08 | 2.58 | 2.42 | 1.38 |
| Civil R&D | 2.1 | 2.7 | 1.7 | 2.8 | 2.0 | 1.4 |
| Government-funded civil R&D | 0.48 | 0.42 | 0.49 | 0.87 | 0.89 | 0.69 |
| Defence R&D | 0.7 | 0.2[a] | 0.4 | 0.1[a] | 0.4 | 0.1 |
| Government-funded defence objectives | 0.71 | 0.03 | 0.39 | 0.11 | 0.53 | 0.06 |
| Business R&D | 1.92 | 2.15 | 1.36 | 1.76 | 1.48 | 0.77 |
| In-government R&D | 0.31 | 0.23 | 0.28 | 0.39 | 0.57 | 0.34 |
| Higher Education R&D | 0.46 | 0.35 | 0.35 | 0.41 | 0.35 | 0.27 |

| Indicator | Indicators of national size and growth | | | | | |
|---|---|---|---|---|---|---|
| | USA | Japan | UK | Germany | France | Italy |
| GDP (£bn. at ppp[b]) | 3,524.2 | 1,502.8 | 572.4 | 857.4 | 660.0 | 619.7 |
| GDP growth rate, 1985–91 (% p.a.) | 8.4 | 11.2 | 8.2 | 11.2 | 9.3 | 9.3 |
| Domestic product of industry (£bn. at ppp) | 2,889.6[c] | 1,191.4[c] | 411.3 | 628.5 | 503.3 | 494.3 |
| Gross expenditure on R&D (£bn. at ppp) | 98.0 | 42.9 | 11.9 | 22.1 | 16.0 | 8.5 |
| GERD growth rate 1985–91 (% p.a.) | 7.5 | 13.0 | 6.6 | 10.3 | 10.6 | 13.1 |

*Note*: Definitional anomalies and rounding can cause seeming inconsistency with national figures.

[a] Data for 1989.
[b] ppp = purchasing power parity.
[c] Data for 1990.

*Source*: OECD, in HMSO (1993*b*).

industrial winners. In the last named context, advice was provided by expert committees such as the Advisory Council for Applied Research and Development (ACARD) and later the Advisory Council on Science and Technology (ACOST).

Following the establishment of an Office of Science and Technology after the 1992 election, UK technology policy has been set out in a recent White Paper, 'Realizing our Potential: A Strategy for Science, Engineering and Technology' (Cm 2250, (1993)). Its central elements include a Technology Foresight Programme, drawing upon industrial and scientific community opinions, which will feed information to a Council for Science and Technology developed from ACOST. The Science and Engineering Research Council is to convert to an Engineering and Physical Sciences Research Council; the Agricultural and Food Research Council becomes the Biotechnology and Biological Research Council. All Research Councils are committed to wealth creation, which some commentators have construed to imply less emphasis on basic science. The Rothschild customer–contractor principle is reaffirmed, as well as improved cross-departmental science and technology co-ordination, and better co-ordination is foreseen for UK government negotiations concerning European and international science and technology programmes.

Table 6.1 shows the national pattern of expenditure on R&D by selected nation states, as percentages of their Gross Domestic Product (GDP). Since some of the countries, notably the United States, Japan, and Germany, have a much larger GDP than the United Kingdom, it is evident from the second half of the table that in absolute terms their R&D expenditure is very much higher than that of the United Kingdom. UK expenditure on R&D has failed over the years to keep pace with its major competitors, and the positive technological balance of payments which existed in 1986 had become significantly negative by 1990. The United States alone of the countries shown in the table has a strongly positive balance of payments on technology account, partly, though not wholly, because the US revenue service is assiduous in requiring US companies to declare every conceivable element of their technology earnings.

## 6.4. THE HISTORY OF THE DEVELOPMENT OF THE EC SCIENCE AND TECHNOLOGY POLICY

The original Treaty of Rome in 1957, signed by Belgium, France, Italy, Luxemburg, the Netherlands, and Germany, concentrated on the abolition of tariffs between the EC6 and on the adoption of a common external tariff (CET) on goods entering from other countries. Matters such as competition policy, freedom of movement for labour and capital, state aid, and the harmonization of national laws fell within the Treaty's area of competence, so that one could say that there were components for an industrial policy but no overall framework, though there was a limited precedent in the experience gained in running the European Coal and Steel Community (ECSC), which had operated since 1951. However, there was no provision in the Treaty for science and technology in the then European Economic Community (EEC), or for the adoption of policy towards them.

This state of affairs fell short of the hopes of the founding fathers of Europe, as Jean Monnet and the Action Committee for a United States of Europe had earlier included plans for a 'European Technological Community' among their proposals. However, there was some recognition of a technological issue, albeit very narrow, in respect of civilian atomic energy. At that time, atomic energy was perceived as one of the most dazzling and important frontiers of science. It was scientifically challenging and exciting. It was expected, in time, to provide very cheap power, and potentially could release Europe from its heavy dependence on deep-mined coal and imported oil. It was an area where there ought to be economies in conducting R&D collectively. And there was an obvious European dimension, in that the United States and the Soviet Union were committed to nuclear-energy programmes, but would probably be secretive about their knowledge because of its military implications. Against this background, the European Atomic Energy Community (Euratom) Treaty was also signed in 1957.

Under the Treaty it was intended that the Euratom Supplies Agency would own and control the supply of all fissile materials in the EC and the Commission would control the distribution of patent rights and the production licences for nuclear-reactor designs and fuel technologies, which were expected to arise from the work of the Joint Nuclear Research Centre (JRNC) which was set up to conduct a five-year research and training programme. Inspired by the examples of Los Alamos and Oak Ridge in the United States and Harwell in the United Kingdom, JRNC was to be established on several sites. As Peterson notes (1991: 269), some commentators at the time foresaw a more influential future for Euratom than for the EEC. Harsh realities soon intruded upon these visionary intentions (Ford and Lake 1991). Rivalry occurred between the German and French nuclear industries, in the early climate of buoyant demand for nuclear power stations. The JRNC's reactor design, described as 'somewhat eccentric', was unsuccessful. Across the 1960s, oil provided increasing rather than shrinking competition under the efficient organization of the multinational oil majors. The JRNC was left with nuclear scientists but little or no nuclear work to do. Gradually it mutated to become the Joint Research Centre (JRC), with a main base at Ispra in northern Italy, with others at Karlsruhe in Germany, Petten in the Netherlands, and Geel in Belgium. In 1993 its mandate was extended to conduct non-nuclear research. The Ispra operation has long been criticized for its inefficiency, with one account reporting that only thirty or forty people from a total staff of 1,600 were qualified and scientifically active (Linkohr 1987). The JRC operation has been described as characterized by 'listlessness, apathy, lack of direction, and lack of conviction' (Ford and Lake 1991; 40). The failure of Euratom was critical: what should have been the exemplary flagship for European technology seemed to have run seriously aground.

The failure of this role model for successful collective international research coincided in the 1960s with strongly interventionist national industrial policies in Europe, particularly in France and the United Kingdom (though the United Kingdom did not enter the EC until 1972). The publication of an influential book by a French journalist, *Le Défi Américain* or *The American Challenge* (Servan Schreiber 1967), added to the pressures on European governments to boost the capacity of their industries to counter the competition of powerful foreign concerns, typified by IBM, the burgeoning US computer giant. The key weapons were mergers and subsidies, which were intended to afford the necessary resource and scale to match foreign competition. There were also several European collaborative initiatives, such as the Anglo-French Concorde airliner project, and the European Space Agency (ESA), but these occurred independently of the EC. Concorde was a technical success but a commerical disaster and one commentator has noted 'the advanced technologies of the 1960s provided suitable objects on to which the fantasies of European unity could be projected, while in reality they did not have any substantial long-term significance in contributing to a process of European integration' (Barry 1990, cited by Ford and Lake 1991).

Potentially more successful was the Airbus commercial airliner project, in which the consortium partners were France (38 per cent), Germany (38 per cent), the United Kingdom (20 per cent), and Spain (4 per cent). This has developed a family of airliners which has gained significant market share from the United States, though it has yet to become profitable and has prompted bitter complaints from US manufacturers that it has been unfairly subsidized. At the end of 1993 there was growing pressure for the consortium to set up a public company, in the interests of internal efficiency and transparency of its accounting procedures. Nevertheless, the venture has shown that commercial companies can collaborate successfully in a high-technology area and compete with world leaders such as Boeing and McDonnell–Douglas.

Another technologically successful example in the space sector was not specifically an EC initiative. In 1962 two organizations were established to foster collaboration in space technology: the European Launcher Development Organization (ELDO) and the European Space Research Organization (ESRO). ELDO became a Franco-German initiative after the United Kingdom withdrew, but, with the merger of the two bodies in 1973 to form the ESA, a more pan-European stance was evident. ESA fared better than its predecessors, partly because of some specific features of its programme. First, inter-institutional collaboration was easier because governments and public agencies were the prime contractors; secondly, the specialized character of the technology led to a closely knit community of policy-makers, engineers, scientists, and industrialists; and, thirdly, its programme was designed so that all the Member States would share formally in the contracts let by the agency. Its thirteen members are Austria, Belgium, Denmark, France, Germany, the Irish Republic, Italy, the Netherlands, Norway, Spain, Sweden, Switzerland, and the United Kingdom, plus Finland as an associate member.

The European Patent Office (EPO), which was founded in 1977 following the European Patent Convention of 1973, was another significant extra-EC development. The EPO provides a single application process for the grant of a 'European patent', which is valid in all the signatory states for twenty years, and saves the administration and expense of applying individually to them. By 1993 membership comprised Switzerland, Austria, Finland, Sweden, and Norway from outside the EC, plus twelve members from within it. Patents issued grew from 1,500 a month in 1980 to over 4,000 a month in 1990. It has headquarters in Munich and the Hague, and sub-offices in Berlin and Vienna. The EPO also distributes patent information, which is an important function of any worthwhile patent system, and it represents Europe in the World Intellectual Property Organization.

Thus by the beginning of the 1980s it seemed rather ironic that the most successful examples of international collaboration were those deriving not from the EC, but from narrower national combinations, like the Airbus project, or wider ones, like the ESA.

## The Shift of Support from Firms to Generic Technologies

Generally, the interventionist policies of support by national governments were not successful. They tended to focus on big firms in industries which the governments perceived as strategically important to the nation (in terms of employment or expected future role or both). By the mid-1970s, after the United Kingdom had joined the EC, it was apparent that this policy of 'picking winners' was beyond the capacity of governments: the phrase was heard increasingly that 'the business of government is not the government of business' (Lawson 1992: 211). One of the most difficult problems was that, if a government selected a firm (sometimes by the merger of former competitors) to be the national champion in an area of technological promise and endowed it with the size and subsidy to compete with the champion of rival states, the most immediate effect was to remove its domestic competition and give it a comfortable, if temporary, feather bed on which it might as readily relax as take up the bruising cudgels of foreign competition. However, there is much evidence that a competitive domestic   market is an important precondition of the vigour required to compete internationally (Porter 1990: ch. 3).

In the 1970s the thrust of policy moved from the selectiveness outlined in the previous paragraph towards the identification and support of selected or 'generic' technologies, which might be expected to impact on a wide range of industries: electronics and biotechnology were probably the foremost examples. Again, it was national governments rather than the EC which were prime movers in the new trend, but the first signs appeared of an EC policy towards science and technology.

On 14 January 1974 the Council decided on the progressive development of 'a common policy in the field of science and technology'. The scope of the policy was twofold: to co-ordinate the policies of the Member States and to implement research programmes and projects of EC interest. This sounds simple but is difficult in practice, since the finance available to the EC for implementation was between 1 and 2 per cent of the public funds spent by the Member States on their own R&D support. Three years later, the Commission produced guidelines for the period 1977–80 (CEC 1977). It set out four prime objectives:

1. securing the long-term supply of resources—namely, raw materials, energy, agriculture and water;
2. the promotion of internationally competitive economic development;
3. improvement of living and working conditions; and
4. protection of the environment and nature.

These pious if worthy aims posed a number of problems of implementation, apart from the modesty of financial resources already noted. How would Member States co-operate, given the record of national divergence discussed earlier in this chapter? Could EC policy be reconciled with the problems which the states themselves faced in their national science and technology policies? How should science and technology relate to other EC policies?

Several criteria for EC support were itemized, four 'general' and eleven 'specific'. The general ones emphasized the need for rationalization and efficiency at EC level, the need for transnational action which would involve several countries, the economic need to spread development costs over several national markets, and the need to meet common national requirements. Specific selection criteria for support included cases where costs or required R&D capacity would be too high for a single nation to bear, or where there would be savings through joint efforts; cases where R&D was in an initial phase, where an EC programme would stand a good chance of competing internationally, as in new transport systems; cases where potential is real, such as new sources of energy; and cases where there is long-term potential, such as nuclear fusion. The need for standardization of measurements and information systems was also noted. The

TABLE 6.2. *Distribution of Direct Action projects, 1977–1980*

| Sectoral policies | Expenditure on direct action projects (m. units of account) | Total expenditure (m. units of account) | Percentage of total expenditure |
|---|---|---|---|
| Energy | 188 | 566 | 58.8 |
| Industrial | — | 137 | 14.2 |
| Environment | 28 | 42 | 4.3 |
| Resource and raw materials | 7 | 28 | 2.9 |
| Transport | — | 19 | 1.9 |
| Agriculture | — | 14 | 1.5 |
| Social | — | 9 | 0.9 |
| Development aid | — | 4 | 0.5 |
| Public service and other | 127 | 144 | 15.0 |
| TOTAL | 350 | 962 | 100.0 |

*Note*: Direct Action projects are carried out by the JRC. Indirect Action projects are 50% funded by the EC.
*Source*: CEC (1977).

distribution of EC financial support for the period 1977–80 is shown in Table 6.2.

The Scientific and Technical Research Committee (CREST) was given responsibility for the development of Community R&D policy and co-ordination at policy level with Member States, and included within its membership senior officials from the member countries as well as Commission officials. The Commission established an internally staffed pilot programme, Forecasting and Assessment in Science and Technology (FAST), to collaborate with outside bodies such as SPRU, the Science Policy Research Unit at the University of Sussex, and DATAR in France. The FAST programme helped to highlight shortcomings in Europe's capacity in capitalizing on basic research, which too seldom produced successful final products. The Commission also acknowledged the importance of evaluating the effectiveness of its research activities and programmes, which we examine later.

Thus by the late 1970s the Commission had begun to address some of the key issues concerning science and technology and to establish tentative proposals for action, but these bore the stamp of a hesitant bureaucracy rather than the confidence which marked the execution of policy by the Ministry of International Trade and Industry (MITI) in Japan.

## The Primacy of US and Japanese Technology

Evidence accumulated in the 1980s that the 'technology gap' noted between US and European industry in the 1960s was widening, and that Japan was also outstripping Europe in many critical industries. One of the most visible industries was electronics, because its products could be seen to pervade industrial and domestic use, including the fashionable information technology (IT) sector. The national governments of France, Germany, and the United Kingdom had all supported their IT industries across the period from the mid-1960s to the early 1980s through subsidy, merger, and procurement preference in government purchases, to little effect (Sandholtz 1992). In 1975 the EC had a positive balance of payments in information technology, but it was in deficit by 1982. Europe's shares of world production in semiconductors and in integrated circuits were declining, foreign penetration of the European market was increasing, and European semiconductor manufacturing was unprofitable. Over four-fifths of the European computer market was held by US firms. Worse still, perhaps, was the fact that the United States and Japan were both pursuing ambitious research programmes in search of future IT supremacy, the former on Very High Speed Integrated Circuits (VHSIC), while the latter, after its successful Very Large Scale Integration (VLSI) programme which had launched Japanese industry into the manufacture of mainstream memory chips in the 1970s, announced an initiative on fifth-generation computers intended, in popular parlance, 'to think for themselves'. Faced with this mounting challenge, a number of leading European IT firms had, with EC encouragement, already begun to collaborate in the late 1970s on 'pre-competitive' research—that is, research on innovations in principle rather than at the level of products for imminent commercial launch.

## The Emergence of Community Programmes

In 1979–80 the Commissioner of DG III, the Directorate-General of Internal Market and Industrial Affairs, Viscount Étienne Davignon of Belgium, invited the heads of Europe's leading IT firms to form a 'Big 12 Roundtable', including ICL, GEC, and Plessey from the United Kingdom; AEG, Nixdorf, and Siemens from Germany; Thomson, Bull, and CGE from France; Olivetti and STET from Italy; and Philips from the Netherlands. As heads, they commanded more authority than the more junior personnel who had attended earlier, less fruitful discussions. And they were well aware of the gravity of their industrial and collective circumstances. Sandholtz (1992) has suggested that, 'in general, states will attempt unilateral strategies first and surrender the goal of autonomy only when unilateral means have proved to be impossible or too costly'. The participant national firms knew that unilateralism had failed, and this recognition gave a climate favourable to co-operation, and Davignon played the key role as the champion of new policies, as described by Sharp (1993). Two years of talks failed to fulfil the early hopes of establishing joint manufacturing companies along the lines of the Airbus consortium, but instead they did establish a consensus for collaborative research. Moral support for such collaboration also followed from the Gyllenhammer group, which was an informal gathering of twenty leading European industrialists, representing Gyllenhammer's Volvo, as well as Pilkington and Philips, and which urged an end to national subsidies, intra-European trade barriers, and divided R&D programmes (Pearce and Sutton 1985: 53–4).

There was, however, a potential conflict with EC competition policy, which forbids collaboration at the stage of developing products for an immediate market. However, Articles 85 and 86 allow collaboration for 'pre-competitive research'. Davignon's alliance of the EC and heavyweight industrialists, supported by the work of 550 industrial, scientific, and university experts (Sandholtz 1992: 14–15), was powerful enough to overcome the doubts of national government officials, and to establish the European Strategic Programme for Research and Development in Information Technology, or ESPRIT. The first outline proposal of September 1980 led to a formal proposal to establish a strategic collaborative IT research programme between the major European companies, together with smaller companies, research institutes, and universities, which was presented on May 1982, and approved by the Commission in December, with funding of Ecu 11.5 million (£8.5 million). Contracts under the pilot programme were invited in February and first signed in May, with thirty-eight projects, chosen from over 200 proposals involving 600 companies and institutes, under way by September 1983. The twelve round-table companies won about 70 per cent of the funds. Davignon's gambit of pilot projects with a streamlined application and vetting procedure paid off in overcoming Member State reservations and led to a ten-year Ecu 1.5 billion (£1 billion) programme for 1984–93.

The first five-year phase, ESPRIT I, 1984–8, was to concentrate on pre-competitive research in microelectronics, advanced information-processing and software technology, as well as applications in computer-integrated manufacturing and office systems. Approval was delayed until February 1984 because of German and UK government concerns about the costs of the programme. There was an enormous response to the first call for proposals in March 1984, with only about one proposal in four winning acceptance. The 227 projects in Phase I involved about 3,000 researchers from 240 companies (of which about 55 per cent were 'small', employing less than 500 workers apiece) and 180 universities and research institutes. Three-quarters of the projects involved firms and academic centres in collaborative work. Of the ten-year budget of Ecu 1.5 billion, Ecu 1.3

billion had been committed by January 1987. The EC funded up to half of the project expenditure, and firms from at least two Member States had to participate.

The successful reception of ESPRIT I was heartening to Europeans, and the consequences were positive.

(a) It created a useful European IT network of researchers, and allowed companies to economize on scarce technological personnel. They could commit one or two researchers to an ESPRIT project, and have their efforts geared up by the joint participation of other institutions' workers, with both short- and long-term benefits of collaboration and familiarity.

(b) Because the research was pre-competitive, collaboration was more open than if it had been near-market, when corporate secrecy would have created inhibitions between the partners.

(c) Collaboration across national boundaries, required intentionally, meant that the narrow horizons of 'national champions' had to widen.

(d) In cases of industrial participation, industry met 50 per cent of the costs, thus enjoying an effective subsidy from the EC.

(e) Although the Commission identified priorities and broad areas of research, actual research projects were nominated by the applicants. Thus, within the restriction that they could not be too near-market, projects became more demand-driven.

(f) Once agreed, each project was subject to a tight timetable and monitored through a system of programme management.

ESPRIT generated a new awareness of Europe's technological strengths, and provided a model for initiatives in other areas of technology. Indeed, it helped establish the climate for the 'Framework' programmes, and produced a tribe of acronyms—RACE, BRITE, BRIDGE, BAP, ECLAIR, FLAIR, COMETT and others—which we detail later.

Another consequence of the success of ESPRIT I was the need to find funds for the remainder of the programme's decade. The Commission brought forward the second phase, ESPRIT II, from 1989 to 1987. The 'Big 12 Roundtable' wanted to triple the budget and scope of ESPRIT II, but the proposal fell foul of UK and German government feelings that the EC R&D budget was too high. Compromises were struck over the Framework programme, and in April 1988 ESPRIT II was formally approved for 1988–92 with a budget of Ecu 1.6 billion (£1.07 billion), which was less than originally proposed but more than double the allocation for ESPRIT I. The Commission received about 1,000 proposals and agreed to fund about half of them. Three principal areas of research were emphasized: microelectronics, IT processing systems, and applications technologies. The emphasis on pre-competitive research, however, still left the difficulty of how to capitalize at market level. ESPRIT II went some way to address this issue by emphasizing 'demand driven aspects of the programme' (Sharp 1993)—for example, Application Specific Integrated Circuit Technology, and Technology Integration Projects (TIP), which were intended to meld different elements of separate work and show how they linked together. Funds for ESPRIT II were all earmarked by the end of 1990, and the Commission launched ESPRIT III with Ecu 1.35 billion (£645 million) for 1990–4, to exploit seven areas—microelectronics, advanced business and home systems peripherals, high-performance computing and networking, technology for software intensive systems, computer-integrated manufacturing and engineering, open microprocessor systems, and basic research to 'contribute to the programme's main objectives from an upstream position' (DTI 1993: 9).

A further development in the 1980s deserves attention. This is the European Research Co-ordination Agency, or EUREKA initiative, which was initiated by France and founded in 1985 as a European response to President Reagan's announcement of the Strategic Defense Initiative (SDI, or 'Star Wars' as it became popularly known) in the United States. EUREKA extends beyond the EC Member States to include the seven countries of the European Free Trade Association (EFTA), Turkey and, latterly, Hungary; but it is managed and co-ordinated by the Commission. It is intended to help industry-led, market-driven projects involving collaboration of at least two organizations from at least two EUREKA member countries. By March 1993 there were 623 projects totalling Ecu 8.8 billion (£6.2 billion). No priority areas are specified, but projects must involve technical innovation, and to that extent it is closer to the market and more concerned with commercial applications than ESPRIT is allowed to be. In practice, most current projects fall into the following areas: communications, energy, environment, IT, lasers, medical and biotechnology, new materials, robotics and automated production, and transport. Specific concerns include high-definition television (HDTV), which has also been the subject of much Japanese R&D, the Prometheus initiative for automatic car navigation systems, and JESSI, the Joint European Structure on Silicon Initiative.

EUREKA has no central funding, simply acting as an umbrella mechanism for encouraging inter-firm collaboration: public funding is granted at the discretion of national governments, which usually follows approval by the EUREKA programme. Thus EUREKA has a large nominal budget but no actual resource: the figures in Table 6.3 reflect a commitment to expenditure by Member States rather than effective expenditure. The partners negotiate the sharing of Intellectual Property Rights (IPRs), for which there are no general rules. Unlike ESPRIT, there is no central monitoring or evaluative role within EUREKA.

EUREKA was conceived as a rival to ESPRIT and other Commission

TABLE **6.3.** *EUREKA funding commitments, September 1992*

| Technology | Number of active projects | Cost (Ecu m.) | Percentage of total expenditure |
|---|---|---|---|
| Medical and biotechnology | 102 | 830 | 9.4 |
| Communications | 28 | 1,452 | 16.4 |
| Energy | 22 | 490 | 5.5 |
| Environment | 117 | 881 | 9.9 |
| IT | 77 | 2,067 | 23.4 |
| Lasers | 14 | 405 | 4.6 |
| New materials | 53 | 317 | 3.6 |
| Robotics and automation | 104 | 1,291 | 14.6 |
| Transport | 22 | 1,110 | 12.6 |
| TOTAL | 539 | 8,843 | 100.0 |

*Source*: EUREKA (1992).

programmes; but, despite occasional overlaps, it has become more complementary, partly because its projects can be more applied than the precompetitive ESPRIT projects. The two programmes, together with others listed in Table 6.2, raised the profile for research in the EC by the mid-1980s. Perceptions were also concentrated by the EC-wide acknowledgment of the technology gap, and of problems of the environment, and by a growing appreciation, through experience, of the benefits of inter-firm and inter-institutional collaboration. Peterson (1991: 270–1) has argued that 'the interests of public and private actors in promoting new collaborative R&D programmes converged as the Framework programme and EUREKA were launched in 1985'.

The instrument which allowed this fuller development of collaborative research was the Single European Act (SEA).

### 6.5. THE SEA OF 1987

The 1987 Act contained an additional section, called Title VI—Research and Technological Development, in which it set out in Article 130*f* the following credo:

The Community's aim shall be to strengthen the scientific and technological base of Europe's industry and to encourage it to become more competitive at international level.

In order to achieve this, it shall encourage undertakings including small and medium-undertakings, research centres and universities in their research and technological development activities; it shall support their efforts to cooperate with one another, aiming notably at enabling undertakings to exploit the Community's internal market potential to the full, in particular through the opening up of national public contracts, the definition of common standards and the removal of legal and fiscal barriers to that cooperation.

In the achievement of these aims, special account shall be taken of the connection between the common research and technological development effort, the establishment of the internal market and the implementation of common policies, particularly as regards competition and trade.

The next Articles, 130*g* to 130*l*, spelt out the means. Research, technological development, and demonstration programmes would promote co-operation between businesses, research centres, and universities. Co-operation would also be promoted with third countries and international organizations, as would the 'dissemination and optimization of results'. Training and mobility would also be stimulated. Member States undertook to coordinate amongst themselves policies and programmes carried out at national level, in liaison with the Commission.

The key provision was the adoption of a multiannual Framework programme setting out all the EC's proposed activities over a five-year period: it would lay down scientific and technical objectives, prioritize them, set out the main lines of activity and the amount deemed necessary, including detailed rules for EC participation, and its distribution across the appropriate activities. The Framework would comprise specific programmes of fixed duration within each activity. An implementation mechanism worked at two levels: the Framework as a whole had to secure unanimous agreement among the Member States; and sub-programmes were to be adopted by the Council by qualified majority voting after consultation with the European Parliament (EP) and the Economic and Social Committee. Programmes subsidiary to the Framework were permissible involving certain Member States only, which could finance them subject to possible EC participation; and co-operation with third states and international organizations was also feasible.

This was a dramatic advance upon the 1956 Treaty of Rome, since it legitimized EC technology policy—as it did industry policy elsewhere in the Act.

In fact, the Framework programme had already been subject to discussions for two years when it was launched in 1987, in the hope of an earlier introduction. The motive of both the Commission and the EP was to break out of the stop–start cycle of *ad hoc* decision-taking and wrangling over funding of research proposals. The first Framework programme, now commonly labelled Framework 1, was scheduled to run from 1987 to 1991. Its budgetary breakdown is shown in Table 6.4. In the event, the take-up of funds for programmes was faster than expected; for example, the most important member programme, ESPRIT, over-ran its budget by Ecu

TABLE **6.4.** *Framework 1 programme of Community activities in research and technological development 1987–1991*

| Activity | Budget (Ecu m.) | |
| --- | --- | --- |
| Quality of Life | | 375 |
| Health | 80 | |
| Radiation protection | 34 | |
| Environment | 261 | |
| Towards large market and an information and communications society | | 2,275 |
| IT | 1,600 | |
| Telecommunications | 550 | |
| New services of common interest, including transport | 125 | |
| Modernization of industrial sectors | | 845 |
| Science and technology for manufacturing industry | 400 | |
| Science and technology of advanced materials | 220 | |
| Raw materials and recycling | 45 | |
| Technical standards, measurement, reference materials | 180 | |
| Exploitation and optimum use of biological resources | | 280 |
| Biotechnology | 120 | |
| Agro-industrial technologies | 105 | |
| Agricultural competitiveness and resource management | 55 | |
| Energy | | 1,173 |
| Fission: nuclear safety | 440 | |
| Controlled thermonuclear fusion | 611 | |
| Non-nuclear energy and rational use of energy | 122 | |
| Science and technology for development | | 80 |
| Marine resources and exploitation of the sea bed | | 80 |
| Marine science and technology | 50 | |
| Fisheries | 30 | |
| Improvement of European science and technology co-operation | | 288 |
| Stimulation, enhancement, and use of human resources | 180 | |
| Use of major installations | 30 | |
| Forecasting, assessment, and other back-up measures | 23 | |
| Dissemination and utilization of science and technology results | 55 | |
| TOTAL | | 5,396 |

*Source*: CREST (1992).

200 million in 1988, in the face of 'the high quality of the proposals, the industrial commitment underlying them and the urgency of the work proposed' (Peterson 1991: 282–3). A second Framework programme had been introduced to run across 1987–91, and by December 1989 the Research Council in Brussels agreed with the new Research Commissioner Pandolfi to establish a third-generation Framework programme: its

TABLE 6.5. Major EC programmes promoting new technology

| Acronym and Full Name | Period | Budget[a] | Prime objectives |
|---|---|---|---|
| ESPRIT: European Strategic Programme for R&D in IT | I 1984–8<br>II 1988–92<br>III 1992–4 | 750<br>1,600<br>1,350 | Promote EC capabilities and competitiveness in IT, especially microelectronics systems. |
| RACE: R&D in Advanced Communications Technologies for Europe | Definition 1985–7<br>RACE I 1990–4<br>RACE II 1992–4 | 21<br>460<br>489 | Help EC competence in broadband communications equipment, standards, and technology. |
| TELEMATICS | 1990–4 | 380 | Develop telematics in e.g. health, transport, and public administration. |
| BRITE/EURAM: Basic Research in Industrial Technologies/Advanced Materials for Europe | BRITE I 1985–8<br>EURAM I 1986–8<br>BRITE/EURAM I 1989–92<br>BRITE/EURAM II 1992–6 | 100<br><br>450<br><br>663 | Support R&D which upgrades technological or materials base of production. |
| BAP: Biotechnology Action Programme | 1985–9 | 75 | Develop infrastructure in biotechnology, esp. research and training. |
| BRIDGE: Biotechnological Research for Innovation, Development and Growth in Europe | 1990–3 | 100 | As BAP, but on large projects, e.g. molecular modelling, advanced cell culture. |
| BIOTECH | 1992–6 | 164 | Prenormative research, more basic than BRIDGE, includes safety. |
| ECLAIR: European Collaborative Linkage of Agriculture and Industry through research | 1989–94 | 80 | Apply advanced biotechnology in agro-industrial sector, esp. using raw materials from agriculture. |
| FLAIR: Food Linked Agro-Industrial Research | 1989–94 | 25 | As ECLAIR, but food oriented, in manufacture and processing. |
| COMMETT: Community Action Programme for Education and Training for Technology | COMETT I 1987–9<br>COMETT II 1990–4 | 30<br><br>200<br>+ 30<br>EFTA | Training programmes between university and industry, via enterprise partnerships and international staff exchange. |
| VALUE | VALUE I<br>VALUE II 1992–4 | 66 | Disseminate and exploit research results of programmes. |

| Acronym and Full Name | Period | Budget[a] | Prime objectives |
|---|---|---|---|
| SPRINT: Strategic Programme for Innovation and Technology Transfer | SPRINT I experiment SPRINT II 1986–9 SPRINT III 1989–94 | 9 90 | Promote innovation and technology transfer, esp. among small and medium enterprises internationally. |
| EURET | 1990–3 | 27 | Rail, sea, and air transport research. |
| MONITOR | 1989–93 | 22 | Identify R&D policy priorities. |

[a] The figures shown as budgeted do not include industrial contributions to ESPRIT and other shared cost programmes: in those cases *actual* expenditure involved in the programmes will approximate twice the budget figure shown above.

funds were topped up in December 1992 from Ecu 5.7 billion to Ecu 6.6 billion.

The total extent of the EC programmes for new technology is wide, and Table 6.5 lists some of the key examples. Often programmes continued through successive generations of Framework, as in the cases of ESPRIT, COMETT, and SPRINT.

### 6.6. EVALUATIONS OF POLICY EFFECTIVENESS

EC-sponsored research is important in both quantity and quality: some system of accountability is, therefore, necessary. Technically the Commission is accountable to the Council, which is made up of national ministers, and to the EP, which scrutinizes legislation and the drafting and execution of budgets. However, science and technology programmes require expert examination of their effectiveness, as to both their scientific and their economic worth, to judge whether the work is worth doing in the first place and whether, once authorized, it has been well accomplished.

One possibility was to employ FAST in the evaluations. But there seemed little enthusiasm at the top of the Commission to involve FAST: its resources were small for such a vast job and independent outside judgement was deemed desirable (Holdsworth and Lake 1988: 424).

When the third Framework programme was adopted, the Council required the Commission to undertake an evaluation of all programmes which operated under the second programme, formally to provide 'an overall appreciation of the current state of execution and achievements of the specific programmes adopted under the second Framework . . . and to set out the principal lessons that have been learned from the execution of these programmes'. The main source of information was the reports of the independent evaluation panels commissioned to examine the operations of specific programmes. In addition, there were reports from consultants commissioned to examine particular questions, internal Commission reviews drawing on the reports of panels or outside experts, reviews and reports of programme committees, plus findings from specially commissioned studies of the horizontal aspects of the effects of EC R&D programmes. An example of commissioned work was a study of the impact of EC policies for R&D on science and technology in the United Kingdom, which was prepared for the UK Office of Science and Technology and the EC Commission (HMSO 1993*a*).

The findings of these studies are generally positive; they chronicle good work and effective international and inter-institutional collaboration. A report from CREST was submitted to the Council in September 1992, giving an evaluation of the second Framework programme (CREST 1992). It addressed three major issues—the quality of programme results and their impact on competitiveness; management and cost-effectiveness of research; and consistency with EC policy and principles. It noted a substantial amount of state-of-the-art research, with a fair balance between incremental and more ambitious research, but intellectual property rights problems were an inhibition on dissemination and exploitation, for which there was, implicitly, more scope. While there were cases of R&D conferring significant technological advantage over international rivals, the most significant impact was felt to be in promoting the idea of collaboration across industry, academia, and nations of the EC. There remained much scope for developing the harmonization of standards across the EC. Though there was general satisfaction over programme management, sometimes project assessment needed more attention, as did the lags between calling for proposals and beginning the research. Programme objectives could be more clearly defined and there was scope for closer and more transparent links with other DGs responsible for policy in areas such as transport, environment, energy, health, and agriculture.

With nearly 18,000 collaborative links within Framework 2, the United Kingdom was its most active participant. In fact, the United Kingdom fared well in the early Framework provisions, as Table 6.6 reveals, though the shares need to be viewed in the light of Member State contributions to the EC budget, shown in Chapter 14. UK views on Framework 2 were analysed by questionnaire and interviews among participants from academia and industry (HMSO 1993*a*). Academics were more positive, but two-thirds of industrial firms involved considered the benefits outweighed the costs, against 21 per cent who did not; and over three-quarters intended to reapply for future participation. It was estimated that about half of EC R&D spending in the United Kingdom was 'additional'—that is, adding to

TABLE **6.6.** *Major recipient countries of Framework funding, 1987–1991*

| Programme area | Percentage granted to | | | |
| --- | --- | --- | --- | --- |
| | UK | Germany | France | Italy |
| IT | 18 | 22 | 25 | 11 |
| Communication technology | 20 | 25 | 22 | 8 |
| Telematics | 20 | 17 | 18 | 9 |
| Industrial and materials | 19 | 20 | 22 | 12 |
| Measurement and testing | 22 | 23 | 15 | 7 |
| Environment | 21 | 19 | 19 | 9 |
| Marine sciences | 22 | 15 | 18 | 9 |
| Biotechnology | 17 | 18 | 14 | 7 |
| Agri and Agro-industrial | 20 | 4 | 22 | 7 |
| Biomedicine | 24 | 10 | 16 | 7 |
| STD | 18 | 10 | 25 | 5 |
| Non-nuclear energy | 14 | 19 | 21 | 11 |
| Fission | 21 | 25 | 22 | 5 |
| Human Capital | 25 | 15 | 25 | 7 |
| TOTAL (weighted average) | 19 | 21 | 23 | 9 |

*Note*: Data exclude Fusion Programme and JRC funding.
*Source*: Cabinet Office 1992.

the total of publicly financed R&D, and not just funding what would have been done without EC monies. Moreover, EC programmes had a bigger impact than the 6 per cent of publicly funded R&D that they constituted, because they were approved by senior staff, concentrated on recently established priorities, eased research-funding scarcities, and were geared up by EC participation.

An independent panel of experts also found in favour of EUREKA's benefits (*Outlook on Science Policy*, 1993: 73–4). Most partnerships were vertical, between firms, customers, and suppliers, rather than horizontal. Collaboration worked best between partners of similar size, with smaller firms more product-oriented than large ones, which focused on longer-term research projects. Over 40 per cent of participants were found to expect substantial sales increases within three years, reflecting the near-market emphasis of EUREKA compared to Framework.

In the discussions leading to the proposed fourth Framework programme, numerous lessons were drawn from earlier experience. The UK government submitted a policy paper in February 1992 (Cabinet Office 1992) drawing together the views of the UK science and technology community. It stressed several points:

1. the need to evaluate Framework 2 before proceeding;

2. that EC spending should be stabilized by a planned profile of annual committments;
3. that Framework 4 should follow the general structure of Framework 3, with additional programmes on transport and the social sciences, plus money for human capital and mobility;
4. that generic technologies, clearly and widely applicable, should be preferred to the needs of specific industrial sectors—this having been the UK view in its domestic R&D support policies;
5. that more resources should be devoted to disseminating technology from research projects;
6. that there should be wide consultation between DGXII and DGXIII and their 'customer' DGs;
7. that the transparent mechanisms for selecting projects—with published criteria, open and competitive tenders, and independent assessment procedures—should continue.

Some of these views have been accepted in CREST (1992), but the fourth Framework proposal remains very controversial at the time of writing (Hill 1993). Its anatomy is shown in Table 6.7.

The programme proposes Ecu 13.1 billion of expenditure, but its adoption requires a unaminous decision from the EC12. However, the three biggest contributors to the EC, Germany, the United Kingdom, and France, are seeking, against the wishes of the other nine, to reduce the Framework

TABLE 6.7. *Proposed fourth Framework programme, 1994–1998*

| Programme area | Budget (Ecu m.) | % R&D |
|---|---|---|
| Information and communications technology | 3,900 | 35.7 |
| Industrial technologies | 1,800 | 16.5 |
| Environment | 970 | 8.9 |
| Life sciences and technologies | 1,325 | 12.1 |
| Clean and efficient energy sources | 1,050 | 9.6 |
| Nuclear safety and security | 495 | 4.5 |
| Controlled thermo-nuclear fusion | 980 | 9.0 |
| Research for European transport policy | 280 | 2.6 |
| Socio-economic research | 125 | 1.1 |
| Co-operation with third countries and international organizations | 790 | n.a. |
| Dissemination and utilization of results | 600 | n.a. |
| Stimulation of training and mobility of researchers | 785 | n.a. |
| TOTAL | 13,100 | 100.0 |

*Note*: n.a. = not available.
*Source*: CEC 1993.

budget by at least Ecu 1 billion. One of the difficulties is that the pay-off to Framework R&D is singularly problematic to assess in financial terms. Since it is not near-market research, it will take time to see clear financial benefit, and the advantages so far ascribed to it by expert analysts are inevitably qualitative rather than measurable in money terms. A cynic might observe that firms will welcome, and laud, Framework programmes if they bring handsome subsidies with them. The EC seems still to be lagging behind its US and Japanese technological competitors in many industries, but this can hardly be laid at the door of the EC programmes, which account for only a very small part of *total* R&D effort across the companies and countries of the EC.

Further, there are a number of fundamental problems which face the EC in the face of changing international relationships and corporate practices.


## 6.7. TECHNOLOGY, INDUSTRIAL, AND TRADE POLICIES: TENSIONS AND CONTRADICTIONS

Industrial policy is traditionally concerned with problems such as influencing industrial and market structure and competitiveness, and encouraging the modernization of capital stock. It shares an uncertain border with technology and trade policies. For example, the desired structure of output cannot be decided independently of trade policies. If a country wishes to develop a new industrial sector in which other countries already have capabilities and experience, it may have to invoke the infant industry argument and offer its industry a period of protection from unrestricted foreign competition. Subsidies to indigenous R&D may also be considered necessary. Technology, industrial, and trade policies clearly overlap here; perhaps the simplest theoretical discriminator is that industry policy emphasizes physical capital, whereas technology policy emphasizes knowledge, creation and utilization.

However, it is a practical and not just a theoretical dilemma. Technology policy seeks to create productive capability, which often requires public sponsorship of R&D. Such support is only compatible with competition (which is a common goal of industrial policy) if the R&D is pre-competitive; but the boundary between pre-competitive and near-market R&D is fuzzy, at best. The tension between protectionism and enhancing capability is exemplified by European attitudes towards micro-electronics and IT. European firms have persistently failed to compete satisfactorily in these sectors in spite of varied forms of protectionism, which are detailed in Chapter 11. How long and how much is it necessary to support the development of European potential, before an infant industry can be weaned? Yet is it possible for the EC to have adequate economic performance and prospects for the future if these strategic industries are allowed to wither?

The tension between a protectionist *Fortress Europa* and an open, competitive EC of the sort which Porter (1990) would consider a pre-requisite for efficiency, is reinforced by the institutional division of labour which assigns technology, industrial, and trade policies to different DGs. Each DG develops its own routines, traditions, and power structure. Programmes once initiated are difficult to terminate, and attitudes harden. Thus the rigidities and contradictions can persist if they are inherent in the priorities of different interest groups. It will take time to reconcile these conflicting forces and establish an acceptable balance of competition, protection, and capability enhancement.

## Interfirm Collaboration and its Implications for EC Technology Policies

As we have seen, EC technology policy has concentrated on sponsoring different forms of collaboration between European countries. Such forms of collaboration are not generally those which participants would choose spontaneously, otherwise the EC initiatives would have been redundant, having been implemented already by the market. Part of the motive for the policy is political, to accelerate European integration. In this context one should note the rise across the late 1970s and 1980s of inter-institutional collaborative agreements or IICAs (Chesnais 1991; Mytelka 1991). They can be of very different scope, varying from licensing agreements, joint R&D, joint development of new products, joint ventures in marketing and distribution, with or without joint equity. The Airbus consortium is just one of many possible manifestations.

The growth of IICAs poses a considerable theoretical and practical problem. From a simple theoretical standpoint, firms are expected to compete rather than collaborate. As they grow in size, we might expect them to integrate vertically and develop internal hierarchical organiza-tional forms. Chandler (1962, 1977) has ably charted the progression of firms from small unstructured enterprises to U- (unitary) and M- (divi-sionalized) forms of companies. Given the realities of market imperfec-tion, firms tend to internalize functions (Coase 1937; Williamson 1975, 1985). Industrial R&D in particular is a function often internalized, because of the difficulties of establishing satisfactory markets in technol-ogy, given the complexities of valuation and the need for secrecy to ensure appropriability of returns to technological effort. The develop-ment of internalized R&D has been one of the most striking institutional changes of this century (Schumpeter 1943; Freeman 1982). In this con-text, inter-institutional collaboration might be considered the exception rather than the rule.

Why then do IICAs happen and why have they proliferated? Several

authors have suggested contributory factors. One is the growing importance of knowledge in production, revealed by the growth of R&D in GDP
and as a proportion of corporate turnover in many industries, and by the
growing percentage of non-material investment (Mytelka 1991). Most
IICAs are in relatively high-technology industries, such as IT, biotechnology, aerospace, or new materials. Other possible contributing factors are
the productivity slow-down of the late 1960s and 1970s, and the observed
shortening of product life cycles, which implies more frequent innovation
with its attendant costs and uncertainties. The decline of traditional mass-
production ('Fordism') and the rise of flexible manufacturing systems also
place a premium on technological capability. Collaborative agreements can
reduce the heavy fixed costs of entry, as well as facilitating exit by
providing a partner to whom an interest might be sold. So long as technology continues to grow in complexity and expense, IICAs are likely to
figure prominently in the corporate landscape.

Collaborative agreements impinge upon technology policies. It might
seem that they are in tune with the collaborative tenor of current EC
technology policy; but IICAs are driven in opportunistic directions, not
those favoured by state or EC governments. Thus Rover chose initially to
collaborate with Honda, rather than an EC firm, though they were subsequently taken over by BMW of Germany. Possibly the EC programmes
may facilitate intra-EC IICAs; but collaboration outside the EC makes it
more difficult to evaluate the pay-off to EC technology policy.

### National Systems of Innovation and EC Technology Policy

The concept of national systems of innovation (NSI) has recently been
proposed by a number of scholars of technology (Freeman 1987, 1988:
Lundvall 1988, 1993; Nelson 1988, 1990; Niosi *et al.*, 1992, 1993) to
interpret the persistence of areas of industrial and technological strength
in national economies, and of very specific institutional congifurations for
very long periods of time. Such areas of industrial strength are chemicals,
luxury cars and machine tools in Germany; cars and consumer electronics
in Japan; and electronics, aircraft, and biotechnology in the United States.
Furthermore, the institutions which control the generation and adoption of
innovations in each country show a high degree of national specificity.
Thus, not only do the degree of centralization and of state intervention, and
the organization of universities and research institutes (to mention just a
few factors) differ widely across countries, but these differences persist
over time. Finally, what contributes even more decisively to the national
specificity of the innovation system is the pattern of interactions between
different institutions. There are true networks formed by research laboratories, government departments, and firms which are extremely important
and, again, very specific.

Pronounced differences exist at the level of national institutions; Lundvall (1988, 1993) laid particular emphasis on user–producer relations. These create institutional networks which communicate and interact, and define a system which may be highly country- (or even region-) specific, as Porter (1990) has noted widely. The role of MITI has been profoundly influential in defining industrial and technological priorities and co-ordinating firms' actions, stressing the role of forecasting and horizontal flows in organizations as significant elements of the Japanese national system of innovation (Freeman 1987, 1988). In particular, information flows in enterprises improve the relationship between R&D and production, in which the Japanese system has been singularly successful.

In this context, EC-sponsored forms of inter-institutional collaboration across national boundaries may establish a new network, with links across the entire Community. This prospect prompts several questions. Will it be a stable network? How will it benefit the EC and Member States? Will there be conflicts between the EC and national systems of innovation? And there is the question of opportunity costs: will the resources allocated to the EC system of innovation impair the performance of NSIs? In essence, this poses the question of subsidiarity on a technological plane.

## 6.8. SUMMARY AND CONCLUSIONS

EC science and technology policy seeks to create new inter-institutional links and forms of collaboration, as well as establishing capabilities in specific sectors. Any such attempt is problematic, because the spontaneous development of the system would be unlikely to replicate those links. However, it can be argued that the EC level of aggregation is the only possible locus at which adequate technological capacity can be established in certain industries or sectors. We began by looking at some national differences of Member States' resources, capabilities, and national systems of innovation, followed by an examination of the emergence of EC collaborative programmes. It will take time to assess the true efficacy of the EC system of innovation; there will probably be continued haggling over its budget; there remain thorny problems of reconciling industrial and trade policies; and the principle of subsidiarity still appears to leave a great deal of autonomy in national hands; but it is highly significant that there seems to be no pressure to abandon the Framework system, and revert to a combination of market-place and nation state. However, the precise role of the EC system of innovation remains to be defined and appraised fully, and it will require a continuous scrutiny, because the interaction of profit-seeking companies will always generate new forms of organization and collaboration, transcending the boundaries of nations and of blocs.

# REFERENCES

Arrow, K. J. (1962), 'Economic Welfare and the Allocation of Resources to Invention', in *The Rate and Direction of Inventive Activity* (Princeton NJ: Princeton University Press, 609–25.

Barry, A. (1990), 'Community and Diversity in European Technology', paper at the Science Museum.

Cabinet Office (1992), *United Kingdom Paper on the Fourth Framework Programme* (London: Office of Science and Technology).

CEC (1977): Commission of the European Communities, 'Common Policy for Science and Technology', *Bulletin of the European Communities*, supplement (Mar.).

——— (1993), Working Document on the Fourth Framework Programme, 22 Apr.

Chandler, A. D., jun. (1962), *Strategy and Structure: Chapters in the History of Industrial Enterprise* (Cambridge, Mass.: MIT Press).

——— (1977), *The Visible Hand: The Managerial Revolution in American Business* (Cambridge, Mass.: Harvard University Press).

Chesnais, F. (1991), 'Technical Cooperation Agreements between Independent Firms: Novel Issues for Economic Analysis and the Formulation of National Technological Policies', *STI Review*, 4: 51–120.

Cm 2250 (1993), *Realising our Potential: A Strategy for Science, Engineering and Technology* (London: HMSO).

Coase, R. H. (1937), 'The Nature of the Firm', *Economica*, 4: 386–405.

Conference on Policies and Publics for Science and Technology, London, Apr. 1990.

CREST (1992), *Evaluation of the Second Framework Programme'* (Brussels: CREST).

DTI (1933): Department of Trade and Industry, *Innovation: A Guide to European Community R&D Programmes* (London: DTI).

EUREKA (1992): EUREKA Secretariat, Annual Progress Report.

Ford, G., and Lake, G. (1991), 'Evolution of European Science and Technology Policy', *Science and Public Policy*, 18: 38–50.

Freeman, C. (1982), *The Economics of Industrial Innovation*, 2nd edn. (London: Pinter).

——— (1987), *Technology Policy and Economic Performance: Lessons from Japan*, (London: Pinter).

——— (1988), 'Japan: A New National System of Innovation?', in G. Dosi, C. Freeman, R. Nelson, G. Silverberg, and L. Soete (eds.), *Technical Change and Economic Theory* (London: Pinter), 330–48.

Gummett, P. (1980), *Scientists in Whitehall* (Manchester: Manchester University Press).

Hill, A. (1993), 'R&D in a Tussle over EC Funding', *Financial Times*, 26 Oct., p. 16.

HMSO (1993a): Cabinet Office, *The Impact of European Community Policies for Research and Technological Development upon Science and Technology in the United Kingdom* (London: HMSO).

———— (1993*b*): Cabinet Office, *Annual Review of Government Funded Research and Development 1993* (London: HMSO).

Holdsworth, D., and Lake, G. (1988), 'Integrating Europe: The New R&D Calculus', *Science and Public Policy*, 15: 411–25.

Knight, F. H. (1921), *Risk, Uncertainty and Profit* (New York: Houghton Mifflin).

Lawson, N. (1992), *The View from Number Eleven* (London: Bantam).

Linkohr, E. (1987), European Parliament document A-2 174/87, p. 18.

Lundvall, B. A. (1988), 'Innovation as an Interactive Process: From User-Producer Interaction to the National System of Innovation' in G. Dosi *et al.* (eds.), *Technical Change and Economic Theory* (London: Pinter), 349–69.

———— (1993) (ed.), *National Systems of Innovation: Towards a Theory of Innovation and Interactive Learning* (London: Pinter).

Mansfield, E., Rapoport, J., Romeo, A., Wagner, S., and Beardsley, G. (1976), 'Social and Private Rates of Return from Industrial Innovations', *Quarterly Journal of Economics*, 91: 221–40.

Mytelka, L. K. (1991) (ed.), *Strategic Partnerships and the World Economy* (London: Pinter).

Nelson, R. R. (1988), 'Institutions Supporting Technical Change in the US', in G. Dosi *et al.* (eds.), *Technical Change and Economic Theory* (London: Pinter), 312–29.

———— (1990), 'Capitalism as an Engine of Progress', *Research Policy*, 19: 193–214.

———— and Wright, G. (1992), 'The Rise and Fall of American Technological Leadership', *Journal of Economic Literature*, 30: 1931–64.

Niosi, J., Bellon, B., Saviotti, P. P., and Crow, M. (1992), 'Les Systèmes nationaux d'innovation: A la recherche d'un concept utilisable', *Revue française d'economie*, 7/1.

———— Saviotti, P. P., Bellon, B., and Crow, M. (1993), 'National Systems of Innovation: In Search of a Workable Concept', *Technology in Society*, 15: 207–27.

OECD (1976): Organization for European Co-operation and Development, *The Measurement of Scientific and Technological Activities* (Frascati Manual) (Paris: OECD).

*Outlook on Science Policy* (1993), 15 (July–Aug.).

Pavitt, K., and Patel, P. (1988), 'The International Distribution and Determinants of Technological Activities', *Oxford Review of Economic Policy*, 4: 35–55.

———— and Soete, L. (1980), 'Innovative Activities and Export Shares: Some Comparisons between Industry and Countries', in K. Pavitt (ed.), *Technical Innovation and British Economic Performance* (London: Macmillan).

Pearce, J., and Sutton, J. (1985), *Protection and Industrial Policy in Europe* (London: Routledge & Kegan Paul).

Peterson, J. (1991), 'Technology Policy in Europe: Explaining the Framework Programme and Eureka in Theory and Practice', *Journal of Common Market Studies*, 29: 269–90.

Porter, M. E. (1990), *The Competitive Advantage of Nations* (London: Macmillan).

Sandholtz, W. (1992), 'ESPRIT and the Politics of International Collective Action', *Journal of Common Market Studies*, 30: 1–24.

Saunders, C. T., Matthews, M., and Patel, P. (1991), 'Structural Change and Patterns of Production and Trade', in C. Freeman, M. Sharp, and W. Walker (eds.), *Technology and the Future of Europe* (London: Pinter), 18–36.

Schumpeter, J. A., (1943), *Capitalism, Socialism and Democracy* (London: Geo. Allen & Unwin).

Servan Schreiber, J.-J. (1967), *Le Défi Américain* (Paris: de Noel; English edn., *The American Challenge*, Harmondsworth, Penguin Books, 1968).

Sharp, M. (1993), 'The Community and the New Technologies', in J. Lodge (ed.), *The EC and the Challenge of the Future*, 2nd edn. (London: Pinter), 200–23.

—— and Holmes, P. (1989) (eds.), *Strategies for New Technologies: Case Studies from Britain and France* (London: Philip Allan).

—— and Pavitt, K. (1993), 'Technology Policy in the 1900s: Old Trends and New Realities', *Journal of Common Market Studies*, 31: 129–51.

—— and Shearman, C. (1987), *European Technological Collaboration* (London: Routledge & Kegan Paul).

Williamson, O. E. (1975), *Markets and Hierarchies* (New York: Free Press).

—— (1985), *The Economic Institutions of Capitalism* (New York: Free Press).

# 7

# Regional Policy

HARVEY ARMSTRONG, JIM TAYLOR, AND ALLAN WILLIAMS

## 7.1. INTRODUCTION

Since 1989 regional policy in the EC has undergone a remarkable change. Whilst always a popular policy among the individual Member States, regional policy at Community level was for many years something of a poor relation among EC common policies. This is no longer the case. While serious weaknesses still remain, regional policy has now moved from the wings to centre stage. It is seen as a central part of the EC's efforts to take economic integration forward. This has been achieved, moreover, without weakening the regional policy efforts of the individual Member States. Any examination of regional policy in the EC must, therefore, consider both the regional policies of the Member States and the policy constructed in recent years by the EC itself.

This chapter considers the structure of existing regional policy in the EC, together with possible future developments. It begins, in Section 7.2, with an examination of regional economic disparities within the EC. These are wide when compared with economic entities of a similar size such as the United States, and are a cause of considerable concern. Section 7.3 explains why governments choose to have a regional policy. This is followed in Section 7.4 by a description of the broad alternative strategies available to regional policy-makers. Section 7.5 considers the regional policies of a number of EC Member States: the Netherlands, Germany, the United Kingdom, France, Italy, and Spain. Space constraints prevent the examination of regional policies for all the EC12; those chosen comprise the larger Member States and also encompass a wide range of different types of regional policies. This is followed in Section 7.6 by a review of the EC's own regional policy. The conclusion points the way forward to regional policy issues in the late 1990s.

## 7.2. REGIONAL ECONOMIC DISPARITIES IN THE EC

Two economic variables are widely used to indicate an economy's current level of economic welfare: GDP per capita and the unemployment rate.

TABLE 7.1. *Regional economic disparities in the EC*

| Member state | GDP per capita (EC = 100) average 1986–8 | | | % unemployed 1990 | | | Participation rate (%) 1988 | | |
|---|---|---|---|---|---|---|---|---|---|
| | National average | Regional maximum | Regional minimum | National average | Regional maximum | Regional minimum | National average | Regional maximum | Regional minimum |
| Belgium | 100.7 | 154.2 | 83.4 | 7.6 | 10.8 | 5.5 | 39.7 | 40.6 | 37.9 |
| Denmark | 112.5 | 132.6 | 94.7 | 7.9 | 9.1 | 6.8 | 56.3 | – | – |
| Germany | 113.6 | 182.7 | 97.8 | 5.2 | 10.4 | 3.0 | 47.8 | 51.7 | 42.1 |
| Greece | 54.8 | 58.5 | 48.5 | 7.5 | 9.7 | 4.2 | 40.7 | 43.6 | 37.6 |
| Spain | 73.6 | 86.6 | 58.5 | 16.1 | 24.1 | 12.4 | 37.8 | 39.9 | 35.3 |
| France | 109.3 | 165.6 | 87.8 | 8.7 | 11.8 | 6.4 | 44.6 | 49.9 | 39.5 |
| Irish Republic | 64.5 | – | – | 16.4 | – | – | 38.0 | – | – |
| Italy | 103.5 | 137.3 | 66.9 | 10.2 | 21.7 | 3.4 | 41.9 | 46.3 | 37.4 |
| Luxemburg | 121.7 | – | – | 1.5 | – | – | 42.5 | – | – |
| Netherlands | 104.2 | 123.6 | 86.6 | 8.0 | 9.4 | 7.5 | 45.4 | 46.7 | 42.0 |
| Portugal | 53.6 | 69.7 | 41.9 | 5.1 | 12.4 | 2.8 | 46.3 | 47.4 | 38.0 |
| UK | 106.5 | 128.3 | 80.6 | 6.3 | 15.7 | 3.9 | 50.2 | 52.3 | 43.1 |

*Note:* The regional maximum and minimum GDP per capita are calculated for sixty-six regions (i.e. at the NUTS1 level using the EC's standard system of Nomenclature des Unités Térritoriales Statistiques). GDP is measured in purchasing power parities (PPPs). All references and data relating to Germany, prior to German unification, apply to West Germany except where stated otherwise.

*Source:* CEC (1991*a*) table A23.

These two variables can be used to provide an indication of national and regional disparities in economic welfare amongst the Member States of the EC. The immensity of the spatial disparities in economic welfare in the EC is clear from Table 7.1, which shows that GDP per capita in Greece and Portugal, for example, was less than half that in (West) Germany in the late 1980s. These apparently huge differences in GDP per capita between Member States, however, conceal equally large disparities within each Member State. In Italy, France, Belgium, and Germany, GDP per capita is nearly twice as high in the region with the highest level as in the region with the lowest level (see Table 7.1). Regional disparities in GDP per capita within the EC as a whole are, therefore, very large, varying from over 180 in Hamburg (Germany) to under fifty in Nisia (Greece).

Regional disparities in GDP per capita will diminish only if those regions with the lowest GDP per capita grow faster than the regions with the highest GDP per capita. Although there is some evidence that this has been occurring since 1950 (Barro and Sala-i-Martin 1991, 1992), the process of convergence is extremely slow and there is no indication that regional disparities in GDP per capita will narrow significantly in the foreseeable future.

Regional unemployment rates also vary substantially between regions both *within* countries as well as between the Member States themselves. Regional unemployment disparities are particularly large in Italy, ranging from under 4 per cent in Lombardy to over 20 per cent in Sicily and other southern regions. No other country in the EC has such large variations in the unemployment rate, but they are nevertheless substantial in the majority of Member States.

A further determinant of economic welfare is a region's participation rate. This is the proportion of the population which is in the labour force. Other things being equal, the higher the participation rate, the higher the level of GDP per capita. Regions with a low participation rate can, therefore, be expected to be less well off than regions with a high participation rate (see Table 7.1).

### 7.3. THE CASE FOR REGIONAL POLICY

Regional economic disparities within the EC are not only substantial; they also show remarkable persistence over long periods of time. Poor regions tend to stay poor and rich regions tend to stay rich. As would be expected, the residents of poor regions are keen to emulate the residents of rich regions, and this is one of the driving forces behind the development of regional policy both within individual Member States and at the supranational EC level. This urge for greater prosperity in less prosperous regions, however, is only one of several reasons for the existence of regional policy, which can be justified on economic efficiency grounds as well as for social and political reasons. The purely economic arguments used to support regional policy stem from the harmful consequences which regional economic disparities can have on the efficiency of the national economy (Taylor 1991; Martin 1992). These harmful effects are as follows:

1. Regional economic disparities lead to a higher *national* unemployment rate than would occur if regional disparities were less severe.
2. Inflationary pressures increase as regional economic disparities increase.
3. Regional economic disparities lead to a sub-optimal use of the nation's economic infrastructure.

Although we concentrate here upon the economic gains from regional policy, it is important not to underestimate the social and political gains which a reduction in regional disparities in living standards may bring. Persistent disparities in living standards between regions can lead to dissatisfaction and resentment with the political process, thereby fuelling the call for devolution. Whether this is regarded as being harmful or beneficial depends upon one's own political ideology.

The argument that a reduction in regional unemployment disparities would result in economic gains for the economy as a whole stems from the mismatch between labour demand and labour supply. This mismatch takes two forms: a geographical mismatch occurs when unemployed workers are located in the wrong place to fill vacant jobs; and a skill mismatch occurs when unemployed workers have the wrong skills to fill vacant jobs. Both types of mismatch unemployment help to explain why unemployment has a tendency to remain permanently higher in some regions than in others. Reducing the geographical or the skill mismatch (through regional policy and training policy) could lead to significant reductions in the national unemployment rate. This would occur if the unemployed could fill job vacancies more quickly, especially during periods of economic expansion. If unemployment could be permanently reduced in the traditionally high unemployment regions without this leading to a loss of jobs in areas of low unemployment, the whole nation would be better off. Those previously unemployed would be producing output and earning a wage instead of being supported by the taxpayer. Lower unemployment could also be expected to reduce crime rates as well as alleviating economic hardship for a large number of people.

The second way in which a reduction in regional economic disparities can provide economic gains to the national economy is related to the first, since it stems from the regional disparities in the balance between labour demand and labour supply. Persistent disparities in the unemployment rate between regions mean that inflationary pressures build up very quickly in low unemployment regions whenever there is a significant business upturn.

As the national demand for goods and services begins to grow more quickly, this puts pressure on the supply of skilled labour in low unemployment areas. The consequence is an increase in wage inflation as firms raise wages to attract more labour (and to discourage their existing workers from looking for jobs elsewhere). These wage increases are then transmitted to other regions, one of the reasons being that firms with plants in several regions have to maintain pay relativities for workers in different parts of the same organization.

Regional policy could help to reduce inflationary pressures by reducing regional differences in labour scarcity during upturns. This could be achieved either by reducing the barriers to labour migration so that labour shortages could be relieved more quickly; or alternatively by diverting the demand for labour from labour-scarce to labour-abundant regions, so that any expansion of the national economy would not hit supply bottlenecks as quickly.

Thirdly, regional disparities in economic growth can inflict severe economic costs on rapidly growing urban areas through the over-utilization of social overhead capital. Exactly the opposite would occur in areas suffering from slow growth: social overhead capital may be under-utilized as workers and their families migrate to more prosperous regions. Roads, rail networks, airports, and housing are often severely over-utilized in rapidly expanding regions. Congestion and pollution are the consequences of over-rapid growth, especially in major cities.

Greater London provides an excellent example of a city-region which has suffered from excessive expansion of economic activity. The popularity of Heathrow with the major airlines means that this airport is persistently short of capacity. The same is true of the motorway system around Greater London. The M25 orbital motorway was expected to relieve road traffic congestion, yet within three years of its opening (in 1987) it became apparent that three lanes each way were grossly inadequate to meet traffic needs. No sooner does supply expand to accommodate demand than the whole cycle begins again; demand increases as supply constraints are relieved and the vicious circle continues.

The classic response by governments to congestion is invariably to relieve it by expanding capacity. There is a great reluctance of governments to tackle congestion by introducing policies to reduce the demand for road space. It is politically more expedient to increase the supply of social overhead capital than it is to reduce demand. The result is a never-ending spiral whereby demand and supply are forever chasing each other. A longer-term solution is offered by regional policy, since the major aim of such policy is to increase economic growth in less prosperous regions so that the migration of workers and their families to the more rapidly growing regions is stifled. Congested regions would benefit from not having to take in more people and the less prosperous regions would benefit by not losing their most productive workers (since the latter are the most likely to migrate to the rapidly growing regions).

## 7.4. REGIONAL POLICY: SOME ALTERNATIVE APPROACHES

Regional policy exists because of market failure. The stability and persistence of regional disparities in unemployment rates and in GDP per capita over long periods of time indicate that market forces are unable to remove these disparities. Governments throughout the EC have, therefore, opted for interventionist policies. These take three main forms:

1. inducing inward investment into high unemployment areas;
2. stimulating indigenous growth in high unemployment areas; and
3. regeneration through investment in economic infrastructure.

Inducing inward investment into high-unemployment areas through offering investment grants and other subsidies to incoming firms typifies the interventionist approach. The policy need not always consist solely of inducements and subsidies. This type of policy, for example, was supplemented in the United Kingdom during 1947–81 by the imposition of location controls on manufacturing firms located in non-designated assisted areas (especially the South East region). The primary purpose of this carrot-and-stick policy was to achieve a better geographical balance between the demand for labour and the supply of labour so that unemployment would fall in areas of high unemployment while inflationary pressures would be lessened in labour-scarce areas (Armstrong and Taylor 1993).

Traditional regional policy, based upon offering subsidies to firms locating their new plant and equipment in designated assisted areas, became less popular in many Member States in the 1980s. The emphasis swung towards stimulating indigenous growth in high unemployment areas. This indigenous-growth approach gained popularity because policy-makers became more interested in the growth of small firms and in the birth of entirely new firms. Moreover, this fitted with the policy shift away from 'state capitalism' towards privatization, deregulation, and the enterprise economy.

The third arm of regional policy which is of crucial significance in any policy designed to reduce regional economic disparities is government investment in the infrastructure of the less prosperous regions. Investment in the infrastructure includes redeveloping derelict areas, improving the transport network, providing better recreational facilities, enhancing the stock of housing, and improving health and educational facilities. Public investment in an area's infrastructure is important, since it acts as a signal to the private sector that the government is committed to the long-term future of the less prosperous regions. It acts as a confidence booster to private sector investors while simultaneously helping the less prosperous regions to retain their most highly skilled workers.

## 7.5. REGIONAL POLICIES IN EC MEMBER STATES

The origin of regional policy in Europe goes back to the global economic crisis of the late 1920s and 1930s. Initially, regional policy emerged as a matter of contingency. Eventually, as the crisis passed, regional policy evolved into a genuine policy for structural change in the economy rather than merely 'fire-fighting' (Bleitrach and Chenu 1982). In the very early days of regional policy, before the existence of the EC, individual Member States pursued their own individual policies.

In practice, the development of regional policy in the European Member States appears to have passed through three stages (Nicoll and Yuill 1980). In the first stage, the emphasis of policy was on *national* economic growth, and regional policy was both weak and confined to only two Member States: Italy with its *Cassa per il Mezzogiorno*, and the United Kingdom with its programme of incentives and controls to assist the Development Areas. Elsewhere there was little in the way of regional policy. The UK case is interesting in that the initial 'fire-fighting' phase was quickly superseded by a switch to longer-term policies designed to engineer structural change. UK regional policy began in the late 1920s when financial help was made available to induce unemployed coal-miners (and later to other unemployed persons) to move to areas where jobs were in more plentiful supply than in their own localities. Although over 200,000 workers received financial assistance under this scheme during the 1930s, the direct targeting of the visible symptom of the problem (i.e. the unemployed themselves) made little impression on regional unemployment disparities. In the immediate post-war years, therefore, the UK government turned to the opposite strategy of 'taking work to the workers' (i.e. enlarging the industrial base and changing the structure of the economies of the disadvantaged regions) as a means of reducing regional unemployment disparities.

The second phase in the development of regional policy in Europe—the 1950s to the early 1970s—saw most West European governments follow the lead of Italy and the United Kingdom and develop some form of regional policy, especially in the face of persistent unemployment and inflationary pressures. Finally, in the third phase—after the mid-1970s— regional policy was given a much lower priority by most Member States in the face of a deepening recession, budgetary constraints, and reductions in the pool of potentially mobile firms that had traditionally been the target of regional policy. Ironically, the period since the mid-1970s, during which Member State regional policies have been cut back, was also the period of rapid expansion of the EC's own regional policy. The retrenchment of the third phase after the mid-1970s was not the result of diminishing pressures for intervention, for, as Albrechts *et al.* (1989) argue, 'the crisis that erupted in the mid-seventies has triggered a range of corporate, social and policy responses' (p. 4). These responses have included an array of local and urban policies (e.g. waterfront redevelopment and inner-city regeneration), but they have become less likely, throughout the EC, to include specifically regional policies.

### Comparing the Rationale for Different Member State Regional Policies

Within the broad framework of the case for regional policy set out in Section 7.2, there are differences among the Member States in the reasons for the development of regional policy. This section considers the cases of the Netherlands, Germany, the United Kingdom, France, Italy, and Spain. These case studies underline the similarities as well as the differences in regional policy within the EC, and also the ways in which the underlying economic rationale of policy is interlinked with social and political considerations.

### The Netherlands
The Netherlands has one of the most all-embracing approaches to regional policy to be found within the EC. This is why it has been selected as a case study, despite the fact that the Netherlands is one of the smaller Member States. There is a long tradition of physical planning in the Netherlands dating from the early 1950s. This tradition is the result of intense pressures on factors of production—especially land—in a relatively small country with Europe's highest population density. The earliest regional planning focused on the reorganization of the war-damaged Rotterdam economy, and the rehabilitation of its economic infrastructure. By the 1950s attention had shifted to the border regions, where there were persistently high levels of unemployment (Gay 1987). Over time, regional policy has become increasingly sophisticated as it has tried to take into account the inter-related requirements of regions in a small and increasingly complex economy. By the 1970s there were distinct policies for three different types of regions: stimulation areas in the north which still had persistent unemployment difficulties; old coal-mining and textiles communities which required major restructuring; and the highly developed Randstadt where production costs were rising as a result of the demands on a relatively inelastic supply of economic infrastructure.

### Germany
Germany shares many of the structural features of the Netherlands in that regional policy has been developed to diffuse inflationary pressures and

maximize national economic potential in an economy experiencing strong economic growth, but where there are also persistently weak regions. There are, however, important differences stemming from both the *Länder* federal structure and the economic and political shock of the sudden unification of East and West Germany. Unification has brought into the most powerful European economy a region which is one of the weakest in the EC. German regional policy faces a pressing need to develop the economy of the Eastern region in a manner which maximizes local job opportunities. If this is not quickly achieved, labour migration may add to the difficulties of all the German regions at a time of slackening economic growth in the national economy.

Despite the distinctive features brought on by reunification, the evolution of German regional policy in the past has broadly followed trends prevalent in northern Europe. There appear to have been four main periods in this evolution in Germany (Blacksell 1987). In the first, in the 1950s, the main concern was with post-war reconstruction. In the 1960s the principal interest was in regional policy as a means of securing a more equitable distribution of the fruits of Germany's economic success. In the third phase there was greater attention to co-ordinating Federal and *Länder* policies. Finally, in common with other North European Member States, there was some withdrawal from regional policy in the cost-conscious 1980s. In general terms, it must be noted that regional policy in Germany has lacked the urgency it has attracted in some of the other Member States with more severe problems.

*The United Kingdom*
The United Kingdom's regional policy has developed against the background of a weaker national economic performance than that of either the Netherlands or Germany, but with a set of problem regions more typical of northern Europe than the south. The overwhelming majority of the United Kingdom's problem regions in the period since the institution of regional policy in the late 1920s have been declining *industrial* areas. The United Kingdom has very few disadvantaged rural regions of the type found in France and in southern Europe. As has already been noted, after an initial attempt to persuade the unemployed to move away from their home localities, UK regional policy rapidly settled, from the mid-1930s onwards, into a policy based on 'taking work to the workers' by restructuring the economies of regions suffering industrial decline. The major phases of UK regional policy since the 1930s have coincided with differing degrees of commitment by successive governments, rather than variations in the fundamental nature of the policies operated. Left-of-centre Labour governments have, on the whole, tended to pursue more active regional policies. The lack of regional governments in the United Kingdom and the weakness of local councils have meant that for most of the post-war period

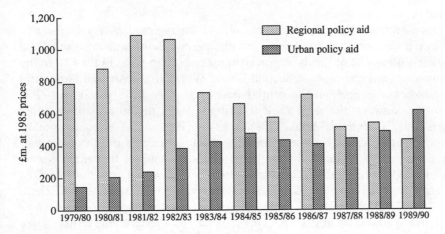

FIG. **7.1.** The switch from regional aid to urban aid in the UK 1979/80–1989/90
*Source*: Martin (1992) and own calculations.

the attitude of the national government has been all important. Regional policy was most actively operated during 1945–51 and 1962–75. Throughout the post-war period up until 1975 the policy concentrated on inward investment. Given the predominance of regions in industrial decline, it is not surprising that particular effort was placed on attracting manufacturing firms to the disadvantaged regions.

From the mid-1970s onwards, UK regional policy, like those in other EC Member States, experienced severe problems associated with a harsher economic climate. This had the twofold effect of cutting back the number of potential manufacturing projects available for inward investment in the disadvantaged regions, and also led to cuts in regional policy funding (Fig. 7.1). The retrenchment in UK regional policy in the 1980s, while similar in kind to that experienced elsewhere in the EC, was accelerated by successive governments ideologically committed to free markets and the 'rolling back of the state'. The 1980s also witnessed the first fundamental change in the *nature* of regional policy in the United Kingdom since the 1930s. Inward investment was partially supplanted by policies designed to encourage indigenous development—renewal 'from within'. The main exception to this process has been the use of regional inducements to attract foreign investment seeking a foothold within the EC (particularly Japanese car manufacturers and electronics firms). Policies designed to help new firm formation, the growth of small businesses, the encouragement of innovation, and the creation of an 'enterprise culture' gradually made their entrance in the 1980s against a background of a continually falling regional policy budget. Interestingly, expenditure on urban policy in the United Kingdom has grown, whilst regional policy spending has fallen (Fig. 7.1).

*France*

France represents a very different context for regional policy in the EC. While it has become one of the most prosperous European economies, and in Paris it has one of the most powerful metropolitan areas in the EC, in the immediate aftermath of the Second World War it also possessed large rural regions whose economic potential had been very little developed. The contrast between the rural regions and the Paris region was highlighted in Gravier's influential book (Gravier 1947). This and other contemporary reports set in train what was to become one of Europe's most comprehensive systems of regional policy. The process was one of four main phases (Clout 1987). In the first, the main aim was to iron out some of the most glaring regional imbalances in the country, primarily as a social goal. Then, in the second phase in the 1960s, there was greater emphasis on comprehensive spatial economic management as part of a programme to maximize national economic growth. In the 1970s an economic recession weakened regional policy. Finally, this was exacerbated in the 1980s when, according to Clout (1987), 'in the present bleak economic climate the chances of effective territorial management have become slim' (p. 171). The overall result is that regional development policy has evolved incrementally and in an *ad hoc* fashion during these years (Flockton and Kofman 1989).

*Italy*

In Italy, regional policies developed differently from France and were dominated by the specific needs of the South. This region continued to experience economic difficulties even during the 'economic miracle' of the late 1950s and early 1960s when the national economy experienced rapid growth. The *Cassa per il Mezzogiorno* was established in 1950 and devoted much of its early attention to land reform, agricultural improvements, and basic infrastructure. These were considered to be essential prerequisites for the integration of the South into the market economy. This emphasis on what can best be described as regional modernization later gave way to more conventional regional policies concerned with the relocation of industry. In the face of strong barriers to development in the *Mezzogiorno*, it was not surprising that regional policy in the 1960s was guided by the concentration of resources into growth centres. The rationale for regional policy in Italy was based on several goals. Initially it aimed to provide the minimum infrastructure necessary for the development of the region's economic potential. A cynical view, however, would suggest that regional policy was only weakly pursued in this period, given the priority allocated to promoting national growth. The latter was premised on the leading role of the North, which in turn relied on the availability of labour supply from the South. However, by the 1960s the North was experiencing increasing inflationary pressures, which were epitomized by the wage inflation which followed the 'Hot Autumn' of 1969 (Williams 1987).

Thereafter, there existed a stronger case for a strategy of balanced economic development typical of other EC Member States.

### Spain

Spain's economy in the 1940s bore many striking resemblances to that of the *Mezzogiorno*: large numbers were employed in relatively unproductive agriculture, regional infrastructures were poorly developed, and there was a strong geographical polarization concentrated on the Madrid–Catalonia–Basque Country triangle. There was the additional dimension, however, of the highly centralized dictatorial government of Franco. Regional policy, such as it was, was not responsive to local needs, was carried out through the poorly co-ordinated actions of individual ministries, and was consistently subordinated to the priority allocated by Madrid to the need to improve national economic performance. Regional policy objectives were inserted into the National Plans as much to please international agencies such as the World Bank as to commit the central government to a more equitable distribution of jobs and income. As a result, while Spain did experience an 'economic miracle' in the 1960s, this was accompanied by wide regional income differentials (Naylon 1987). The restoration of democracy after 1975 changed the accountability of regional policy, but occurred at a time of recessionary constraints and was followed in the 1980s by the transfer of powers to the autonomous regions.

### Comparing Regional Policy Instruments in the Different Member States

As has been shown above, the individual Member States of the EC operate regional policies which differ significantly in their rationale, but which also show considerable similarities. This is also the case when the policy instruments used to implement regional policy are considered. Indeed, while a lot of variation still exists from country to country, 'the multiple ideas on tools of regional policy development in the Member States of the European Community are settling in a kind of pattern, and some consensus is gradually crystallising out' (Molle 1990: 424). The various instruments can be disaggregated into those aimed at labour, those aimed at industries, and those involving improvement in infrastructure. While some states have policies in one or more of these categories, only rarely have they been linked in integrated programmes, as in France, for example, with its *aménagement du territoire*.

There are few examples of policies to promote labour mobility, even though the reduction of regional unemployment differentials has been one of the primary objectives of regional strategies. In part, the reluctance to employ such measures is political, stemming from the unwillingness of governments to be seen to promote the break-up of communities. There is also the economic argument that interregional transfers of labour on a large scale would add to the inflationary pressures in the more dynamic regions. Nevertheless, there have been some examples of labour-transfer policies, including the United Kingdom's Employment Transfer Scheme in the 1970s, which provided grants to help offset the costs of workers moving to other regions to obtain jobs. This was, however, only a minor component in UK regional policy. The depth and persistence of the economic crisis in recent years—leading to the more generalized distribution of high unemployment rates across all regions—has further eroded the economic rationale for labour-transfer policy instruments. The speed of technological change and the pace of economic restructuring have also meant that labour-market policies have focused more on general training programmes than on specific regional measures.

Instruments aimed at particular industries have usually sought to influence the location of new investment and the relocation of existing capacity. There have been two types of measures: restrictions on investment in the more prosperous regions, and incentives to attract investment projects to the poorer regions. These are commonly known as 'carrot-and-stick' policies. Locational constraints are less widely used now than financial incentives. Examples of locational constraints in the past have included the United Kingdom's Industrial Development Certificate scheme, which restricted investment projects in the south and the Midlands between 1947 and 1981. In France a system of *agréments* was introduced in 1955 to regulate new and existing developments in the Paris region. At first the *agréments* applied only to manufacturing but were later extended to services. Italy also developed a system of location controls for the Milan and Turin areas in 1971 in response to the inflationary pressures which followed the 'Hot Autumn' of 1969. In the Netherlands, a Selective Investment Levy was introduced for new office construction in the prosperous and congested Randstadt area in the mid-1970s, supplementing earlier controls on the location of manufacturing industry investment in this region. In all of the countries which experimented with locational constraints, the policies lost favour during the persistent economic crises of the 1970s and 1980s. These crises have led governments to reduce most constraints—locational or otherwise—on economic activity and expansion. In France, for example, locational controls on new office developments in Paris were relaxed in the late 1980s in response to fears that jobs could be lost to other European capital cities.

While locational controls aimed at the private sector have had only a limited impact, they do seem to have been important in the public sector. King (1987), for example, argues that the Italian regional policy instrument which was most effective in bringing industry to the South was that which compelled nationalized and state-holding industries to locate at least 60 per cent of all their new investment in the *Mezzogiorno*. In contrast, it is symptomatic of the neglect of regional policy in Spain that the Franco government never required the Instituto Nacional de Industria, the industrially dominant state-holding company, to locate activities in the poorer regions.

Financial incentives have been more important than controls amongst the policy instruments which have sought to redirect industries from richer to poorer regions. The precise form of incentives is variable but may include grants, loans at below market rates of interest, tax concessions, and transport subsidies. Under the 1957 Industrial Areas Law, Italy was able to bring all of these financial incentives to bear on the relocation of private-sector investment to the South. In France, the main emphasis was on a system of grants and subsidized loans to encourage firms to relocate from Paris. These instruments were most effective in the economically buoyant early-1960s when more than 250 relocations a year took place from Paris (Clout 1987). The Netherlands also employed financial incentives to encourage private-sector relocations, especially to the border regions and to Limburg, a traditional coal-mining centre.

In the United Kingdom, for most of the post-war period, the main type of incentive has taken the form of investment grants to businesses. The nature of UK investment incentives has changed several times, however, since 1945. In the early years up until the mid-1970s *automatic* investment grants tended to predominate. From the mid-1970s onwards this instrument was supplemented by more *selective* investment assistance. Since 1988, UK regional investment incentives have been almost entirely discretionary; the amount of assistance provided to individual firms is now determined mainly by government officials (after negotiation with each individual applicant for financial aid). As has already been shown, UK investment incentives are now more closely focused on local indigenous firms than on inward investment.

The switch from automatic to discretionary incentives in the United Kingdom has not been followed by all Member States of the EC. Differences remain in the balance between discretionary and automatic financial assistance. The latter is usually preferred by industry, as automatic assistance is simpler and more transparent. Many governments now prefer discretionary assistance, however, since it is more flexible and cost efficient. With discretionary assistance, judgements can be made concerning the contributions of individual projects to the regional economy and also on whether the investment would occur anyway irrespective of the availability of financial assistance (a phenomenon known as 'deadweight' spending). There is some evidence from research in the United Kingdom (Wren 1987, 1989) that 'deadweight' spending is indeed a problem when automatic incentives are used. The problem with discretionary incentives, however, is that, while they avoid wasted 'deadweight' spending, the associated spending cuts tend to reduce the overall volume of investment in the disadvantaged regions. The Netherlands has attempted to get the best of

TABLE 7.2. *Selected features of the regional policies of EC Member States 1990*

| Member State | Type of regional policy incentive | Automatic (A), or discretionary (D) | Labour-related (L) | Eligible services |
|---|---|---|---|---|
| France | Regional policy grant | D | L | Research. |
| | Business tax concessions | A | — | Non-local markets. |
| Germany | Investment grant | D | — | Export-based. |
| | Special depreciation allowance | A | — | All. |
| | Regional soft loans | A | — | Export-based. |
| UK | Regional selective assistance | D | — | Non-local consumer. |
| | Regional enterprise grant | A | — | Non-local and non-financial. |
| | N. Ireland selective assistance | D | L | Export-based. |
| Italy | Capital grant | A | — | Consultancy and producer. |
| | National fund scheme | A | — | Consultancy and producer. |
| | Social security concession | A | L | Tourism, R&D, transport, producer. |
| | Tax concession | A | — | R&D, data-processing. |
| Spain | Regional incentives grant | D | — | Tourism, producer. |

*Source:* Yuill *et al.* (1991).

both worlds by combining the two types of investment incentives. The rate of award of the Netherlands Investment Premium scheme is automatic up to a fixed limit, and therafter it is discretionary. In recent years, however, the general trend has been away from automatic incentives towards discretionary incentives, particularly in response to budgetary constraints (Allen, Yuill, and Bachtler 1989). The current pattern of financial incentives is set out in Table 7.2.

Financial incentives differ in a variety of other ways between the Member States of the EC. Incentives can be either capital related (usually expressed as a proportion of project costs), or labour related (according to the number of jobs created by the investment). Traditionally most incentives have been capital based. With the growing pressure of unemployment, however, there has been a shift to labour related schemes. Other differences among Member States are a function of whether the financial incentives are available over large areas of the national economy (e.g. Italy) or are highly spatially selective (e.g. the Netherlands). If the overall level of resources available for regional policy is limited, then there is an economic argument for concentration so as to optimize the external economies of scale realized by such investments. A combination of budgetary constraints and the EC's competition-policy requirements is leading to steady reductions in the spatial coverage of Member States' regional policies.

Finally, there is considerable variation between Member States in the sectors included within the regional policy remit. Traditionally, manufacturing was favoured on the grounds that it was more likely to be export orientated and to be locationally mobile. Tourism has also been included in the regional policies of some countries for the same reasons. In contrast, other countries, such as Germany and the Netherlands, have long recognized the potential contribution of the service sector to regional development, particularly as many service industries are labour intensive. The general trend in recent years has been for regional policies of EC Member States to become more inclusive of the service sector (see Table 7.2). Financial incentives have also begun increasingly to be focused more specifically on certain *types* of firms such as small firms and high-technology firms (Mason and Harrison 1990; Thwaites and Alderman 1990).

The third main arm of regional policy in Europe has been state investment in economic infrastructure as a means of changing the comparative advantage of poorer regions. A considerable variety of options is available, but of particular importance has been the provision of transport infrastructure and serviced (usually subsidized) industrial land and buildings. Industrial estates were one of the mainstays of regional policy in the 1950s and 1960s, but, given the crisis facing the traditional manufacturing sectors in the 1970s and 1980s, this policy has given way to an increasing emphasis on office parks and science parks. The Tecnopolis Novus Ortis near Bari in southern Italy is an outstanding example of the latter, as is the Cambridge Science Park in the United Kingdom.

One of the most popular forms of infrastructure investment has been the growth centre, representing the concentration of state investment in particular locations with the aim of building up interlinked industrial complexes which, it is then hoped, will diffuse growth outward into the surrounding region. The idea has its origins in the theoretical work of Perroux in the early 1950s on growth poles in economic space. This work emphasizes the growth potential of clusters of interlinked, innovative firms. Growth centres have extended this concept to the notion that *spatial* concentrations of industry can realize these growth advantages and achieve self-sustaining growth. Some would argue, however, that the real attraction of growth centres to policy-makers has been the economies of scale offered in terms of urbanization costs.

It is symbolic of the internationalization of regional policy that growth centres have been essential policy instruments in five of the six countries considered here (the exception being the United Kingdom). France has had a particularly well-developed strategy, including both industrial poles and *métropoles d'équilibre* for tertiary activities. Growth centres also provided one of the main arms of Italian regional policy under the landmark 1957 Industrial Areas Law, with incentives initially concentrated on twelve growth areas and thirty growth nuclei. As a result of political pressures (King 1987), they encompassed more than 50 per cent of the total population of the *Mezzogiorno*, a far higher proportion than would be expected in terms of the economic rationale of concentration. Growth centres are also to be found in the Netherlands and Germany, where there have been attempts to channel growth into, respectively, 18 and 312 development centres. The wide differences from country to country in the number of growth centres reflect the lack of theoretical and empirical guidance on the most effective means of implementing a growth-centre strategy. Finally, Spain, too, has had a growth-centre strategy which dates back to the first National Development Plan (1964–7). The policy in Spain seems to have been only weakly implemented in practice (Naylon 1987), with the result that little employment was generated and overall costs were high.

*Evaluating the Effectiveness of Member State Regional Policies*
After more than forty years of regional policy in the Member States of the EC, there is considerable evidence of the relative strengths and weaknesses of the various instruments. Nevertheless, there are difficulties involved in any such evaluation. Not least, there is the critical question of whether some of the plant relocations would have occurred anyway, even in the absence of regional policy, perhaps as a consequence of the reorganization of production linked to technological change (Massey 1979). Both econometric and survey techniques can be used to investigate the impact of

TABLE 7.3. *The ranking of regional incentives by firms as a factor affecting a region's competitiveness*

| Member State | Type of region | Rank of regional policy as a factor affecting a region's competitiveness for the location of firms | |
|---|---|---|---|
| | | Positive factor | Negative factor |
| France | Control | 15 of 19 | |
| | Declining | 15 of 19 | |
| | Lagging | | 7 of 19 |
| Germany | Control | | 6 of 8 |
| | Declining | | 3 of 5 |
| UK | Control | | 2 of 2 |
| | Declining | 12 of 22 | |
| | Lagging | 3 of 18 | |
| Italy | Control | 10 of 21 | |
| | Lagging | 7 of 8 | |
| Netherlands | Control | | 3 of 3 |
| | Declining | 18 of 21 | |
| Spain | Control | 18 of 19 | |
| | Declining | 11 of 16 | |
| | Lagging | | 6 of 9 |

*Note*: Terms such as '15 of 19' mean that regional policy is ranked as 15th of 19 factors affecting the competitiveness of the region.
*Source*: CEC (1990*a*: 86).

regional policy, but neither approach has proved to be entirely satisfactory. The EC has undertaken one of the few cross-Member State surveys of the effectiveness of regional policy. Firms in declining/lagging regions and in control regions were asked to rank the importance of regional incentives as positive or negative factors in regional competitiveness. The results are set out in Table 7.3 and show that regional policy was considered to be a negative rather than a positive influence by firms in lagging or declining regions in France, Spain, and Germany, while in Italy firms in the control regions viewed it more favourably than did those in the lagging regions. Even where it is ranked positively, as in the declining regions of France and Spain, and in the lagging regions of Italy, it receives a relatively low priority compared to other competitive factors.

A number of criticisms have been levelled at regional policies, and these are remarkably consistent across the Member States. First, the location controls have been criticized for being one-sided. While they restrict investment in the more prosperous regions, they cannot influence the destination of the diverted production capacity. Thus in France manufacturing decentralization from Paris in the 1960s seems mainly to have benefited the outer Paris region rather than poorer regions such as Brittany or Limousin. Secondly, there has been criticism of the kinds of plants established by industrial relocations from richer to poorer regions. The classic criticism is that branch plants are established which are externally controlled, have few intra-regional linkages, lack R&D content, specialize in less skilled assembly work, and are vulnerable to closure in times of recession. Thirdly, the policies of growth centres have been criticized for polarizing growth intra-regionally. In Italy this has been labelled the 'cathedrals-in-the-desert' effect, reflecting the lack of linkages between the capital-intensive industries of the growth centres and their surrounding hinterlands (King 1987). Hermansen (1971) explains this in terms of a lack of complementarities between the economic structures of the growth centres and their hinterlands. Fourthly, the recent switch to promoting small firms as part of the emphasis on indigenous development has been criticized because of the limited number of jobs created, the low quality of jobs in small firms, and the limited innovation potential of small firms (Mason and Harrison 1990). Regional incentive schemes also tend to be too complicated for most small firms (Allen, Yuill, and Bachtler 1989). Fifthly, infrastructure investments are criticized as being permissive. If they fail to generate additional economic activity, then regions may simply be endowed with expensive but under-utilized fixed capital in the form of roads or airports. Nevertheless, evidence does exist that there is a strong correlation between infrastructure endowment and levels of regional income, employment and productivity (CEC 1986).

Member State regional policies have diminished in importance since the mid-1970s for several reasons. The EC is seeking to reduce the level of assistance as part of a general programme of removing barriers to competition. At the same time, an economic crisis and budgetary constraints have limited the amount of discretionary expenditure available to governments. Finally, there is constant tension between policy objectives and the means of policy implementation. For the most part, the objectives are set by the government, but the majority of the means of implementation rest with the private sector, which regional policy can seek to influence but cannot control.

## 7.6. EC REGIONAL POLICY

Most of the individual Member States of the EC operate their own regional policies.These Member State regional policies co-exist alongside a central EC regional policy, which in recent years has been greatly strengthened. The individual Member State policies differ substantially from one another in both the size of resources devoted to them and in the types of policies utilized. It is clear, therefore, that the principle of subsidiarity is alive and well in the field of regional policy. No attempt has been made to bring about the complete central control of EC regional policy. Indeed, in recent years the role of local and regional governments in regional industrial regeneration has, if anything, been strengthened in many of the Member States.

The continued vitality of the Member States in the operation of regional policy raises an obvious but key question: what is the justification for an EC regional policy running alongside those of the Member States? In the aftermath of the Maastricht Treaty and the 1992 Edinburgh Summit, in which the debate on subsidiarity has been greatly intensified, this question is attracting renewed interest. The arguments advanced for a central EC regional policy are crucial not only to justify its continued existence, but also to determine what the nature of the EC's role in regional policy should be.

A number of different reasons can be advanced in support of a separate central EC role in regional policy. The first is concerned with the concept of 'cohesion'. This concept is most clearly identified in the Maastricht Treaty, which states that: 'In order to promote its overall harmonious development, the Community shall develop and pursue its action leading to the strengthening of its economic and social cohesion. In particular the Community shall aim at reducing the disparities between the various regions and the backwardness of the least favoured regions, including the rural areas' (Article 130*a*).

The importance of cohesion, and the key role to be played by regional policy in achieving it, is the result of the quickening pace of integration. The Single European Market (SEM) legislation introduced during 1989–92, its extension to some of the European Free Trade Association (EFTA) countries with the creation of a European Economic Area (EEA), the prospect of European Monetary Union (EMU) in the years ahead, and the likelihood of a wave of new entrants in the 1990s, have all combined to raise concern on the issue of cohesion. In principle, the integration process does not necessarily threaten cohesion by widening regional disparities. As was shown earlier, there is some evidence (particularly from the United States) that highly integrated economies experience a gradual narrowing of regional disparities (Barro and Sala-i-Martin 1991, 1992). These are, however, very long-term effects. In the short and medium term there is no doubt that the effects of the SEM and EMU on the various regions of the EC will be profound. EC regional disparities are already wide by international standards (OECD 1991; CEC 1991*a*). Further EC integration may well lead to a further widening of disparities (Camagni 1992; Steinle 1992). Even on the most optimistic scenarios, the integration processes set in motion by the SEM and EMU will cause profound structural changes among the regions of the EC. In order to reap the static and dynamic gains from integration, most of the major industries of the EC must rationalize their production processes. The effects of this will be felt in every region of the EC, in some more than others.

The regional effects of further integration have been widely used to justify the existence of an EC regional policy and its recent strengthening. There are two aspects to this argument. First, a strong EC regional policy is necessary because the EC is itself the *cause* of part of the regional problem as a side-effect of the integration process it has set in motion. Secondly, a strong EC regional policy is vital if the SEM and EMU are to be *achieved*. Wide differences in the performance of the different regional economies pose a threat to the attainment of integration just as the lack of convergence between Member State economies does.

In addition to the link between EC regional policy and the integration process, supporters of EC regional policy point to additional arguments in its favour. First, the more prosperous Member States tend to have fewer regional problems but also have the greater financial resources. Without EC intervention, the outcome will be that richer Member States can spend more on their problem regions than can poorer Member States (CEC 1990*b*). Indeed, some Member States such as the Irish Republic and Greece are virtually disadvantaged regions in their own right and face severe financial constraints in trying to fund an active regional policy. An EC regional policy is vital if resources are to be concentrated in those regions of the EC in greatest need.

The need for an EC regional policy as a means of targeting help where it is most needed is really part of a broader *co-ordination* case for an EC regional policy. Money, however, is only part of the solution to the regional problems of Europe. The efficiency with which regional policy is operated is also important. The EC has an important role to play in co-ordinating the activities of the EC12. At one level this involves simple but effective actions, such as ensuring that Member States sharing a common frontier tackle regional problems on either side of the frontier in a sensible co-ordinated manner, or in ensuring that cross-Community transport and other links are highly integrated. At another level, co-ordination involves bringing the Member States, regional, and local organizations together, so that a common integrated strategy for tackling the EC's regional problems can be hammered out. Co-ordination is also necessary as part of EC competition policy to prevent Member States from using regional policy subsidies to bid against one another for 'mobile' investment projects.

Finally, it is important not to lose sight of the fundamental reason for regional policy: that regional disparities are socially inequitable. The EC aspires to be more than just an economic entity. To be an EC citizen means being part of a community of interest in which equity is just as important as economic efficiency. Regional policy at EC level can, therefore, be seen as a way of expressing the desire to help fellow EC citizens in poorer regions to realize their potential. In addition, the presence of low-income and high-unemployment regions with depressed spending power is not in the interests of the more prosperous parts of the EC.

## EC Regional Policy since 1989

Despite a recent set of reforms (CEC 1993*a*), the current EC regional policy was moulded by a set of major reforms introduced in 1989 as part of the SEM process (CEC 1989*a*). These reforms were extremely far-reaching and radically altered the nature of EC regional policy, which began with the creation of the European Regional Development Fund (ERDF) in 1975 (CEC 1975; Armstrong 1978).

The 1989 reforms were designed as a complete revamp of the EC's three *structural funds*. The three structural funds are the ERDF, the European Social Fund (ESF), and the Guidance Section of the European Agricultural Guidance and Guarantee Fund (EAGGF). All three funds had been in existence for many years before the 1989 reforms. The gradual introduction of the SEM legislation between 1988 and 1992 proved to be the catalyst for the design of a co-ordinated framework for administering these three structural funds. The new framework, in addition to attempting to co-ordinate the activities of the structural funds, also sought to integrate the actions of two other EC financial instruments providing help to the disadvantaged regions: the European Investment Bank (EIB) and the European Coal and Steel Community (ECSC).

Under the 1989 reforms, the structural funds were set five common objectives:

1. *The development of structurally backward regions.* These are defined as regions with GDP per capita under 75 per cent of the EC average (see Fig. 7.2). They comprise the most disadvantaged of the EC's problem regions and are dominated by the Mediterranean South together with the Irish Republic. In addition, the East German *Länder*, given special EC aid prior to 1994, will become an EC Objective 1 region in future budgets. Objective 1 regions comprise some 22 per cent of the EC's population. All three structural funds, together with the EIB, are charged with their redevelopment.

2. *The conversion of regions in industrial decline.* These comprise some 16 per cent of the EC's population. The ERDF and ESF, together with the EIB and, where appropriate the ECSC, are charged with helping these regions.

3. *Combating long-term unemployment.* This objective is not specifically a regional one, and does not therefore appear in Fig. 7.2. The ESF has the main responsibility for achieving this objective.

4. *The increase in the employment opportunities for young people.* This

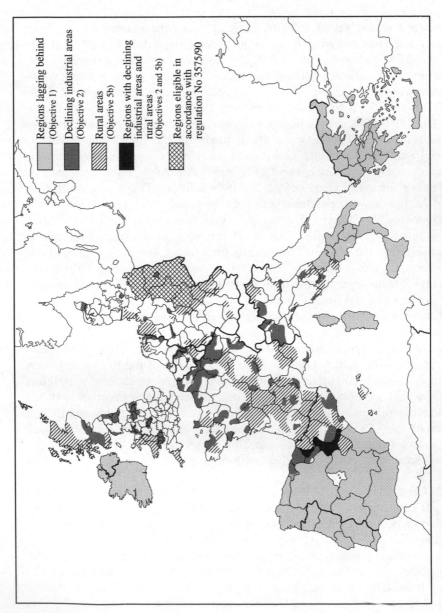

Fɪɢ. 7.2 European Community assisted areas, 1989–93

too is a 'non-regional' objective and again is the responsibility of the ESF rather than the ERDF.

5. This objective is in two parts. Objective 5A (*the adjustment of agricultural structures* arising from reforms to the EC's agriculture policy) is a non-regional objective for which the EAGGF has prime responsibility. Objective 5B (*promoting the development of rural areas*), however, is a regional objective. Eligible areas are shown in Fig. 7.2. Objective 5B regions comprise some 5 per cent of the EC's population. All three structural funds, including the ERDF, are charged with attaining this objective.

The 1989 reforms led to a doubling (*in real terms*) of EC assistance to the disadvantaged regions between 1988 and 1993. This reflects the determination of the EC to develop a powerful and effective regional policy of its own. It also reflects fears that the SEM may exacerbate regional disparities in the EC unless remedial measures are put in place. The doubling of financial resources in the 1989 reforms was accompanied by measures designed to ensure that EC resources are *concentrated* on those objectives and those regions which are in greatest need. As was shown earlier, one of the main arguments in favour of an EC-level regional policy is its inherent ability to direct resources to the regions in greatest distress. It is the Objective 1 regions which are by far the most disadvantaged. The 1989–93 EC budget allocated Ecu 38.3 billion (at 1989 prices) to the Objective 1 regions (for all three structural funds), while Objective 2 regions were allocated Ecu 7.2 billion, and Objective 5B regions were allocated Ecu 2.8 billion. The individual structural funds have also reflected this pattern of concentration. Some 80 per cent of ERDF resources, for example, are earmarked for Objective 1 regions. The 1989 reforms also laid down rules for targeting money on those Member States with the most severe regional problems. Table 7.4 shows the 'indicative allocations' for the various EC Member States for ERDF money. These signal the EC's intentions on the state-by-state division of (85 per cent of) ERDF funds for the period 1989–93. The remaining 15 per cent of the ERDF budget is available for spending in a manner which is not predetermined.

The ERDF (and the other structural funds) are essentially grant-giving financial instruments. Other types of financial assistance, such as loans, are the province of agencies such as the EIB and ECSC. Before 1989 most of the assistance provided by the ERDF was in the form of project-by-project grants, given mainly to large infrastructure projects and with lesser amounts going to industrial projects. This approach tended to draw the EC into detailed work requiring expertise and information not available in Brussels. The 1989 reforms sought to bring about a fundamental change in the manner in which EC regional policy is administered. The key features of the 1989 reforms were *planning*, *partnership*, and *additionality*. The

**TABLE 7.4.** *ERDF indicative allocations 1989–1993 (%)*

| Member State | Objective 1 regions | Objective 2 regions | Objective 5B regions |
| --- | --- | --- | --- |
| Belgium | 0.0 | 4.3 | 1.2 |
| Denmark | 0.0 | 0.4 | 0.7 |
| Germany | 0.0 | 8.9 | 27.5 |
| Greece | 16.2 | 0.0 | 0.0 |
| Spain | 32.6 | 20.7 | 7.2 |
| France | 2.0 | 18.3 | 37.2 |
| Irish Republic | 5.4 | 0.0 | 0.0 |
| Italy | 24.5 | 6.3 | 16.4 |
| Luxemburg | 0.0 | 0.2 | 0.1 |
| Netherlands | 0.0 | 2.6 | 2.2 |
| Portugal | 17.5 | 0.0 | 0.0 |
| UK | 1.7 | 38.3 | 7.5 |
| TOTAL | 100.0 | 100.0 | 100.0 |

*Note*: Objective 1 regions are structurally backward regions; Objective 2 regions are regions in industrial decline; Objective 5B regions are rural areas.
*Source*: CEC (1989*b*, 1989*c*, 1989*d*).

1989 reforms have attempted to create a comprehensive system of regional planning. The planning process is designed to be a collaborative one, drawing the Member States together with regional and local organizations (hence the term 'partnership').

The planning process represents the most determined attempt yet by the EC to capitalize upon its key role as a policy co-ordinator. The planning process set up by the 1989 reforms has several distinct phases. At the first stage the Member States (and lower-level authorities) are required to submit regional plans to the Commission. After detailed negotiations between the EC and the Member States, the Commission produces Community Support Frameworks (CSFs). These set out the contribution which the EC's structural funds will make to the attainment of the regional plan, and also indicate the role which the Member States' own regional policy will play (see CEC (1991*b*) for an example of a CSF). Once the regional plan and CSF have been agreed, the next stage is implementation. This is undertaken partly via assistance to individual projects (particularly large infrastructure projects). In an attempt to move away from project-by-project assistance, much greater emphasis since 1989 has been placed on Operational Programmes (OPs). These are carefully co-ordinated packages, in which EC aid is only one part. A programme will be designed to run for several years, have a clear and precise set of goals, comprise a variety of individual projects and other initiatives (e.g. help for small firms), and will involve the Member States, regional, and local organizations. The EC provides partial funding for the OPs but does not directly administer them; this is left to the Member States. The programming approach to regional policy is not new. Before 1989 the EC had developed a range of Community programmes such as STAR (improvement of telecommunications in disadvantaged regions). These Community-level programmes (now called Community Initiatives (CIs)), encompassing several Member States, have been retained and expanded by the 1989 reforms. The bulk of ERDF money, however, is channelled through OPs, which are specific to individual Member States. As well as programmes such as the OPs and CIs, some ERDF money is still given as project-by-project assistance. The 1989 reforms also allow ERDF money to be used to part-finance *Member State* regional policy schemes, or to be given by way of *global grants* (e.g. as grants to financial intermediaries such as banks or development agencies which then undertake the detailed distribution of the funds). The final stage in the post-1989 planning system is the monitoring and assessment of the CSFs and the associated programmes of help. Once this is done, the whole process is repeated, with new plans being agreed and new CSFs and programmes being developed. At no stage does the EC act on its own. The key principle, therefore, is that of partnership between the EC, the Member States, and regional and local organizations. The expectation is that, in return for close involvement, the Member States will commit money of their own in an 'additional' manner (i.e. as a complement to ERDF funds and not as a substitute). Whether the new system can genuinely stimulate 'additionality' remains to be seen. The past record of some Member States has not been good.

The initial implementation of the 1989 reforms stimulated considerable discussion (EP 1991; CEC 1992*a*). The rapid pace of change in the EC in the period since 1989 led to the need to think again on EC regional policy. Economic and monetary union will have important implications for the EC's disadvantaged regions. So, too, will the establishment of an EEA with EFTA members and the likelihood of new entrants to the EC in the mid-1990s. As a result, a new set of EC regional policy reforms designed to encompass the period 1994–9, was introduced in 1992 and 1993. The Edinburgh Summit of heads of state in December 1992 agreed a new seven-year budget (1994–9). Although an overall budget-ceiling equivalent to 1.27 per cent of EC GDP (by 1999) was set at Edinburgh, the structural funds have been granted a further major expansion. The total budget for the structural funds will rise to Ecu 27.4 billion by 1999. In addition, the EC at Edinburgh agreed to the creation of a new Cohesion Fund (worth Ecu 2.6 billion by 1999). Although not strictly a regional policy instrument, the Cohesion Fund is important as it is earmarked for the EC Member States with the most severe regional problems (Spain, Portugal, Greece, and the Irish Republic). Cohesion Fund money will be targeted on transport and environmental infrastructure projects. It effectively reinforces the EC's attempts to help the Objective 1 regions. These major budget changes have been accompanied by a new set of reforms for the EC's structural funds (CEC: 1993*a*, 1993*b*). The new reforms are designed to reinforce the system put in place in 1989 and do not represent a radical revision of the whole policy. The principal amendments being brought in for the period 1994–9 are: (*a*) an additional new objective for the structural funds (the reintegration of workers affected by industrial change), (*b*) additional help for fishing communities, (*c*) simplified procedures for drawing up programmes of assistance, and (*d*) procedures to strengthen the role of regional and local level partners in the EC's regional policy decision-making. A new map of eligible assisted areas designed to replace that shown in Fig. 7.2 was also being drawn at the time of writing.

## 7.7. CONCLUSION

Regional policy has become one of the key policies within the EC. The Maastricht Treaty and the 1992 Edinburgh Summit have reinforced a trend towards the strengthening of EC regional policy which has been apparent since the major reforms of EC regional policy introduced in 1989 (designed to accompany the SEM process). The rapid growth of EC regional policy in recent years is welcome in that it has occurred at a time when the regional policies of the individual Member States have been under tight fiscal constraints. The EC, however, has not supplanted the Member States. Individual Member States continue to operate strong regional policies of their own. A situation of considerable complexity has, therefore, emerged, particularly as the current fashion for assisting small firms and other types of 'indigenous development' has given a new lease of life to regional and local development organizations.

In the mid- to late 1990s the EC is likely to play an increasing role in regional policy. A further large expansion of resources devoted to regional policy has been earmarked for the period 1994–9. The EC's system of regional planning and close co-ordination with Member States first introduced in 1989 is now fully operational.

A number of key issues are likely to dominate regional policy in the EC in the remainder of the 1990s. The first will be the issue of the size of the regional policy budget. Further EC integration combined with the gradual adoption of the SEM will place further strains on the weaker regional economies. Regional disparities in the EC remain wide, despite persistent attempts to narrow them. A second issue likely to be of importance is the effectiveness of EC regional policy and the 'indigenous-development' strategies of the Member States. Neither has yet been fully evaluated. The 1990s will produce evidence of whether or not they are successful strategies for achieving regional policy objectives. Failure would force a major rethink of regional policy. Other issues likely to continue to be important in the years ahead are subsidiarity and additionality. The final division of regional policy powers between the EC and the Member States (subsidiarity) has not yet been decided, and further evolution of the situation is bound to occur. Additionality will be important because, as the EC regional policy budget expands further during the 1990s, some Member States will be tempted to use EC regional policy spending as a substitute for their own.

# REFERENCES

Allbrechts, L., Moulaert, F., Roberts, P., and Swyngedouw, E. (1989), 'New Perspectives for Regional Policy and Development in the 1990s', in L. Albrechts, F. Moulaert, P. Roberts, and E. Swyngedouw (eds.), *Regional Policy at the Crossroads* (London: Jessica Kingsley).

Allen, K., Yuill, D., and Bachtler, J. (1989), 'Requirements for an Effective Regional Policy', in L. Albrechts, F. Moulaert, P. Roberts, and E. Swyngedouw (eds.), *Regional Policy at the Crossroads* (London: Jessica Kingsley).

Armstrong, H. W. (1978), 'Community Regional Policy: Survey and Critique', *Regional Studies*, 12: 511–18.

―― and Taylor, J. (1993), *Regional Economics and Policy*, 2nd edn. (Hemel Hempstead: Harvester Wheatsheaf).

Barro, R. J., and Sala-i-Martin, X. (1991), 'Convergence across States and Regions', *Brookings Papers*, 1: 107–82.

―― (1992), 'Convergence', *Journal of Political Economy*, 100: 223–51.

Blacksell, M. (1987), 'West Germany', in H. Clout (ed.), *Regional Development in Western Europe*, 3rd edn. (London: Fulton), 229–56.

Bleitrach, D., and Chenu, A. (1982), 'Regional Planning: Regulation or Deepening of Social Contradictions?', in R. Hudson and J. R. Lewis (eds.), *Regional Planning in Europe* (London: Pion).

Camagni, R. P. (1992), 'Development Scenarios and Policy Guidelines for the Lagging Regions in the 1990s', *Regional Studies*, 26: 361–74.

Clout, H. (1987), 'France', in H. Clout (ed.), *Regional Development in Western Europe*, 3rd edn. (London: Fulton).

CEC (1975): Commission of the European Communities, 'Regulation Establishing a Community Regional Policy', *Official Journal of the European Communities*, L73 (21 Mar.).

―― (1986), *The Contribution of Infrastructure to Regional Development* (Brussels: CEC).

―― (1989*a*), *Guide to the Reform of the Community's Structural Funds* (Brussels: CEC).

―― (1989*b*), 'Commission Decision fixing an Indicative Allocation between

Member States of 85% of the Commitment Appropriations of the ERDF under Objective 1 as Defined by Council Regulation (EEC) No. 2052/88', *Official Journal of the European Communities*, L101 (13 Apr.), 41–2.

—— (1989c), 'Commission Decision fixing an Indicative Allocation between Member States of 85% of the Commitment Appropriations of the ERDF under Objective 2 as Defined by Council Regulation (EEC) No. 2052/88', *Official Journal of the European Communities*, L113 (26 Apr.), 29–30.

—— (1989d), 'Commission Decision fixing an Indicative Allocation between Member States of 85% of the Commitment Appropriations of the ERDF under Objective 5b as Defined by Council Regulation (EEC) No. 2052/88', *Official Journal of the European Communities*, L180 (27 June), 54–5.

—— (1990a), *An Empirical Assessment of Factors Shaping Regional Competitiveness in Problem Regions* (Brussels–Luxemburg: CEC).

—— (1990b), *Second Survey on State Aids in the European Community in Manufacturing and Other Sectors* (Brussels: CEC).

—— (1991a), *The Regions in the 1990s: Fourth Periodic Report on the Social and Economic Situation and Development of the Regions of the Community* (Brussels: CEC).

—— (1991b), *Community Support Frameworks 1989–1993 for the Development of Rural Areas: United Kingdom* (Brussels: CEC).

—— (1992a), *The ERDF in 1990* (Brussels–Luxemburg: CEC).

—— (1992b), *Community Structural Policies: Mid-Term Assessment and Outlook* (Brussels: CEC).

—— (1993a), *Community Structural Funds 1994–1999* (Brussels: CEC).

—— (1993b), *The Community's Structural Fund Operations 1994–1999*, COM (93) 67 final–SYN 455 (Brussels: CEC).

Council of Ministers (1992), *Treaty on European Union* (Brussels: Commission of the European Communities).

EP (1991): European Parliament, *A New Strategy for Social and Economic Cohesion after 1992*, Study by National Institute of Economic and Social Research for European Parliament (Brussels–Luxemburg: EP).

Flockton, C., and Kofman, E. (1989), *France* (London: Harper and Row).

Gay, F. J. (1987), 'Benelux', in H. Clout (ed.), *Regional Development in Western Europe*, 3rd edn. (London: Fulton).

Gravier, J. (1947), *Paris et le désert français* (Paris: Plaminiarian).

Hermansen, T. (1971), 'Development Poles and Development Centres in National and Regional Development', in UNRISD (ed.), *Growth Poles and Growth Centres in Regional Policies and Planning* (Geneva: UNRISD).

Keeble, D., and Wever, E. (1986), 'Introduction', in D. Keeble and E. Wever (eds.), *New Firms and Regional Development in Europe* (London: Croom Helm), 1–34.

King, R. (1987), *Italy* (London: Harper and Row).

Lewis, J. R. (1984), 'Regional Policy and Planning', in S. Bornstein, D. Held, and J. Krieger (eds.), *The State in Capitalist Europe* (London: George Allen and Unwin), 138–55.

Martin, R. (1992), 'Reviving the Economic Case for Regional Policy', in M. Hart and R. Harrison (eds.), *Spatial Policy in a Divided Nation* (London: Jessica Kingsley), 270–90.

Mason, C. M., and Harrison, R. T. (1990), 'Small Firms: Phoenix from the Ashes', in D. Pinter (ed.), *Western Europe: Challenge and Change* (London: Belhaven), 72–90.

Massey, D. (1979), 'In What Sense a Regional Problem?', *Regional Studies*, 13: 233–44.

Molle, W. (1990), *The Economics of European Integration: Theory, Practice, Policy* (Aldershot: Dartmouth Publishing Co.).

Naylon, J. (1987), 'Iberia', in H. Clout (ed.), *Regional Development in Western Europe*, 3rd edn. (London: Fulton), 383–418.

Nicoll, W. R., and Yuill, D. (1980), *Regional Problems and Policies in Europe: The Postwar Experience* (Studies in Public Policy No. 53; Glasgow: University of Strathclyde).

OECD (1989): Organization for Economic Co-operation and Development, *Economic Outlook, July*, (Paris: OECD).

Perroux, F. (1950), 'Economic Space: Theory and Applications', *Quarterly Journal of Economics*, vol. 64.

Steinle, W. J. (1992), 'Regional Competitiveness and the Single Market', *Regional Studies*, 26: 307–18.

Taylor, J. (1991), *Reviving the Regions* (Fabian Society Pamphlet, No. 551; London).

Thwaites, A. T., and Alderman, N. (1990), 'Technological Change and Regional Economic Advance', in D. Pinder (ed.), *Western Europe: Challenge and Change* (London: Belhaven), 91–107.

Williams, A. M. (1987), *The Western European Economy: A Geography of Postwar Development* (London: Hutchinson).

Wren, C. (1987), 'The Relative Effects of Local Authority Financial Assistance Policies', *Urban Studies*, 24: 268–78.

—— (1989), 'The Revised Regional Development Grant Scheme: A Case Study in Cleveland County of a Marginal Employment Subsidy', *Regional Studies*, 23: 127–38.

Yuill, D., Allen, K., Bachtler, J., Clement, K., and Wishlade, F. (1991), *European Regional Incentives 1991* (London: Bowker Saur).

# 8

# Transport Policy

NORMAN LEE

## 8.1. INTRODUCTION

Transport is an important sector in the economies of all Member States of the European Community (EC) (with approximately 7–8 per cent of GNP being spent each year on transport activities). Typically, it has been expected to serve a variety of different, sometimes conflicting, objectives—economic, social, and environmental. Given this, it became one of the most regulated sectors in most European economies, although the nature and extent of such regulations varied greatly between them. Therefore, it was not surprising that, when it was first established, the EC attempted to develop a common transport policy for the Community as a whole.

This chapter contains a review and evaluation of the Common Transport Policy (CTP). The next section describes its origins and subsequent development. There is then a brief review of the main characteristics of the EC transport sector and the problems that transport policies need to address. This is followed by an economic analysis of certain general efficiency and equity issues raised by such problems and policies. Thereafter, EC transport policy and its effects are analysed in each of a number of policy areas—road freight and passenger transport, rail and inland waterways transport, maritime and air transport, and transport infrastructures. The chapter concludes with an overall evaluation of the current CTP and its future development.

## 8.2. ORIGINS AND DEVELOPMENT OF THE CTP

The Treaty of Rome (1957) established, in Articles 3e and 74–84, the legal basis for a CTP within the EC. This is one of only three common policies specifically mentioned in the original Treaty—the others being agriculture and external commerce.

Prior to this, the European Coal and Steel Community (ECSC), established by the Treaty of Paris (1951), had been developing its own common transport policy (Erdmenger 1983). This was because discrimination in transport rates and related practices by member countries were being used to favour domestic exporters and to penalize imports and this was considered harmful to the establishment of a common market in coal and steel within the ECSC.

Continuing concern over similar issues resulted in provision for a CTP within the Treaty of Rome. The following features are worth noting:

1. Article 84 restricts the automatic application of the CTP to road, rail, and waterway transport, whilst giving the Council of Ministers powers to add marine and aviation transport if they unanimously agree (eventually this was agreed in 1974).
2. Article 74 establishes the fundamental objectives of the CTP as being the overall objectives of the Treaty itself (see Article 2). These objectives are broadly defined and leave considerable discretion in interpretation to the Commission and Council of Ministers. They have also been subsequently amended, as discussed later, through the Single European Act (SEA) (1987) and the Treaty on European Union (TEU) (1992) which was ratified in 1993.
3. Articles 75–84 contain a mixture of more specific requirements of the CTP which relate to the elimination of discriminatory practices but also permit state subsidies for transport activities under certain circumstances.

The principles and guidelines to be followed by the CTP were set down in the Schaus Memorandum of 1961 and the types of measures to be introduced in implementing these were listed in the Commission's first Action Programme of 1962 (Despicht 1969). These proposed measures were of the following main kinds:

- *Anti-discrimination* measures: these were intended to eliminate discrimination between Member States and between different modes of transport.
- *Liberalization* measures: carriers were to be given additional opportunities to supply services across national frontiers within the EC.
- *Harmonization* measures: these proposed standardization of provisions, across Member States, relating to such matters as the weights and dimensions of road vehicles, conditions of work in road transport, and the taxation of vehicles.

Additionally, the Commission proposed an EC role in co-ordinating transport investment relating to 'trunk routes of Community importance'.

However, progress in implementing many of these measures was very slow. Then, the enlargement of the EC in 1973 led the Commission to review the future development of the CTP and, *inter alia*, it proposed the establishment of an EC transport system (Erdmenger 1983)—but progress continued to be limited.

There were many reasons for slow progress, but a principal factor has been conflicts of interest between different Member States and between those providing different forms of transport. Some interests, for example, favoured 'harmonization' measures which might protect or strengthen their own competitive and financial position; others favoured 'liberalization' measures because they believed they would benefit from greater access to other Member State markets. The differing attitudes of Member States in the early 1980s can be seen from the following statement by the then Director of Transport in the Commission:

The Benelux countries and the peripheral Member States—the United Kingdom, Denmark, Greece and Ireland—primarily seek freedom of movement in the Community for their road haulage and inland waterway companies in order to open up a large economic area for their transport operations. The Federal Republic of Germany and Italy, however, stress the need for harmonising the conditions of competition. This has the twin aim of protecting their own road haulage companies and their national railways . . . The United Kingdom, Denmark and Greece are the strongest advocates of the traditional freedom of navigation (in sea transport). Belgium, France, the Federal Republic of Germany and Italy are inclined to allow their own fleet to benefit from the fact that their industries have a high level of imports and exports . . . The traditional air transport policy of the Member States is mainly directed at gaining a share of traffic for their national airline . . . The Member States are reluctant therefore to make any promises in Brussels. However, the United Kingdom, which has a policy of admitting several airlines—and, to a certain extent, the Netherlands as well—advocates specific European solutions. (Erdmenger 1983: 7–8)

However, the pace of change in the CTP has accelerated considerably since the mid-1980s. This has been mainly for two reasons:

1. The Judgment of the European Court of Justice (ECJ) in May 1985, which, *inter alia*, required the Council of Transport Ministers to adopt 'within a reasonable time' measures to liberalize transport services. This was in response to an action brought by the European Parliament (EP) against the Council of Ministers for failing to introduce and implement a common transport policy. (DG for Research 1991)
2. The political initiative to establish, by 1993, a single market in Europe. 'The abolition of frontiers and the concrete implementation of the freedom of movement for people, goods and capital could not, in fact, be conceived without an internal market for transport' (DG for Research 1991: 21).

In effect, these two changes, supported by an international trend towards deregulation (Button and Pitfield 1991), broadened the political support for the liberalization and anti-discrimination measures which had previously been lacking. In November 1985 the Council of Transport Ministers agreed a work programme comprising:

- the creation of a free transport market, without quantitative restrictions, no later than 1992; and
- a progressive liberalization of transport services and elimination of distortions to competition within the EC transport market, in the intervening period.

The progress made in implementing this work programme is reviewed, for each main policy area, later in the chapter. Measured according to the scope and number of new regulations and directives approved at EC level, the overall progress has been impressive. However, account has to be taken of provisions for exemptions and delays in implementation which occur at the Member State level. In most cases it is only since the late 1980s that certain of these measures have begun to have significant, practical consequences, and their full effects have not yet been fully experienced.

Also, from the mid-1980s, the Commission has made further efforts to strengthen the infrastructure investment component of the CTP. In 1986 it identified its medium-term policy objectives as:

- improvement of transport communications in land–sea corridors;
- reduction in the transport costs incurred within 'transit' countries;
- integration of the peripheral regions within the EC's network; and
- construction of links offering a high level of service between major Member State cities, particularly high-speed rail links (Lee 1992).

However, some Member States, including the United Kingdom, have not supported the development of a substantial EC transport fund for these purposes, and its impact has been relatively limited. Much larger financial support for transport infrastructure has been available through the European Regional Development Fund (ERDF).

The future role and operations of EC transport policy will also be affected by the provisions of the SEA (1987) and the TEU (the 'Maastricht Treaty'). *Inter alia*, they provide for:

- the introduction of majority voting on certain transport-policy issues;
- the need to respect the subsidiarity principle within the CTP;
- the need to reflect the new statement of EC objectives (in Article 2 of the Treaty) following the Maastricht agreement—that is, of promoting throughout the EC: a harmonious and balanced development of economic activities; sustainable and non-inflationary growth respecting the environment; a high degree of convergence of economic performance; a high level of employment and of social protection; the raising of the standard of living and quality of life, and economic and social cohesion and solidarity among Member States; and
- the need to include, within the CTP, measures to improve transport safety.

It is clear that the existence of multiple objectives for a Common Transport Policy will continue, and the need to reconcile these, where they conflict, will remain. The Commission has indicated how the CTP might evolve in the future, in its report on *The Future Development of the Common Transport Policy* (CEC 1992). This identifies three main goals:

1. the removal of any remaining restrictions or distortions in the single market;
2. the proper functioning of EC transport systems; and
3. the integration of environmental objectives within the CTP.

These will be re-examined in the final section of this chapter.

## 8.3. EC AND MEMBER STATE TRANSPORT SECTORS

Within the EC as a whole, between 1970 and 1990, passenger transport (measured by total passenger kilometres travelled) increased by 3.1 per cent per annum and goods transport (measured by tonne kilometres moved)

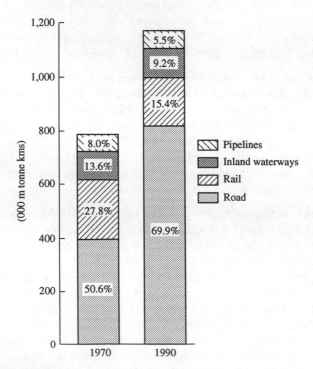

FIG. **8.1.** EC freight transport 1970 and 1990
*Source*: CEC (1992).

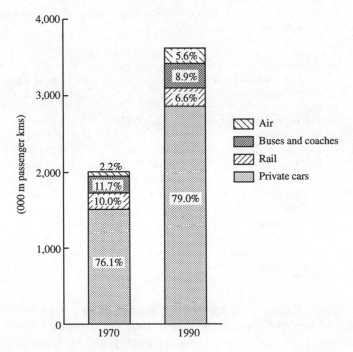

**Fɪɢ. 8.2.** EC passenger transport 1970 and 1990
*Source*: CEC (1992).

by 2.3 per cent per annum. This compares with an annual growth rate in GDP, in real terms, of 2.6 per cent (CEC 1992). In the absence of major policy changes, these kinds of growth rates are likely to continue in the future.

The relative shares of the different modes in the EC transport market have changed considerably over the period, as illustrated in Figs. 8.1 and 8.2. In the case of *inland freight* movements, the dominance of road transport has increased. Its share of the total market has risen from 50 to 70 per cent, whilst the shares of the other three modes have declined—rail transport from 28 to 15 per cent, inland waterways from 14 to 9 per cent, and pipelines from 8 to 6 per cent. Comparable data are not available for *sea transport*, but it has been estimated that this accounts for at least 30 per cent of all freight transported between Member States, though for only 2–3 per cent, on average, of all domestic transport within Member States (CEC 1992).

In the case of the EC *passenger transport* market, private car transport was already dominant in 1970 and this has increased further over the period (from 76 to 79 per cent). The modal share of air transport has also risen from 2 to 6 per cent. In contrast, the bus and coach share has declined from 12 to 9 per cent and the rail transport share from 10 to 7 per cent.

**TABLE 8.1.** *Range of variation in the relative importance of different transport modes between the Member States (1988)*

| Freight movements | | Passenger movements | |
|---|---|---|---|
| Mode | % of total movements in Member State | Mode | % of total passenger traffic in Member State |
| Road | 34.1 (Netherlands) – 75.5 (Spain) | Cars and taxis | 73.2 (Spain) – 87.3 (UK) |
| Rail | 6.8 (Netherlands) – 24.5 (Germany) | Buses and coaches | 6.6 (France) – 18.4 (Spain) |
| Inland waterway | 0.1 (UK) – 54.4 (Netherlands) | Rail (excluding metro) | 5.8 (UK) – 9.7 (France) |
| Sea-going | 0.2 (Germany) – 27.1 (UK) | | |
| Pipeline | 2.2 (Spain) – 10.8 (Denmark) | | |

*Source*: DoT (1991).

The relative shares of the different transport modes vary considerably between the Member States. In the case of freight movements, for example, road haulage is of much greater relative importance in Spain than in the Netherlands. In contrast, inland waterways are of major significance in the Netherlands but are insignificant in the United Kingdom. In the case of passenger transport, the differences are less pronounced, but, for example, the private road transport shares of the northern, higher-income, countries are greater and those of bus and coach transport considerably lower than in the southern, lower-income Member States. Other examples of these differences are shown in Table 8.1.

The trends within certain transport modes also differ between Member States (DoT 1991). The growth in both freight and passenger transport by road in many of the southern countries has been considerably above the EC average. Some Member States have experienced a significant absolute increase in rail freight traffic (e.g. Portugal, Italy, the Netherlands), whilst others (e.g. United Kingdom) have experienced an absolute decline.

These differences help to explain why the transport problems and policy interests of different Member States do not always coincide. Additionally, they may adopt different policies because their transport philosophies are different. Some adopt more narrowly defined economic objectives for transport policy, whilst others emphasize its broader social and environmental role.

Despite such differences, there are a number of common problems which face most Member States or are likely to do so in the near future. These include:

- Increasing pressure on the transport infrastructure, especially roads, as traffic continues to increase. This is reflected in a number of different policy issues: growing concern over the financing of new infrastructure, increasing congestion and road-safety problems, problems of pollution and resource conservation, and growing interest in traffic constraint by regulatory or fiscal measures.
- Increasing pressure on the provision and funding of public passenger transport facilities as car-ownership levels continue to rise. This reflects in a growing pre-occupation with the mobility of lower-income groups and the use of state subsidies to support this.

These transport trends and concerns, although manifest in individual Member States to different degrees and in somewhat different ways, provide the context within which the CTP has to operate in pursuit of the objectives described at the end of the previous section. The Commission's proposals for addressing these, according to its *Programme for Sustainable Mobility* (CEC 1992) are to:

- promote the proper functioning of the internal market by facilitating the free movement of goods and persons within the EC;
- remove distortions and inefficiencies within the transport market;
- assist, through investment in new transport infrastructure, in reducing regional disparities in economic and social development;
- ensure that the development of transport systems contributes to a sustainable pattern of development by respecting the environment; and
- improve transport safety.

The next section examines, at a general and more theoretical level, how these different types of goals might be simultaneously achieved.


## 8.4. ECONOMIC ANALYSIS OF TRANSPORT POLICIES

The transport-policy goals listed at the end of the previous section can be regrouped into three categories for the purpose of economic analysis:

1. those relating to an efficient allocation of resources within the transport sector and between that sector and other economic sectors (the *allocative-efficiency* objective);
2. those concerned with meeting individual transport market requirements at least resource cost (*marketing* and *productive-efficiency* objectives); and
3. those relating to an equitable distribution of benefits and costs from transport and other economic activities (*equity* objectives—inter-personal, inter-generation, and geographic).

A CTP which meets these three sets of objectives should satisfy the CTP goals which were previously listed. The types of policy measures which, within the framework of a single, internal market, are likely to achieve these objectives, are now considered. This provides an analytical basis for evaluating developments in a number of more specific policy areas in the following sections of the chapter. Allocative-efficiency and equity objectives are discussed first of all, followed by marketing and productive-efficiency objectives.

### Allocative-Efficiency and Equity Objectives

Welfare economics demonstrates, on certain market assumptions, that welfare will be maximized, for any given distribution of income, if prices are set equal to the marginal social costs of production (Laidler and Estrin 1989). This is automatically achieved in perfectly competitive markets, but not in the imperfect markets which are typically found in real-world situations. Inefficiencies result from 'market failures', and it is part of the purpose of transport (and other) policies to address these.

Traditionally, many transport markets have been very imperfectly competitive. In some cases, this is because the available transport technology has favoured large, relatively indivisible, infrastructure systems (e.g. railways, ports), which have led to high seller concentration. In other cases, it has been consciously fostered through agreements between operators (e.g. shipping conferences). Additionally, competition within the transport market has been restricted by governments nationalizing transport undertakings and regulating transport activities in the belief that this would better serve a wider range of economic and social objectives. In the event, it is questionable whether the forms that these interventions took actually achieved their goals. Therefore, today, a CTP has to address both 'market-failure' and 'regulatory-failure' problems.

One kind of policy response to this situation is to try to make transport markets more 'workable' or 'contestable'—that is, 'more competitive' (Clark 1940; Baumol 1982). This approach is examined later when reviewing the role that deregulation and anti-discriminatory measures might play within a CTP. A second approach, which under certain circumstances may be complementary to the first, is to improve transport-pricing and investment decision-making so that they are more consistent with allocative-efficiency objectives.

The transport-pricing principle which is often advocated to achieve allocative efficiency is the marginal social cost (MSC) rule of pricing. According to this, the transport user is expected to pay a price equal to the social-opportunity cost of the service with which he is provided.

This is illustrated, in a simple form, in Fig. 8.3. The transport operator is assumed to produce under conditions of constant returns to scale; that is

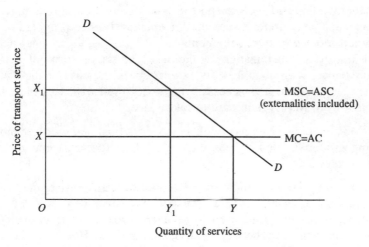

FIG. **8.3.** An illustration of MSC pricing

long-run marginal costs and long-run average costs are equal. Therefore, in long-run equilibrium, if there are no external costs for which he is responsible and given the market-demand conditions (DD), he should supply $OY$ services at a price of $OX$.

However, the provision of transport services often causes additional costs to fall on other members of society—for example, road accidents to pedestrians, delays to other road users, noise and air pollution impacts on nearby residents. These external costs should also be taken into account and, in Fig. 8.3, would justify raising the transport price to $OX_1$ and reducing the supply of services to $OY_1$.

Where competing transport services are not charged according to their MSCs, there may be a case for departing from strict MSC pricing on 'second-best' grounds (Lipsey and Lancaster 1956). For example, it has been argued that, if motorists pay less than their MSCs on congested roads, bus and coach operators should charge their customers less than their MSC by a similar proportion. If this applied in Fig. 8.3, there would be a case for lowering price below $OX_1$ *by a specified amount.*

A second type of justification for departing from MSC pricing may be on equity grounds. In this case, it is argued that those with low incomes cannot adequately reflect the strength of their demand for certain transport services in the market and that they should be compensated for this by paying lower fares than strict MSC pricing would imply. Given the case for assisting low-income consumers, the issues to be considered are twofold:

1. Is the subsidization of transport services the best way of providing assistance? An alternative (such as redistributive direct taxation) may

be preferable, since it may be difficult, in practice, to confine the benefits of subsidized transport to low-income householders, who, in any case, may prefer to use the financial assistance provided to meet other, more urgent, requirements.

2. If transport subsidization is the most effective form of financial assistance, what should be its extent? As in the case of the 'second-best' arguments, it is necessary to justify the *extent* to which departures from MSC pricing are to take place.

The MSC-pricing principle (with reasoned adjustments on second-best or equity grounds), has not been widely used, in transport markets, for a variety of reasons.

1. Estimating the marginal costs of providing transport services can be complex, especially where transport facilities (e.g. railway track, roads, ports, etc.) are used by many services and it is difficult to allocate their costs between individual services. However, this is not the fundamental explanation, especially as some degree of 'cost averaging' is permissible.

2. In unregulated, imperfect markets, operators have been free to charge profit-maximizing (MC (marginal cost) = MR (marginal revenue)) prices.

3. In regulated markets, prices have often been controlled on the basis of quite different criteria, for example:
   - some rail freight charges used to be related to the value of the commodities being carried;
   - in both passenger and freight markets, standardized charging schemes (i.e. the same charge made for a given distance, irrespective of location or time) were commonplace. The consequence was that high-cost services were commonly cross-subsidized by low-cost services. This internal cross-subsidization was often regarded as part of a 'public-service obligation' to help in providing 'necessary', but unremunerative, services; and
   - sometimes, minimum charges were established to ensure the long-run viability of the operators and the continued provision of their services.

4. In the case of roads, the charges payable for their use (mainly vehicle-licence duties and fuel duties) have often been determined by general fiscal requirements rather than by the marginal social costs incurred by different categories of road users.

5. Externalities have not, in most cases, been internalized in operators' costs and charging schemes.

6. Grants and subsidies have been paid to transport producers and users without sufficient attention to their justification on efficiency or equity grounds.

In principle, transport investment schemes should be justified by the same efficiency and equity criteria as apply to transport pricing. All costs and benefits (including externalities) should be taken into account in a scheme's appraisal. Also, any costs or benefits in the more distant future should be given a sufficient weighting to reflect society's views on inter-generational equity. Similarly, if the benefits and costs affecting particular income groups or regions are considered to be of particular importance, this should be consciously reflected in the weighting they receive in the project's appraisal.

In practice, though formal social cost-benefit appraisal studies have been carried out on a number of occasions, they are not yet widely used in reaching decisions on new scheme proposals. The reasons for this are often similar to those for the limited use of MSC pricing:

- it is often difficult to place reliable monetary measures on all costs and benefits, especially externalities;
- financial criteria (such as the ability of the investment to be self-financing) may be used instead of the economic criteria described above;
- the availability of grants, rather than the justification upon which their payment is based, may have the stronger influence upon whether a scheme proceeds; and
- broad equity considerations may have a strong influence on scheme approval, but not necessarily within a systematic, well-justified project appraisal.

In summary, the economic logic relating to transport-pricing and investment appraisal which has been described above has not had a strong influence on transport policy. As a result, both market and regulatory failures have continued, and in some cases they have been intensified. However, there is some indication that this economic logic *may* influence the CTP to a greater degree in the future. For example, the Commission has suggested, in its report on the future development of the CTP, that:

- the strong shift to the use of roads by both passenger and freight transport may be partly due to the under-pricing of road use and proposes 'incorporating, into the transport prices, the infrastructure and external costs which are presently not taken into account' (CEC 1992: para. 97);
- internalizing external costs (especially environmental costs) will be necessary to ensure the development of a sustainable transport system:

  Such a policy will influence the demand for all modes by increasing the price of individual modes to the extent that they impose costs on society which are presently not paid for by the respective transport users. As the external costs associated with various modes differ significantly . . . the price increases will also vary across transport modes leading transport users to adjust their demand, in particular, to favour those forms of transport that impose fewer external costs or even to reduce or avoid unnecessary movements. (CEC 1992: para. 95)

### Marketing and Productive-Efficiency Objectives

Marketing and productive-efficiency objectives are concerned with ensuring that:

- the transport services provided, in terms of their combined attributes of price and quality, are those most preferred by consumers in the market (market efficiency); and
- services are produced at least resource cost (productive efficiency).

Other things being equal, improvements in market efficiency are reflected in increases in demand, and improvements in productive efficiency in a reduction in the marginal and average costs of production. An illustration of the benefits of a simultaneous improvement in the marketing and productive efficiency of a transport service is given in Fig. 8.4.

In the past there have been two contrasting views of how marketing and productive-efficiency improvements might be best achieved. One favoured the establishment of larger integrated transport undertakings through which it was hoped to achieve more technical harmonization between different parts of the transport system, greater economics of scale in production, and more effective marketing of transport services. The second favoured the removal of restrictions on the competitive process

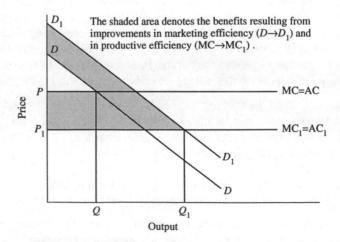

FIG. **8.4.** Benefits of a simultaneous improvement in marketing and productive efficiency

(sometimes loosely described as deregulation, but also including anti-discrimination measures), believing that increased consumer choice would raise marketing efficiency, and greater rivalry between operators would result in increased productive efficiency and cost reductions.

The former viewpoint tended to dominate transport policy thinking in most Member States until the 1980s. However, there has been a shift of opinion, starting in the late 1960s, towards the latter view. This has probably been most evident in the United Kingdom, which liberalized its own road-haulage industry in the late 1960s, its bus and coach services in the 1980s, and proposes to extend this approach to its railways in the mid-1990s. However, most other Member States have changed the orientation of their transport policies much later and to a more limited extent. Inevitably, therefore, changes in the CTP, which, until recently, required the unanimous support of all Member States, were very slow to occur.

The economic consequences of deregulation are fairly straightforward to predict if it is assumed that this will result in a perfectly competitive or perfectly contestable transport market (Baumol 1982). In these circumstances, the welfare gains from improvements in marketing and productive efficiency are unambiguous and are additional to those resulting from improved allocative efficiency, as described previously. However, deregulation is unlikely completely to realize either of the above market forms in practice, and, therefore, the market outcomes are less certain.

For example, following deregulation there may still be a small number of sellers within the market, new entry may still be difficult, and consumers may have imperfect knowledge of the services being supplied. In the more oligopolistic, rather than perfectly competitive, transport markets that result, anti-competitive practices may continue and mergers may further limit the effectiveness of the competitive process over the longer term. Marketing and productive-efficiency benefits may be reduced—as may allocative-efficiency benefits, if operators have commercial freedom to price and make investments as they choose. Without some form of intervention, broader equity objectives may also be unfulfilled. Evaluations of the effects of transport deregulation in the United Kingdom and the United States (which have the greatest experience of deregulation to date) tend to support the conclusion that these have been of a mixed nature (Kahn 1988; Gwilliam 1989; McGowan and Seabright 1989; Doganis 1991).

### Harmonization Measures

Harmonization measures have traditionally formed an important part of the CTP and therefore it is worth analysing how they relate to the efficiency and equity objectives described earlier. Their economic consequences can differ considerably as illustrated below.

- *Technical harmonization.* Member States may agree to common technical specifications for specific types of transport equipment because of the potential benefits from economies of scale in production which this can bring. However, if the market is not satisfied with the supply of standard equipment, there will be some loss of marketing efficiency. There may also be a case for technical harmonization to promote the inter-connection of transport systems and operation of rolling stock between Member States. However, if existing systems and rolling stock are not to be retired prematurely, this type of technical harmonization may only be gradually achieved over a considerable period of time.
- *Charge and tax harmonization.* There are good reasons to base transport charges and taxes on the same pricing principles (e.g. an agreed form of MSC pricing). However, this does not support the establishment of uniform levels of charges and taxes in all Member States, if their MSC levels vary. Similarly, there are good reasons for applying the same principles to the payment of transport grants and subsidies (e.g. in accordance with MSC pricing, with agreed adjustments for 'second-best' and equity reasons). Again, however, this does not imply that the same level of grants and subsidies must apply throughout the Member States.
- *Harmonization of conditions of employment.* To the extent that the EC accepts minimum conditions of employment for all workers, as one of its social objectives, this should be reflected in its CTP. However, the opportunity costs of labour do vary between Member States. To go beyond the basic social objective and harmonize actual conditions of employment of all transport workers could provide unjustified protection to the Member State transport industry with the highest per capita incomes and conditions of employment.

Thus, proposals for harmonization measures across Members States need to be carefully evaluated to check their consistency with efficiency and equity objectives.

In summary, economic analysis provides useful criteria and guidelines to evaluate both existing and new CTP measures. However, it cannot be expected to supply simple transport-policy solutions, because the context in which the CTP has to operate is itself inherently complex:

- the objectives it is expected to pursue are multiple—economic, social, and environmental—and, from time to time, will conflict;
- the Member States, whose support for new CTP measures is needed, have different sectional interests and their transport-policy philosophies may also conflict; and
- the CTP is not being designed for an idealized, perfectly competitive,

market system but for one in which market and regulatory failures are endemic.

## 8.5. ROAD FREIGHT AND PASSENGER TRANSPORT

### Road Freight Transport

Road transport is the major means of moving freight within the EC (see Fig. 8.1). The haulage industry contains a large number of operators, many of whom are relatively small scale. Some carry only materials and goods belonging to their own business ('own-account' operators), whilst others are commercial hauliers (carrying for 'hire and reward'). Many operate only at a local or, at most, national market level. Others engage in international transport between Member States and/or with non-EC countries.

At the time when the EC was first established, most Member States tightly regulated their road-haulage activities, for two reasons.

1. To reduce competition between road haulage and their national railway systems. The railways were already subject to considerable regulation and their financial performance had previously been undermined by the growth of the road-haulage industry.
2. To reduce competition within the road-haulage industry. The unregulated industry was characterized by a large number of sellers and relative ease of entry by new operators. It was felt that these conditions had led to excessive cost and rate cutting, neglect of road safety, high rates of bankruptcy, and undesirable instability within the industry.

The regulations which existed were of two main kinds: those intended to preserve the quality and safety of the services provided (qualitative controls), and those controlling their quantity and price (quantitative controls). The latter took somewhat different forms in different countries (Button 1984) but included:

● preventing own-account operators from obtaining 'hire-and-reward' work;
● restricting the geographic area within which a commercial operator might operate, or the types of goods he might carry;
● restrictions on the charges that might be levied;
● restrictions on the numbers of vehicles licensed to engage in hire and reward work; and
● restrictions on the transport of goods to or from other countries and on 'cabotage'—i.e. undertaking road-haulage business *within* other countries on the return journey.

Many of these practices were considered to conflict with the objectives of the CTP, as established in the Treaty of Rome, but, for many years, there was resistance to major changes. Slowly, attitudes began to alter. In 1968 the United Kingdom removed the quantitative restrictions on its own road-haulage industry and, when it entered the EC in 1973, it began to support similar changes within the Community. However, a number of other Member States (notably France, Germany, Italy, and, later, Spain) continued to resist radical changes. After the mid-1980s, for reasons that have been previously described, the pace of change accelerated, especially as 1992 approached. The potential benefits of greater productive efficiency, according to Emerson (CEC 1988), were considerable—he suggested that the removal of any remaining regulatory restrictions in the road-haulage industry could be equivalent to a 5 per cent reduction in road-haulage costs and charges. The main changes that have been made to road-haulage operations, through the CTP, are summarized below.

1. *Harmonization measures.* Typically, these EC measures have been justified on the grounds that they prevent distortions of competition between carriers from different Member States operating within the EC market. In many cases the measures have been relatively non-controversial, but in others the standardization they sought may have created rather than removed distortions in competition. The harmonization measures fall into three categories—technical, social, and fiscal—and most EC measures have fallen within the first two categories. The first relates to vehicle standards and to such matters as brakes, lighting, windscreens, noise, emissions, weights and measures, road-worthiness tests, etc. Of all of these measures, the most controversial (at least from a UK viewpoint) have related to the maximum size of lorries. Social harmonization measures have been of two kinds. The first relates to maximum driving-hours per day, installation of tachographs, training and certification of drivers, etc. The second relates to the requirements for obtaining EC operator licences, which have become increasingly important as the liberalization of the EC market has taken place (see below). Fiscal harmonization measures, for example, designed to reduce disparities between fuel taxes and licence duties for lorries, have been little evident until the 1990s. This issue is discussed more fully in the later section dealing with transport infrastructure investment and pricing.

2. *Controls over haulage charges.* When the EC was first formed, some Member States operated a fixed-freight-charges system (e.g. Germany) whilst others had a relatively free-market system (e.g. Netherlands). The EC initially responded to this by establishing a system of maximum and minimum rates for traffic between Member States. From 1977 onwards, pairs of Member States could continue

with this system or with a reference rate system in which the reference rate only had the status of a recommendation. From 1983 onwards, the system of recommended prices became the norm. Then, from 1 January 1990 (according to Council Regulation 4058/89), it was decided that all rates should be set by free negotiation between the parties to the haulage contract. Thus, all price regulation should have ceased, although it is not certain that this had occurred by the end of 1993.

3. *Licensing, quotas, and cabotage.* As previously explained, the EC inherited a situation in which road-haulage transport between Member States was regulated by a series of bilateral agreements, most Member States applied fairly restrictive arrangements in their own domestic markets, and opportunities for cabotage were limited.

In 1968 (under Regulation 1018/68) the Council agreed, initially on an experimental basis, to introduce a Community Quota System (CQS) which provided for a specified number of vehicle permits to be allocated between the Member States, which allowed their holders to carry goods within the EC without the need to negotiate bilateral agreements (Button 1984). This became a permanent system, and the number of CQS permits was progressively increased over the years, but, even by the early 1980s, they accounted for only around 5 per cent of total intra-EC road haulage (Whitelegg 1988). The slow rate of liberalizing the EC road-haulage market was severely criticized in the 1985 Judgement of the European Court of Justice (ECJ). Since then the process has been considerably accelerated.

- According to Regulation 1841/88, all quantitative restrictions on inter-Member State road-haulage operations, for hire and reward, were to be terminated by the end of 1992. This was later confirmed in Regulation 881/92. In the intervening period, the number of CQS permits issued was to be substantially increased each year. As from 1 January 1993, all Member State hauliers may engage in inter-Member State haulage activities provided they have an EC authorization. This is granted automatically provided certain 'quality' requirements (professional competence, financial probity, etc.) are met. There is, however, provision for a surveillance system (Regulation 3916/90), which would, in the event of chronic over-supply, enable the Commission to intervene.
- The removal of cabotage restrictions has been more recent. In 1990 a limited number of EC cabotage permits were made available. According to an agreement reached in 1993, cabotage will be fully liberalized within the EC by July 1998. This will, in effect, allow qualified EC carriers in one Member State to engage (whilst undertaking

inter-Member State haulage work) in temporary domestic road-haulage operations in another Member State.

Whilst the overall pace of policy change in the EC haulage market has accelerated, the Commission still has 'unfinished business', additional to the complete liberalization of cabotage. This includes extending the opportunities for 'own-account' operators to engage in 'hire-and-reward' operations between and within Member States, and facilitating road-haulage operations with non-EC countries. Crucially, the differences between Member States in road-user charging systems still need to be addressed.

### Road Passenger Transport

The CTP has paid much less attention to road passenger transport operations than it has to road haulage. This is partly because a high proportion of bus and coach travel is of a local or regional nature, which, except in border areas, does not pass from one Member State to another.

The bus and coach market has experienced considerable competition from increased car-ownership during the lifetime of the EC. Typically, it has been highly regulated, particularly for local services (Tyson 1991), although in the United Kingdom there has been a considerable degree of deregulation through the Transport Acts of 1980 and 1985 (Gwilliam 1989). Again, typically, local bus undertakings have been expected to meet a range of 'public-service' obligations, rather than simply act

TABLE 8.2. *Revenue/cost ratios for urban passenger transport systems in Member States, various years (%)*

| Member State | Revenue/cost ratios |
| --- | --- |
| Denmark | 55–6 |
| Belgium | 30–40 |
| France | 53 |
| Germany | 54 |
| Greece | 40–50 |
| Irish Republic | 80–95 |
| Italy | 24–8 |
| Netherlands | 28–40 |
| Portugal | 67 |
| Spain | 70–90 |
| UK | n.a. |

*Note*: n.a = not available.
*Source*: Andersen (1992).

commercially. As a consequence they often require subsidization on a considerable scale (see Table 8.2).

The inter-Member State market is of a somewhat different character, since it contains a significant proportion of tourist and scheduled long-distance coach services. Here, also, few significant policy changes have been implemented until very recently. Since the mid-1980s the main thrust of policy has been to liberalize the coach market, though it was never regulated to the degree existing in local transport markets.

Two main regulations were approved during 1992. Regulation 684/92, which came into operation in June 1992, removed the requirement for authorizations for certain inter-Member State coach services (principally, package-holiday tourist services). Authorizations were still required for other types of services, but the grounds on which these could be refused were curtailed. Additionally, Regulation 2454/92, which came into operation in January 1993, made provision for a limited form of cabotage to be practised by international coach operators. The scope of its application will be extended in 1996, when, subject to a review of the remaining types of services, it may become generally applicable. These two measures increase the freedom to operate between Member States and, on a temporary basis, within the domestic market of another Member State, but they stop well short of full, immediate liberalization.

## 8.6. RAIL AND INLAND WATERWAY TRANSPORT

### Rail Transport

As Figs. 8.1 and 8.2 show, railways account for a significant but declining share of EC freight and passenger transport markets. The rail systems are predominantly in public ownership and, traditionally, have been expected to shoulder a wide range of 'public-service' obligations which have been a major source of their unprofitability. As Table 8.3 illustrates, all Member State rail systems make operating financial losses (though to varying degrees) and all are dependent on substantial state aids.

One of the principal objectives of the CTP, since its inception, has been to enable the railway systems to compete more effectively with other modes of transport, particularly in the freight market. With this in mind, efforts have been made to:

- eliminate distortions of competition which arose from state intervention in railway operations; and
- achieve better transparency of state financial contributions to railway undertakings (Erdmenger 1983). An intermediate aim was to segregate the public-service element from the commercial-service element

TABLE 8.3. *Operating revenue/cost ratios for Member State railway systems 1983 (%)*

| Member State | Revenue/cost ratios |
|---|---|
| Belgium | 25.6 |
| Denmark | 48.5 |
| France | 52.0 |
| Germany | 55.9 |
| Greece | 39.4 |
| Irish Republic | 64.5 |
| Italy | 20.5 |
| Luxemburg | 21.3 |
| Netherlands | 49.0 |
| Portugal | 41.9 |
| Spain | 56.9 |
| UK | 64.5 |

*Source*: Whitelegg (1988).

and to reflect this in the system of railway accounting and state subsidization that was adopted. A series of Regulations was passed to this end in the late 1960s and early 1970s (1191/69, 1192/69, 1107/ 70). This was reinforced by a Council Decision in 1975 that railway management should become more independent of state governments and develop more effective business and financial planning.

Despite these measures, progress in their practical implementation has been slow, because of resistance from the Member States. The situation at the beginning of the 1990s was described in the following terms:

The practical application of these principles has left something to be desired. The public service obligations, with the characteristics specific to each individual country, have been changed very little or not at all and the public service charges are, in most countries, still not identifiably shown in the accounts of the companies; and the system of state aids which eliminates the financial imbalances of the railways is still not entirely clear and has yet to be resolved. (DG for Research 1991: 14)

However, in 1989 the Commission issued a new set of proposals relating to the future development of rail services within the single market (CEC 1990). These addressed a number of long-standing issues and contained a mixture of familiar and new suggestions whose purpose was to strengthen the management of the railway systems by increasing the degree of their independence from the state. *Inter alia*, it proposed:

- separating, into two distinct units, the management of the rail infrastructure (e.g. track and signalling systems) from the management of the rail services operating on that infrastructure;

- operating railway services according to commercial criteria with the state becoming 'a mere customer of railway companies [which] would have to pay for the services required in order to meet public needs, in a proper, open and fair manner' (DG for Research 1991: 15);
- free access to the use of all rail systems within the EC by international groupings operating rail services between Member States; and
- responsibility for the provision of the rail infrastructure remaining with the Member State, which has a choice between retaining it in the public sector or privatizing its management and investment. However, whichever is adopted, there should be a clear separation of the accounts and management between the provision of infrastructure and rail-service operations.

These proposals were largely agreed and then incorporated into Directive 91/440/EEC, which required Member States to take the necessary measures to implement these by January 1993. The progress made in achieving this, in each of the Member States, has yet to be assessed, but delays in its implementation are believed to have occurred. So far as the United Kingdom is concerned, a number of the measures proposed in the Directive (e.g. separation of responsibilities for infrastructure and opera-tion, increasing access to service operation, separation of commercial and public-service provision and financing) have been reflected in the government's privatization proposals for British Rail (Cm. 2012 (1992)).

Directive 91/440 is, in many respects, a framework directive and, as the Commission has noted, it may be necessary to establish detailed criteria relating to such matters as access to and charging for the use of the infrastructure, the setting-up of railway operating undertakings, the deter-minants of financial aids to recompense public-service obligations, etc. The directive provides for a review of its application by January 1995. Very considerable progress would need to be achieved in a very short time if satisfactory *practical* compliance is to be achieved by that date; previous experience suggests this is unlikely.

Within the framework of an EC investment programme in transport infrastructures, the Council of Ministers agreed, in 1990, to provide some financial assistance for the development of a European high-speed rail network (Regulation 3359/90). Provision is also made for measures to develop a combined transport network (i.e. to facilitate trans-shipment of freight between transport modes, such as road to rail). Additionally, as part of the EC's regional policy (see Chapter 7), assistance is provided for investments in rail and other transport infrastructures in the poorer (mainly southern) Member States. Transport infrastructure investment and pricing is reviewed in Section 8.8.

## Inland Waterways

As previously explained, inland waterways are of limited significance as a means of freight transport in such countries as the United Kingdom but are of considerable importance in the Netherlands, Belgium, and Germany. For these Member States in particular, the Rhine is the backbone of the European inland navigation system. However, the Rhine is also recognized as an international river regime in which certain non-EC members also have navigation rights. This has both complicated and delayed policy actions by the EC relating to Community inland waterways as a whole.

Over at least the past twenty-five years, the share of inland waterways in the EC market has declined and Member State carriers have experienced a prolonged period of overcapacity. By the late 1980s it was urgently necessary for the CTP to address this issue as well as the creation of a single market by 1992.

A programme for the reorganization of inland waterway transport was approved in 1989 (Regulations 1101/89 and 1102/89). It provided for each Member State to establish a dismantling fund to reduce total carrying capacity which was to be mainly financed by vessel owners but with some assistance from EC funds. The programme also provided for some restrictions to be imposed on bringing new vessels into the market. Its practical consequences have still to be evaluated, but the potential conflict of these restrictions with the objective of liberalizing access to the single market is evident.

A number of preparatory measures for the single market have also been approved, notably relating to the elimination of border controls. However, studies have identified a number of other 'single-market' issues that need to be addressed. These include restrictions on captains sailing the waterways of certain Member States because their qualifications were not recognized, certain market-sharing arrangements which restrict competition, the operation of mandatary scales of charges for certain national waterway carriers, and the existence of some restrictions on cabotage (DG for Research 1991). Regulation 3921/91, approved in December 1991, provided for the removal of cabotage restrictions on inland waterways from the beginning of 1993, but certain exemptions apply in France and Germany until the beginning of 1995.

## 8.7. MARITIME AND AIR TRANSPORT

### Maritime Transport

Around 95 per cent of the tonnage of Community trade with non-EC states and some 30 per cent of intra-Community traffic is carried by sea (Kreis

1992). Community-based shippers have experienced increasing international competition over the last thirty or more years from non-EC fleets which have benefited from lower costs partly resulting from their non-EC registration and financial assistance from their own governments. The consequences for EC-based shipping operations have been overcapacity in the industry, a pronounced decline in the shipping tonnage registered under EC Member State flags, as EC shippers switched to 'off-shore' registration, and pressures on Member States to continue and/or extend state aids to shipping and to continue certain restrictive measures to protect 'home' fleets (Brooks and Button 1992). Certain of these pressures potentially conflict with the objective of liberalizing maritime shipping operations within the single market.

As previously explained, maritime shipping was not included in the provisions relating to the CTP within the Treaty of Rome. This, combined with the lesser interest of the original Community members in intra-Community sea transport, helps to explain the limited progress in developing a Community shipping policy until the mid-1970s. However, action was precipitated in 1974 by the finding of the European Court of Justice (ECJ) that the UN Code of Conduct for Liner Conferences, which the Member States were prepared to accept, was in violation of the competition rules of the Treaty of Rome. This was subsequently resolved by granting a block exemption for liner conferences from compliance with these rules provided they met with certain conditions—but the potential conflict between traditional shipping policies (of which restrictive agreements between operators within liner conferences is one example) and the EC's competition policies was apparent.

It was not until 1986 that the Council agreed a package of measures, comprising four regulations (Regulations 4055/86–4058/86), which established the legal foundations of an EC maritime policy. In brief, the package:

- establishes the principle of freedom to provide maritime services, without discrimination, for intra-EC traffic and traffic between Member States and third countries (but not for domestic traffic within a Member State);
- provides for the application of the Treaty of Rome's competition rules to liner shipping, but with a conditional exemption for liner cargo conferences, as described above; and
- provides for measures to be taken to deal with unfair pricing and other practices by non-EC shipowners and third countries (Erdmenger and Stasinopoulos 1988).

However, the flight from registering ships under Member State flags continued, and the Commission became increasingly concerned that differences in fiscal and employment conditions between different flags of registration were distorting competitive conditions within the EC. This led it to propose the establishment of an EC shipping register (EUROS) which aimed to offer some economic attractions (see below) to encourage EC-based fleets to register but was also intended to harmonize registration conditions within the EC. However, successive forms of this proposal had not (by end-1993) been found acceptable (Brooks and Button 1992).

Another continuing area of concern has been the role of subsidies, tax exemptions, and other forms of fiscal assistance within the maritime market. State aids of different kinds are provided by virtually all Member States as well as by third countries (Brooks and Button 1992). The EC's response has been to encourage a more consistent approach between Member States by issuing guidelines which list seven categories of aid which are permissible under the Treaty and the detailed criteria to be applied in their calculation. The seven categories cover: aids to reduce manning levels, reimbursement of costs of repatriating seafarers, assistance with training costs, special tax treatment of shipping earnings, operating aids, investment aids, and aids through public authority holdings (CEC 1989). The maximum amount of aid is to be defined by reference to the cost difference with the cheapest EC flag and is more likely to be acceptable where ships are registered with EUROS. The extent to which these guidelines are now being applied and their practical consequences have not yet been evaluated.

A long-standing problem has been the continuation of restrictions on cabotage in maritime shipping within the EC. These restrictions were not removed by the First Package of regulations in 1986, and, though their partial removal was proposed in 1989, this was not formally approved until 1992. According to Regulation 3577/92, cabotage rights may be exercised by all EC shipowners registered with EUROS. This was due to come into operation for coastal trade at the beginning of 1993 (or as soon as EUROS is approved by the Council of Ministers) but inter-island and mainland–island cabotage will operate only from 1999 (2004 in the case of Greece).

Another continuing issue has been whether agreements between shipping consortia should comply with EC competition law or, like liner conference agreements, should have a block exemption. The issue is a complex one, both because of the variety of activities in which a consortia may engage but also because they may yield some economic benefits in the process of reducing competition between their members. These benefits are discussed in Kreis (1992). In February 1992 Regulation 479/92 was finally approved; this permits, subject to certain safeguards, the exclusion of particular categories of agreements by consortia from the general prohibition of cartels contained in the Treaty.

In summary, some significant steps have been taken towards the establishment of a single, liberalized market in maritime transport but there are a number of ways in which competition is still restricted and where state aids continue to have a distorting influence on market conditions.

### Air Transport

Air transport accounts for a small but increasing share of intra-EC traffic. Until the mid-1980s scheduled air-transport services were tightly regulated, although there was greater freedom in the provision of charter-flight services (Van de Voorde 1992). Tight regulation originally arose as a consequence of nations being granted sovereignty over their own airspace at the Chicago conference of 1944. The exercise of this sovereignty led to a form of regulation comprising the following elements:

- Each state had its own flag-carrying airline, which was usually in public ownership. It was often expected to serve some non-commercial objectives, as part of its general remit, and was accustomed to receive state aids to assist in this.
- States made bilateral agreements with each other about landing rights and flight routes between their two countries. Typically, scheduled services were shared on a 50 : 50 basis between the two flag carriers. In this way, capacity was controlled and arrangements for revenue-sharing made.
- Negotiations about fares were held within the framework of IATA (International Air Transport Association). However, government approval was needed once these fares had been negotiated (Button 1992).

Though this regulatory system had certain attractions to Member State governments, it was also seen to have some undesirable features (Van de Voorde 1992), for example:

- fare levels were likely to be higher than in a more competitive market environment;
- cost levels were likely to be higher (because of lower productive efficiency and higher 'rental' payments to factors of production) than would otherwise have been the case; and
- consumer choice was more limited, and the absence of price competition led to an over-stimulus of quality of service competition (e.g. 'in-flight' refreshments).

These matters received little attention from the EC until the ECJ ruling in 1974 that air and maritime transport within the EC was subject to the Treaty of Rome's general rules. Even then, little substantive action was taken until the mid-1980s. This was triggered by a number of developments, including:

- the recommendations of the Cockfield Report (CEC 1985) relating to the measures necessary to complete the single market and, more specifically, proposing changes to the system for setting and approving tariffs, and limiting the rights of governments to restrict capacity and access to the market;
- the ECJ ruling in the *Nouvelles Frontières* case (1986), which stimulated investigation of the application of the Treaty's competition rules to the aviation sector; and
- growing international interest in the deregulation of air transport, in part stimulated by deregulation experience in the United States (McGowan and Seabright 1989; Doganis 1991).

This led to the first Liberalization Package for air transport, approved in December 1987.

*First Package* (1987). The Package consisted of two Council Decisions (601/87 and 602/87) and two regulations which came into force on 1 January 1988 (Vincent and Stasinopoulos 1990). It applied only to scheduled services between Member States and contained some block exemptions, for certain traffic categories, until 1991. However, it did provide for:

- greater fares flexibility, by making provision for discount fares;
- greater capacity flexibility by allowing limited variations in the 50 : 50 traffic sharing rule; and
- some easing of market access.

Its overall impact was fairly limited because some of these changes had already been incorporated into earlier bilateral agreements. Its main significance, according to Stasinopoulos (1992), was that it set up a mechanism through which gradual liberalization could be realized.

*Second Package* (1990). A further package of measures (Regulations 82/91–84/91) was agreed in June 1990 (Stasinopoulos 1992). This provided for more extensive fares-discounting, greater variations in the 50 : 50 rule, and greater market access, including some limited provision for cabotage. Block exemptions were to continue to January 1993, but it was envisaged that full liberalization would be achieved by that date.

*Third Package* (1992). This package of measures comprised three regulations (2407/92–2409/92), covering scheduled, non-scheduled, and cargo services, and came into force on 1 January 1993 (CEC 1993; International Aviation Directorate 1993). It provides that:

- Any carrier satisfying safety, financial fitness, and EC nationality tests is entitled to an EC operator's licence.
- Virtually all intra-EC air routes are open to recognized EC operators. Cabotage restrictions are further reduced, with full cabotage rights

being established by April 1997 (but with a delay of ten years in the case of the Greek Islands and the Azores).
- Airlines are free to determine their own scheduled passenger fares, subject to certain safeguards. All restrictions on charter fares are removed and cargo rates continue to be unregulated.

Regulations have been approved and brought into force relating to competition rules, block exemptions, and allocation of slots at EC airports.

The extent to which the EC's aviation market has been liberalized since 1987 has been substantial, the pace of change almost certainly being greater than in any other sector of the transport market. It is too early to assess what the practical consequences of this will be. However, any evaluation should take into account the following:

- certain exemptions still apply and their effects (e.g. in the allocation of landing/take-off slots) are difficult to gauge;
- cabotage restrictions are not due to be fully removed for a number of years;
- state aids continue, and, though there is provision to update the guidelines for these, their market significance could increase in the more competitive environment which has been created; and
- as experience elsewhere has shown (Kahn 1988; Doganis 1991), not all of the outcomes of a deregulated air-transport market may be desirable. In particular, the effects of mergers between airline operators, which may be stimulated by deregulation, are uncertain (Van de Voorde 1992).

## 8.8. TRANSPORT INFRASTRUCTURE

Each of the forms of transport operation which has been reviewed makes use of a different form of transport infrastructure—the road system, railway track and signalling system, waterways, ports, and/or airports. Transport policy has to consider in each case:

- how to make best use of *existing* infrastructure facilities, and the role of user charges in achieving this (*infrastructure pricing*); and
- how best to develop *future* infrastructure facilities (*infrastructure investment*).

The problems which exist in these two areas, and the attempts to address these through EC-level transport policy, are reviewed below.

### Infrastructure Pricing

The charging systems which exist for the use of transport infrastructures vary considerably. Users pay tolls on some roads in certain Member States (e.g. France and Italy) but, more generally, pay road-user taxes (e.g. annual vehicle licence and fuel duties). Airlines pay landing charges for the use of airports and shippers pay berthing charges for port facilities. Railway undertakings typically own the rail track and do not pay separately for its use (as mentioned in Section 8.6, this may change in the future).

The principles upon which charges schemes have been based are also highly variable. In some cases, commercial criteria ('what the market will bear') apply; in others, the objective is cost recovery (in some cases, after deduction of any state aids received); in other cases (e.g. certain road-user tax systems), the level of charges depends upon the general fiscal requirements of the government.

From at least the mid-1960s, the Commission has been concerned about the distortions to competition which could result from different approaches to infrastructure pricing in the Member States (Whitelegg 1988). In 1971 it proposed the introduction of a system of infrastructure pricing for all inland transport modes, based on the MSCs of using the infrastructure. However, it was not implemented and only limited progress has been made in achieving this subsequently, as illustrated below in the case of road-user pricing.

The first task, in applying the MSC pricing principle to road use, is to estimate the marginal social costs incurred by the main categories of road user. The United Kingdom probably has the greatest experience in attempting to calculate these costs, which are published annually (see e.g. DoT 1993*a*). However, these calculations do not cover all cost items (notably they exclude road congestion and environmental costs), and the methods used to calculate certain cost items that are included have been criticized (DoT 1993*b*: annex A). Fowkes, Nash, and Tweddle (1992) suggest that UK road cost estimates might need to be increased, on average, by 50 per cent to cover the excluded cost items.

Fowkes, Nash, and Tweddle (1992) also compare the annual road-track costs of a 'reference' vehicle (38 tonnes gross weight averaging 74,000 kilometres per year), as estimated by the Department of Transport in the mid-1980s, with the total road-user taxes (from licence and fuel duties) that would have been paid in a number of different European countries (see Table 8.4). Assuming the road-track costs for the reference vehicle were broadly similar in all of these countries, it would seem that, in all of them, heavy lorries were charged less than their MSCs, and in certain countries (e.g. Italy, Netherlands) charges were substantially below these MSCs. The inclusion of tolls revenue in the calculations would not substantially alter the conclusion.

The movement to establish the SEM by the end of 1992 provided a new impetus to harmonize excise and other duties relating to vehicle use. Two Council Directives (92/81 and 92/82) provided for the adoption, by the beginning of 1993, of common minimum rates of excise duty on petrol and diesel oil in all Member States. However, they also permit a number of

TABLE **8.4.** *Highway revenue/cost ratios for selected EC countries, mid-1980s*

| Member State | Fuel and annual licence duty revenues as % of highway costs (excluding externalities) |
|---|---|
| Denmark | 41 |
| Germany | 96 |
| France | 60 |
| Italy | 27 |
| Netherlands | 38 |
| UK | 119 |

*Source*: Fowkes, Nash, and Tweddle (1992).

TABLE **8.5.** *Variations in road-user charges between Member States 1993*

| Type of charge | Lowest charge | Highest charge |
|---|---|---|
| Four-star petrol duty (pence per litre) | 32 (Luxemburg) | 52 (Netherlands) |
| Diesel duty (pence per litre) | 20 (Luxemburg) | 34 (Italy) |
| Annual car licence duty or equivalent (£) | 15 (Spain) | 270 (Denmark) |
| Annual heavy goods vehicle (38t.) licence duty (£) | 318 (Greece) | 3,900 (Germany) |

*Source*: DoT 1993*b*.

important delays and exemptions in their application. Table 8.5 shows that, even by 1993, there were still considerable differences in the levels of the major road-user charges, particularly in the case of annual vehicle licence duties. Subsequently, proposals were submitted to establish common minimum rates for annual vehicle licence duties/taxes, and to regulate tolls, but these would only operate from 1994 and some delays and/or exemptions would be permitted beyond this year.

An additional problem, in the case of inter-Member State road transport, is that the revenue from road-user charges does not necessarily accrue to the Member State which incurs the road-track costs. Various devices have been proposed to satisfy the so-called 'territoriality' principle, including the transfer of payments between Member States to settle any net imbalances (Crowley 1992). More recently, it has been proposed that Member States should be encouraged to establish common systems of user charges, including provisions for balancing payments of road-user charge revenues between them.

For its part, the Commission has indicated the importance it attaches to the development of an EC framework for charging users according to the infrastructure costs they incur. However, because of the complexities involved, it proposes this should be done in phases—first developing a satisfactory costing system for allocating capital and maintenance costs to main user groups, then applying this to heavy goods vehicles, and later devising a satisfactory system for reflecting externalities in charges.

## Infrastructure Investment

Community-level investment in transport infrastructure did not become a CTP issue until the late 1970s (Whitelegg 1988). Once it did, the extent to which EC-level institutions should become involved in transport investment planning, financing, and decision-making become a subject of continuing debate.

The main reasons advanced for Community-level involvement have been:

- the absence of adequate interconnections between national transport networks because of missing links, bottlenecks, and technical incompatibilities between systems; and
- unbalanced economic development within the EC, because of previous under-investment in transport infrastructure in the (mainly) peripheral regions.

The stated goal of EC action is 'the integration of the Community's transport system through the completion and combination of its networks, taking particular account of the needs of its more geographically isolated regions' (CEC 1993: para. 140). The first type of deficiency has been mainly addressed through the CTP itself and is examined immediately below; the second has been mainly tackled through the EC's regional policy (see Chapter 7) and is briefly discussed at the end of this section.

The first deficiency is essentially due to a 'market-failure' problem. The economic case for Community-level intervention is that it may be able to assist by taking account of cross-border spillovers of costs and benefits and through access to the geographically, broader-based information needed for infrastructure planning and investment appraisal. Whether this necessitates Community-level involvement in decision-making and the financing of new transport infrastructures, or engaging in a more limited role in facilitating transport planning by the Member States themselves, remains an unresolved issue.

In 1979 the Commission outlined its overall transport infrastructure policy, stating that 'the CTP will not achieve the objectives defined for it in the Treaty and play its part in the economy as a whole unless it relates more and more to transport infrastructure' (CEC 1979). It defined the types of investment that it considered necessary and later provided lists of projects that it believed met these criteria. However, the Council of Ministers agreed to allocate only relatively small amounts of investment finance for this purpose. In 1986 the Commission published its medium-term transport infrastructure policy, which restated its earlier objectives but added support for 'the general Community objective of completing the internal market and strengthening its economic and social cohesion' (Crowley 1992). It also proposed support for the construction of links in a European high-speed rail network (see Section 8.6 for further details). However, the Council was reluctant to accept this policy statement or the five-year plan identifying infrastructure programmes that might be financed by the EC. As a result, prior to 1990, financial support for such measures was largely provided, on a case-by-case basis, by the EP (DG for Research 1991).

Finally, in 1990, the Council approved more modest proposals for financing certain transport infrastructure schemes between 1990 and 1992 (Regulation 3359/90). Similar kinds of provisions were made for 1993 and 1994 but are not envisaged to continue. The financial assistance provided (*c*. Ecu 180 million per annum) is still at a relatively low level for this type of investment in the E12.

The Treaty on European Union (TEU), ratified in 1993, contains new provisions relating to the establishment and development of trans-European transport networks, and, according to the Commission, they 'provide a new basis for Community action, define more clearly the objectives and limits of Community involvement, and introduce a new decision-making process as well as a new approach to financing' (CEC 1992: para. 139). Following ratification, the Commission is expected to prepare indicative guidelines 'covering the objectives, priorities and broad lines of the measures envisaged in the sphere of European transport networks'. Once these guidelines are approved by the Council of Ministers, their application will be a Member State responsibility. The EC will make a financial contribution, but it will not be the major source of finance. 'The Community contribution is to provide the financial leverage that will ensure that infrastructure programmes funded primarily at national or regional level will nevertheless integrate into the larger framework and priorities which the Community as a whole has decided that it needs' (CEC 1993: para. 143).

Additional to the above arrangements, within the framework of the CTP, there has been much more substantial Community-level financial assistance for investments in transport infrastructure through the Structural Funds (especially the ERDF). According to Commission estimates, since 1975 approximately Ecu 16,000 million have been invested in transport infrastructures through the ERDF. Additionally, the European Investment Bank (EIB) loaned approximately Ecu 14,000 million for financing transport infrastructures between 1982 and 1991, whilst the ECSC has contributed a further Ecu 1,200 approximately since 1987 (CEC 1992: para. 137). Financial support for these types of transport infrastructure investments are expected to grow, post-Maastricht, through the Cohesion and Regional Development Funds.

## 8.9. OVERALL EVALUATION

The progress made in implementing a CTP within the EC was very limited during the first thirty years of its existence. The measures that were introduced largely related to particular aspects of harmonization and reduction in discriminatory practices in the provision of transport services between Member States. Community-level investments in transport infra-structures were mainly undertaken as part of regional, rather than transport, policy. Little progress was made in realizing the kinds of efficiency and equity objectives specified in Section 8.4.

Since the mid-1980s the pace of change in policy formation and implementation has accelerated and its focus has changed, placing greater emphasis on liberalization than harmonization (CEC 1993). This was stimulated by the ECJ judgment in 1985, which criticized the lack of progress with the CTP, and by the political drive to establish a single European market by the beginning of 1993.

The principal measures which have been brought into force since the mid-1980s, in each of the main transport sectors, have been reviewed in the preceding sections of this chapter. Given the relatively short time period over which they have been introduced, the aggregate level of Community-level activity has been substantial—especially in such sectors as air transport and road haulage. However, in evaluating their likely effects, it is important to note that:

- a significant proportion of these measures has been brought into force only since 1990;
- in a number of cases, they provide for exemptions and/or delayed application until later in the decade;
- their practical effects depend to a large degree on the speed and extent of their implementation by the individual Member States. In the past, examples of delayed and/or incomplete compliance have been quite common; and
- not all of the Community-level measures that were envisaged have yet been agreed—there is still some 'unfinished business' (CEC 1993).

The Emerson Report concluded that the economic benefits of transport liberalization could be substantial. For example, it indicated that the removal of regulatory restrictions in the road-haulage and air-transport markets could cause road-haulage and air-transport costs and prices within the single market to fall by 5 and 10 per cent respectively (CEC 1988). It also suggested that there could be significant transport-cost savings through the simplification and/or removal of customs procedures. However, it is far too early to assess the actual scale of the economic effects of the measures that have been implemented—it will be at least five years before these can be properly evaluated.

There are, however, a number of issues which remain unresolved and need to be addressed in any future development of the CTP:

- The liberalization of the single market will not establish a perfectly competitive, or perfectly contestable, market. Therefore, it will be necessary to address those types of transport problems which can occur in liberalized imperfect markets, such as arise from increased merger activity (e.g. among airlines) or the neglect of environmental externalities.
- Public-service obligations (i.e. commitments to non-commercial objectives, such as certain equity objectives) will remain. Cost-effective means of achieving these within liberalized markets will have to be devised, and existing systems of state aid for transport services will need to be restructured in the light of these.
- Given the differences in transport arrangements between Member States, some conflicts of interest will continue. More effective ways of resolving these will need to be found whilst, at the same time, respecting the subsidiarity principle.
- So far, the main focus of the CTP has been on inter-Member State transport policy. In the future it will be necessary to clarify its relationship to the regulatory systems for intra (domestic) Member State transport and for transport with non-EC countries.
- In the light of each of the above, the role of EC transport policy in planning and financing investments in the EC transport infrastructure will also have to be more clearly defined.

In summary, the increase in EC transport-policy activities, since the mid-1980s, has not dealt with all of the deficiencies that previously existed. A number of fairly complex problems remain. Careful evaluation of the economic consequences of those measures that have been introduced, and of the deficiencies that remain, should be used to guide the future development of the CTP.

# REFERENCES

Anderson, B. (1992), *Transport Research*, 26A: 179–91, quoted in K. Button, *Transport, the Environment and Economic Policy* (Aldershot: Edward Elgar, 1993).

Baumol, W. J. (1982), 'Contestable Markets: An Uprising in the Theory of Industry Structure', *American Economic Review*, 72/1: 1–15.

Brooks, M. R., and Button, K. J. (1992), 'Shipping within the Framework of a Single European Market', *Transport Reviews*, 12/3: 237–51.

Button, K. J. (1984), *Road Haulage Licensing and EC Transport Policy* (Aldershot: Gower).

—— (1992), 'The Liberalisation of Transport Services', in D. Swann (ed.), *The Single European Market and Beyond* (London: Routledge), 146–61.

—— and Pitfield, D. (1991) (eds.), *Transport De-regulation: An International Movement* (London: MacMillan).

Clark, J. M. (1940), 'Towards a Concept of Workable Competition', *American Economic Review*, 30: 241–56.

CEC (1979): Commission of the European Communities, *A Transport Network for Europe: Outline of a Policy* (Brussels: CEC).

—— (1985), *Completing the Internal Market*, COM (85) 310 final (Brussels: CEC).

—— (1988), 'The Economics of 1992: An Assessment of the Potential Economical Effects of Completing the Internal Market of the European Community' (the Emerson Report), *European Economy*, 35 (Mar.).

—— (1989), *Financial and Fiscal Measures Concerning Shipping Operations with Ships Registered in the Community*, SEC (89) 921 (Brussels: CEC).

—— (1990), *Communication on a Community Railway Policy*, COM (89) 564 (Brussels: CEC).

—— (1991), *Council Directive of 29 July 1991 on the Development of the Community's Railways* (91/440/EEC) *Official Journal of the European Communities*, L237/25 (24 Aug.).

—— (1992), *The Future Development of the Common Transport Policy* (Brussels: CEC).

—— (1993), *A Common Market for Services: Current Status 1 January 1993* (Brussels: CEC).

Council of the European Communities (1990), Council Regulation 3359/90/EEC for an *Action Programme in the Field of Transport Infrastructure with a view to the Completion of an Integrated Transport Market in 1992* (Brussels).

Cm 2012 (1992), *New Opportunities for the Railways: The Privatisation of British Rail* (London: HMSO).

Crowley, J. A. (1992), 'Inland Transport in the European Community following 1992', *Antitrust Bulletin*, 37/1: 453–80.

Despicht, N. (1969), *The Transport Policy of the European Communities* (European Series, No. 12 (PEP); London: Chatham House).

DG for Research (1991): Directorate-General for Research, *The Judgement of the Court of Justice of the European Communities in Case 13/83 and the Development of the Common Transport Policy* (Regional Policy and Transport Series 21; Luxemburg: CEC).

Doganis, R. (1991), *Flying Off Course: The Economics of International Airlines* (London: Harper Collins Academic).

DoT (1991): Department of Transport, *International Comparisons of Transport Statistics 1970–88* (London: HMSO).

—— (1993*a*), 'The Allocation of Road Track Costs', *Statistical Bulletin*, 3/31 (London: DoT).

—— (1993*b*), *Paying for Better Motorways* (London: HMSO).

Erdmenger, J. (1983), *The European Community Transport Policy—Towards a Common Transport Policy* (Aldershot: Gower).

—— and Stasinopoulos, D. (1988), 'The Shipping Policy of the European Community', *Journal of Transport Economics and Policy*, 22/3: 355–60.

Fowkes, A. S., Nash, C. A., and Tweddle, G. (1992), 'Harmonizing Heavy Goods Vehicle Taxes in Europe: A British View', *Transport Reviews*, 12/3:199–217.

Gwilliam, K. M. (1989), 'Setting the Market Free—Deregulation of the Bus Industry', *Journal of Transport Economics and Policy*, 23/1: 29–43.

International Aviation Directorate (1993), *EC Aviation Liberalisation: Information Pack* (London: International Aviation Directorate, Department of Transport).

Kahn, A. E. (1988), 'Surprises of Airline Deregulation, *American Economic Review*, Papers and Proceedings, 78: 316–22.

Kreis, H. W. R. (1992), 'EC Competition Law and Maritime Transport', *Antitrust Bulletin*, 37/1 (summer), 481–505.

Laidler, D., and Estrin, S. (1989), *An Introduction to Microeconomics*, 3rd edn. (Deddington: Philip Allan).

Lee, N. (1992), 'Transport Policy', in S. Bulmer, S. George, and A. Scott (eds.), *The United Kingdom and EC Membership Evaluated* (London: Pinter), 83–8.

Lipsey, R., and Lancaster, K. (1956), 'The General Theory of Second Best', *Review of Economic Studies*, 24: 11–32.

McGowan, F., and Seabright, P. (1989), 'Deregulating European Airlines', *Economic Policy*, 9 Oct., 283–344.

Ross, J. (forthcoming), 'European High Speed Rail: Expensive Showpiece or Catalyst for Integration?', *Journal of Common Market Studies*.

Stasinopoulos, D. (1992), 'The Second Aviation Package of the European Community', *Journal of Transport Economics and Policy*, 26/1: 83–7.

Tyson, W. J. (1991), 'Analysis of the Organisation of Local Public Transport in the European Community', in International Union of Public Transport, *Public Service and Competition*, (Brussels: UITP).

Van de Voorde, E. E. (1992), 'European Air Transport after 1992: De-regulation or Re-regulation?' *Antitrust Bulletin*, 37/1: 507–28.

Vincent, D., and Stasinopoulos, D. (1990), 'The Aviation Policy of the European Community', *Journal of Transport Economics and Policy*, 24/1: 95–100.

Whitelegg, J. (1988), *Transport Policy in the EEC* (London: Routledge).

# 9

# Environmental Policy

## 9.1. INTRODUCTION

Environmental problems have traditionally been viewed as unwanted side-effects of economic activities which should be controlled by a range of regulatory measures. A less widely held view is that environmental problems stem from market failures within economies—and, therefore, market-based measures are needed to resolve them. Though the former approach has dominated EC and Member State environmental policies so far, the balance of view is changing.

The next section of this chapter surveys the historical development of EC environmental policy which has enlarged in scope and changed its emphasis over the years—from a reactive to a more anticipatory approach and from reliance on control and command (regulatory) instruments towards greater use of economic (market-based) measures. The following three sections (9.3–9.5) examine the essentially economic nature of environmental problems within the EC and the logical case for using economic instruments to help in dealing with them. They also identify the weaknesses inherent in both regulatory and economic instruments, as practical tools of environmental policy, and the need to use different types of instruments in a complementary manner. Section 9.6 contains a review and evaluation of the practical use made of economic instruments within the European Community (EC) and some other member countries of the Organization for Economic Co-operation and Development (OECD), which further demonstrates their particular strengths and limitations. Section 9.7 reviews a proposal for an EC energy/carbon tax to help in reducing the risks of global warming. Section 9.8 analyses the attempts that have been made to assess, in economic terms, the benefits and costs of environmental policies and their likely consequential effects on Member States within the EC. The chapter concludes, in Section 9.9, with a review of possible future developments in EC environmental policy.

## 9.2. EVOLUTION OF EC ENVIRONMENTAL POLICY

The Treaty of Rome (1957), which led to the establishment of the EC, contains no reference to environmental protection. Indeed, it is only through the enactment of the Single European Act (SEA) (1987) that the EC explicitly adopted environmental objectives, namely:

(i)   to preserve, protect and improve the quality of the environment
(ii)  to contribute towards protecting human health
(iii) to ensure a prudent and rational utilization of natural resources.

(Article 130R)

More recently, the Treaty on European Union (TEU) (1992) extended the EC's environmental-policy objectives to include the goals of 'sustainable and non-inflationary growth respecting the environment' (Article 2) and promoting measures to help resolve global environmental problems (Article 130R).

Despite the absence of an explicit legal basis, the Heads of the Member States, meeting shortly after the UN Stockholm Conference on the Environment in 1972, invited the European Commission to prepare the first Environmental Action Programme. To date, the Commission has prepared five Action Programmes for approval by the Council of Ministers (1973–6, 1977–81, 1982–6, 1987–92, 1993–2000 (with provision for a review in 1995)).

These Programmes contain the environmental-policy intentions of the Commission and the Council of Ministers. To varying degrees, and often after a considerable period of negotiation with Member State governments, these result in Council Decisions in the form of regulations, directives, recommendations, and non-binding opinions. In turn, after a further interval and to varying degrees, these are transposed into Member States' laws and practice. The delayed and incomplete implementation of Community-level actions is, in effect, one of the important mechanisms by which Community-level and individual Member State interests are reconciled. Such mechanisms need to be taken into consideration when assessing the actual costs and benefits to individual Member States which result from Community-level actions.

Since the preparation of the first Environmental Action Programme, the EC had approved, by the end of 1992, over 175 legally binding acts as well as a considerable number of non-binding measures relating to the protection of the environment (CEC 1992*a*). These related to:

● water quality: the quality of drinking water, surface waters in rivers and the sea, bathing waters, ground waters, and discharges of pollutants into water;

- air quality: the concentration of pollutants in the atmosphere and emissions from stationary and mobile (transport) sources of pollution;
- wastes: the collection, treatment, and disposal of solid and semi-solid wastes;
- chemicals and other dangerous substances: the testing, marketing, and use of dangerous substances, and the regulation of major accident hazards and of chlorofluorocarbons (CFCs);
- noise: maximum noise levels from stationary and mobile sources;
- wildlife and countryside protection: the protection of wildlife, their habitats, and environmentally sensitive areas, and the regulation of trade in endangered species; and
- the 'polluter-pays' principle: originally formulated as an EC Recommendation in 1975 (and based on an earlier OECD Recommendation of 1972). It establishes the general principle, subject to certain possible exemptions, that polluters should pay for the full costs of their pollution.

These actions have taken place within a policy framework which has changed in emphasis over time, as the EC's approach to environmental policy has itself developed. In the early 1970s its policies primarily emphasized the need for corrective measures to 'clean up' specific pollution problems through the use of regulatory instruments. By contrast, its latest action programme, whilst not abandoning the more traditional types of corrective measures, gives a new emphasis to:

- anticipatory measures (i.e. planning and related actions designed to prevent new environmental problems being created, e.g. environmental assessment of new development projects; testing, before use, of new chemicals; etc.);
- multi-media measures (which recognize that pollution problems in one environmental medium cannot be satisfactorily resolved, in many cases, without considering possible repercussions on other environmental media);
- integrative measures (the integration of environmental-protection measures into the policies and programmes of development for the main economic sectors);
- sustainable development measures (the complementary use of resource-conservation and pollution-control measures to promote sustainable development both within the EC and in other parts of the world); and
- market-based measures (i.e. financial/economic instruments to encourage environmental costs being fully taken into account in all decisions relating to the allocation and use of resources).

The most recent Action Programme, which covers the period 1992–2000, emphasizes the long-term objective of sustainable development. This is summarily defined, in the 1987 Report of the World Commission on Environment and Development, as 'development which meets the needs of the present without comprising the ability of future generations to meet their own needs'. According to the European Commission, 'it entails preserving the overall balance and value of the natural capital stock, redefinition of short, medium and long-term cost/benefit evaluation criteria and instruments to reflect the real socio-economic effects and values of consumption and conservation, and the equitable distribution and use of resources between nations and regions over the world' (CEC 1992*a*: 18). The Action Programme states that the main environmental policy issues facing the EC—of climate change, acidification and air pollution, depletion of natural resources and biodiversity, pollution of water resources, deterioration of the urban environment and coastal zones—are themselves symptoms of more fundamental resource-management problems. To address these, the Commission proposes to broaden the range of policy instruments which are applied. In particular, it recommends the greater use of *market-based* instruments 'designed to sensitise both producers and consumers towards responsible use of natural resources [and] avoidance of pollution and waste by internalising of external costs' and notes 'it will be necessary to ensure that all Community funding operations and, in particular, those involving the Structural Funds, will be as sensitive as possible to environmental considerations' (CEC 1992*a*: 8).

Thus, the intention is to integrate environmental policy considerations into the future development and operation of those sectors (notably industry, energy, transport, agriculture, and tourism) which are considered to be the main contributors to current environmental problems, and, at EC level, into those of its own policies and programmes (relating to agriculture and fisheries, energy and transport, regional development and overseas aid, etc.) which, in the past, may have been environmentally damaging on a considerable scale.

## 9.3. LINKAGES BETWEEN ENVIRONMENTAL AND ECONOMIC SYSTEMS

Environmental problems are essentially economic in nature. Therefore, not surprisingly, economic-policy instruments have a role to play in their resolution. The purpose of this and the following two sections is to explore the economic nature of environmental problems and the theoretical justification for using economic instruments, as well as regulatory instruments, to deal with these.

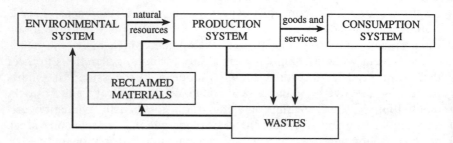

**Fig. 9.1.** Linkages between environmental and economic systems

Environmental and economic systems are inextricably linked (see Fig. 9.1). Production entails the *abstraction* of natural resources (water, minerals, forest products, etc.) which, depending upon the rate of abstraction, renewability, etc., may result in a resource-conservation problem. Production and consumption involve the *transformation* and *use* of materials which create wastes (gaseous, aqueous, solid, etc.) which, when returned to the environmental system, may result in an environmental pollution problem.

Other things being equal (notably resource/output and waste/output ratios remaining constant), economic growth results in faster rates of natural-resource depletion and higher levels of waste disposal. On these assumptions, and given limits to the stock of natural resources and the capacity of the environment to assimilate increased wastes, continuing economic growth eventually ceases to be sustainable. In other words, the environmental system is no longer able to sustain the levels and quality of production and consumption which have previously been achieved within the economic system.

This type of reasoning underlines the approach of the 'limits-to-growth' school which was presented in the late 1960s and, in a modified form, more recently (Meadows *et al.* 1972; Meadows, Meadows, and Randers 1992). It was used to suggest that there was an inherent conflict between economic growth and the maintenance of environmental quality—hence the arguments in favouring of 'limiting growth'.

However, in market systems, these simplifying assumptions rarely hold, and the resulting relationships between economic growth and environmental quality are more complex than the above analysis implies (Beckerman 1974; Pearce, Markandya, and Barbier 1989). Under certain circumstances, especially where markets work efficiently, a number of the above effects may be reduced, delayed, or not occur at all. For example:

- The increased scarcity of particular natural resources will lead to increases in their prices. This may encourage greater economy in their use, higher rates of reclamation and re-use, and the development of substitute materials.

- Increased difficulties in finding suitable waste-disposal sites are associated with increased disposal costs. This provides a financial incentive to reduce wastes at source, and to increase waste reclamation and recycling.
- Products which use the scarcest natural resources or cause the greatest waste-disposal problems become relatively more expensive, causing production and consumption patterns to alter in favour of more 'environmentally friendly' activities.

However, in practice, the conditions necessary for markets to work efficiently may not apply. For example:

- The prices charged for the use of natural resources should fully reflect their social opportunity costs. Yet, in practice, prices may be substantially below these levels because of price regulation (e.g. for the use of water), neglect of long-term social opportunity costs (e.g. costs of forest clearance to future generations), or the absence of markets (e.g. for nature reserves or natural landscapes).
- The costs of environmental pollution should be fully borne by those responsible (i.e. the producers or consumers of the goods and services concerned). Yet, in practice, the 'polluter-pays' principle may not operate, either because the law does not so provide or because of its unsatisfactory implementation.
- Governmental interventions for other policy purposes, in the absence of satisfactory resource and pollution charging, may intensify environmental problems. For example, fertilizer subsidies originally designed to increase agricultural production have encouraged excessive fertilizer use leading to increased water-pollution problems. Similarly, policies designed to encourage the provision of 'cheap' energy and transport have contributed to increased consumption and adverse environmental effects in both sectors.

Thus, the underpricing of natural resources and the failure to internalize environmental externalities reduce the capacity to resolve resource conservation and environmental problems—and certain forms of market intervention inadvertently increase these problems.

## 9.4. ROLE OF REGULATORY INSTRUMENTS IN ENVIRONMENTAL POLICY

The traditional approach to problems of over-use of natural resources and of excessive pollution has been to curb these excesses by regulation. These regulations take a variety of forms which include:

- prohibiting the abstraction, use, or disposal of particular substances, products, processes, etc., which are considered to be environmentally damaging (e.g. hunting wildlife, use of prescribed chemicals, discharge of particular radio-active substances);
- setting of maximum limits for the abstraction of particular natural resources (e.g. water abstraction, minerals extraction, fish catches);
- setting of maximum limits (i.e. emission standards) for discharges of pollutants to air, water, or land;
- prescribing the technology which may be used for particular processes of production or the materials which may be used in particular processes (e.g. cement manufacturing processes, sulphur content of fuels used in certain industrial boilers); and
- establishing ambient quality standards (e.g. minimum water quality standards to be achieved in a river receiving polluting discharges).

The achievements of this traditional approach have been considerable, as comparisons between the environmental quality in countries within the EC which have effective environmental regulations, and those in parts of Central and Eastern Europe which do not, amply demonstrate.

However, the regulatory approach is not without its problems, for example:

- The criteria by which environmental standards have been set are often unclear or are insufficiently justified in terms of their benefits and costs.
- Standards may not be enforced: problems of non-compliance are pervasive in some countries.
- Uniform emission standards are not the most cost-effective methods of achieving environmental quality standards.
- At best, regulations provide only limited incentives to cost-reducing innovations in pollution-control technology.

More fundamentally, the regulatory approach tends to be directed at the *symptoms* of the environmental problem (i.e. observed pollution and resource-use levels) rather than at its underlying socio-economic *causes* (i.e. failure of those engaging in environmentally damaging activities to take the externalities for which they are responsible into account in their own decision-making). Given this, exclusive reliance on regulations to control a specific pollution or conservation problem is likely to result in its eventual re-emergence in another form or location rather than provide a comprehensive solution.

## 9.5. ROLE OF ECONOMIC INSTRUMENTS IN ENVIRONMENTAL POLICY

Economic instruments aim to achieve environmental objectives by using financial incentives and disincentives to encourage more 'environmentally friendly' behaviour by producers and consumers. This section contains a theoretical analysis of economic instruments, whilst the two following sections examine their use in practice.

The environmental objectives which economic instruments serve should be consistent with the broader socio-economic objectives of society. These are often characterized by economists as *efficiency* and *equity* objectives, where

- the efficiency objective is to promote the efficient allocation and use of resources within society; and
- the equity objective is to promote an equitable distribution of goods and services both between different sectors of society and between different generations of society (intra- and inter-generational equity, respectively).

In order to use these two objectives, it is necessary to have an operational definition of such terms as '*efficient* allocation of resource' and '*equitable* distribution of goods and services'. In the former case, this has typically been based on the use of market prices as expressions of value and the application of the Pareto criterion or potential Pareto criterion. Thus, an efficient allocation of resources exists where it is not possible to make one member of society better off without making another worse off or, in the case of the potential Pareto criterion, to do so after allowance for those made better off compensating those made worse off.

Within a market system, efficiency is to be achieved through the price mechanism, with governments intervening to correct for imperfections in the market system and/or in the operations of the price mechanism. Central to this approach is the notion that prices for environmental services or the use of natural resources should reflect their full social opportunity costs. For example, in the case of abstracting a mineral from land or sea, these should cover:

- the marginal private opportunity cost of its abstraction;
- the marginal external cost of the environmental damage that its abstraction causes; and
- the future net benefit of the consumption forgone by its earlier exhaustion (if it is a non-renewable resource).

This implies a fairly broad definition of the 'polluter-pays' principle contained in the 1975 EC Recommendation. As will be seen later, narrower interpretations of this principle are often adopted in practice.

The objective of an 'equitable distribution of goods and services' does not have a widely accepted operational definition. Typically, it is not interpreted to imply strict equality in the distribution of income and wealth. Frequently it is expressed in a weaker and broader form, such that policy instruments which increase income and wealth inequalities tend to be regarded as undesirable. The *extent* to which any distributional changes are desirable or undesirable is usually considered to be a matter of value judgement, on which economists can provide little professional guidance.

### Bargaining, Based on Environmental Rights

If the legal rights to use all natural resources (including air, water, land, etc.) are well defined, then the efficient allocation of those resources should be automatically achieved (*without* government intervention) *in a perfectly competitive market system*. This is illustrated, in simple form, in Figs. 9.2–9.5 below.

Fig. 9.2 illustrates the case where industrialists, producing a given level of output, negotiate with fishermen (who own the water rights) to accept the discharge of their waste-water into the river. The payments acceptable to the fishermen depend upon the damage which the waste-water will cause to their fishing activities; the higher the level of waste-water treatment by the industrialist prior to its disposal, the more the damage will fall (this being reflected in the shape of the marginal reduction in damage (MRD) function in Fig. 9.2). Thus profit-maximizing industrialists will be prepared, on a voluntary basis, to treat their waste-water to a higher level so long as the reduction in damage to fishing activities (which is reflected in a reduction in compensation payable to fishermen) exceeds the increase in their waste-water treatment costs (shown in the marginal pollution treatment cost (MPTC) function in Fig. 9.2). Thus, the outcome of the negotiations between industrialists and fishermen is that the industrialists

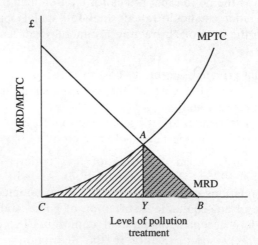

**FIG. 9.2.** Optimal level of pollution control (product output level given)

*Note*: It is assumed that fishermen own the water rights.

are permitted to discharge into the river provided the waste-water is treated to a level of *CY* and that compensation is paid by them equal to the area *YAB*.

At this level, the combined total pollution damage and pollution control costs are at a minimum, which is consistent with the efficiency objective. In this situation, also, the 'polluter pays' in two senses: industrialists are paying all of their pollution-treatment costs (area *YAC* in Fig. 9.2) and are paying full compensation for any remaining pollution damage (*YAB*)

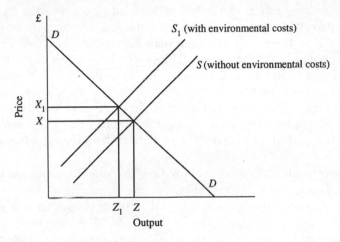

**FIG. 9.3.** Product–market equilibrium (with and without environmental costs being internalized)

*Note*: It is assumed that fishermen own the water rights.

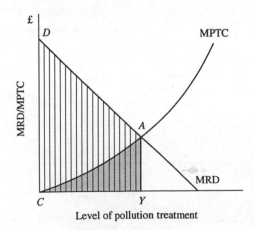

**FIG. 9.4.** Optimal level of pollution control (product output level given)

*Note*: It is assumed that industrialists own the water rights.

which is caused. In effect, what is happening is that the environmental costs are being fully internalized within the costing and decision-making systems of the industrialists. This, as shown in Fig. 9.3, will tend also to reduce total output of their (polluting) products and raise their prices.

Fig. 9.4 illustrates the same case as Fig. 9.2, except that it is assumed that the water rights are held by the industrialists. As a consequence, the fishermen have to make payments to the industrialists to persuade them to treat their waste-waters before discharging them to the river. The maximum payments that fishermen are prepared to pay are based on the marginal damage to them that would be avoided by waste-water treatment. For their part, the industrialists will treat the waste-waters so long as the extra payments (based on the marginal damage avoided) exceed their marginal pollution-treatment costs. The outcome, in terms of the mutually agreed level of treatment, is the same (i.e. $CY$) as in Fig. 9.2. However, the distributional consequences are different (reflecting the different distribution of property rights). In this latter case, the polluter is 'bribed' to pollute less than he would have done. Also, the output effects are different— polluters produce more output than in the 'no-bargaining' situation (see Fig. 9.5).

The above analysis is used to show how markets might respond, in the absence of government intervention, to the presence of environmental pollution. However, its practical value is limited, given that real markets are often imperfect and legal rights to the use of the environment are often inadequately or unsatisfactorily (from an equity viewpoint) defined.

One possible type of policy response to this situation would be to define

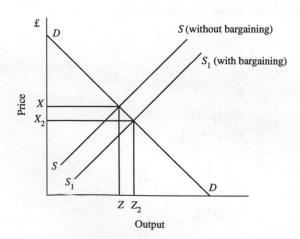

**Fig. 9.5.** Product–market equilibrium (with and without bargaining over pollution treatment)

*Note*: It is assumed that industrialists own the water rights.

legal rights to the environment more clearly and, from an equity viewpoint, more satisfactorily and to improve the functioning of the relevant markets so that the bargaining process works more efficiently. In this context, various measures might be considered, for example:

- clearer specification of rights relating to natural resources, especially common property natural resources;
- transfer of certain rights (e.g. to discharge into air and water) from private to public ownership;
- improvements to the judicial system, including provisions relating to strict liability for environmental damage (i.e. onus of proof placed on the polluter), legal aid to finance environmental protection cases, and reductions in the transactions costs and uncertainties of outcome within the judicial system;
- improvements to the knowledge about pollution damage held by those involved in the bargaining process; and
- institutional strengthening to support the development of markets for environmental resources. The development of emission permit trading systems is one example of this kind of policy initiative and is discussed in more detail later in the chapter.

However, reliance on these types of market instruments is still likely to be limited where:

- there are many sources of a pollutant (e.g. sulphur oxides), many receptors are affected by it, and the legal rights to the use of the environment are in multiple ownership. In these circumstances it will always be difficult, in both a technical and a legal sense, to establish liability for damage to particular receptors and to conduct negotiations without high transactions costs and great uncertainties about outcomes;
- the pollutant is more localized and there are few sources and affected parties involved. In such cases, because of the small numbers involved, the market may be oligopolistic and the efficient solution may not emerge (see the later review of emission trading experience in Section 9.6 for further details).

Therefore, other types of economic instrument, involving some form of government intervention, are likely to be needed. These are examined below.

## Charging Systems

Suppose that legal rights to the environment are vested in a public authority which is empowered to charge for their use. Assume further that these charges should reflect the efficiency and equity objectives identified earlier.

So far as efficiency is concerned, this implies that users should be charged the marginal social costs (MSC) incurred from their use of the environment (it is assumed, for expository purposes, that there are no 'second-best' or other market distortions which justify departures, on efficiency grounds, from the MSC pricing rule (see Laidler and Estrin (1989) for further details). This implies, in the case of a waste discharge, that the user should be charged according to the estimated damage his discharge causes to the environment in addition to covering any costs incurred by the public authority in providing disposal services for him.

So far as the first component of the charge is concerned, this will vary according to the degree of pre-treatment by the user and the resulting reduction in damage caused. Faced by a schedule of charges, reflecting different levels of environmental damage, the profit-maximizing user will choose the level of pre-treatment where the marginal reduction in the charges bill (which reflects the marginal reduction in pollution damage) is just equal to the marginal cost of pre-treatment.

This is, seemingly, the same response as in the bargaining solution in Fig. 9.2. At first sight, this charging system appears to offer the same efficiency benefits as the bargaining solution, without the difficulties high-lighted above. However, there are some differences between the two approaches and this type of charging system also has its own drawbacks.

1. Unlike in the bargaining case shown in Fig. 9.2, those damaged by the residual pollution do not necessarily receive compensation and therefore its distributional consequences also need to be considered.
2. The public authority has to assess the likely damage, at each level of treatment, and express this in monetary terms in order to construct its charges schedule. To do this, in a way that is generally acceptable to all of the parties involved, is a very difficult task. In many cases, scientific knowledge on the environmental effects of pollutants is incomplete or subject to considerable uncertainty. Additionally, many types of environmental resources (e.g. air, sea water, nature reserves, archaeological sites) have no market price, or, if there is a price, it is fixed at a level unrelated to its social value. Therefore, other methods have to be used in an attempt to derive suitable market values. A number of such methods exist, which are briefly reviewed in a later section of this chapter (see Section 9.8), but there is a continuing debate over their validity, and examples of their practical application, although increasing, are still relatively few.

In the absence of sufficiently reliable monetary measures of damage on which to base charges schedules which will 'steer' polluters to apply optimal (i.e. efficient) levels of pollution control, charges systems may still be used to serve a more modest objective. This is to curtail, in a cost-effective manner, the use of, or damage to, a particular environmental

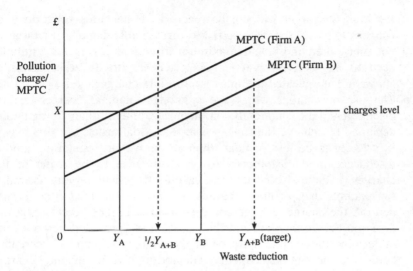

FIG. 9.6. Use of charges to achieve a waste-reduction target

resource, to a target level which is predetermined by the environmental control authority. This is illustrated in Fig. 9.6, where a charge of $OX$ per unit of waste is imposed on each of two dischargers, A and B, as a means of achieving a combined target waste reduction of $OY_{A+B}$ waste units. Each finds it profitable to reduce the wastes it discharges so long as the savings in charges ($OX$ per unit) are greater than its MPTC. Since Firm B is more cost efficient in waste reduction than Firm A, it finds it profitable to abate its wastes to a greater extent and therefore it makes a greater contribution to the overall waste-reduction target.

This type of charging system has certain advantages over a regulatory system which, for example, may achieve its overall waste reduction target by requiring all dischargers to achieve the same waste reduction (e.g. $\frac{1}{2}OY_{A+B}$ in Fig. 9.6):

- the target is achieved at the lowest total treatment cost (note that total cost minimization is achieved where the MPTC for the last unit of waste reduction achieved is the same for all dischargers); and
- it provides a stronger financial incentive to all dischargers to reduce their MPTCs (thereby further reducing the total resource cost of achieving any waste target) in the future.

However, even this more modest charging system has its problems.

- If the public authority does not have accurate information on the individual MPTCs, it cannot correctly identify the level of charge needed to achieve the overall target waste reduction. If, because of this, the charge level is set too high, the target will be exceeded; if it is too low, the target will not be reached. If the latter situation is of concern (e.g. where there is a risk of irreversible damage if a target is not met), then individual maximum discharge levels may initially need to be set until practical experience with different levels of charging has revealed the most appropriate charge level.

- The use of charges will place a greater financial cost on certain dischargers (and, indirectly on their customers) than a regulation designed to achieve the same waste-reduction target. For this reason it is likely to be less popular, than an equivalent regulation, among dischargers and customers. However, the use to be made of the charges revenue also needs to be taken into consideration. Assuming for example that pollution charges systems are intended to be fiscally neutral, the charge revenue could be used to reduce other charges or taxes on the dischargers and their customers (provided this does not undermine the original purpose of the charges scheme) or to reduce taxes elsewhere in the economy. The notion of environmental charges providing a 'double dividend'—improving the quality of the environment and enabling other tax rates to be reduced—can help to reduce their unpopularity in some quarters.

### Marketable Permits

An alternative approach to achieve a target level of total discharges is to introduce a system of marketable permits. In this case, the public authority provides a fixed quantity of permits, each of which contains an authorization to discharge a given quantity of wastes. The owner of such a permit (or permits) may freely sell it to others. Thus, in principle, a market for discharge permits is established. A number of benefits are claimed for such a system, for example:

- The total number of permits issued is controlled by the authorities, who can then ensure that any target for total authorized discharges is respected.
- The authorities do not need to know the marginal damage or MPTC functions of the individual dischargers.
- The establishment of an effective market for permits would lead to those dischargers who value the permits most highly (because, for example, of their high MPTCs) acquiring them by offering the highest prices. Those with low MPTCs would find it more profitable to sell some of their permits and reduce their own discharges through higher levels of treatment. In this way, the total costs incurred in reaching the target for total discharges are minimized.
- If permits have a market price, this provides a financial incentive to all dischargers to reduce their MPTCs in order to lower their future

permit requirements. This should stimulate further cost savings in pollution control over the longer term.

However, there are a number of concerns about marketable permit systems:

- There is concern over how the initial allocation of permits by the authorities should be undertaken. Some favour the use of an auction, others support their allocation, free of charge, to the existing holders of waste-disposal authorizations. Clearly, the distributional consequences of the two approaches are quite different.
- The transfer of permits between dischargers at different locations within a market can result in serious environmental problems where environmental impacts are very location-specific.
- Markets work well only if there are a sufficient number of buyers and sellers and there is reasonable freedom of market entry and exit. In most, small area, permit markets there will be very few buyers and sellers. Also, those who possess permits may prefer to retain them (either to hold back opportunities for expansion by their rivals or because they are uncertain whether they could buy them back should they need them again in the future) rather than sell them, even when they are surplus to their current requirements.

A fuller treatment of these, and related issues, is to be found in OECD (1992c).

## Grants and Subsidies

Grants and subsidies are often provided in support of pollution-control activities, despite concerns that this might conflict with the 'polluter-pays' principle. Therefore, it is necessary to clarify the circumstances in which different forms of financial assistance for environmental protection may be acceptable, on efficiency or equity grounds, and where they are not.

Figs. 9.4 and 9.5, earlier in the chapter, establish that the optimal level of pollution can, in principle, be achieved by those who are damaged by pollution-making payments to the polluters to induce them to treat or abate their wastes to the desired level. Alternatively, this could be achieved by a public authority offering payments to polluters up to the value of the marginal damage reduction they are prepared to achieve. Or, such payments to polluters may be fixed at a level which provides sufficient incentive to achieve the target reduction in wastes set by the authorities.

Thus, in addition to economic instruments which involve payments *by* polluters to achieve environmental goals in an efficient or cost-effective manner, one can envisage instruments which involve payments *to* polluters to achieve the same objectives. However, the effects of the two types of economic investments are not identical in all respects, notably:

- their *output* effects are different, charges being output-contracting and grants/subsidies output-expanding (compare Figs. 9.4 and 9.6);
- their *distributional* effects are different, charges being imposed upon polluters and grants/subsidies being received by them.

Other reasons have also been given to justify grants or subsidies, such as:

- where developments give rise to external environmental benefits—for example, where a river-bank improvement scheme leads to environmental benefits which are not reflected in financial benefits to the developer. The maximum grant justified in this case would correspond to the value placed on the external environmental benefit; and
- transitional assistance to polluters where environmental quality standards are raised substantially and at relatively short notice. This may be justified, as a temporary measure, where the short-term adjustment costs are high; however, there is a danger that such financial assistance schemes will continue where the original justification no longer applies.

### *Summary*

Environmental policy-makers within the EC and its Member States have a potentially wide range of instruments—regulatory and economic— available to them. However, there is a need for careful selection and specification of the instruments to be used. The types of criteria by which this might be carried out are listed below and are closely modelled on those described in Opschoor and Vans (1989):

- *economic efficiency*: is the instrument likely to assist in achieving 'optimal' environmental quality (i.e. minimize the sum of environmental damage and treatment costs)?
- *environmental effectiveness*: is the instrument likely to be effective in achieving and preserving the prescribed level of environmental quality?
- *cost effectiveness*: is the instrument likely to assist in achieving the required environmental quality at least resource cost, both at present and in the future?
- *equity*: is the distributional effect of the instrument likely to be broadly acceptable?
- *administrative feasibility*: is the use of the instrument feasible in terms of its information requirements, administrative demands, and political acceptability?
- *institutional compatibility*: is the instrument compatible with the approach to environmental policy and the existing administrative framework in the countries in which it would operate?

It is evident from the above review that all of the types of instruments that have been examined—regulatory and economic—are likely to have some deficiencies when measured against one or more of these criteria. However, the strengths and weaknesses of each do not always coincide. Regulatory instruments tend to perform relatively better in terms of their administrative feasibility, institutional compatibility, and, in certain cases, their environmental effectiveness. In contrast, economic instruments have greater potential in terms of cost effectiveness and, in certain cases, economic efficiency. Because of this it has been argued that the use of 'hybrid' systems, which combine regulatory and economic instruments, is preferable to realize the principal benefits of each. Finally, in the case of all instruments, their merits and limitations vary according to how well or poorly they are designed and used in practice. This becomes more evident in the review of the uses made of economic instruments in the next section.

## 9.6. USE OF ECONOMIC INSTRUMENTS IN PRACTICE

A number of surveys of the use of economic instruments in developed economies, including certain EC countries, have been carried out by OECD and others (Opschoor and Vans 1989; Huppes *et al*. 1992; OECD 1992*a*, 1992*b*, 1993). The following review is based upon these studies, supplemented by more recent OECD data. It mainly highlights their use within EC countries but also includes data relating to other OECD countries for comparative purposes. The next section (9.7) examines one specific economic instrument proposal—for an energy-carbon tax to reduce carbon dioxide ($CO_2$) emissions.

The economic instruments in use may be classified as follows:

- *charges and taxes*: these include effluent charges, user charges, product charges and taxes, and administrative charges. They may be used to reduce consumption of specific natural resources, to discourage polluting activities, and/or to provide financial assistance to achieve reductions in pollution by other technical means;
- *grants and subsidies*: these include grants, soft loans, and tax allowances which may be used to encourage less polluting, or more 'environmentally friendly', forms of behaviour;
- *deposit-refund schemes*: for example, on beverage containers, to encourage re-use and/or more environmentally acceptable means of their disposal;
- *market-creation arrangements*: for example, emission permit trading arrangements, to encourage more efficient and cost-effective use of emission permits; and

- *financial enforcement incentives*: for example, non-compliance fees and performance bonds, which provide a financial inducement to comply with existing environmental regulations.

A survey of OECD member countries, undertaken in 1988, identified 153 economic instruments in use, of which eighty-one took the form of charges and taxes, forty-one consisted of some type of subsidy, and thirty-one fell within the other three categories mentioned above (Opschoor and Vans 1989). More recent OECD data suggest that the number of economic instruments known to be in use may have increased by 50 per cent over the following five years. Additional economic instruments are known to have been approved or submitted for approval in Austria, Belgium, Canada, Denmark, Finland, France, Germany, Italy, Norway, and Sweden (OECD 1991). There is also growing interest in promoting the use of environmental charges and taxes as part of a more comprehensive process of tax reform—for example, linking the revenues raised to reductions in other taxes or to the funding of particular expenditures (OECD 1993).

However, the increasingly large numbers of economic instruments in use reveal little about the comprehensiveness of their coverage or of the extent to which they conform with the efficiency and equity principles described in the previous section. Some indication of this is provided below, where each main type of economic instrument is discussed in greater detail.

### Charges

Table 9.1 summarizes the types of charges in force in 1988, with some updating from more recent sources. It shows that each of the five types of charges which are listed are in use but their extent is highly variable.

#### Effluent charges
These are charges related to the size and/or composition of the polluting discharge to the environment. They are applied only to a limited extent to atmospheric emissions within EC countries but are more commonly used in the case of aqueous waste discharges (e.g. in France, Germany, Italy, and the Netherlands). Noise charges are common in many EC countries but are mainly confined to aircraft landing charges. Overall, effluent charges are set at relatively low levels and their incentive effect in reducing discharges is weak. Also, the motivation of these charges may vary; for example, water effluent charges in France are more closely linked to revenue-raising to finance investment in pollution control facilities than directly internalizing externalities.

TABLE **9.1.** *Types of charges in use in selected EC and OECD countries (1988 updated)*

| Country | Types of charges | | | | User | Product | Admini-strative | Tax diffe-rentiation |
|---|---|---|---|---|---|---|---|---|
| | Effluent | | | | | | | |
| | Air | Water | Waste | Noise | | | | |
| Canada | | | | | X | X | | X |
| USA | | | X | | X | X | X | |
| Australia | X | X | | | X | | X | |
| Japan | X | | | X | | | | |
| Austria | | X | | | X | | | X |
| Belgium | X | X | | | X | | X | X |
| Denmark | | X | | | X | X | X | X |
| Finland | | | | | X | X | X | X |
| France | X | X | | X | X | X | | |
| Germany | X | (X) | X | | X | X | X | (X) |
| Greece | X | | | | X | | X | X |
| Italy | X | | | | X | X | | |
| Netherlands | X | X | X | | X | X | X | X |
| Norway | | | | | X | X | X | X |
| Portugal | X | | | | | | X | |
| Spain | | X | | | X | | X | |
| Sweden | X | | | | X | X | X | X |
| Switzerland | (X) | | X | | X | (X) | | X |
| Turkey | | X | | | | | | |
| UK | X | | X | | X | | X | X |

*Note*: X = applied, (X) = under consideration.
*Source*: OECD (1991).

*User charges*

These are charges for the use of natural resources (e.g. water) or for the use of waste treatment and disposal facilities. According to the efficiency principle, these should cover at least the private opportunity cost of the resource or facility provided and, if not covered by an effluent or similar charge, any external costs incurred.

Water use and effluent disposal charges (in some cases combined within a single charge) are commonly applied within the EC and elsewhere. However, in a number of cases the charges appear to be below the marginal social costs incurred. User charges are also frequently applied for the collection and treatment of municipal solid wastes but are often fixed charges based on covering the overall accounting costs of the service.

*Product charges and taxes*
There are charges imposed on products that are considered polluting in their manufacturing or consuming phase. They include charges on fuels (reflecting the presence of pollutants such as sulphur or carbon) and on non-returnable containers. So far, these charges are confined to a limited range of products and, with the possible exception of the Netherlands, the level of the charges has been too small to have a significant environmental effect. A variation on the product charge is the use of differential rates in taxes to favour the purchase of 'environmentally friendly' products—notably 'clean' cars and unleaded petrol (International Energy Agency 1993).

*Administrative charges*
These are charges used in a number of EC countries, principally in the form of licence and registration fees. Their intended purpose is often to help in financing the administrative costs of pollution regulation activities. However, they are often too low for this purpose and this results either in their implicit subsidization or in under-funding leading to ineffective administration of the pollution regulations.

### Grants and Subsidies

According to OECD surveys, the majority of member countries for which data are available provide some financial assistance for their pollution control activities. In certain cases, these payments are linked to charges schemes where revenues are then used to help finance investment in pollution control equipment. In other cases, subsidies appear to be hidden in 'below-cost' charges for environmental services or take the form of grants, soft loans, or special tax allowances.

For a number of years, OECD has operated a procedure for the 'Notification of Financial Assistance Systems for Pollution Prevention and Control'. Taken at face value, the amounts of financial assistance provided do not suggest significant departures from the 'polluter-pays' principle, especially as, in some cases, they are justified as 'transitional' arrangements. However, not all member countries comply with the notification procedure, nor do the data necessarily cover all forms of pollution control expenditure. For these reasons the extent to which pollution control activities are subsidized on a continuing basis within the EC remains in some doubt.

### Deposit-Refund Schemes

These are quite widely used for beer and soft-drink bottles in a number of EC countries and especially in Scandinavia. Up to a certain level, companies find such schemes commercially viable and require no financial assistance unless governments wish to raise the proportion of bottles returned above the commercial level. The range of containers to which these schemes relate is limited and, though they have a useful demonstration value, their overall contribution to environmental protection is probably fairly small.

## Market-Creation Arrangements

Practical experience in tradeable permit systems is, to date, largely confined to the United States (OECD 1992c). This system provides for internal trading within the same plants (through 'bubble' and 'offset' arrangements) and external trading between different enterprises (through the buying and selling of emission licences). The former has introduced a welcome degree of internal flexibility into the US regulatory framework, which, to a varying degree, already existed in other European countries. However, external trading has occurred to a much less extent and no effective market for emissions trading has yet been established. In contrast, stronger provisions for strict liability (i.e. where the onus of proof, relating to liability for environmental damage, resides with the polluter) are being reflected in higher insurance claims and higher insurance for polluters or those who acquire their liabilities when they purchase contaminated land. In this way, the insurance market, both in North America and Europe, is beginning to internalize these environmental damage costs and secure greater adherence to the 'polluter-pays' principle (OECD 1992b).

## Enforcement Incentives

The main form of enforcement incentives used within Europe are non-compliance charges when polluters' emissions exceed those permitted by regulations. In the past, these charges have been set at very low levels and this, combined with low rates of detection and action for non-compliance, has meant that the financial incentive to comply has been very weak. The situation is gradually changing as some countries (e.g. Norway, the United States, the United Kingdom) begin to raise the level of these charges.

## Overall Assessment of Current Practice

The numbers and types of economic instruments of environmental policy in use within the EC has grown considerably over recent years. However, closer examination suggests that they play a limited, if expanding, role in environmental protection. Charges schemes, though relatively numerous, are still confined to a small range of polluting activities and products and are mainly set at too low a level to have a major incentive effect. Grants and subsidies are still used and their full extent may be underestimated— but the environmental rationale for their use is not always clear and, in some cases, their consistency with the 'polluter-pays' principle is in doubt. Deposit-refund schemes play a limited, but useful, role in pollution control. Market-creation schemes are still in their infancy in Europe. Financial enforcement incentives have been very weak in the past but, in some EC countries at least, are getting stronger.

However, as the Fifth Action Programme (CEC 1992*a*) indicates, the intention is to make greater use of economic instruments in the future. This is typified by the interest shown in the possible use of such instruments to control $CO_2$ emissions and reduce the risks of global warming. This is briefly examined in the next section.

## 9.7. REDUCING $CO_2$ EMISSIONS

Of all the recent environmental policy issues facing the EC and the international community, the most widely publicized has been the threat of global warming from increased emissions to the atmosphere. The precise causes, likely extent, and consequences of global warming continue to be debated. However, it is clear that, if the more pessimistic 'do-nothing' scenarios were to be realized, the resulting environmental and economic consequences would be of enormous scale. In these circumstances, the precautionary policy response has been to set target levels which should not be exceeded for the main emissions believed to contribute to global warming, and then to determine, and hopefully reach political agreement on, the best ways of achieving these.

The major type of emission believed to contribute to global warming is $CO_2$. In October 1990 the Council of Ministers undertook to stabilize $CO_2$ emissions in the EC at 1990 levels by the year 2000. In the absence of any specific measures to curb emissions, total energy use has been predicted to grow by more than 12 per cent, and $CO_2$ emissions by more than 11 per cent, over this period.

In order to achieve these targets, the EC proposed a package of measures which included:

- voluntary, regulatory, and other related measures to encourage energy conservation and switching to lower carbon fuels;
- a combined energy and carbon tax whose level would be progressively raised between 1993 (the originally assumed start date) and 2000 (with provision for certain exemptions and tax reductions);
- increases in annual vehicle licence duties; and

- a redistribution of the tax revenue through reductions in other taxes so as to achieve tax neutrality.

It is envisaged that approximately one-third of the target reductions in energy use and $CO_2$ emissions would be achieved by the non-tax measures, leaving the remainder to be achieved by the energy-carbon tax and the increased vehicle licence duties (DRI 1992). The tax and licence duty levels needed to achieve the required reductions are considerable and would be reflected in substantial increases in the prices of particular fuels (by year 2000, over 60 per cent for coal and 40 per cent for heavy fuel oil used by industry, and 10–20 per cent for residential/commercial fuel prices). However, it was envisaged that certain of the high energy industrial users would benefit from exemptions or tax-rate reductions and, most importantly, the very considerable tax revenues generated would be used to reduce other tax rates (e.g. personal income taxes, social security charges, etc.).

The likely economic consequences of this package of measures have been assessed using a linked set of energy, industry, and macroeconomic models (DRI 1992). The results are sensitive to the precise form of the package, the technical properties of the particular models used, and the assumptions made about the levels of energy-carbon taxes that will be adopted by non-EC countries over this period. For the EC as a whole, the average rate of inflation is estimated to rise by 0.25 per cent per annum more, and GDP to increase by 0.07 per cent per annum less, than if the package was not introduced. These small, but not insignificant, economic consequences would be more limited if other OECD countries adopted similar packages. However, the averages conceal considerable variations in impacts between Member States and regions, economic sectors, and different socio-economic groups. For example, carbon taxes tend to be regressive, and, on equity grounds, careful attention needs to be given to the income distribution effects of any tax reductions introduced to achieve tax neutrality (Pearson 1992).

In June 1992 the EC presented a proposal for a Council Directive to introduce an energy-carbon tax along the lines described above (CEC 1992). However, by the end of 1993 there had been little sign of its impending adoption, partly because of sensitivities over the subsidiarity issue but, even more so, because of concern over the likely public reaction to substantial increases in energy prices.

## 9.8. BENEFITS AND COSTS OF ENVIRONMENTAL POLICIES: AN OVERVIEW

This section examines how the benefits and costs of environmental policies might be assessed and compared and reviews the limited estimates which are available.

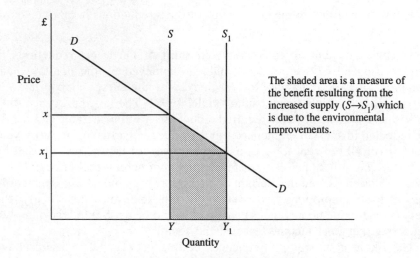

The shaded area is a measure of the benefit resulting from the increased supply $(S \rightarrow S_1)$ which is due to the environmental improvements.

**Fig. 9.7.** Valuation of the increased supply of an agricultural crop, due to environmental improvements

## Measuring Environmental Benefits

*Conceptually*, the measurement of environmental benefits is relatively straightforward. It involves calculating the *welfare gain* from the environmental improvement to which the policy gives rise. *In practice*, measuring the size of this gain is often difficult. In part, the difficulty stems from incomplete *scientific* knowledge about the bio-physical effects of the policy. However, even where these are reasonably well known, problems remain in placing an *economic value* upon them.

Where improvements in environmental quality result in increased yields of commercial crops, forests, or fisheries, then market prices may be used in their economic valuation, provided these prices are competitively determined. This is illustrated in Fig. 9.7. However, many environmental benefits and dis-benefits relate to receptors and natural resources which do not have a market value—for example, human life and well-being, nature conservation sites, famous landscapes, etc. In these cases, alternative, more indirect, methods of economic valuation have to be used. Over recent years a number of these methods have been developed, as illustrated in Table 9.2. However, outside the United States, their practical application has been quite limited and their usefulness continues to be debated (OECD 1989; Winpenny 1991; Kuik *et al.* 1992; OECD 1992*a*).

The available estimates of the country-wide benefits of existing environmental policies, and of the potential benefits of new policies, are very approximate and incomplete. However, they do suggest that both types of benefits are considerable. For example, a very incomplete estimate of

TABLE **9.2.** *Examples of economic valuation methods for assessing environmental benefits*

| Environmental benefits | Economic valuation methods |
| --- | --- |
| Reductions in crop losses | Quantity of crop loss is valued at its mean market price (see Fig.9.7). |
| Savings in expenditure | Reductions in costs associated with materials corrosion, cleaning of structures, sound-proofing, etc., due to reduction in pollution and noise are estimated. |
| Increases in property prices | Increases in property prices (and numbers of properties affected) due to reductions in air and road traffic noise, improvements in air quality, etc., are estimated. |
| Wage-risk studies | Wage differentials, reflecting risk premiums in dangerous occupations, are used to value reductions in the probability of accidents from pollution. |
| Travel cost approaches | Increased visit rates, combined with travel cost data, are used to value improvements to natural amenities and associated recreational facilities. |
| Contingent valuation studies | Questionnaire and survey techniques are used to deduce how much respondents would be willing to pay for specified environmental improvements or how much they would need to accept if agreeing to particular environmental benefits being withdrawn. |

annual air and water pollution damage in the Netherlands in the mid-1980s calculated that this was equivalent to 0.5–0.9 per cent of the Netherlands GNP. A corresponding, but more broadly based, estimate of annual pollution damage costs in Germany was found to be equivalent to 6 per cent of that country's GNP (OECD 1989; Pearce, Markandya, and Barbier 1989).

### Measuring Pollution Control and other Environmental Policy Costs

In principle, these costs should be straightforward to estimate—they are the costs which would be saved if the pollution control and other policy measures did not apply. However, applying this costing principle in practice is problematic because:

- many enterprises and authorities do not keep separate cost data for their pollution control activities and, in any case, some of these costs are jointly incurred with other activities;
- cost-accounting methods are not standardized and this creates problems of comparability, especially in the treatment of capital expenditures on pollution control; and

- some pollution control costs are 'hidden' in higher process design costs.

OECD collects and periodically publishes Pollution Abatement and Control (PAC) annual expenditures for its member countries (OECD, various years). The data are incomplete and very approximate but indicate, at least on the basis of mid-1980s data, that PAC expenditures in the higher income EC countries range between 0.8 per cent and 1.5 per cent of their GDP. These percentages are considerably lower in the poorer, southern regions of the EC. The trend in PAC expenditures is probably rising in absolute terms, but, relative to GDP, any increase since the mid-1980s has probably been quite modest (OECD 1993). The incidence of PAC expenditures does, however, vary considerably between sectors and, for this reason, is considerably higher than the percentages quoted above in parts of the electricity, mining and quarrying, chemicals, petroleum, and other polluting industries.

## Economic Impacts of Environmental Control

Considerable concern is expressed, especially in times of recession, about the likely economic consequences of stricter environmental controls. In broad terms, the fear is that, in the Member State concerned, increased expenditure on such controls will raise the general level of production costs and prices, lower the competitiveness of exports, reduce the overall growth rate of the economy, and raise the level of unemployment. In contrast, others have argued that, in addition to the environmental benefits it may bring, increased investment in pollution controls may be a useful, counter-cyclical measure in periods of unemployment.

Attempts have been made to model the macroeconomic consequences of particular policy measures (such as the energy-carbon tax described previously), and of entire pollution control programmes in a number of OECD countries. An OECD survey, mainly based on six OECD countries (including France and the Netherlands within the EC), examined the macroeconomic consequences of the PAC expenditures in place or projected in the late 1970s and early 1980s (OECD 1985). At the aggregate level, in all cases, the economic consequences were assessed to be very small and to be an insignificant factor in the overall performance of the countries concerned. The effects on output and unemployment were both extremely limited and in a mixed direction—typically having limited positive effects in the initial years of implementation followed by equally limited negative effects in the following years. More recently a task force of the Commission used the HERMES macroeconomic model to predict the likely effects, over a five-year period, of increased expenditure on environmental controls, equivalent to 1 per cent of GDP, in each of five Member

States—Belgium, Germany, France, Greece, and the United Kingdom—based upon alternative assumptions about the method of financing to be used (Task Force 1990). On the basis of the 'combined' scenario (which was believed to be the most realistic scenario) GDP was predicted to change, by the end of the five-year period, between −0.10 per cent (in the United Kingdom) and +0.14 per cent (in France). Similarly, unemployment was predicted to fall by approximately 14,000 in Germany and increase by approximately 13,000 in the United Kingdom.

Though these overall changes appear to be relatively small, and would be smaller if all developed economies made similar changes at the same time, it should be noted that:

- the impacts on individual economic sectors, geographic areas, and socio-economic groups within these countries differ considerably from the average changes described above; and
- beyond a certain point the marginal costs of achieving stricter environmental controls can rise sharply. Therefore, the economic consequences of further substantial increases in PAC expenditures on a country, especially if it pursues such a policy unilaterally, could be very considerable.

This implies that all major *new* policy initiatives should be carefully examined to ensure that their likely benefits, costs, and economic consequences (including their distributional effects) are properly assessed before they are approved.

## 9.9. FUTURE DEVELOPMENTS

The status and scale of EC environmental policy activities have increased substantially since 1973 when the first Action Programme was approved. The achievements have certainly fallen short of the ambitions, but this is not particularly surprising given reliance on (currently twelve) Member States for the approval and implementation of new policy initiatives. However, the new long-term goal, of promoting sustainable development within and outside the EC, is extremely ambitious and is unlikely to be achieved, in any meaningful sense, if existing policy measures are not strengthened.

A basic prerequisite is to provide the objective of sustainable development with operational meaning so that the measures required to achieve it can be sufficiently clearly identified. Also it will be necessary to clarify the interpretation of the subsidiarity principle in the formulation and implementation of environmental policies. This will probably result in some responsibilities for environmental protection passing from Community to Member State, or more local, levels. However, increasing awareness of transboundary and global environmental problems will probably lead to Community institutions assuming some new environmental responsibilities. Similarly, it will be necessary to clarify how the TEU's requirements relating to environmental protection are to be accommodated within the economic logic of the 'single market' which will involve 'internalizing' the environmental externalities which it generates.

Some strengthening of institutional procedures, policy instruments, and methods of evaluation will be needed. At the procedural level, the greatest challenge lies in integrating environmental considerations into the future planning and development of the major economic sectors and into land-use planning activities. At Community level this requires strengthening procedures for integrating environmental measures into such programmes as those for the development of agriculture, forestry and fishing, energy and transport, regional development, and overseas aid. This will not be achieved easily or quickly, but progress is being made (see e.g. OECD (1992*d*), (1992*e*)). Parallel developments are needed at the Member State level, where, typically, environmental ministries are still relatively weak compared with the more powerful 'economic' ministries with which they will need to work more closely. Again, realistically, progress will be slow in some areas.

A number of the policy instruments will also need to be strengthened and their use extended. More attention is needed to the development of instruments which promote resource conservation which are less developed than those dealing with pollution problems. Economic instruments have a potentially important role to play in both resource conservation and pollution control. Their current contribution is limited, partly because they are not widely applied but, more fundamentally, because they do not closely conform with the efficiency and equity objectives they are supposed to serve. They are in need of comprehensive review, and this should probably be linked to wider tax-reform studies. More appropriate economic instruments may help to deliver the 'double dividend' of a better system of environmental protection and a better tax regime.

Even if economic instruments play a larger and more effective role in environmental protection, there will still be a major role for other planning and regulatory instruments. Many of these are seen to be under-performing when measured against the evaluation criteria outlined in Section 9.5. Paralleling a review of economic instruments, there should be a similar review of regulatory instruments.

If the various proposed changes outlined above are to be satisfactorily implemented, then better quality data and analysis, both environmental and economic, will be needed. Whilst some progress has been made in measuring the benefits and costs of environmental policies in economic terms, much more work of this kind is needed. Improvements in evaluation practice, drawing upon both environmental and economic data, are also required. Finally, more attention is needed to modelling the linkages between economic and environmental systems and to modelling the economic consequences of environmental policies within the EC.

The agenda is very demanding, and, being realistic, it is unlikely to be completed by the year 2000. However, there is no reason why substantial progress cannot be made in these directions over the intervening period.

# REFERENCES

Beckerman, W. (1974), *In Defence of Economic Growth* (London: Cape).

CEC (1992*a*): Commission of the European Communities, *Towards Sustainability: A European Community Programme of Policy and Action in relation to the Environment and Sustainable Development*, 2 vols., COM 23 (Brussels: CEC).

—— (1992*b*), *Proposal for a Council Directive Introducing a Tax on Carbon Dioxide Emissions and Energy*, COM 226 final (Brussels: CEC).

DRI (1992): European Industry Service, *Impact of a Package of EC Measures to Control $CO_2$ Emissions on European Industry*, DG XI (Brussels: CEC).

Haigh, N. (1989), *EEC Environmental Policy and Britain* (Harlow: Longman).

Huppes, G., van der Voet, E., Van der Naald, W. G. H., Vonkeman, G. H., and Maxson, P. (1992) (eds.), *New Market-Oriented Instruments for Environmental Policy* (London: Graham & Trotman).

International Energy Agency (1993), *Cars and Climate Change* (Paris: Organization for Economic Co-operation and Development/International Energy Agency).

Kuik, O. J., Oosterhuis, F. H., Jansen, H. M. A., Holm, K., and Ewers, H. J. (1992) (eds.), *Assessment of Benefits of Environmental Measures* (London: Graham & Trotman).

Laidler, D., and Estrin, S. (1989), *An Introduction to Microeconomics*, 3rd edn. (Deddington: Philip Allan).

Meadows, D. H., Meadows, D. L., Randers, J., and Behrens, W. W. (1970), *The Limits to Growth* (London: Earth Island).

Meadows, D. L., Meadows, D. H., and Randers, J. (1992), *Beyond the Limits: Global Collapse or a Sustainable Future* (London: Earthscan).

OECD (1985): Organization for Economic Co-operation and Development, *Macro-economic Impact of Environmental Expenditure* (Paris: OECD).

OECD (1989), *Environmental Policy Benefits: Monetary Valuation* (Paris: OECD).

—— (1991), *The State of the Environment* (Paris: OECD).

—— (1992*a*), *Benefit Estimates and Environmental Decision-Making* (Paris: OECD).

—— (1992*b*), *Pollution Insurance in OECD Countries*, Environmental Monograph (Paris: OECD).

OECD (1992*c*), *Climate Change—Designing a Tradeable Permit System* (Paris: OECD).

—— (1992*d*), *Agricultural and Environmental Policy Integration–Implementation—*(Paris: OECD).

—— (1992*e*), *Market and Government Failures in Environmental Management: The Case of Transport* (Paris: OECD).

—— (1993), *Taxation and the Environment: Complementary Policies* (Paris: OECD).

Opschoor, J. B., and Vans, H. B. (1989), *Economic Instruments for Environmental Protection* (Paris: OECD).

Pearce, D., Markandya, A., and Barbier, E. B. (1989), *Blueprint for a Green Economy* (London: Earthscan).

Pearson, M. (1992), 'Equity issues and Carbon Taxes', in OECD', *Climate Change—Designing a Practical Tax System* (Paris), 213–40.

Task Force on the Environment and the Internal Market (1990), *1992: the Environmental Dimension*, DG XI (Brussels: CEC).

Winpenny, J. T. (1991), *Values for the Environment: A Guide to Economic Appraisal* (London: HMSO).

# 10

# Social Policy

DAVID PURDY AND PAT DEVINE

## 10.1. INTRODUCTION

A social dimension has been present within the EC since its foundation, broadly shaped by the process of economic integration, but continually evolving and always contested. One reason why the EC's social arrangements have remained unsettled is that the policy regimes of its Member States continue to diverge. Although the very existence of the EC imposes *some* degree of commonality, the possibility that initial divergences might eventually wither away has so far been blocked by fundamental disagreements, both about the 'proper' scope and objects of social policy, and about the 'proper' division of responsibility and power between the Community and its Member States. One of the main aims of this chapter is to clarify these differences of policy regime and policy paradigm.

Before one can appreciate how regimes and paradigms differ, one needs some idea of the field over which social provisions and prescriptions may range. Accordingly, Section 10.2 examines the remit of social policy in a 'typical' advanced capitalist democracy. The perspective adopted invokes the now familiar distinction, first formulated by Marshall (1950), between three aspects of citizenship—civil, political, and social—and encompasses both the world of work and the various branches of the welfare state.

Section 10.3 draws on recent comparative literature to propose a typology of social policy regimes in contemporary Western Europe. Four 'ideal types' are distinguished: traditional–rudimentary, liberal–individualist, conservative–corporatist, and social democratic. It is stressed that, since actual states normally combine the characteristics of more than one type, what varies from one state to another is the mix between different principles of social organization. The resulting amalgam may be stable or unstable. In the latter case, the regime in question will be in a state of flux or transition.

Analogous points apply to a union of states: the character of the union's policy regime depends on the balance between the regimes of its member states and on the way in which issues requiring union-wide co-ordination are handled. At one extreme, for example, national regimes could all cluster round a single centre of gravity, and the role of union institutions could be limited to removing or correcting for minor discrepancies. Alternatively, national regimes may pull in different directions. In this case, the Member States must either forge a new, union-wide social settlement or, failing that, acquiesce in whatever arrangement is thrown up by spontaneous social evolution. Of course, without an agreed design for their union, Member States will be reluctant to cede sovereignty over social policy. Indeed, if the tensions and discords are strong enough, the union may dissolve.

In the final two sections of the chapter this general scheme is applied to the framework and development of EC social policy. Section 10.4 focuses on the factors which have constrained its role: disparities of economic condition and differences of social regime among Member States; and the policy-making institutions of the EC itself. Section 10.5 seeks to explain why periods of policy activism have alternated with periods of stagnation, and briefly speculates about the shape of things to come as the states of Europe struggle to cope with the pressures of global competition, mass unemployment, and the fiscal crisis of the welfare state.

## 10.2. THE REMIT OF SOCIAL POLICY

The scope and character of social policy vary from one society and era to another. They are also deeply controversial. In Table 10.1 the issues involved are grouped under two broad headings: 'work' and 'welfare'. 'Work' is not, of course, confined to the activities of gainfully employed persons; it also includes the domestic and caring services that people (mostly women) perform outside the cash nexus for the benefit of partners, children, and other dependent relatives.

In reality, the various aspects of social policy are intertwined. Consider, for example, the distribution of work between men and women, referred to in Table 10.1 as 'the sexual division of labour'. Whether the working lives and occupational profiles of men and women are symmetrical and integrated or divergent and segregated depends very largely on the ways in which boys and girls are reared, schooled, and generally socialized by parents, teachers, and others employed in the social services. The social transfer side of the welfare state also plays a part in determining how far *biological* differences between males and females become the basis of systematic *social* inequalities between men and women. Income tax and social security are not just devices for redistributing purchasing power from net taxpayers to net beneficiaries; they also embody certain more or less questionable presumptions about how people do in fact or should ideally live their lives: for example, in relation to the respective responsibilities of mothers and fathers towards their children and towards each other. Analogous points apply to social divisions based on race, ethnicity, and disability.

TABLE **10.1.** *The remit of social policy in the advanced capitalist democracies*

| Work | Welfare |
|---|---|
| *Labour-market management and human-resource development*<br>   macroeconomic policy<br>   active manpower policy<br><br>*Regulation of employment standards and conditions*<br>   health and safety<br>   minimum wages and other employee rights<br>   working time and the quality of working life<br><br>*Industrial relations*<br>   the framework of collective bargaining<br>   workplace/enterprise democracy<br>   social dialogue and policy bargaining<br><br>*Gender, difference, and social inequality*<br>   sex and race discrimination in employment<br>   the sexual division of labour<br>   other social divisions (e.g. of race, ethnicity, disability) | *Social transfers*<br> *direct*<br>   social insurance<br>   social assistance<br>   'universal' grants (e.g. child benefits; citizen entitlements)<br><br> *indirect*<br>   personal tax allowances and tax reliefs<br>   some producer subsidies (e.g. agricultural price support and deficiency payment schemes)<br><br>*Social services*<br>   compulsory schooling<br>   health care<br>   housing policy<br>   social work |

Table 10.1 outlines the agenda of social policy in a 'typical' advanced capitalist democracy. It is instructive to approach the issues at stake by asking: what is the basis of citizenship in a state of this kind? And what does this status entail? Nowadays, as a rule, the sole qualification for becoming a citizen is permanent (legal) residence, though some states continue to discriminate against 'resident aliens' by restricting eligibility to those with appropriate ancestry, as laid down in nationality law. In theory at least, all citizens enjoy extensive and equal freedom of thought, expression, movement, organization, and worship. Similarly, all adult citizens are equally entitled to vote in elections for government and to hold public office. People's *social* rights, however, are more recent in origin than these *civil* and *political* attributes of citizenship, and are correspondingly less secure. They are also more limited in scope and uneven in coverage. Indeed, to the extent that people who belong to the

same political community hold unequal social rights, we are dealing not with social citizenship, but with social privilege. The citizens of a given state may all be privileged by comparison with outsiders, and their holdings of private wealth and other assets may be highly unequal. But their common status as citizens is inherently egalitarian.

The underdeveloped condition of social citizenship has an important bearing on the distribution of income, work, and power under democratic capitalism. Given that only a few people own more than modest amounts of income-yielding property, most depend for their livelihood on continuous access to paid work, whether in their own right or as dependants of others who are continuously willing, or legally obliged, to support them. And regular employment gives access to other life-enhancing resources besides money income: valuable experience, self-esteem, social identity, public recognition, and political clout. Moreover, by virtue of having paid the requisite social insurance contributions, regular jobholders are more or less adequately protected against temporary or permanent loss of earning power as a result of workplace accidents and occupational disease, other kinds of illness, unemployment, and old age; and protection normally extends to their dependants and survivors as well.

Most, though not all, of the states in question provide some kind of 'safety net' outside the framework of social insurance. But 'social assistance'—to use a generic name for schemes which vary widely in operational detail—is almost always means-tested, and able-bodied claimants of conventional working age are normally subjected to some form of work test. They may simply be required to show that they are 'available for' or 'genuinely seeking' (paid) work. Alternatively, they may be obliged to enrol in 'workfare' schemes organized or financed by the state, and variously intended to serve the community, deter 'scrounging', impart training, or prevent social exclusion.

The only major contemporary type of social transfer which is 'universal', in the sense that it is neither contributory, means-tested, nor work-tested, but can be claimed without further ado by everyone who belongs to the relevant social category, is Child Benefit—a recurrent, tax-free cash payment granted automatically to anyone with primary responsibility for the care of a child. No state has yet introduced a universal grant which *all* its citizens are entitled to receive throughout their lives, each in his or her own right.

Besides using insurance contributions and general tax revenue to finance *direct* social transfers, modern states also preside over a variety of selective transfers which, being *indirect*, are often known as 'the hidden welfare state'. They consist mainly of personal tax allowances and reliefs, the effect of which is to drive a wedge between *gross* and *taxable* income, thereby raising the *net* incomes of eligible taxpayers just as cash grants boost the net incomes of eligible claimants. Some quasi-permanent producer subsidies also provide income support for the employers and workers concerned. Agricultural price support and deficiency payment schemes furnish the main examples.

Given the primacy of employment as a source of income and other social advantages, it is hardly surprising that both the macro- and microeconomic aspects of what Table 10.1 calls 'labour-market management and human-resource development' loom large in public debate. By design or default, and for better or worse, a government's macroeconomic stance is a potent force: it helps to determine how much labour employers in the aggregate wish to hire at any given real wage, and hence, given the pattern of working time, the total number of jobs on offer in the monetized economy. The demand for waged labour, taken in conjunction with the size and skills of the labour force, the allocative efficiency of the labour market, and the degree of real wage flexibility, determines the overall level of unemployment. 'Macroeconomic policy' must here be broadly construed to include not just budgetary, monetary, and exchange-rate policy, but also the full panoply of weapons, remote-control as well as hand held, which governments may bring to bear in the perennial struggle to restrain the growth of money wages and non-wage incomes.

The mere existence of a unitary state with a common currency and centralized fiscal arrangements automatically affects the spatial pattern of production, employment, and income within its borders. In addition, most governments make piecemeal or wholesale attempts at 'active man-power policy'. This, too, is an umbrella term. It covers regional policies intended to influence the geographical distribution of jobs and/or workers; auxiliary services designed to reduce the time, trouble, and expense involved in filling or finding vacant job-slots; and all provisions affecting post-school education, vocational training, and work experience, whether to relieve specific skill shortages, upgrade the general quality of the labour force, reintegrate the long-term unemployed into the mainstream of society, or reinforce the work ethic.

Whilst none of these matters is uncontroversial, their *presence* on the policy agenda has become commonplace. All governments, whatever their political persuasion, are nowadays obliged to formulate reasonably coherent policies for the labour market. The same applies to certain other tasks which are generally acknowledged—by economic liberals no less than by social collectivists—to necessitate positive public action: notably, the regulation of health and safety at work and the prevention of discrimination by sex and race in pay and conditions, hiring and firing, training and promotion, and tax and social security legislation. The status of other work-related issues is more contentious. Economic liberals argue that, the broader the remit of social policy, the greater the threat to individual freedom (conceived as the freedom to seek out or choose between alternative market options), and the greater the damage to social welfare (likewise evaluated by reference to market outcomes). The implication is that, apart from providing certain recognized public goods, including a minimally intrusive framework of contract law, governments should leave employers and employees to work out their own salvation subject to the 'impersonal' discipline of the market.

The leading exponent of this doctrine within the EC has been the UK government. Since the demise of what Marquand (1988) calls 'Keynesian social democracy', the policy paradigm which dominated public life in the United Kingdom from the Second World War to the advent of Mrs Thatcher, successive Conservative governments have sought to recast the relationship between state and civil society in the name of market freedom, competition, privatization, self-help, and selectivity. One must, however, distinguish between economic liberalism as a timeless theoretical ideal and the practical steps which are intended to bring it into being. During the process of 'transition', when the old regime is being dismantled and a new one put in its place, it would be specious to claim that government had somehow given up trying to shape the pattern of social development. On the contrary, a government that sets out to deregulate the labour market, weaken trade unions, privatize retirement pensions, or encourage commercial child-minding is bent on transforming social institutions and mores no less than a government that enacts minimum wage laws, parleys with industrial organizations, enhances the social rights of citizens, or invests in pre-school education. On this understanding, Table 10.1 accurately summarizes the remit of social policy in all the EC states, the United Kingdom included.

## 10.3. SOCIAL POLICY REGIMES

If the remit of social policy is much the same throughout the EC, the way it is handled is not. Transnational differences in work and welfare arrangements range from minor variations in official definitions of 'industrial accidents' to deep-seated and long-lasting contrasts of historical formation, social philosophy, and institutional design. To mark this latter, *systemic* source of diversity, several writers have employed the concept of a *social policy regime*. (See, in particular, Titmuss (1974); Therborn (1987); Esping-Andersen (1990); Leibfried (1990); Langan and Ostner (1991); Pierson (1991).)

As might be expected in what is still a fairly new field, the study of comparative social policy has generated vigorous debate about what exactly needs to be investigated and how to go about it. Nevertheless, some common ground does exist. All the authors just cited insist that the mere presence of a particular kind of provision in a given state at a given time matters less for the lives of its citizens and their mutual relations than the *character* of its overall policy regime. The same goes for related quantitative indicators such as the proportion of GDP absorbed by social expenditure. Researchers also agree that it is no use generalizing from the experience of one country or sticking to one academic discipline: the study of social policy regimes must be comparative and cross-disciplinary. Whilst the eventual aim is to understand *why* states have different regimes and what causes them to change, an essential intermediate step is to classify states in ways that clarify *how* they differ and change. Accordingly, most writers seek to delineate certain 'ideal types', to which actual states approximate more or less closely, it being understood that in practice regimes tend to be mixed. What follows is a composite and somewhat reconstructed account of their principal conclusions.

Within Western Europe since the Second World War, four ideal types of regime can be identified: traditional–rudimentary, liberal–individualist, conservative–corporatist, and social democratic. Each of these types is also known by the name of the region or culture which best exemplifies it: Latin Rim, Anglo-American, Germanic, and Nordic, respectively. The former nomenclature seems preferable: it lessens the risk of confusing abstract models with actual states; and it conveys the idea that the first case stands somewhat apart from the others.

Nowadays, the *traditional–rudimentary* model is largely, though not entirely, obsolete. The states or regions most often cited as rough approximations are Greece, Spain, Portugal, and the Italian *Mezzogiorno*, which in this, as in many other respects, is unlike the northern and central regions of Italy. As its name suggests, the model evokes a way of life which predates modernity. The state does little to regulate employment or redistribute income. From this standpoint, it resembles its liberal counterpart. But the ambient culture is quite different. A single, dominant religion retains a strong hold on both state and civil society; kinship ties, local loyalties, codes of honour, and informal reciprocity count for more than market rationality, shared citizenship, and the rule of law; agriculture remains the mainstay of the economy, and domestic 'subsistence' production is common; the extended family caters for children and old people, absorbs social distress, and perpetuates the subjection of women; and against the background of a thriving black economy, politics is 'clientelist' and government corrupt—a pattern which, as the case of Italy shows, is perfectly capable of surviving the late arrival of 'modern' industry, bureaucracy, and democracy.

The *liberal–individualist* model celebrates markets, property, and the work ethic. Its basic presumption is that all those who are not incapacitated by age, disability, or illness are free to choose between selling their labour power and subsisting in poverty—apart, that is, from the wealthy minority who have no need to earn a living. The aim of welfare policy is to encourage participation in the labour market. The state provides a safety net for market casualties and social misfits, offering residual cash benefits which are strictly targeted, means-tested, and stigmatizing. Social services are similarly designed to meet the minimum needs of 'second-class' citizens who lack recourse to the private education, health care, insurance services, and retirement pensions that 'first-class' citizens are encouraged to buy for themselves.

In the Anglo-American countries, where this social philosophy has become hegemonic, the family has been virtually excluded from public discourse, at any rate until recently. Women were simply subsumed as appendages of male bread-winners, their work unpaid and unseen. This has changed with the steady rise in female employment and one-parent families. Nevertheless, public provision for mothers and children, in cash and in kind, remains scanty and equivocal. The remedy, according to economic liberals, is to readjust the structure of incentives and penalties. Government should phase out child benefits in favour of selective social assistance, simultaneously offering tax relief on childcare costs so as to induce women to enter or stay in the labour market. The state should also be more zealous in pursuing absentee fathers who fail to maintain their children, and should compel single mothers who claim state benefits to take part in some form of training or public service. These reforms mesh neatly with the growing trend towards 'atypical' employment. By employing women and young people on a part-time, temporary, on-call, or home-working basis, firms in fiercely competitive product markets expect to be able to cut their wage bills, gain greater flexibility in staffing, and impair the capacity of their employees to organize and act in concert.

*Conservative–corporatist* regimes are less obsessed with the market. Nor are they hostile to social rights. Indeed, they favour the fullest development of social insurance, with the proviso that separate and/or appropriately differentiated schemes should apply to each officially recognized category of employee: manual and non-manual; private and public; male and female; married and unmarried; and so on. The aim is to compensate for undeserved loss of earning power, whilst avoiding any vertical redistribution of income and preserving the established hierarchy of class, status and gender.

Historically, this model originated in the efforts of Bismarck to pre-empt the appeal of socialism by securing the allegiance of the German working class to the newly unified German state. The influence of Catholic social thought is also evident: in the provision of 'family wage' supplements for (male) bread-winners; in the principle of subsidiarity, whereby the legitimate role of the state is limited to matters which cannot be handled by voluntary agencies—notably, the Church; and in a system of industrial relations designed to uphold the dignity of labour, prevent class conflict, and incorporate workers' representatives in both enterprise management and national policy formation.

*Social democratic* regimes are also committed to social insurance and social partnership, but as components in a strategy of 'democratic class struggle' aimed at securing universal social rights within the framework of a capitalist economy. The state is not a second or last resort, but the primary agency for enabling every citizen to enjoy the highest attainable degree of economic security and to benefit from a wide range of high-class social services. Esping-Andersen (1990) describes this project as an attempt to 'decommodify' the labour market. Whilst this term captures the sense in which workers in a social democratic state are protected from market contingency, it is not entirely apt. For, as we shall see, this kind of regime is not only firmly wedded to traditional forms of employment, but can even be said to 'commodify' work to the extent that the state becomes a major provider or purchaser of caring services that were formerly performed unpaid in homes and families.

Social insurance plays a key role in mitigating market insecurity. Contributions and benefits are earnings related, not 'flat rate'. But everyone belongs to a common, unified scheme. Apart from its symbolic value, this inclusive arrangement secures the allegiance of professional and skilled workers to the welfare state, thus making it easier to gain support for general welfare expansion. Moreover, to the extent that an expanding resource base makes it easier to raise the ratio of benefits to earnings, income is redistributed not only over each worker's life cycle, but also from incumbent jobholders to those who are currently unemployed or 'economically inactive'.

The viability of a system that guarantees all citizens paid work or generous transfer incomes from cradle to grave depends on the maintenance of full employment, not just as a state of equilibrium between labour demand and supply, but in the more vital sense that the size of the active labour force is maximized. Certain strategic imperatives follow. Some way has to be found of ensuring that uncoordinated wage-bargaining in an open economy at full employment does not set off a destabilizing wage–price spiral. Government cannot deliver this outcome single-handed: it needs the collaboration of trade unions and employers' associations which can speak with authority and act with discipline. And, having established a perpetual round of three-way bargaining over economic and social policy, government must somehow contrive to reconcile conflicts of interest between workers and employers, not only over wages, but also over industrial democracy. It must also perfect the art of active manpower policy, absorbing labour that is surplus to the requirements of private industry, and drawing women out of the home, by expanding employment in the public sector. In the process, childcare is partially socialized and issues of gender division become more salient. At the same time, to the extent that the state is simply paying some women to look after other women's children, the underlying sexual division of labour remains intact.

## 10.4. THE FRAMEWORK OF EC SOCIAL POLICY

So far we have focused on social policy in one state. We now turn our attention to the EC as a whole. In this section we examine the constraints which continue to inhibit EC action in the social field: disparities of economic condition and differences of social regime *between* EC members; and the institutions of the EC itself. In the next section we review the history of EC social policy and speculate about its future. It must be said at once that the various programmes and measures which answer to the name of 'EC social policy' are in no way comparable with the work and welfare regimes of individual states, even if the comparison is restricted to the *federal* level of states such as Germany or the United States. Nor, indeed, do they resemble the more ambitious policies of the EC itself such as the Common Agricultural Policy (CAP). Of course, a social dimension has been present in the EC since its inception. But EC social policy has always been limited in both scope and impact. And, although social issues have become more prominent as the EC has evolved, after the upheavals of the early 1990s the prospects for EC social policy in the future, as for the EC itself, are more uncertain than they have ever been.

### Disparities and Differences between Member States

Because Member States differ in demographic and social structure, they generate different demands for social expenditure. Because their economies are at different levels of development or display different standards of performance, they differ in their capacity to respond to these demands. And, as we have seen, the *character* of each state's response depends on its historically evolved policy regime.

Tables 10.2, 10.3, and 10.4 illustrate the resulting disparities within the EC and highlight recent social trends. Table 10.2 shows that, apart from the case of the Irish Republic, roughly two-thirds of each Member State's population falls within the conventional 'working age' range from 15 to 64. By contrast, economic activity rates vary widely, as do unemployment rates. The general upward trend in unemployment over the 1980s is also evident. Table 10.3 shows that per capita income in the richest Member State is roughly two and a half times as high as per capita income in the poorest. The incidence of poverty also varies from one country to another: thus, in 1985 the proportion of persons belonging to households with incomes less than 50 per cent of 'equivalent mean national expenditure' ranged from 5.9 per cent in Belgium to 32.7 per cent in Portugal. Furthermore, between 1980 and 1985 poverty rates as thus defined fell or remained more or less unchanged in most EC states, but rose in Italy, the Netherlands, and the United Kingdom, the rise in the United Kingdom being particularly marked. Table 10.4 reveals continuing disparities in the

TABLE **10.2.** *EC selected demographic and labour market indicators 1979–1989*

| Member State | Population age 15 to 64 | | Labour force | | Unemployment | |
|---|---|---|---|---|---|---|
| | As % of total population | Average annual % change | As % of total population | Average annual % change | As % of labour force | |
| | 1989 | 1979–89 | 1989 | 1979–89 | 1979 | 1989 |
| Belgium | 67.0 | 0.3 | 41.7 | 0.2 | 7.5 | 9.3 |
| Denmark | 67.2 | 0.5 | 56.1 | 0.9 | 6.0 | 8.1 |
| Germany | 69.7 | 0.7 | 48.0 | 0.8 | 3.2 | 6.8 |
| Spain | 66.5 | 1.0 | 39.0 | 1.2 | 8.4 | 16.9 |
| France | 65.9 | 0.9 | 43.3 | 0.4 | 5.9 | 9.4 |
| Greece | 66.8 | 1.0 | 39.5 | 1.6 | 1.9 | 7.5 |
| Irish Republic | 60.9 | 0.8 | 36.8 | 0.5 | 7.1 | 15.6 |
| Italy | 69.7 | 0.7 | 42.7 | 0.9 | 7.6 | 11.8 |
| Luxemburg | 69.3 | 0.6 | 48.7 | 1.5 | 0.6 | 1.1 |
| Netherlands | 69.0 | 1.0 | 45.2 | 2.5 | 5.4 | 8.3 |
| Portugal | 66.0 | 0.7 | 47.3 | 0.9 | 8.1 | 5.0 |
| UK | 65.4 | 0.5 | 49.7 | 0.7 | 4.6 | 6.1 |
| EC | 67.3 | 0.7 | 44.8 | 0.8 | 5.6 | 9.2 |

*Source*: OECD (1992).

proportions of GDP which EC governments devote to education, health care, and social security. In some countries, though not in all, the share of GDP absorbed by social security rose between 1979 and 1989. This trend reflects the toll exacted by higher unemployment, rather than the introduction of new programmes, the liberalization of eligibility conditions, or the enhancement of benefit standards: in general, the 1980s was a decade of fiscal retrenchment.

It is also worth noting that the convergence criteria for monetary union make no reference to any of the factors likely to affect either the demand for social expenditure or the capacity to sustain it. This is hardly surprising. Social policy has played a secondary role in the development of the EC, and social conditions do not *directly* affect the conditions necessary for monetary stability. Nevertheless, the deflationary policies which several EC governments adopted in an attempt to satisfy the convergence criteria undoubtedly contributed to high unemployment rates, high interest rates, and low growth rates, thereby increasing the demand for social expenditure at the same time as making it harder for governments to finance it. Since the resulting 'fiscal crisis' was an element in the monetary and exchange-rate crises of 1992/3, there is a

TABLE 10.3. *EC GDP per head and rates of poverty 1979–1989*

| Member State | GDP per head | | Percentage rates of poverty[a] | | | |
|---|---|---|---|---|---|---|
| | At current purchasing power parities | Average annual % change | Percentage of households | | Percentage of persons | |
| | 1989 | 1979–89 | 1980 | 1985 | 1980 | 1985 |
| Belgium | 103.7 | 1.9 | 6.3 | 5.2 | 7.1 | 5.9 |
| Denmark | 106.7 | 1.8 | 8.0 | 8.0 | 7.9 | 8.0 |
| Germany | 116.2 | 1.6 | 10.3 | 9.2 | 10.5 | 9.9 |
| Spain | 74.3 | 2.2 | 20.3 | 17.8 | 20.9 | 18.9 |
| France | 111.3 | 1.6 | 18.0 | 14.8 | 19.1 | 15.7 |
| Greece | 49.0 | 1.2 | 20.5 | 17.4 | 21.5 | 18.4 |
| Irish Republic | 65.4 | 2.7 | 18.5 | 17.4 | 18.4 | 19.5 |
| Italy | 102.7 | 2.2 | 12.0 | 14.7 | 14.1 | 15.5 |
| Luxemburg | 127.3 | 2.9 | n.a. | n.a. | n.a. | n.a. |
| Netherlands | 101.2 | 1.0 | 6.9 | 7.9 | 9.6 | 11.4 |
| Portugal | 52.5 | 2.1 | 31.4 | 31.7 | 32.4 | 32.7 |
| UK | 103.6 | 2.1 | 14.1 | 18.9 | 14.6 | 18.2 |
| EC | 100.0 | 1.8 | — | — | — | — |

*Note*: n.a. = not available.

[a] Households/persons are counted as experiencing poverty if their income does not exceed 50% of equivalent mean national expenditure in their country of residence.

*Sources*: OECD (1993); CEC (1991).

clear sense in which the inadequacy of EC social policy played an *indirect* role in derailing plans for monetary union.

Even if Europe's economies had been less divergent, and their recent history less turbulent, the differences of policy regime described in the previous section would still be a powerful obstacle to any Community-wide social policy. Whilst some resolution of these differences cannot be ruled out—indeed, *some* convergence is already evident—the process is bound to be partial and protracted. The issues involved are explored in the final section of this chapter.

## The Institutions of the EC

The legal basis of EC social policy is set out in the Treaty of Rome (1957), as modified by the Single European Act (SEA) (1987) and the Treaty on European Union (TEU) (1993), the 'Maastricht Treaty'. The relevant legal

**TABLE 10.4.** *EC social expenditure 1979–1989[a]*

| | Total government outlays at current market prices as % of GDP at current market prices on | | | | | |
| | Education | | Health | | Social security and welfare | |
| | 1979 | 1989 | 1979 | 1989 | 1979 | 1989 |
|---|---|---|---|---|---|---|
| Belgium | n.a. | 7.3[b] | n.a. | 6.0[b] | n.a. | 20.4[b] |
| Denmark | 7.3 | 7.0 | 5.6 | 5.2 | 20.4 | 23.3 |
| Germany | 5.0 | 4.2 | 6.1 | 6.0 | 19.5 | 18.5 |
| Spain | n.a. | 3.9[c] | n.a. | 4.7[c] | n.a. | 14.0[c] |
| France | n.a. | 5.3 | n.a. | 6.9 | n.a. | 19.6 |
| Italy | 4.8[d] | 5.1 | 5.6[d] | 5.9 | 13.2[d] | 16.1 |
| Netherlands | 7.4[e] | 5.4[e] | n.a. | n.a. | 21.2[f] | 19.3[f] |
| Portugal | 3.9 | 4.7[b] | 3.9 | 3.8[b] | 8.8 | 10.7[b] |
| UK | 5.2 | 4.7 | 4.6 | 4.9 | 11.9 | 12.7 |

*Note*: n.a. = not available.

[a] no data available for Greece, the Irish Republic, and Luxemburg.
[b] 1986.
[c] 1988.
[d] 1980.
[e] schools only.
[f] social security only.

*Source*: OECD (1993).

instruments consist of Regulations, Directives, and Decisions. The principal agency responsible for formulating and implementing social policy is the Commission's Directorate-General (DG) V, which deals with Employment, Social Affairs, and Education. Other important policy-making bodies include the Administrative Commission for Social Security, made up of one representative from each Member State; and a number of corporatist advisory committees, consisting of government, trade-union, and employer representatives from each Member State, the most important of which is the Economic and Social Committee.

The provisions of the Treaty of Rome relating to social policy are contained mainly in Articles 117–28, though relevant matters are also referred to in a number of other Articles. Articles 117 and 118 record the agreement of Member States to promote improved standards of living and working conditions. They also charge the Commission with responsibility for promoting co-operation among Member States in the social field. This is defined as covering vocational training, employment, working conditions, occupational health and safety, labour law, the rights of association and collective bargaining, and social security. The scope of social policy is thus explicitly confined to matters affecting *employees* rather than *citizens*. Moreover, the role of the Commission in relation to these matters is restricted by Treaty to conducting research and offering opinions.

Articles 119–22 proclaim the objectives of equal pay for equal work and equal provisions for paid holidays; establish links with Articles 48–51, which seek to facilitate labour migration—*between* Member States, that is—by various means including, in particular, the co-ordination of social security arrangements; and empower the Commission to report on social conditions in the Community. Articles 123–28 establish the European Social Fund with a view to promoting employment opportunities and supporting geographical and occupational labour mobility within the EC. They also authorize the Council of Ministers to develop a common vocational training policy.

The operational design of the Social Fund has changed several times in the course of its history. In its most recent guise, the Fund supports a variety of projects, some organized centrally by the Commission, but most sponsored by public and private sector organizations at national, regional, and local levels. Eligible projects must be directed towards reducing unemployment in designated regions suffering from rural underdevelopment or industrial decline, and among specified groups experiencing social disadvantage—young people, the long-term unemployed, women seeking to re-enter employment, disabled people, and migrants. The scale of the Fund, however, remains small, and applications for support have consistently outstripped appropriations, despite a threefold expansion in its budget since 1988. Furthermore, although Article 104 of the Rome Treaty declares that one of the EC's general objectives is to ensure a 'high' level of employment, even these modest essays in active manpower policy have not been matched by any comparable institutional commitment in the macroeconomic sphere, beyond the limited degree of policy co-ordination required to run the European Monetary System (EMS).

The minor role assigned to social policy by the Treaty of Rome reflects the fact that the EC was originally envisaged as a strictly economic union: issues which had no direct bearing on this goal were ignored or discounted. Accordingly, except in the case of agriculture, the EC lacked the attributes of a federal state processing demands, allocating resources, and securing legitimacy. Rather, the emphasis was on standardizing access to the market through law. Whilst this might be seen as adding a European layer to the *civil* rights of citizenship, the *political*, and still more the *social*, rights of citizenship remained at a pre-European, national level. This state of affairs did not really change until the mid-1980s when the Commission's new President, Jacques Delors, seized the opportunity presented by the Single Market programme to argue and campaign for the idea that social cohesion was just as important as market integration. Even then, the preoccupation with *employment* remained, and the concept of a European 'social space' was fiercely contested by Delors's opponents, who were by no means confined to the United Kingdom.

Articles 100*a* and 118*a* of the SEA commit the EC to improving and harmonizing national standards of health and safety and of environmental and consumer protection. Article 118*b* gives the Commission responsibility for promoting a social dialogue between management and labour at the European level. Articles 130*a* and 130*b* seek to strengthen 'economic and social cohesion' through the use of reformed structural funds, including the European Social Fund.

These additions to the EC's remit were accompanied by significant changes of legislative procedure. Except for certain reserved issues, the SEA introduced qualified majority voting in the Council of Ministers, and strengthened the powers of the European Parliament (EP) in relation to the Council. Proposals on taxes and transfers, the free movement of people, and the rights and interests of employees are still subject to the unanimity rule and can, therefore, still be blocked if a single Member State chooses to exercise its veto. There is also a grey area in which it is open to argument which procedure should be used, and which both the Commission and those, like the UK government, who have no time for the 'social dimension' have made active efforts to exploit. Nevertheless, as Springer (1992) shows convincingly, the introduction of qualified majority voting has facilitated some important new initiatives in the social field by helping to expedite action in Council, expand the scope for coalition-building between Commission, Parliament, and Council, and reduce the scope for obstructionism.

The fall-out from the SEA both reflected and reinforced a wider shift among opinion-makers. Political, business, and labour leaders were all keen to relaunch the project of European union and revitalize Europe's economies, and were all happy to embrace an activist conception of EC social policy. Statesmen and industrialists, noting the real or apparent dynamism of the American and East Asian economies, sought antidotes to 'Eurosclerosis'. The labour movement, devastated by mass unemployment and political defeat, was desperate for new jobs and new horizons. The high point of this new mood was reached at the Strasburg Summit in December 1989, which, with the dissent of the United Kingdom, adopted the 'Social Charter'—or, to give it its full title, the Community Charter of Fundamental Rights.

The significance of this event was largely symbolic. Despite the controversy it aroused, the Charter, whose final draft had, in any case, been diluted for the sake of consensus, was purely declaratory and had no legal force. The pointed reference which its Preamble makes to the principle of subsidiarity was a coded way of acknowledging limitations on the EC's authority to enact and enforce social legislation. Even so, the importance of symbols should not be underrated. The immediate reason for treating the 'social dimension' as a second pillar of the Single Europe project had been to alleviate dislocations caused by economic restructuring and to reassure workers that existing, nationally guaranteed rights and standards would not be undermined by intensified competitive pressure. Beyond this, however, lay a wider, political purpose. Supporters of the social dimension saw it as a building block in the creation of a 'people's Europe', which would, in time, rival the older nation-states as a focus of social identity. From this standpoint, the Social Charter was less a statement of legislative intent than the proclamation of a social ideal to stand alongside the market economy and parliamentary democracy as an emblem of European civilization.

The Social Charter formed the basis of the Social Chapter of the Maastricht Treaty agreed in December 1991, and ratified by all Member States in 1993. At the insistence of the United Kingdom, the Social Chapter was formally excluded from the main body of the Treaty. But a Protocol was adopted by all twelve Member States which referred to an Agreement among the eleven Member States other than the United Kingdom to comply with the terms of the omitted Social Chapter. Thus, on matters covered by the Treaty of Rome, as amended by the SEA, or on matters covered by the Social Chapter in which the United Kingdom wished to participate, decision-making would proceed in the normal way among all twelve Member States. On matters covered by the Social Chapter in which the United Kingdom did *not* wish to participate, decisions would be made by the other eleven Member States only, acting under the terms of the Protocol.

The Social Chapter adds to Article 117 of the Treaty of Rome the new objectives of 'proper social protection', dialogue between management and labour, and the 'development of human resources to achieve lasting employment'. The EC is empowered by Article 118 to legislate by qualified majority voting on questions of health and safety, working conditions, sex equality at work, and the integration of excluded social groups into the labour force. Unanimity is still required for legislation on social security, redundancy procedures, the funding of job creation, the working conditions of third-country nationals, and worker representation. The Commission is obliged to consult representatives of management and labour before introducing proposals in any of these areas. Note, however, that questions of pay, the right of association, and the right to resort to strikes or lock-outs are expressly excluded from Article 118. Furthermore, under the terms of the new Article 3*b* on subsidiarity, the EC is authorized to act only when its objectives can be achieved better by action taken at the Community level than by the actions of Member States.

## 10.5. THE DEVELOPMENT OF EC SOCIAL POLICY

Besides being tightly constrained, EC social policy has developed in fits and starts. Sometimes it has been consigned to a minor role either by general consent or because any other course was blocked by an adverse balance of forces. But there have also been spurts of activism as those who favoured a collectivist, Community-wide approach to social issues— whether in the conservative–corporatist or social democratic mould— temporarily gained ground over the supporters of economic liberalism and national autonomy, groups which often, though not invariably, coincide. In general, the policy activists have included the Commission, the majority groupings within the EP, and the European Trade Union Confederation (ETUC). They have been opposed by the Union of the Industries of the European Community (UNICE), which speaks for European employers and normally favours an internal market as free as possible from physical, technical, fiscal, and social 'distortions'. The UK government has also taken this view, sometimes gaining the backing of other Member States which had pragmatic objections to specific policy proposals and found it convenient to let the bellicose British do their fighting for them. In the end, the fate of social policy has depended on the Council of Ministers. But the Council is the focus of efforts by the Member States to uphold what they take to be their national interests. It is, therefore, the least 'European' of the EC's policy-making bodies.

Given this general line-up of forces, raising the profile of social policy has usually required the assistance of one or both of two conditions: an easing of the institutional constraints—as with the introduction of qualified majority voting—or a change in the political complexion of the Council, preferably accompanied by a change of heart on the part of UNICE. Suitable conjunctures have arisen either at times when the EC is being enlarged through new accessions, or when it is about to embark on some wider policy initiative such as closer monetary union or the Single Market project, the success of which can plausibly be shown to depend on stronger supranational social regulation.

### Modest Beginnings: From the Treaty of Rome to the late 1960s

EC social policy was originally envisaged as a minor adjunct to economic integration, focused almost exclusively on the labour market with particular reference to labour mobility and the impact of internal free trade on working conditions, wages, and social insurance. Policy-makers assumed that aspirations for higher wages and social expenditure would be met from the economies of scale and more rapid economic growth which they expected to result from market liberalization. Since the 1960s were indeed years of unprecedented economic growth in the founding Member States, there was little pressure for anything more substantial.

Nor, it could be argued, was there much *need* for policy harmonization among the original EC6. Leibfried (1990) notes that, apart from the Italian *Mezzogiorno*, these states formed a relatively homogeneous bloc. There was a rough balance in the overall configuration of factors governing their competitive relations—economic structure, technical proficiency, wage levels, social insurance levies, labour productivity, transport costs, and exchange rates. Their policy regimes were all designed in the conservative–corporatist mould, with certain local peculiarities, liberal or social democratic, as the case might be. This homogeneity was disrupted by the successive enlargements of the EC in the 1970s and the 1980s, which introduced a new pole of liberal-individualism in the west and extended the sway of social traditionalism in the south. Once the spontaneous equilibrium underlying the original Treaty of Rome had been disturbed in this way, it could be regained, if at all, only by deliberate negotiation.

During the 1960s, then, EC social policy was modest in both intention and achievement. Some progress was made in redeploying redundant workers, especially in unskilled trades, with the European Social Fund being used to support national retraining and resettlement schemes. But hopes that the Fund would redistribute resources towards the less-developed regions of the EC were thwarted. The total size of the Fund was left unspecified, but the proportions in which Member States contributed were predetermined. Thus, France and Germany were to contribute 32 per cent each, while Italy's contribution was fixed at 20 per cent. The expectation was that France and Germany, with lower unemployment rates, would be net losers. However, since the Fund operated by reimbursing Member States 50 per cent of approved national expenditure, the amount which each state received depended critically on the scale of its own training efforts. As a result, Germany became a net beneficiary, receiving over 40 per cent of Fund expenditure during this period.

The goal of harmonizing social insurance systems proved equally elusive. In part, this was because initial variations in coverage, scope, standards, costs, methods of finance, and administrative regulations were too wide to permit any easy or rapid convergence. But a more serious problem was that any uniform, Community-wide scheme would have entailed interstate transfers on a scale that Germany, as the principal prospective net loser, was unwilling to countenance. The only concession to harmonization was an agreement to introduce equal pay for equal work throughout the EC. This move was instigated by France, where the law already prohibited sex discrimination with respect to rates of pay. The motive was strictly commercial: French employers were anxious not to be saddled with a competitive handicap. It was, nevertheless, an important precedent. Over the next thirty years both the Commission and the European Court of Justice exerted consistent pressure on Member States to equalize the terms on which women participate in the labour market. This said, it is pertinent to point out that equalizing market opportunities does not in itself redress structural inequalities between men and women rooted in the sexual division of labour. The achievements and limitations of EC legislation with special relevance for women are discussed by Hoskyns (1985), Mazey (1988), Meehan (1990), and Springer (1992: ch. 6).

*Hopes and Disappointments: The Social Action Programme of the 1970s*

By the end of the 1960s the EC's low-key approach to social issues came to seem less and less appropriate. Several developments conspired to stimulate this perception. The deliberations of the Werner Committee on Monetary Union prompted the realization that a system of 'irrevocably' fixed exchange rates would lead to regional imbalance and political tension if it were not complemented by an adequately funded and centrally directed programme of regional support. At the same time, the EC was about to undergo its first enlargement, with the impending accession of the United Kingdom, the Irish Republic, Denmark, and Norway (whose voters, in the event, withheld their approval). As indicated earlier, this meant that matters which the original EC6 had been able to take for granted now required explicit attention. Meanwhile, the explosion of working-class militancy and youth revolt in the late 1960s left its mark on the political scene. Political élites could no longer disregard either the social costs of economic growth or the widespread popular impression that the Common Market was a club for big business. On both counts, the EC needed a 'human face'.

The new initiative was launched at the 1972 Paris Summit after several years of preparation. The Heads of State undertook to establish a Community regional policy, complete with a Regional Commissioner and a European Regional Development Fund (discussed in Chapter 7). They also instructed the Commission to draw up a Social Action Programme with the aims of promoting 'full and better employment'; improved living and working conditions; social dialogue between employers, unions, and government; and workers' participation in enterprise management.

The Commission's proposals, unveiled in 1974, spawned a stream of new Directives. Two of these conferred rights of information and consultation on employees in firms which were proposing to institute collective redundancies or were involved in a change of ownership as a result of mergers, take-overs, or acquisitions. Other Directives obliged Member States to guarantee women equal access to vocational training and social security; and imposed tougher standards of workplace health and safety. In addition, the European Social Fund was given a larger budget and a new, more tightly specified list of priorities. However, by the time these measures were implemented, the economic and political context had changed radically, and in the end the high hopes which had been vested in the Social Action Programme were largely disappointed.

The recession which hit the advanced capitalist democracies in the mid-1970s marked the end of the long post-war boom and transformed both the character and scale of the social problems facing the EC. Member States responded by seeking national rather than Community solutions. One reason was that the Commission's efforts to promulgate Community-wide rights and standards tended to level up existing national provisions (or would have done had they been implemented). But the richer states were unwilling to pay for EC policies that would mainly benefit the poorer states, and the poorer states were unwilling to agree to EC policies that they were unable to pay for themselves.

The least successful parts of the Social Action Programme were those concerned with industrial democracy. The idea that trade unions had a right to participate in policy-making, at national and Community levels, and that workers likewise had a right to participate in enterprise decision-making, was deeply rooted in the social policy regimes of the EC's core states, and was strongly supported by the Commission. But policy regimes are organic formations and cannot easily be transplanted from one state to another. The United Kingdom's experience offers a case in point.

The UK system of industrial relations, at any rate prior to the neo-liberal revolution of the 1980s, was steeped in the tradition of free collective bargaining. Trade unions reserved the right to oppose specific manage-ment decisions of which they disapproved, but refrained from seeking formal rights of co-decision—whether on the lines of the German system of co-determination, under which worker directors are appointed to the supervisory boards of large enterprises; or even in the less exalted form of workplace councils, which are a standard feature of industrial life in most EC countries. UK employers, for their part, broadly accepted the need to recognize and negotiate with the unions over a narrow range of issues—chiefly, wages and working conditions—but jealously guarded the right of unilateral control over corporate investment, technical innovation, and other managerial decisions. It was not, therefore, surprising that UK trade unions, which were, in any case, opposed to the United Kingdom's mem-bership of the EC, showed little enthusiasm for 'foreign' notions of industrial democracy, or that UK employers flatly rejected proposals that they perceived as a threat to their 'prerogatives'.

Throughout the 1970s the Commission laboured to find an acceptable way of establishing a common commitment to workers' participation. But, even though it abandoned its preference for the German model and was prepared to allow for several alternative systems from which governments could choose according to their national traditions, this effort failed. The final act in the cycle of social legislation that had begun a decade earlier was the 'Vredeling' Directive of 1980. This was a proposal to extend the EC's disclosure laws to transnational companies, obliging them to inform and consult their employees on a regular basis and with respect to their global operations, not just those in the EC. It aroused strong opposition from UNICE and was thrown out by the Council of Ministers after orchestrated resistance led by the United Kingdom. Between 1980 and 1986 there were no major new employment laws.

### *The 1980s: The SEA and the Social Charter*

After the doldrums into which it drifted in the late 1970s, social policy received a new impetus in the early 1980s, following the electoral victory of the French socialists in 1981. The crucial turning-points were the Fontainebleau Summit in 1984 and the arrival in 1985 of a new Commission headed by Jacques Delors. Building on the decisions of the Summit, the Commission proposed a new Action Programme with four major themes: (i) the completion of the Single European Market (SEM) by the end of 1992; (ii) the adoption of an SEA, which would complement the Treaty of Rome with provisions relating to the working environment; (iii) a package of reforms covering the CAP, the EC's finances, and the three structural funds; and (iv) a revival of the practice of social dialogue.

From 1985 onwards all shades of opinion paid greater heed than before to what came to be known as the 'social dimension' of European integration. The rationale and significance of this development were briefly touched on in the previous section. It is, however, important to bear in mind that social policy did not suddenly cease to be a battleground. For market enthusiasts the 'social dimension' meant removing obstacles to the free movement of labour by improving information about job prospects and establishing uniform professional standards and job qualifications. Pragmatists, more alert to the negative consequences of closer economic union, stressed the need to compensate those regions and social groups which stood to lose from economic restructuring, and urged that action be taken to prevent 'social dumping'—the levelling *down* of established wages, standards, and rights which, it was feared, would result from the removal of barriers to pan-European competition. As we noted earlier, ardent 'Europeans' saw the 'social dimension' as a means of winning popular support for the goal of closer political union, or at any rate allaying the fears which many ordinary people harbour towards the EC, and which surfaced with dramatic consequences during the process of ratifying the Maastricht Treaty.

By the end of the 1980s the Social Charter had emerged as the principal focus of conflict. Mrs Thatcher denounced it as 'Marxist interventionism'. Rhetoric aside, this was, on the face of it, a bizarre thing to say. The Charter was non-binding and most of its specific principles, such as the right to belong or not to belong to a trade union, had long been observed in most Member States, or indeed, as in the case of equal treatment for women at work, had been enshrined in Community law. What the Charter's opponents chiefly took exception to was its underlying philosophy of social regulation. In so far as they had specific, practical criticisms to make, the provisions singled out for attack were those which would, or might, add to employers' costs or limit their room for manœuvre: notably, the right of workers employed on 'atypical' terms to benefit from an 'equitable' reference wage; the potential extension of disclosure rights; and the aspiration, long held by the Commission, but loathed by UNICE, towards Community-wide collective bargaining in transnational companies. Hackles were also raised at the licence which the Commission was given to compile an annual report on the application of the Charter throughout the EC.

In fact, as Springer (1992: 88–96) notes, except in relation to health and safety standards, which are somewhat technical, and which no one is anxious to appear to be weakening, the Commission tended to soft-pedal the implementation and monitoring of the Social Charter. There was no new stream of Directives on the pattern of the 1970s. The Directive is, in any case, of limited value as an instrument of social protection. The latitude it gives Member States in choosing the means of attaining specified targets necessarily complicates the Commission's responsibility for ensuring that different means really are equivalent—the more so when the targets in question are difficult, if not impossible, to quantify.

## Maastricht and after

By the time the ratification of the Maastricht Treaty had been completed in 1993, the Exchange Rate Mechanism (ERM) had effectively broken down and prospects for closer European Union, if not for the EC itself, were very uncertain. In the early 1990s many of the underlying worries which had been largely submerged during the heady years of 1986–91 resurfaced. The special dispensations obtained by the United Kingdom and Denmark interacted with a shift in public opinion to create a general reluctance, even in those Member States most committed to the European ideal, to cede any more sovereignty to the Community. It is, therefore, impossible to do more than speculate about the future of EC social policy.

One factor that will certainly influence the course of events, however, is the tension that exists in the Single Market project between the integration of product and capital markets, and the integration of the labour market. The opening-up of national markets to pan-European competition calls for deregulation, whereas the establishment of common social rights and uniform standards of treatment in the labour market can only be achieved by positive regulation. Yet the labour market is regulated in different ways in different states according to their respective policy regimes, and these, as we have seen, have so far resisted assimilation.

The difficulties which have beset attempts to harmonize social policy have led to a lowering of sights. Harmonization was conceived as a dynamic process in which diverse national systems would gradually converge as the ground that they shared in common was continually enlarged. The aim of the new approach, which some observers describe as 'negative co-ordination', is simply to render distinctive national regimes compatible by organizing the areas in which they overlap and, in particular, by arranging for mutual recognition of national standards, subject to an agreed minimum. In this context, the provisions of the Social Charter/ Chapter can be seen as an attempt to formulate a common set of general norms, based on an agreed view about the role of labour in European society, which is nevertheless capable of accommodating economic disparities and institutional differences among EC members.

Both 'positive harmonization' and 'negative co-ordination' are to be contrasted with a third approach to social policy, which might be called 'European social citizenship'. This would involve supranational initiatives designed to institute common rights of social citizenship throughout the EC as an integral part of a federal European state. Social policy would cease to focus exclusively or predominantly on the labour market. Rather, its remit would become universal, affecting everyone—men and women, young and old, employed and non-employed—in their shared capacity as citizens of the EC.

Hitherto, most ordinary people have experienced the EC as remote and irrelevant or labyrinthine and sinister: either way, they had little reason to love or trust it. If EC social policy impinged on them at all, it was as the outcome of multi-levelled bargaining between sectional interest groups, national governments, and EC agencies over the allocation of structural funds or the framing and enforcement of EC law. By contrast, the links between European social citizenship and an emergent federal state would be direct and transparent. For this to happen there would, of course, need to be a separate EC tier of taxes and transfers, over and above the transfers and services that continued to be provided by each national state. And Eurofiscal policy would, in turn, need to be conducted in tandem with macroeconomic and active manpower policies framed on a Community-wide basis. It would, moreover, be essential that the integration of social policy be matched by a corresponding degree of political integration: Eurocitizenship could be legitimized only by the EP, whose powers of initiative, amendment, supervision, and inquiry would need to be expanded accordingly.

In the prevailing climate of disillusion and cynicism, it is easy to dismiss this vision as hopelessly utopian. Before leaping to this conclusion, however, readers are asked to ponder the social condition of contemporary Europe. The entire continent, from Scandinavia to Sicily and from Russia to the Republic of Ireland, is plagued by problems of mass unemployment, poverty, and social exclusion, against which all established policy regimes have proved ineffective, even those of the Nordic states, which succeeded in hanging on to full employment and the world's most advanced welfare standards throughout the upheavals of the 1970s and 1980s. Yet history provides no warrant for the view that attempts to reconstruct social institutions and international relations are doomed to failure. Consider, for example, the role of creative statesmanship in overcoming the dislocation of the world economy after the Second World War. The lesson to be drawn is that Europe's current social disorders *can* be tackled, but it is going to need the kind of breadth and boldness of vision which gave its peoples a new lease of life half a century ago.

It is also important to realize that the alternative to European social citizenship will not be the indefinite continuation of the status quo. Willy nilly, existing work and welfare arrangements are being reshaped in response to global competition, European recession, and national budget deficits. The consequence of further market integration in the EC, unaccompanied by any serious attempt to enhance the EC's social competency, will be the withering away of welfare states, even in their present battered and beleaguered forms. And any further erosion of social rights which were never very ample, equal, or well founded in the first place is bound to deepen the gulf that divides secure and well-paid jobholders in the core of the labour market from both the working poor on its margins and the disinherited poor beyond the pale. In short, European social policy is at a turning-point. The choices made over the next few years are likely to prove fateful.

# REFERENCES

CEC (1991): Commission of the European Communities, *A Social Portrait of Europe* (Brussels: CEC).

Esping-Andersen, G. (1990), *The Three Worlds of Welfare Capitalism* (Cambridge: Polity Press).

Hoskyns, C. (1985), 'Women's Equality and the European Community', *Feminist Review*, 20 (June), 71–88.

Langan, M., and Ostner, I. (1991), 'Gender and Welfare: Towards a Comparative Framework', in Room (1991), 127–50.

Leibfried, S. (1990), 'Sozialstaat Europa? Intergrationsperspektiven Europäischer Armutsregimes', in *Nachrichtendienst des Deutschen Vereins fur Offentliche und Private Fürsorge (NDV)*, 70/9 (Sept.), 296–305.

Marquand, D. (1988), *The Unprincipled Society* (London: Jonathan Cape).

Marshall, T. H. (1950), *Citizenship and Social Class and Other Essays* (Cambridge: Cambridge University Press).

Mazey, S. (1988), 'European Community Action on behalf of Women: The Limits of Legislation', *Journal of Common Market Studies*, 27: 63–84.

Meehan, E. (1993), *Citizenship and the European Community* (London: Sage).

OECD (1992): Organization for Economic Co-operation and Development, *Labour Force Statistics 1970–90* (Paris: OECD).

—— (1993), *National Accounts 1979–91* (Paris: OECD).

Pierson, C. (1991), *Beyond the Welfare State* (Cambridge: Polity Press).

Room, G. (1991) (ed.), *Towards a European Welfare State* (Bristol: School for Advanced Urban Studies Publications).

Springer, B. (1992), *The Social Dimension of 1992: Europe Faces a New EC* (New York: Praeger).

Therborn, G. (1987), 'Welfare States and Capitalist Markets', *Acta Sociologica*, 30: 237–54.

Titmuss, R. (1974), *Social Policy* (London: Allen and Unwin).

# 11

# Developments in Trade and Trade Policy

LYNDEN MOORE

## 11.1. INTRODUCTION

The increase in trade between member countries of a preferential trading area is often taken as an indication of how successful the area is in integrating the countries' economies. As can be seen from Fig. 11.1, EC trade in total increased very rapidly in the thirty years from 1958, whilst an increasing proportion has been intra-EC trade, such that by 1989 it accounted for roughly 60 per cent of total EC exports and imports.

However, some of the increase in total trade simply represents the expansion in membership of the EC and some of the increase is just due to inflation. It is difficult to correct for this because *relative* prices have also changed. In particular, the price of oil quadrupled from 1973 to 1974 and then doubled again from 1978 to 1980, since when it has tended to decline. As fuel represented 38 per cent of imports by the EC12 from other countries in 1981, declining to 15 per cent in 1988, this has had an appreciable effect on the overall result. Furthermore, as tariffs on oil are zero or negligible, membership of the EC has not affected Member States' imports of oil. In the circumstances, it seems more appropriate to look at EC trade as a proportion of world trade. The increase in EC trade relative to that of the world as a whole between 1958 and 1989 for the EC of the time and for the EC12 is shown in Figure 11.2*a*.

In Chapter 3 the expansion of trade was examined from the point of view of Member States in terms of trade creation and trade diversion. It was mentioned there that Balassa had suggested that, when the impact of the formation of the EC6 on total trade from 1959 to 1970 was considered, the effect on trade appeared to be one of trade creation; but that, when individual sectors were considered, there was evidence of trade diversion for non-tropical food, chemicals, and other manufactured goods (Balassa 1974).

There has been no equivalent analysis of the effect of the expansion of the EC6 to the EC12. However, many economists have pointed out that there is not much evidence of emerging specialization between the EC economies, as would be expected from trade creation. Rather there has been a rapid increase in intra-industry trade. This is generally attributed to

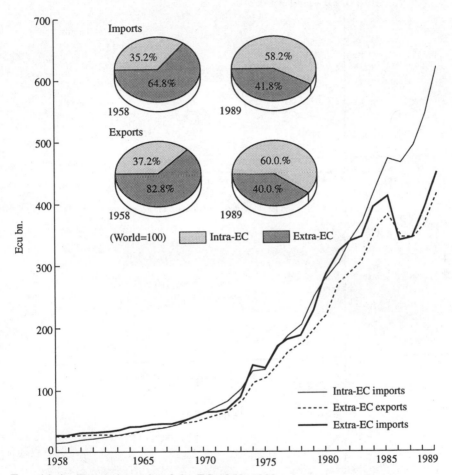

**Fig. 11.1.** Trends in trade of the EC 1958–1989
*Source*: GATT (1991: ii).

the exploitation of economies of scale. Clearly what is regarded as intra-industry trade will depend on how fine a break-down of industries is used in the study and this in turn will determine its empirical magnitude. (See Greenaway, Hyclak, and Thornton 1989; Tharakan and Kol 1989).

The question asked in world fora, such as GATT, is how far this increase in intra-EC trade has been at the expense of trade with third countries. What has been the effect on them of the discrimination inherent in EC policy favouring EC and European Free Trade Association (EFTA) expor-

External and internal exports of the EC in world trade

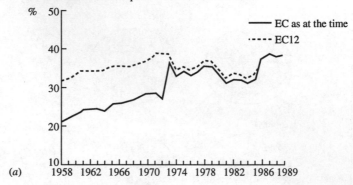

(a)

External exports of the EC in world trade (excluding internal exports of the EC)

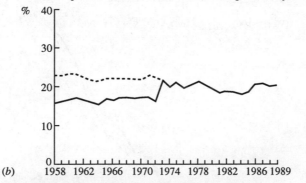

(b)

Share of external exports in total exports of the EC

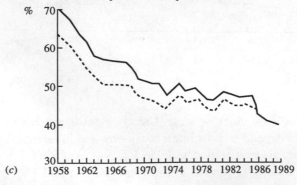

(c)

FIG. 11.2. Merchandise exports of the EC 1958–1989
*Note*: EC as at the time = EC6 from 1958 to 1972; EC9 from 1973 to 1980; EC10 from 1981 to 1985; EC12 from 1986 to the present time.
*Source*: Gatt (1991ii).

ters to the EC markets, and the movement away from multilateralism to the regionalization of trade?

As can be seen from Fig. 11.2*b* and *c*, EC external trade has been declining as a proportion of world trade, and it has been declining even more dramatically as a proportion of total EC trade (GATT 1991: 1, 303). Within this total the position of developing countries has come in for particular scrutiny. Their share in external EC trade declined from 44.5 per cent (exports) and 45.5 per cent (imports) in 1981 to 32 per cent and 31 per cent respectively in 1989. This partly reflects the relative decline in the price of oil, and the deteriorating trade position of oil-exporting countries (GATT 1991: 1, 3).

However, the proportion of the EC's trade with EFTA has been increasing and in 1990 it accounted for 27 per cent of EC exports and 24 per cent of EC imports. Indeed, in 1990 intra-West European trade accounted for a third of total world merchandise trade.

In this chapter we will concentrate on trade in manufactures. Let us begin by considering the overall structure of such trade. Table 11.1 shows the distribution of trade between the major commodity categories, and the proportion of EC exports going to other EC countries, the remainder of Western Europe to which an EC exporter has privileged access, and the rest of the world. The proportional distribution varies considerably. It is interesting to observe that the relative importance of intra-EC exports is highest for products for which there are many non-tariff barriers—for example, iron and steel, office and telecommunications equipment, automotive products, textiles, and clothing. The same conclusion would almost certainly apply to some items such as footwear which are included in the very disparate category of 'other consumer goods'.

Thus, although developments in trade are partly the result of exogenous changes in the relative costs of production and technological change, they are also the result of trade policy. We begin the review of this policy by considering the international institutional framework for trade within which the EC was established. Then we will consider the development of internal EC trade policy: first, in terms of the provisions of the Treaty of Rome and how they have been interpreted by the Commission and the European Court of Justice (ECJ); and, secondly, their extension through the Single European Act (SEA) of 1986. The EC has devoted far more attention to the removal of barriers to intra-EC trade than to the liberalization of world trade—that is, until the 1990s, when efforts to conclude the Uruguay Round of tariff reductions forced the EC to take the international dimension of its policies more seriously.

This will be followed by a consideration of policies on trade in some important sectors—notably, steel, automobiles, and textiles and clothing. Finally, we will consider how national aspirations to be at the leading edge of new technologies, particularly electronics, have been transferred to an

TABLE 11.1. *EC trade in manufactures in 1990*

| Manufactures | Exports Total (US$bn) | Percentage distribution | | | Imports (US$bn.) | Net exports (US$bn.) |
|---|---|---|---|---|---|---|
| | | Intra-EC | Other West European | Rest of world | | |
| Iron and steel | 52.4 | 65 | 11 | 24 | 45.56 | 6.48 |
| Chemicals | 162.71 | 60 | 12 | 28 | 141.19 | 21.52 |
| Other semi-manufactures | 124.66 | 61 | 13 | 26 | 125.99 | −1.33 |
| Machinery and transport equipment | 518.50 | 58 | 12 | 30 | 464.94 | 53.56 |
| Power-generating equipment | 20.92 | 37 | 9 | 53 | 17.28 | 3.64 |
| Other non-electrical machinery | 142.26 | 48 | 14 | 38 | 104.81 | 37.45 |
| Office and telecommunications equipment | 82.98 | 67 | 11 | 22 | 115.91 | −32.93 |
| Electrical machinery | 54.36 | 56 | 15 | 29 | 49.33 | 5.03 |
| Automotive products | 158.38 | 69 | 10 | 21 | 130.43 | 27.95 |
| Other transport equipment | 53.25 | 50 | 9 | 41 | 47.17 | 6.08 |
| Textiles | 47.15 | 65 | 13 | 22 | 46.00 | 1.15 |
| Clothing | 37.89 | 65 | 19 | 17 | 50.68 | −12.79 |
| Other consumer goods | 133.83 | 55 | 16 | 28 | 128.68 | 5.15 |
| TOTAL | 1,076.79 | 59 | 13 | 28 | 1,003.03 | 73.76 |

*Note:* Product Groups are defined according to Revision 3 of the Standard International Trade Classification (SITC Rev. 3).
*Source:* GATT (1992).

EC level, and we will review the various trade devices that have been exploited in pursuance of this, and their apparent effect.

## 11.2. THE INTERNATIONAL CONTEXT

The formation of the EC and its free trade area in manufactures with EFTA took place within an international legal framework provided by the General Agreement on Tariffs and Trade (GATT), to which all West European countries belonged. GATT was established in 1948 to remove discrimination and impediments to trade between its members. On becoming a member, each nation had extended to it the most-favoured-nation (m.f.n.) tariff—that is, the lowest tariff—of every other member, and vice versa.

However, an exception was made with respect to the formation of custom unions and free trade areas, which were regarded as a further step to the liberalization of trade, provided that 'the [external] duties . . . shall not on the whole be higher or more restrictive than . . . prior to the formation of such a union' and also provided they 'shall include a plan and schedule for [their] . . . formation within a reasonable length of time' (GATT 1986*a*: 41, Article XXIV). The EC has conformed to these requirements. Initially, the EC countries continued to negotiate individually within GATT, but since 1980 the EC has been negotiating for its membership as a whole.

GATT's first priority was to remove all quantitative restrictions (quotas) on trade. It has also conducted a series of tariff-cutting rounds, the latest of which has been the Uruguay Round, from 1986 to 1993. In former rounds the EC countries insisted on excluding 'sensitive'—that is, declining—industries, such as agriculture and textiles and clothing. In the Uruguay Round GATT insisted that they be included, and it was negotiation in these areas that delayed the completion of this round. The negotiations were also extended, for the first time, to include services.

An additional problem has been that, as tariffs on manufactures were reduced under the previous seven rounds, countries have increasingly made use of non-tariff barriers to trade, which are quite inconsistent with the ethos and legal requirements of GATT. Prominent among these devices has been the 'voluntary' export restraint (VER) by which the importing country negotiates a physical limit on exports from a particular country. The VER is in effect a bilateral quota. It has a similar effect to a tariff in raising the price of the product on the market of the importing country. But no tariff revenue is gained. Instead, there is an 'economic rent' associated with the quota, because the product is sold on the domestic market at a much higher price than it can command on the international market. Who gains the economic rent depends on how the quota is allocated. When VERs are imposed on developing countries, those countries are generally given the entitlement to export and are therefore generally regarded as acquiring the rent from the quota.

On the other hand, in the case of Japan, the entitlement may be given to importing firms who then acquire the rent. In 1990 there were quantitative restrictions on a variety of machinery exports to certain Member States: machine tools, ship's cranes, forklift trucks, and agricultural machines to Spain, and engines and sewing machines to Italy, Spain, and Portugal. Between 1981 and 1991 France accepted only 260 machining centres and 360 numerically controlled lathes per annum from Japan. In addition to these, Japan has 'monitored' its exports to the EC of colour TV sets, colour TV tubes, and video tape recorders since 1983 (GATT 1991: 1, 105, 211–15).

In addition, there has been a widespread use by both the EC and the United States of countervailing and anti-dumping duties. Dumping is defined as the situation in which a product is sold in a market at less than its 'normal' value, which is regarded as either being 'the comparable price . . . when [the product is] destined for consumption in the exporting country, or, in the absence of such domestic price, is less than either the highest comparable price . . . [of the] product for export to any third country . . . or the cost of production of the product in the country of origin plus a reasonable addition for selling cost and profit' (GATT 1986*a*: 10, Article VI). The importing firm country can levy an anti-dumping duty not greater than the margin of dumping on the exports of the firm. Alternatively, if the difference is due to a government subsidy, a countervailing duty may be imposed to offset it. Sometimes firms avoid anti-dumping duties by accepting a 'price under-taking'—that is, a minimum import price, by which the exporting firms lose their competitive advantage but gain a higher price.

The problem with these non-tariff barriers is their arbitrary nature, the way they discriminate not only between countries but also between firms, penalizing the most efficient producer. In calculating the size of anti-dumping duties the EC is also accused of the dubious use of statistics.

Thus the protective ring around the EC is not only that of the common external tariff (CET), which for industrial products is (on average) very low at 6.4 per cent (GATT 1991: 1, 90), but also a widespread use of these non-tariff barriers to external trade. Economists have expressed much concern about these, but the Commission itself has paid much more attention to the internal barriers to intra-EC trade.

## 11.3. EC POLICY TOWARDS INTERNAL TRADE

Article 3 of the Treaty of Rome included provisions for

(a) the elimination, as between Member States, of customs and of quantitative restrictions in regard to the import and export of goods as well as of all other measures having equivalent effect;

(b) the establishment of a common customs tariff and of a common commercial policy towards third countries.

These provisions were expanded in the following articles, but then in Article 36 it was stated that these 'shall not preclude prohibitions or restrictions on imports, exports, or goods in transit justified on the grounds of public morality; public policy; public security; the protection of health and life of humans, animals or plants . . . Provided always that such prohibitions or restrictions shall not be used as a means of arbitrary discrimination nor as a disguised restriction on trade between Member States.' Articles 100–2 provided the legal framework for 'harmonizing' these national restrictions if they affect trade.

Thus not only were all tariffs and quotas to be abolished but so also was any national regulation that interfered with intra-EC trade. Thus was the Commission set upon the road to 'harmonization', which proved to be very slow and arduous.

Soon after the United Kingdom joined the EC in 1973, instances of 'harmonization' aroused the ire of the UK populace, as one consumer product after the other appeared under threat: British beer because it was made with male and female hops, the British sausage because it contained less meat than the continental sausage, and British chocolate because British manufacturers were not required, as on the Continent, to include cocoa butter and generally used a cheaper vegetable oil as a substitute. Controversy over standards was not resolved until a legal case was brought by a German company, Rewe-Zentral, which was trying to import the French blackcurrant liqueur *cassis*, which had a lower alcohol content than required by German law. The ECJ ruled in 1978 that consumer protection could have been achieved by a label indicating the alcohol content: the German requirement was not essential. The 'Cassis de Dijon' principle, essentially one of mutual recognition of standards, has become of increasing importance ever since.

However, there are areas in which the process of harmonization has been more fruitful, in particular with regard to the safety requirements for motor vehicles; by 1991 forty-one directives for the technical harmonization of cars had been adopted (GATT 1991: 1, 220). There are other areas where agreements on standards have become very important and sometimes essential to communication—as, for instance, in the case of electronics—and they will be discussed later.

The Commission has also been engaged in removing other obstacles to trade. Some of these have been erected by firms to protect their markets. For instance, in 1984 the Commission fined British Leyland £210,000 for trying to prevent the reimportation of left-hand-drive metros for conversion (Swann 1988: 91). There are also the collusive practices discussed in Chapter 5.

Under Articles 92-4 of the Treaty, the Commission forbids national governments subsidizing the direct costs of its domestic firms in a way which distorts competition between Member States. There are some escape clauses, but export aid is not allowed. Indeed in 1990 Renault was forced to pay back the French government FF6 billion for not following proper procedures in this respect (Swann 1992: 154). More recently, British Aerospace had to pay back the government the aid it received on taking over the Rover car group in 1988 (£11 million for the aid it received and £46.6 million in interest payments on this) (*Financial Times,* 25 May 1993).

By the 1980s there were still in being a large number of non-tariff barriers to trade. They applied not only to goods but also to services. Under the SEA of 1986 these were supposed to have been removed by the beginning of 1993. They include all Member States' individual non-tariff barriers on imports from third countries. The most noticeable of these has been in the car industry, where there was a wide variation in the restrictions imposed by individual Member States on imports from Japan. In theory these have been replaced by an EC quota and this quota itself should be lifted by 2000.

Another major area of non-tariff barriers has been in the VERs negotiated with developing countries, but these will be discussed later.

One of the most important barriers to trade is that associated with public procurement. In 1987 public procurement accounted for 16 per cent of GDP (GATT 1991: 1, 15), and in 1984 a third of these were manufactures (CEC 1988: 55). Traditionally, national firms considered they had a right to supply their own government and nationalized industries, and therefore the proportion of public procurement supplied by imports was very much less than in the private sector. This is inconsistent with the ethos of the EC. Under the SEA, public procurement orders have to be submitted for tenders, which are open to suppliers in all Member States. This represents a very important breakthrough in, for example, the market for telecommunications equipment, which is growing fast but which in many European countries is still under the control of a nationalized industry. Particular attention is being paid to the Bundespost in Germany, which is regarded as being both slow to innovate and as exploiting its monopoly position with very high telephone call charges.

In tandem with the reduction in barriers to intra-EC trade, negotiations have also been taking place under, first, the Tokyo 1973-9 Round and then the Uruguay 1986-93 Round; the latter included further proposals for opening up public procurement to international competition. In this forum, the EC endeavoured to maintain some degree of protection, a 3 per cent tariff, on tenders from outside the EC to supply the EC markets. But this was not agreed to by EC's trading partners and the area of public procurement subject to international competition agreed to in the Tokyo

Round was extended by the Uruguay Round concluded in December 1993. Separate telecommunication negotiations are due to take place in 1994.

## 11.4. THE STEEL INDUSTRY

The iron and steel industry has been of major concern to the Member States of the EC from the outset. Indeed, the Treaty of Paris establishing the European Coal and Steel Community (ESCS) in 1951 preceded the establishment of the EC. The original objective was to remove discrimination by ESCS producers—whether that discrimination was exercised by direct or by indirect means (e.g. via distorted transport cost schedules)—and thus to open up the markets and promote the integration of these industries. This, it was considered, would deprive Germany of the ability again to use its own industry as the base for a large armaments programme.

The EC steel producers were also considerable suppliers on the world market. But steel was one of the first industries to be established by any major developing country starting to industrialize, and there soon developed a world overcapacity in steel production. Then, in the late 1950s and 1960s, the Japanese built a number of plants incorporating technological developments such as continuous casting, a more fuel-efficient method of production, and computer process control, and this was accompanied by a very rapid increase in labour productivity. Thus Japan became the lowest-cost producer of steel (Walter 1983).

The rise in the price of fuel in the early 1970s significantly raised the level of costs in steel production, and the downturn in international economic activity in the latter half of the 1970s imposed great competitive strains on all the steel industries. In 1977 Viscount Davignon became the Commissioner for industry, and his devices for keeping up the price of steel are called the Davignon Plan. He introduced a system of recommended minimum prices for certain iron and steel products which was extended in 1978, whilst minimum prices were also established for imports and VERs were negotiated with foreign suppliers (Swann 1992: 325).

When in 1980 prices resumed their downward slide, production was restricted under 'the manifest crisis' Article 58 of the ECSC Treaty by allocating quotas to the different firms based on mill capacity. This system lasted, with some misbehaviour on the part of participants, from 1980 to 1988. It can be argued that this effectively ossified the industry. Weaker firms did not go out of business and the German industry remained very fragmented (HMSO 1993).

Many of the firms were state owned, and, in order to reduce the enormous losses of major steel producers, national governments had to close some obsolete and unprofitable plants. All leading European producers cut back capacity, and for the EC as a whole it was reduced by 31 million tonnes between 1981 and 1986.

However, the EC market did not appear to be working effectively, with wide discrepancies between the prices of the same steel products in different national markets. This, together with the endeavours to establish a high minimum price in the EC, must inevitably have affected other industries. Steel is an important intermediate product: a 10 per cent rise in the price of steel raises the price of a car by 0.5 per cent and the price of metal products by between 1.5 and 2 per cent (CEC 1988).

The Commission tried to reduce state aid and prohibited all subsidization of direct costs and investment. Aid was allowed for the protection of the environment, for research and development expenditure, and for closures under strict conditions (CEC 1988: 82).

There was a slight increase in domestic demand in the early 1980s which then ceased; exports in 1991 and 1992 were lower than in the mid-1980s. From September 1989 to May 1993 steel prices fell by 35 per cent (HMSO 1993: 27). At present, overall demand for steel is static. The political problems in adjusting to this are that steel mills have been established in areas of high unemployment, deliberately, in the United Kingdom, Italy, and Spain, and it is in these areas in which steel-making has become most unprofitable. The United Kingdom, having carried out the rationalization of its industry prior to its privatization, is now the lowest-cost producer in the world in terms of the integrated steel-making route of blast furnace–basic oxygen steel-making, and its industry is the most profitable in the EC. But the Italians and Spanish are finding it very difficult to close down their high-cost plants, which appear to be heavily subsidized by their governments. Parts of the West German as well as the East German industry also appear to be making losses.

This subsidization by EC governments provides a pretext for the United States to impose countervailing duties on steel, and in January 1993 the United States duly imposed dumping duties of up to 110 per cent on imports of carbon steel from the EC. At the same time the EC's net exports to Eastern Europe went into reverse, with the EC trying to prevent an anticipated flood of low-quality steel from Eastern Europe, without at the same time discouraging producers too much. For Poland, Hungary, and Czechoslavakia, trade has been completely liberalized, but VERs have been negotiated with the other countries of Central and Eastern Europe (CEC 1993: 34). At the end of 1992 the EC imposed anti-dumping duties on imports from Eastern Europe whilst pressing governments there to agree to minimum import prices (*Financial Times*, 1 Dec. 1992). The actual level of imports from Eastern Europe has been kept low; in 1992 it was only 4 million tonnes compared with an EC production of 132 million tonnes (HMSO 1993).

During 1993 the Commission tried to persuade the industry to close 30 million tonnes of excess crude steel capacity. But it found it difficult to get the co-operation of the private producers, British Steel and the German companies Thyssen and Krupp-Hoesch, without some reduction in the subsidies paid to the state-owned producers in Spain and Italy (*Financial Times*, 13 Sept. 1993). The plan involved a 50,000 cut in the labour force, which would require compensation. It was suggested that a levy be put on the firms remaining in the industry to finance the social costs of those closing down capacity, but this would reduce the profits of a not very profitable industry. Alternatively, the fund collected by the ECSC could be used for this purpose.

By December 1993 the Commission appeared to have given in to the political exigencies of governments involved in steel production. Industry ministers unanimously approved state subsidies for public-sector production in East Germany, Italy, Spain, and Portugal worth Ecu 6.79 billion (£5.17 billion), involving only a 5 million tonne reduction in capacity, and a restructuring of Ekostahl, the East German producer, which will involve an expansion in production. This is a derogation under Article 95 of the ECSC Treaty, which otherwise bans such subsidies. The Commission hoped that the other 25 million tonnes reduction in capacity would be contributed by the private sector in exchange for assistance in financing redundancies and limitations on imports from Eastern Europe (*Financial Times*, 18 Dec. 1993, 20 Dec. 1993). Although the Commission's long-term aim is to abolish subsidies and to allow trade in steel to take place on the basis of relative cost advantage, in the short term this objective appears to have been abandoned.

## 11.5. TEXTILES AND CLOTHING

### Protective Measures

The most elaborate system of protection the EC has engaged in has been for the benefit of its textile and clothing industries. These are classic declining industries. The textile industry was in the forefront of European industrialization and its position was later reinforced by its uptake of man-made fibres, the production of which became particularly important in Germany from the 1930s onwards. The clothing industry developed later, and in France and Italy it is best known for high fashion often set by its couture houses. Thus, continental European countries have regarded themselves as exporters of these products, although it has become increasingly obvious that the costs of production in developing countries are much lower.

When the EC was formed, most of the EC6 continued to maintain their own severe restrictions on imports of textiles and clothing from Japan and developing countries. However, developing countries were increasing their exports of cotton textiles to the more liberal countries such as the United States, and the United Kingdom and Denmark, which, however, eventually responded by introducing quotas on them (at the same time the United Kingdom removed all restrictions on imports from members of EFTA when it was formed in 1959). In an endeavour to halt this proliferation of quotas, GATT introduced, in 1961, a Short Term Arrangement and then, in 1962, a Long Term Arrangement (LTA) for cotton textiles. The LTA permitted the bilateral negotiation of quotas but stated that they should not be less than the actual imports of the previous year and were normally to be increased by 5 per cent a year. Although the LTA violated the main principle of non-discrimination, GATT hoped that its provisions would restrict unbridled protectionism. Under the LTA the EC agreed to increase its import quotas by 88 per cent, a development dourly dismissed by a Lancashire millowner as '88% of nowt is nowt'.

In 1967 30 per cent of UK consumption and even more of Danish consumption of cotton yarn, cloth, and made-up articles came from Japan and developing countries compared with only 5 per cent for the EC as a whole; the Netherlands was the most liberal Member State, with 11 per cent (Textile Council 1969: 22).

Thus the entry of the United Kingdom, Denmark, and the Irish Republic into the EC in 1973 brought in two of the most open economies with respect to cotton textiles. However, textile producers in the United Kingdom were looking forward to entry, anticipating a much greater degree of protection from developing countries.

Developing countries had increased their export earnings, in spite of the LTA, by increasing their exports of items with higher value added such as clothing. They had also increased their exports of textiles with less than 50 per cent cotton which were not covered by the LTA. The United States responded in 1971 by negotiating quotas on imports of man-made fibre textiles and clothing. Once more GATT endeavoured to control their proliferation, in this case by agreeing to extend the LTA to include most fibres. The Arrangement Regarding International Trade in Textiles—the Multi-Fibre Arrangement (MFA)—came into operation in 1974. It embraced textiles and clothing of most textile fibres (excluding hard fibres and initially ramie and silk). Bilateral agreements were negotiable under it but were to be expanded by 6 per cent a year. The MFA was subsequently renewed three times, with new versions coming into operation in 1978, 1982, and 1986, and was then extended further in 1991. In 1986 the scope of the Agreement was expanded to cover goods made from silk blends and vegetable fibres.

The grouping of products to which the quotas are applied differs between industrialized countries, and has varied over time; in 1984 the EC had 114 categories. Some flexibility was introduced into this system by a 'swing' provision whereby an exporting country could transfer a quota between product categories in the same year, a provision by which up to 10 per cent of the unused portion of its previous year's quota could be 'carried over', and a 'carry-forward' provision by which it could utilize up to 5 per cent of the following year's quota.

The EC had to negotiate overall quotas and then to distribute them by agreement between Member States—'burden-sharing', as it was called! With the delay in obtaining statistics and in getting agreement, the EC first reached a bilateral agreement in 1975. Meanwhile, imports into the EC increased by 41 per cent over two years in comparison with a 3 per cent increase for imports into the United States. This led the EC to adopt a much more restrictive approach in the next round of negotiations.

It divided products according to 'sensitivity'. Group 1 included the eight most sensitive products, selected by a process of political bargaining: cotton yarn, cotton fabric, fabrics of synthetic fibres, T-shirts, pullovers, trousers including jeans, blouses, and shirts. For these categories the growth rate of import quotas was limited to 1–2 per cent per annum, and exports by Hong Kong, South Korea, and Taiwan were restricted to levels below those reached in 1976. Group 2 included other sensitive products for which imports from outside the EC accounted for at least 20 per cent of the EC market in terms of physical units in 1976; quotas for these categories were allowed to increase by between 2 and 4 per cent a year, with lower rates for the largest suppliers, for which import quotas were allowed to increase by 4 per cent per annum. The growth rates for Group 3, other textile products, Group 4, other clothing, and Group 5, articles for technical use, were set in relation to market penetration levels. In addition, as a further safeguard to home producers, there was a 'basket' mechanism by which restrictions were imposed on previously unrestricted exporters if their exports reached a certain proportion of imports from third countries in the previous year (Keesing and Wolf 1980: 65–6).

The 'burden-sharing' was supposed to be arranged so that Germany would have 28.5 per cent, Benelux 10.5 per cent, France 18.5 per cent, Italy 15 per cent, Denmark 3 per cent, the Irish Republic 1 per cent, and the United Kingdom 23.5 per cent of the total quota. But by 1981 the United Kingdom, Germany, and Benelux still had higher proportions than these, and France a lower proportion.

When the EC was negotiating for the renewal of the MFA in 1978, under the guise of helping the least-developed countries, the EC was relatively more 'generous' with its quotas to countries with relatively little productive capacity but *reduced* its quotas for imports from Hong Kong and Taiwan. Again, when the MFA was renewed in 1982, quotas on imports from Hong Kong, South Korea, Macao, and Taiwan were *reduced*.

But at the same time the EC concluded a series of preferential trade agreements with Mediterranean countries and African, Caribbean, and

Pacific (ACP) states which had signed the Lomé agreement under which manufactures from these countries were allowed into the EC market freely.

In addition, there are special provisions for 'outward processing traffic' (OPT). This generally involves continental EC countries contracting out their more labour-intensive processes to Eastern Europe, and formerly to Yugoslavia. When an EC country exports textiles or clothing for further processing in another country and then reimports it, the only tariff imposed is on the value added. In 1989 OPT accounted for 12 per cent of EC imports of clothing (GATT 1991: 1, 193).

This account does not cover all the EC provisions relating to trade in textiles and clothing but it demonstrates its main features—namely, that they involve:

1. a hierarchy of discrimination, in ascending order of restraints:
   (a) barrier-free access for members of EC and EFTA;
   (b) ACP states' free access (although this appears limited in practice) and zero tariffs up to a certain import quantity under the Generalized System of Preferences (GSP), which the EC signed in 1971 and modified in 1981. If this amount is exceeded, customs duties are reimposed;
   (c) preferential access for Mediterranean countries;
   (d) outward processing provisions;
   (e) tariffs on imports from other industrialized countries;
   (f) VERs on MFA developing countries, though they may be free of tariffs if under the GSP.
2. a categorization of imports and grouping according to 'sensitivity'.

### Effectiveness of the MFA

In discussing the MFA, it should be clear that the most stringent barriers are being placed on imports from the cheapest sources. Wage and labour costs are very much lower in the developing countries than in industrial countries, and, even allowing for differences in productivity and quality, all the evidence shows that developing countries' costs of production are lower (Silberston 1984, 1989; Moore 1991). But has this elaborate system actually reduced imports into the EC from developing countries? Indications of the effectiveness of a quota in restricting imports are taken to be as follows:

1. *A high degree of quota utilization.* The MFA quotas for 1989 for Group 1 products plus those for terry towelling and bed linen, together with the rate of quota utilization for the EC as a whole, are shown in Tables 11.2 and 11.3. The last column shows the Member State markets in which quotas appear to have been particularly restrictive—i.e. where the rate of quota utilization is over 90 per cent.

TABLE 11.2. *MFA quotas on imports of textiles and their utilization 1989*

| Quota number and category, and major suppliers | EC quotas in tonnes | % of total EC market utilization | Member State markets in which 90% or more of quota is utilized |
|---|---|---|---|
| 10 Cotton yarn not for retail sale | | | |
| Brazil | 33,268 | 55 | |
| India | 30,600 | 37 | |
| 20 Woven cotton fabrics | | | |
| India | 43,969 | 74 | |
| Pakistan | 23,324 | 84 | France, UK, Spain |
| China | 23,100 | 68 | Spain |
| Brazil | 18,332 | 49 | |
| Indonesia | 15,142 | 53 | |
| Hong Kong | 13,340 | 70 | |
| 30 Woven synthetic fabrics | | | |
| Hong Kong | 11,107 | 35 | |
| Malaysia | 9,450 | 51 | Irish Republic |
| Taiwan | 8,276 | 52 | |
| Pakistan | 5,511 | 50 | |
| China | 4,750 | 40 | UK, Irish Republic, Denmark, Spain |
| 90 Cotton terry towelling | | | |
| Brazil | 9,280 | 56 | France, Irish Republic, Spain |
| China | 3,624 | 44 | Spain |
| Pakistan | 2,865 | 79 | UK, Denmark, Spain |
| 200 Woven bed linen | | | |
| India | 9,280 | 56 | France |

*Source:* Textile Surveillance Report.

Table 11.3. *MFA quotas on imports of clothing and their utilization 1989*

| Quota number and category, and major suppliers | EC quotas 1,000 pieces | % of total EC market utilization | Member State markets in which 90% or more of quota is utilized |
|---|---|---|---|
| 40 Knitted shirts, T. shirts | | | |
| Hong Kong | 36,351 | 77 | UK |
| China | 32,800 | 31 | |
| India | 29,754 | 80 | UK |
| Indonesia | 23,355 | 47 | |
| Singapore | 15,142 | 59 | UK |
| Pakistan | 14,494 | 67 | Irish Republic, Spain |
| South Korea | 11,903 | 45 | Spain |
| Thailand | 11,735 | 85 | Germany, UK, Spain |
| Macao | 11,434 | 77 | Portugal |
| Taiwan | 10,132 | 55 | UK |
| | | | |
| 50 Knitted sweaters | | | |
| Hong Kong | 27,553 | 88 | Germany |
| South Korea | 27,405 | 32 | |
| Taiwan | 20,922 | 68 | |
| India | 18,500 | 54 | |
| Macao | 10,497 | 85 | France |
| Thailand | 9,261 | 82 | France, UK |
| Singapore | 8,761 | 65 | UK |

| 60 Woven trousers and men's shorts | | | |
|---|---|---|---|
| Hong Kong | 52,973 | 85 | UK |
| Macao | 10,844 | 94 | Germany, France, UK, Denmark |
| China | 9,650 | 64 | UK |
| Indonesia | 5,506 | 74 | Germany, UK |
| Taiwan | 5,195 | 77 | |
| Thailand | 3,608 | 81 | Germany |
| South Korea | 4,877 | 45 | Irish Republic |
| 70 Woven/knitted blouses | | | |
| India | 43,701 | 82 | France, UK, Spain |
| Hong Kong | 30,643 | 90 | Germany, UK, Denmark |
| South Korea | 8,364 | 55 | |
| Singapore | 7,652 | 29 | |
| Indonesia | 4,607 | 61 | Germany |
| Macao | 4,769 | 92 | Germany, France, UK |
| Thailand | 4,420 | 55 | UK |
| 80 Men's woven shirts | | | |
| Hong Kong | 47,550 | 84 | France, UK, Spain |
| India | 30,029 | 96 | Germany, France, Benelux, UK, Irish Republic, Denmark, Spain |
| South Korea | 28,578 | 63 | Spain |
| China | 9,000 | 52 | UK |
| Taiwan | 8,655 | 46 | Benelux |
| Indonesia | 7,393 | 62 | |
| Macao | 6,397 | 90 | Germany, France, Benelux, UK, Denmark |

*Source:* Textile Surveillance Report.

2. *The existence of quota premia.* Producers are willing to pay for the
right to export textiles and clothing to the EC market. Unfortunately,
Hong Kong is the only country with a free market in quota permits.
Hamilton (1986) estimated that during 1980–4 for exports to the EC
the premia on such permits were on average 14 per cent. Silberston
(1989) calculated that in 1988 they amounted to up to 26 per cent of
the export price for shirts. But within Pakistan the quota premia
appear much higher, varying between 50 per cent of the export price
of clothing and cloth to 80 per cent for knitwear.

In addition, there may be a long-run effect, in so far as the existence of
restrictions on exports may discourage investment in production in a
developing country.

## Trade in Textiles and Clothing

Recent statistics show that in 1990 EC countries were some of the largest
exporters of *textiles* but that only West Germany and Italy had exports
greater than imports. Indeed Germany, which has very high wage costs and
relatively low machine utilization, increased the quantity and value of its
exports of yarn and woven textiles, and remained the world's largest
exporter, accounting for 12 per cent by value. Its strength is mainly in
man-made fibre products. Italy, whose strength is mainly in wool products
and to a lesser extent man-made fibre products, was the second largest
exporter, accounting for 8.5 per cent of world trade (Moore 1991; GATT
1992). Trade is heavily regionalized, with 79 per cent of EC exports and
imports being with other West European countries.

Italy and Germany were also leading exporters of *clothing* but only Italy
was a net exporter. Germany was the second largest importer after the
United States. Although 83 per cent of West European exports went to
other West European countries, only 62 per cent of their imports came from
them; 26 per cent came from Asia, 6 per cent from Africa, and 3 per cent
from Eastern Europe.

It is easiest to identify trade-creation and trade-diversion effects by
considering the entry of the United Kingdom into the EC. It initially
had, as recounted, a high proportion of imports from developing countries
and its producers expected to benefit from the greater restrictions entailed
by the MFA. However, between 1973 and 1988—as can be seen from
Table 11.4—its output of all types of textiles fell. Its domestic consumption of textiles fell, largely because of the decline in production of the UK
clothing industry which takes up roughly half its output, and so did its
exports, except for man-made fibre fabric. Its total imports of textiles and
clothing increased but almost all of this increase came from other EC
countries. Only in the case of man-made-fibre fabrics did an appreciable

TABLE 11.4. *UK changes in Production (P), Consumption (C), Imports (M), and Exports (%) 1973–1988*

| Category | ΔP | ΔC | ΔX | ΔM | ΔM of which from | | |
| --- | --- | --- | --- | --- | --- | --- | --- |
| | | | | | ΔEC8[a] | ΔEC11 | ΔMFA countries |
| Cotton yarn (m. kg.) | −71.7 | −12.1 | −10.0 | 49.6 | 19.1 | 28.6 | 2.7 |
| Spun m.m.f. yarns (m. kg.) | −66.2 | −27.0 | −3.5 | 35.7 | 18.3 | | 3.9 |
| Wool yarns (m. kg.) | −58.3 | −44.1 | −4.4 | 9.8 | 7.4 | | 0.3 |
| Wool cotton fabric (m. sq. m.) | −271.0 | −97.0 | −8.0 | 182.0 | 131.9 | | −41.8 |
| Woven m.m.f. (m. sq. m.) | −261.0 | 178.0 | 67.0 | 506.0 | 250.7 | 255.3 | 174.3 |
| Wool fabrics (m. sq. m.) | −86.0 | −51.0 | −22.0 | 13.0 | 11.7 | | 0.3 |
| Knitted fabrics (m. kg.) | −44.0 | −31.0 | −6.0 | 7.0 | 4.0 | | 0.3 |

*Note*: m.m.f. = man-made fibres.
[a] Denmark excluded from 1973 for all except wool yarns.
*Sources*: Silberston (1984, 1989).

proportion come from MFA countries. For other textile products the increase in imports from the MFA countries was very small and for woven cotton fabric it actually fell. This suggests some trade creation took place in relation to other EC countries, but probably on the basis of superior quality rather than lower costs. However, it also suggests that, in view of the very small or negative increase in imports from developing countries, there has also been a considerable amount of trade diversion.

### Effect of the MFA on Welfare

The welfare gain to the EC from removing all MFA bilateral quotas and tariffs on textiles and clothing has been estimated within a general equilibrium framework to be US$3,487 billion at 1986 prices. If quotas, but not tariffs, were removed, the welfare gain would be US$5,029 billion (Hamilton 1990). Furthermore, the impact of the higher prices resulting from the MFA are borne more than proportionally by the poorer sections within the EC.

So why is the EC afraid of relinquishing the MFA? It is worried about its effect on employment, in particular because employment in textiles and clothing tends to be regionally concentrated. However, Silberston calculated in 1988 that in the United Kingdom the cost per job 'saved' by the MFA was about £29,700 per annum—some three or four times the annual average earnings of an employee in these industries.

### The Uruguay Round

The GATT agreement reached as the conclusion of the Uruguay Round in December 1993 incorporated a plan for phasing out the bilateral quotas of the MFA after 1995 and for their elimination by 2005. Tariffs on textiles and clothing are also to be reduced. But they will still remain relatively high in the United States and Australia, areas to which EC countries export these products (*Financial Times,* 16 Dec. 1993).

### 11.6. MOTOR VEHICLES

The car industry has been an 'engine of growth' in the EC. Between 1960 and 1982 the number of cars produced by the seven major countries (West Germany, Belgium, France, Italy, Netherlands, the United Kingdom, and Spain) more than doubled. Many of them were to supply the home market, which was expanding at 3.2 per cent per annum between 1970 and 1980 (OECD 1983). But the EC was also a major exporter, supplying more than half by value of developed countries' exports of automotive products. In terms of units, the EC countries supplied 51 per cent of industrial countries' exports of passenger cars, and 21 per cent of their exports of commercial vehicles—i.e. trucks and buses—in this period. The value of exports has continued to rise but at a decelerating rate, whereas imports have been rising faster at an accelerating rate. As a result, the EC positive trade balance in motor vehicles with the rest of the world is declining. Output in the 1990s started to decline in the major countries except for the United Kingdom.

The Commission regards motor vehicles as a strategically important industry with a significant effect on upstream and downstream activities. The industry accounted for 8 per cent of all manufacturing employment and 9 per cent of industrial value added in 1988 (GATT 1991: 1, 215). Automotive products represented 13 per cent of intra-EC trade, and 9 per cent of exports to the rest of the world in 1990.

Each of the larger European countries has at least one indigenous manufacturer of mass-produced cars, its 'champion', which is regarded as having political as well as economic significance. There are also a number of luxury car producers—for example, Rolls Royce, Jaguar, BMW, Mercedes-Benz, and Alfa Romeo, though several have now lost their independence (Jaguar to Ford and Alfa Romeo to Fiat). In addition there are a number of van and lorry producers.

The trading position of the individual vehicle manufacturers and Member States has changed considerably over time. In the 1950s the United Kingdom was the largest exporter of cars and commercial vehicles in the world. Then France and Germany rapidly increased their exports, so that Germany became the largest exporter in the 1960s. Cars have now become the most important manufacture in the struggle between the large industrial countries, with each supporting its 'champions' in the trading arena.

The Commission has endeavoured to restrict the amount of assistance that governments give to their national 'champions'. It was expected that the removal of trade barriers between Member States would lead to greater competition and the demise of the weaker firms—i.e. trade creation. In particular, the French and German firms expected to oust Austin Rover (previously British Leyland) when the United Kingdom entered the EC in 1973. In the event, UK imports increased rapidly and Austin Rover lost much of its domestic market. On the verge of bankruptcy, it had to be nationalized in 1975. The fact that it survived is due partly to a co-operation agreement with Honda. In 1988 British Aerospace took it over.

At present the 'champions' are still heavily dependent on sales to their home markets—for example, the UK market accounts for 80 per cent of the sales of Rover, the Italian market accounts for 62 per cent of the sales of Fiat, Peugeot and Renault are each dependent on the French market for 54 per cent of their sales, whilst Daimler-Benz and Volkswagen are dependent on the German market for 47 and 38 per cent respectively of their sales

(GATT 1991: i. 216). This might be regarded as reflecting different national preferences. But the Commission regards it as also indicating the existence of barriers to trade. Another indication of this is the disparity in prices of the same model of car throughout the EC, even allowing for the differences in car taxes.

The Commission has regarded the car industry as the manufacturing industry likely to provide some of the greatest benefits from the creation of the Single European Market (SEM) (CEC 1988: 186). The market for cars is regarded as an example of an imperfectly competitive market. Consumers can distinguish the products of each firm and firms compete as much in the provision of new models as by price. In the model used by Smith and Venables (see Chapter 3), each firm is regarded as producing in its home country, and in selling abroad it is 'invading' the territory of another. It reduces prices in its export market partly by reducing the monopoly power of the firms already there. Consumption increases. As the firm expands its output, it can exploit further its economies of scale and thus costs also fall. This is an attractive picture of consumers benefiting without producers losing as a result of international trade. Furthermore, this enables producers to expand not only to reduce imports but also to increase exports.

This kind of calculation can be criticized on a number of counts. Most of the data used relating to economies of scale were drawn from the 1960s (Pratten 1988), and the greater use of computers, particularly in changing from one specification to another, must have considerably affected the value of scale economies.

However, the most important omission from the Commission's analysis was to ignore the importance of multinationals, in particular foreign multinationals. In the exercise, foreign subsidiaries operating in the EC were treated like domestic firms.

Before discussing further the activities of the multinationals, let us take note of the ring of protection round the EC. By July 1968, when the CET first became effective, it was at a level of 22 per cent for assembled cars and of 14 per cent for components. As a result of the Kennedy Round of 1964–7, these had been reduced to 11 and 7 per cent respectively by 1972, with the duty on commercial vehicles remaining at 22 per cent (Maxcy 1981: 96). In 1991 the average EC CET was 9.5 per cent (GATT 1991: 1, 216). However, in addition to these tariffs, individual Members States of the EC had widely different restraints on vehicle imports from Japan before 1993 (GATT 1991: 1, 216), namely:

France  3 per cent of market share
Italy   2,500 cars, direct imports; 750 light commercial vehicles since 1986
Spain   1,000 cars, direct imports; 200 commercial vehicles
UK      11 per cent of market share

Under the SEM these individual quotas are due to be phased out and to be replaced by a system of monitoring, with a removal of restraints by the year 2000.

The US multinationals—Ford, General Motors, and Chrysler—had established subsidiaries in European countries before the Second World War. They supplied the European markets from these plants rather than exporting from the United States. This was not only because of the European tariffs but also because the cars they produced in the United States tended to be much larger than required for the European market. The formation and expansion of the EC, by reducing the costs of sending products across national boundaries, made it easier for them to locate production in the lowest cost source within the EC. They were attracted to Belgium in the 1960s by a plentiful supply of male labour willing to work shifts (because of the closure of the coal mines). Thus, although it had no indigenous producers, Belgium emerged as a significant producer and exporter of cars in the 1970s.

Then in the 1970s the multinationals were attracted to Spain, which, at that time, was not yet a member of the EC. This was partly due to the low wage rates in the country but also to make it easier to supply the rapidly expanding, but highly protected, Spanish home market. Ford succeeded in persuading the Spanish government to lower its tariffs on imported components to 5 per cent, and to allow it 100 per cent ownership (previously foreign firms had been limited to 50 per cent) and to reduce its national content requirement from 95 to 50 per cent, provided two-thirds of production was exported. Thus began the integration of Spanish vehicle production into the European market and a very rapid increase in Spanish exports (Dicken 1992). Also, over the succeeding period, Volkswagen eventually took over one of Spain's largest vehicle assembly plants, SEAT, as the manufacturing base for its small car, the Polo.

Meanwhile, in the 1970s, Japan had emerged as the lowest cost and most efficient producer of small and medium-sized cars. Exports had increased but as detailed above their entry into the EC was restricted. Then, in the 1980s, the Japanese producers Nissan, Toyota, and Honda began to invest in the EC, particularly in the United Kingdom. Rather than setting up in the traditional areas of volume car production, which had acquired a reputation for being strike-prone, they invested in greenfield sites (see Table 11.5). From the outset, production was intended not only for the UK domestic market but also for export to the rest of Europe. The United Kingdom's car production, which had declined after its entry into the EC, began to increase, and so did its exports.

The French regarded this establishment of Japanese 'transplant' factories in the United Kingdom with dislike and suspicion. Peugeot's chairman has described them as a 'Japanese aircraft carrier' off the coast of Europe (*Independent*, 4 Jan. 1993). At first France threatened to include imports

TABLE 11.5. *Japanese motor capacity in Europe*

| Manufacturer | Location | Models | Capacity | Start-up |
|---|---|---|---|---|
| Nissan | UK | Bluebird | 50,000 (200,000 by 1992) | 1986 (July) |
| | Spain | Patrol | 70,000 | 1983 (Jan.) |
| | | Vanette | | |
| | | Trucks | | |
| | | Buses | (100,000–150,000 by 1991) | |
| | Greece | Cherry | 10,000 | 1980 |
| | | Sunny | | |
| | | Pickup | | |
| Toyota | West Germany | Hllux Pickup | 8,000 (15,000 by 1990) | 1989 |
| | Derbyshire, UK | Cars | 31,000 (100,000 by 1995) (200,000 by 1997) | 1993 |
| Honda | N. Wales | Engines | | |
| | Swindon, UK | Engines | 70,000 | 1989 |
| | Longbridge, UK | Legend | | |
| | | Ballade | | |
| Suzuki | UK | Microvans | 5,000 | 1981 |
| | Spain | SJ410/413 | 15,000 | 1986 |
| Fuji | France | 4WD cars | 20,000 | 1985 |
| Isuzu | UK | Light vans | 30,000 | 1993 |
| Daihatsu | Italy | 4WD Rocky | 20,000 | 1986 |
| | | | 4,000 | 1989 |
| Hino | Irish Republic | Med/Hvy/Trucks | 300 | 1980 |

(In addition, Nissan, Toyota, Mazda, Mitsubishi and Daihatsu operate local assembly bases in Portugal.)

*Source:* Economist Intelligence Unit, quoted in *Financial Times*, 20 Oct. 1988, 8 Dec. 1991.

from Nissan's UK plant within its overall Japanese quota unless the imports had an EC content of 80 per cent. However, this would have been inconsistent with the EC definition whereby 'origin is assigned to the country where a product has been wholly obtained or where it has undergone its *"last substantial working or processing"'* (GATT 1991: 1, 118–19). Eventually, the Commission persuaded France to accept these cars as being of UK origin, and, in any case, the local content very soon reached 80 per cent.

The national quotas on motor-vehicle imports from Japan have to be phased out under the SEM. Under an agreement reached with Japan in July 1991, these individual quotas are to be replaced by an overall quota which will increase to 1.23 million units of cars and light commercial vehicles and trucks (up to 5 tonnes) by 1999, calculated on the basis of a forecast 15.1 million vehicle market for the EC as a whole. By 2000 the quotas will be abolished. During the transitional period, EC and Japanese officials will meet twice a year to monitor the past and forecast future level of imports, both in total and to each restricted market, in relation to the size of the market as a whole. There are to be 'no restrictions on Japanese investment or on the free circulation of its products in the Community'—i.e. on motor vehicles produced by Japanese 'transplants' (*Financial Times*, 5 Aug. 1991).

However, this raises the question of what is meant by car-manufacturing. Assembly itself accounts for about 10 per cent of the value of a car; prior to that the main activities are the production of engines and transmission, the production of bodies, and the manufacture of a wide range of components ranging from spark plugs to windscreen wipers. Some companies, such as Ford, have maintained a high degree of vertical integration in their production activities. On the other hand, until they were persuaded to amalgamate by the Industrial Reorganization Corporation, the UK producers had a low level of integration. Thus in many circumstances, the transfer of the final stage of production from one country to another tends to affect the trade in intermediate products. The extent of the type of trade has also been affected by the just-in-time (JIT) methods introduced by the Japanese manufacturers. These require the component suppliers to be able to deliver their products within a certain time to the final producers. As a result, although the establishment of Japanese production in the United Kingdom initially led to increased imports of components, this has tailed off as more components came to be purchased from domestic suppliers—and, in some cases, the Japanese component manufacturers also invested in production facilities within the United Kingdom.

The Commission's anticipation of the benefits that indigenous car producers would derive from the removal of barriers to intra-EC trade appears to have been fundamentally misconceived. By concentrating on the benefits from the economies of scale in plant size, it has tended to ignore, on the one hand, the much greater organizational efficiency of Japanese firms, and, on the other hand, the efforts of other firms to emulate them by implementing new working practices, including twenty-four hour, three-shift working. Three-shift working can, in general, only be realized in the poorer parts of Europe, and thus there has been both an inflow of Japanese direct investment into the United Kingdom and a transfer of production by already existing producers to these poorer areas. Eastern Europe may soon become another such area of development; Volkswagen's acquisition of a stake in Skoda, Czechslovakia, is just the beginning of this trend. In addition, the production of multinationals has become organized on a global basis with the sourcing of components (e.g. for the Ford Fiesta and the Ford Escort) taking place throughout Western Europe (Dicken 1992).

All of these changes are reflected in trade patterns. EC exports of automotive products were US$158 billion in 1990, of which 69 per cent was intra-EC and 10 per cent went to other countries in Western Europe (see Table 11.1). Of EC imports of automotive products of US$130 billion, 80 per cent were from other EC countries and a further 7 per cent from other countries of Western Europe. The argument here is that this very high degree of regionalization in production and trade is a result of the operations of multinationals unencumbered by tariff barriers within the free-trade area of EC and EFTA. However, it is also the result of the restrictions imposed on the entry of imports from Japan. It will be interesting to see whether this trade pattern is maintained when the restrictions are removed in the year 2000, and also how successful developing countries such as South Korea and Malaysia are in increasing their exports to the EC.

### Developments in 1993

Recently, with the world recession, there has been a sharp decline in European sales, and West European car production is forecast to decline by 2 million units in 1993, that is 15 per cent. The United Kingdom initially was the exception; its output was expected to rise because of the development of the Japanese plants which now account for 37 per cent of UK output (*Financial Times*, 23 Aug. 1993). There is continuing pressure on Japan itself to reduce its exports to the EC.

In Germany both Volkswagen and Mercedes-Benz negotiated reductions in the emoluments package of their work-forces in 1993, holding out the threat of compulsory redundancies if agreement was not reached; Mercedes-Benz reinforced this threat by surveying other sites within the EC for its venture into small-car production (*Financial Times*, 26 Nov. 1993, 20 Dec, 1993). But some operations continue to be transferred to cheaper areas: Audi, for instance, now purchases wiring systems from Poland and Hungary (*Financial Times*, 23 June 1992).

## 11.7. HIGH-TECHNOLOGY INDUSTRIES

The EC's policy towards high-technology industries reflects the concern of its Member States that Europe is being left behind in the race for innovations, and, increasingly, is becoming technologically dependent on the United States and Japan.

The OECD has defined 'research-intensive' industries as those 'based not on a once-and-for-all dose of technology, but for which a continuous stream of new products and processes is necessary in order to keep in the market' (OECD 1970: 123, 135). But for practical purposes they are classified according to the proportion of their research and development (R&D) expenditure to output: where the ratio is above 4 per cent, they are regarded as 'research-intensive' or 'high-technology industries'. These include pharmaceuticals, aerospace, and electrical and electronic equipment industries.

### Pharmaceuticals

Europe has traditionally been a net exporter of pharmaceuticals. The Commission's primary policy concern has been over the fragmentation of the internal market which allows average pharmaceutical prices in Germany and the Netherlands to be more than twice those in France and Italy. This is largely due to the market freedom in setting prices in Germany, and to a lesser extent in the Netherlands and Denmark, in contrast to the government control over pharmaceutical prices exercised in the United Kingdom, Ireland, France, and Belgium (CEC 1988).

### Aircraft

A number of EC countries became worried that they were almost totally dependent on two large US firms, Boeing and McDonnell-Douglas, for the supply of commercial aircraft. In 1966 France and Germany, later joined by the United Kingdom and Spain, established a consortium consisting of one firm from each country to develop a wide-bodied jet, called the Airbus. The four governments contributed a considerable amount towards the estimated $2 billion development costs, Germany alone contributing almost DM11 billion between the mid-1960s and 1989. This has been a continuing source of conflict with the United States. The importance of the project can be gauged from the fact that it accounts for about half the EC output of aircraft (GATT 1991: 1, 224). In July 1992 the United States and EC agreed to limit government financial support to their aviation industry: production and marketing subsidies are outlawed and aid for development is to be no more than 33 per cent (*Financial Times,* 24 Feb. 1993).

*Electronics*

The EC has appeared most concerned about EC firms being at the leading edge of technology with respect to the electrical and electronics industries. Most government assistance to this industry in the United Kingdom and France, as in the United States, went initially for defence purposes. This was not permitted in Germay and Japan and as a result their firms appear to have developed a more commercial orientation. Japan purchased the right to use US innovations and was very adept at developing them for consumer products.

In the 1980s Japan became the leading producer of 'active' electronic components—i.e. semi-conductors, integrated circuits, and microprocessors. In 1989 it accounted for 42 per cent of the total world production, with the United States accounting for 26 per cent, and Europe only 12 per cent. Of the European total, West Germany accounted for 31 per cent, France 19 per cent and the United Kingdom 16 per cent (Dicken 1992: 311). Recently the United States appears to have reclaimed its position as the largest producer (*Financial Times,* 11 Dec. 1992). As far as can be ascertained, the EC is a net importer of most types of electronic products.

The EC has sought to strengthen its position in these industries by the direct subsidization of research, as described in Chapter 6. In November 1992 the French and Italian governments announced an investment of $2 billion over five years into SGS–Thomson (of which France and Italy each owned 45 per cent), the world's twelfth largest microchip maker. However, Siemens and Philips refused to participate in this venture. Heinz Hagmaster, head of the semi-conductor division at Philips, said: 'The same [semi-conductor] plant, of the same size, making the same product in the same production volumes, will have 10 to 20 per cent higher costs in Europe than its identical sisters in the US and Japan, and more than 30 per cent higher costs than an identical plant in a newly industrialised country.' As a result, there is a consistent tendency for the European firms to transfer operations to the South-East Asia region (*Financial Times,* 16 Nov. 1992).

The EC also protects its electrical and electronic industry with a relatively high CET of 14 per cent on integrated circuits, radios, television receivers, and video recorders imported into the EC. The EC would like to have discriminated against Japanese producers, but this was not permitted by GATT in the Tokyo Round. Instead, individual Member States have made extensive use of non-tariff barriers such as VERS; in mid-1990 the following Japanese products were subject to bilateral quotas: radio and TV sets (France, Italy, Spain), colour TV sets, transistors, and integrated circuits (France and Italy), TV cameras, TV tubes, car radios, hi-fi radios, radio recorders and antennae (Italy) (GATT 1991: 1 213–14). Faced with these limitations, Japanese firms began to invest in other parts of South-East Asia to supply the EC market. The EC then extended the VERs to include these countries as well.

Many of these electrical consumer products might not be regarded as representing the leading edge of technology; indeed, many of them are produced in developing countries with very little R&D expenditure. However, the argument appears to be that EC firms must be profitable in these in order to remain in the high-technology sector of the industry. There are now only two indigenous producers of consumer electronic products left, Philips (Netherlands) and SGS–Thomson (France).

In the 1980s the EC also used anti-dumping procedures as a form of protective policy. Between 1983 and 1989 nine investigations were initiated involving imports of electronic consumer and office-equipment goods: video casette recorders from Japan and South Korea (1988–9), videotapes from Hong Kong and South Korea (1987–9), small-screen colour TV sets from South Korea, Hong Kong, and China (1988–90), compact-disc players from Japan and South Korea (1987–90), electronic typewriters from Japan (1984–8), photocopiers from Japan (1986–9), dot-matrix computer printers (1988–9), daisy-wheel computer printers (1988–9), and microwave ovens (1986). All of these investigations resulted in anti-dumping duties or price undertakings being introduced, except in the case of microwave ovens (National Consumer Council 1990*a*: 17).

In addition, after an anti-dumping investigation, in 1990, the Commission negotiated a minimum import price with eleven Japanese semi-conductor producers of dynamic random access memory (DRAM) chips; an anti-dumping duty of 60 per cent was imposed on exporters who did not participate in the undertaking (GATT 1991: 1, 214).The EC also imposed a provisional anti-dumping duty of 10.1 per cent on imports of memory chips from South Korea, as it began an investigation into dumping (*Financial Times,* 18 Sept. 1992). This has buttressed the position of European electronic firms already established in Europe (often to supply the defence industries), and induced US and Japanese firms to establish subsidiaries. In 1988 five of the ten leading semi-conductor firms in Europe were American. In addition there was IBM (US), which produces its own semiconductors and which for a long time has dominated the world market in mainframe computers. Since Fujitsu took over ICL (UK) in the 1980s there has been no European producer of mainframe computers (Dicken 1992). However, there are a number of European producers in the personal computer market, the largest being Olivetti with 6.4 per cent of the market (*Financial Times,* 19 Feb. 1993).

There has been strong criticism of the EC for introducing these measures. The GATT's anti-dumping provision was meant to prevent a firm selling in a particular market below its price in other markets, or below the cost of production, as a temporary competitive strategy, to bankrupt competitors, after which prices would be raised again. It was not meant to be used to exclude external competitors whose long-term costs were lower. The EC's method of calculation and its use of statistics have been severely criticized. The anti-dumping duties imposed have often been very high and have varied greatly between firms exporting from the same country. The lowest cost and most efficient firms appear to have been the most penalized. Sometimes, in order to avoid their imposition, Japanese firms have agreed not to sell below a certain price.

These non-tariff barriers have similar effects to a tariff in raising the price of the products on the EC market. The national Consumer Council of the UK calculated that the annual cost to EC consumers of anti-dumping duties on video cassette recorders was Ecu 272.5 million (1989); on compact disc players, Ecu 146.1 million (1989); on video cassettes, Ecu 48 million (1987); on dot-matrix printers, Ecu 512.6 million (1988); on electronic typewriters, Ecu 104.5 million (1987); and on photocopiers, Ecu 339.5 million (1988) (quoted in GATT 1991: i. 213).

The high prices in the EC protected market have encouraged investment, though not necessarily by European firms. Colour-television production in the United Kingdom was ceded first to European firms—to Philips (Netherlands) and to Thomson (France), which had acquired Ferguson in 1987— and then to inward investing Japanese firms. Now virtually all colour televisions and video recorders produced in the United Kingdom are made by foreign firms (Eltis and Fraser 1992). The United Kingdom also imports more than it exports, although it would be necessary to know the imported inputs in order to calculate the effect on the balance of payments. The EC is very concerned that such inward investment should not be of 'screwdriver' firms, mere assemblers of imported components. In order to prevent this the EC has sometimes tried to impose duties on the imported components. In many cases it has treated the foreign subsidiary more harshly than its indigenous firm, which may be importing a relatively higher proportion of its components.

Another area of operation has been in the establishment of standards. In the Tokyo Round the EC agreed not to use its establishment of standards as a form of protection for its domestic industry. None the less, at the 1986 meeting of the International Radio Consultative Committee (CCIR) it refused to agree to a Japanese–US standard for a high definition television system (HDTV) because it wanted to insulate the European market from competition from US and Japanese producers. The EC adopted a rival 1250 line system and proposed an evolutionary MAC system claiming that this would minimize the transition costs for EC consumers, although EC consumer organizations complained that they had not been consulted. After the EC taxpayer had invested Ecu 625 million (£516 million) on R&D with additional funds by Philips (Netherlands) and Thomson (France), the United Kingdom blocked any further expenditure which it said would serve no good purpose. Then at the beginning of 1993 Philips announced that, although it had carried out the development work, it would not produce any HDTVs because there were no programmes to transmit on it. Meanwhile the Japanese had begun broadcasting eight hours a day on their HDTV system and US firms had developed a digital technology which appeared likely to sweep the board (*Financial Times,* 17 Nov. 1992, 9 Feb. 1993 and 11 Feb. 1993). At the beginning of 1993 the programme was cancelled and the incoming EC commissioner, Mr Martin Bangemann, said that the EC would have to adopt the US standard (*Financial Times,* 19 Feb. 1993).

Thus the EC has endeavoured to achieve its aim of placing the EC at the leading edge of developments in the electronics industry by protecting and subsidizing indigenous firms. But some of the largest of these firms benefiting from protection, such as Siemens (Germany) and GEC (UK) have been better known for their large cash balances and financial conservatism than for innovation. It has also encouraged mergers between EC firms in order to be able to exploit economies of scale—such as, for instance the Siemens take-over of GPT from Plessey. However, most of the alliances formed by EC firms in computing and telecommunications have been with North American or Japanese firms.

The emphasis of the Commission in its trade-policy measures on the nationality of the firms operating within its borders has tended to detract from the EC obtaining the full potential benefits of the new technologies. Prices to consumers have been raised, which has discouraged the use of the new equipment. The indigenous firms which were the object of this protection have not been particularly successful, whereas some of those taken over by Japanese firms have been.

## 11.8. CONCLUSION

The EC appears to have been relatively successful in removing barriers to trade in manufactures between members of the EC and between the EC and EFTA.

However, the description 'fortress Europe', which has been applied to its relationship with the rest of the world, appears to be partially justified. The EC has endeavoured to protect its declining industries, notably textiles and clothing and steel, and its precariously performing motor-vehicle industry, as well as its high-technology industries, such as aircraft and electronics. This is a form of modern-day mercantilism. However, a country or region cannot effectively protect all of its industries. Inevitably, the protection it gives to industries which compete with imports from third countries discriminates against those industries that export to them— because foreigners are unable to earn enough export proceeds to purchase EC products. This also leads exporters within a Member State to become very dependent on the EC market—that is, it leads to a high degree of regionalization of EC trade.

Inevitably this has caused the EC to come into conflict with non-EC trading partners, notably the United States. Japan has acted more circumspectly and her firms have endeavoured to overcome such trade restraints by producing goods within the EC rather than exporting them from Japan; or, alternatively, investing in South East Asian countries which have less impeded access to the EC market. Thus, of all developing countries the Asian countries have been the most successful in increasing their exports to the EC. The Lomé countries with far more preferential trading arrangements have been very much less successful, and this has contributed to their more general economic difficulties (see Chapter 15).

# REFERENCES

Balassa, B. (1974), 'Trade Creation and Trade Diversion in the European Common Market', *Manchester School*, 62/2: 93–135.

CEC (1988): Commission of the European Communities, *European Economy* (Mar.).

——— (1993), *European Economy*.

Cline, W. R. (1993) (ed.), *Trade Policy in the 1980s* (Washington DC: Institute for International Economics).

Dicken, P. (1992), *Global Shift*, 2nd edn. (London: Paul Chapman).

Eltis, W., and Fraser, D. (1992), 'The Contribution of Japanese Industrial Success to Britain and to Europe', *National Westminster Bank Quarterly Review* (Nov.), 2–19.

GATT (1986a): General Agreement of Tariffs and Trade, *The Text of the General Agreement on Tariffs and Trade* (Geneva: GATT).

——— (1986b), *The Texts of the Tokyo Round Agreements* (Geneva: GATT).

——— (1991), *Trade Policy Review: The European Communities 1991*, 2 vols. (Geneva: GATT).

——— (1992), *International Trade 90–91*, ii (Geneva: GATT).

Greenaway, D., Hylak, T., and Thornton, R. (1989) (eds.), *Economic Aspects of Regional Trading Arrangements* (London: Harvester Wheatsheaf).

Hamilton, C. B. (1986), 'An Assessment of Voluntary Restraints on Hong Kong Exports to Europe and the USA', *Economica*, 53: 339–50.

——— (1990), *Textiles Trade and the Developing Countries: Eliminating the Multi-Fibre Arrangement in the 1990s* (Washington DC: World Bank).

Hine, R. C. (1985), *The Political Economy of European Trade* (Brighton: Harvester Wheatsheaf).

HMSO (1993), House of Lords Session 1992–3, Select Committee on the European

Communities, *Restructuring the EC Steel Industry* (HL Paper 111) (London: HMSO).

Keesing, D. B., and Wolf, M. (1980), *Textile Quotas against Developing Countries* (Thames Essay No. 23; London: Trade Policy Research Centre).

Maxcy, G. (1981), *The Multinational Motor Industry* (London: Croom Helm).

Moore, L. (1991), 'International Trade in Textiles and Clothing', *Journal of the Textile Institute*, 82/2: 145–59.

NCC (1990a): National Consumer Council, *International Trade and the Consumer*, Working Paper 1. *Consumer Electronics and the EC's Anti-Dumping policy* (London: NCC).

—— (1990b), *International Trade and the Consumer*, Working Paper 2. *Textiles and Clothes* (London: NCC).

OECD (1970): Organization for Economic Co-operation and Development, *Gaps in Technology: Analytical Report* (Paris: OECD).

—— (1983), *Long Term Outlook for the World Automobile Industry* (Paris: OECD).

Pratten, C. (1988) 'A Survey of the Economics of Scale', in Commission of the European Communities, *Research on the ' Cost of Non-Europe'* — *Basic Findings*, ii. *Studies on the Economics of Integration* (Luxemburg: Office for Official Publications of the European Communities).

Silberston, Z. A. (1984), *The Multi-Fibre Arrangement and the UK Economy* (London: HMSO).

—— (1989), *The Future of the Multi-fibre Arrangement: Implications for the UK Economy* (London: HMSO).

Swann, D. (1992), *The Economics of the Common Market*, 6th edn. (Harmondsworth: Penguin).

Textile Council (1969), *Cotton and Allied Textiles* (Manchester: Textile Council).

Tharakan, P. K. M., and Kol, J. (1989), *Intra-Industry Trade* (London: Macmillan).

Walter, I. (1983), 'Structural Adjustment and Trade Policy in the International Steel Industry', in W. R. Cline (ed.), *Trade Policy in the 1980s* (Washington, DC: Institute for International Economics), 483–518.

# 12

# The European Monetary System

## ROBIN BLADEN-HOVELL

### 12.1. INTRODUCTION

Before the turbulence experienced on the foreign-exchange markets during 1992 and 1993, the Exchange Rate Mechanism (ERM) of the European Monetary System (EMS) represented the cornerstone of international monetary arrangements within Europe and looked set to provide the operational framework that would lead eventually to complete monetary union among EC Member States. Bilateral exchange rates between the EC countries had remained remarkably stable for an extended period within the ERM framework and appeared to exhibit lower levels of variability than other, non-ERM, rates. The last major adjustment of European exchange rates had occurred in 1987, and since that date the system had successfully incorporated three additional currencies—the Spanish peseta in June 1989, UK sterling in October 1990, and the Portuguese escudo in April 1992—and had witnessed German monetary unification in 1990. The success of the system seemed further underlined by the decisions of some non-EC countries (Sweden, Norway, and Finland) unilaterally to tie their currencies to the ERM. By the end of the period of turbulence, however, the framework appeared to be in crisis. Two major currencies, the Italian lira and UK sterling, had suspended their membership; the Spanish peseta and Portuguese escudo had devalued within the system; the permissible band of fluctuation around central parity rates had been substantially widened to 15 per cent; the non-ERM adherents to the system (in the Swedish case, after a spectacular but unsuccessful defence) had severed their links with the system.

The purpose of this chapter is to survey the performance and achievements of the system and to highlight the factors that led up to the events of September 1992, when the lira and pound sterling suspended their membership of the system, and the subsequent crisis of 1993. The chapter contains five sections. The key provisions of the system are outlined in Section 12.2, this is followed by a discussion of the performance of the EMS from its inception to 1989. The issue of whether the ERM is simply a Deutschmark zone is considered in Section 12.4, whilst the question of whether capital controls are necessary for the system to function is tackled in Section 12.5.

Of course, the turbulence experienced in the foreign-exchange markets during 1992 and 1993 is not entirely independent of these two issues. The virtual freedom of movement for international capital, together with the dominant position of Germany and its unwillingness to operate monetary policy from a European (rather than a German) perspective, is frequently blamed for the crisis in the system. These questions are considered in detail in Section 12.6. A brief summary of the main points and conclusions complete the chapter.

## 12.2. PROVISIONS OF THE MECHANISM

The EMS was established in March 1979 with the intention of creating a 'zone of monetary stability' within Europe. The origins of the system may be traced to the 1970 Werner Report, which proposed the achievement of complete monetary union within the EC by 1980. Although circumstances at the time led to the original timetable for this proposal being abandoned almost immediately, a further attempt to relaunch the idea of a European zone of exchange-rate stability was made in the aftermath of the break-down of the Bretton Woods system and the Smithsonian Agreement of December 1971. In March of the following year the EC countries embarked on an experiment to restrict the range of fluctuation between their currencies to a band of ±2.25 per cent. Anticipating imminent accession to the EC, the United Kingdom, Norway, Denmark, and the Irish Republic also participated in this scheme, which became known as the Snake. The Snake system was unable to withstand the considerable turbulence in the currency markets; some countries left the system quite soon after joining (the United Kingdom and the Irish Republic), whilst others left and rejoined only to leave again (France). By 1977 only a core group of five countries (Germany, Denmark, the Netherlands, Belgium, and Luxemburg) remained. Nevertheless, the desire remained strong to stabilize exchange rates between the EC Member States and agreement of a more effective means for achieving this was finally achieved at the Council of Ministers meeting held in Brussels in December 1978.[1] The EMS began operation from the following March.

The EMS is formally organized around a basket of EC currencies that comprise the European Currency Unit (Ecu) which acts as the numeraire for the ERM and the unit of account for all EC transactions. The Ecu is a composite currency that contains specific amounts of the currencies of all Member States, including those which do not participate in the ERM. Thus, at the end of 1993, the Ecu contains the Greek drachma, the Italian lira, and the UK pound sterling even though Greece has never participated in the ERM, whilst Italy and the United Kingdom both suspended their membership in September 1992. The composition of the Ecu has been subject to periodic review, the review period being set initially as every five years.

The composition of the Ecu set at each of the quinquennial reviews, together with the weight of each currency in the Ecu, is shown in Table 12.1. From this we can see that the Ecu consists literally of so many Deutschmarks, so many French francs, so many pounds sterling, and so on. However, the actual weight of each currency in the basket will change because of exchange-rate movements, and the weights shown in the table are those prevailing on 12 October 1990, following the decision of the UK government to join the ERM.

The centrepiece of the EMS is its ERM. This provides for a 'currency grid', a set of all bilateral exchange rates between participating countries with a nominated central rate for each and a permissible band of fluctuation. As a matter of arithmetic, a currency's central rate is re-expressed in terms of Ecu; but the essence of the ERM is the obligation to maintain bilateral exchange rates within the permitted bands of fluctuation. Prior to the decision taken by European finance ministers in August 1992 to allow ERM currencies to float within a margin of ±15 per cent, the size of this band was set at ±2.25 per cent for the majority of participating countries. Italy, however, had negotiated a transitional arrangement which allowed it

TABLE 12.1. *Composition and weighting of the Ecu and divergence-indicator threshold*

| Country and currency | Composition of the Ecu | | | Weight at 12 Oct. 1990 | Divergence-indicator at Oct. 1990 |
|---|---|---|---|---|---|
| | 13 Mar. 1979–14 Sept. 1984 | 17 Sept. 1984–20 Sept. 1989 | 20 Sept. 1989–? | | |
| Belgium/Luxemburg (franc) | 3.800 | 3.850 | 3.431 | 8.1 | 1.55 |
| Denmark (krone) | 0.217 | 0.219 | 0.1976 | 2.5 | 1.65 |
| France (franc) | 1.150 | 1.310 | 1.332 | 19.3 | 1.36 |
| Germany (mark) | 0.828 | 0.719 | 0.6242 | 30.2 | 1.18 |
| Greece (drachma) | n.a. | 1.150 | 1.440 | 0.7 | n.a. |
| Irish Republic (pound) | 0.00759 | 0.00871 | 0.008552 | 1.1 | 1.69 |
| Italy (lira) | 100.000 | 140.000 | 151.8 | 9.8 | 1.52 |
| Netherlands (guilder) | 0.286 | 0.256 | 0.2198 | 9.4 | 1.53 |
| Portugal (escudo) | n.a. | n.a. | 1.04741 | 0.8 | n.a. |
| Spain (peseta) | n.a. | n.a. | 6.885 | 0.7 | 4.47 |
| UK (sterling) | 0.0885 | 0.0878 | 0.08784 | 12.8 | 3.92 |
| | | | | 100.0 | |

*Note*: n.a. = not applicable.

to operate within a wider, ±6 per cent, band of fluctuation.[2] This transitional arrangement was subsequently extended to three new participants: Spain (June 1989), the United Kingdom (October 1990), and Portugal (April 1992) upon their joining the mechanism.

Central rates are not irrevocably fixed within the system, but may be adjusted, or realigned, after consultation among EMS members. One of the principal objectives of the ERM, however, has been to keep such realignments to a minimum and especially to prevent devaluation being used as a competitive instrument of policy within Europe.

To this end, central banks are obliged to intervene in the foreign-exchange market in order to keep their currencies within the permitted margins of fluctuation. The intervention rules themselves are relatively straightforward and designed to impose symmetry of adjustment on the system.[3] When a currency diverges from its central rate by the amount permitted by its band of fluctuation, say ±2.25 per cent, the central banks of the strongest and the weakest currency within the system are equally obliged to intervene in order to stabilize the currency. Since any of the bilateral exchange rates can trigger an intervention, measuring the maximum appreciation and depreciation against the weakest and strongest currency respectively means that the effective band of fluctuation is narrower than the 2.25 per cent margin would suggest in practice. Moreover, this effective width will adjust continually, as the weights of individual currencies in the Ecu change with exchange-rate movements.

The innovation in the EMS of the divergence indicator, based upon the concept of the Maximum Divergence Spread (MDS), provides a further example of the desire to promote symmetry of adjustment within the system. The MDS, calculated as $\pm 2.25 \, (1 - w_i)$, where $w_i$ denotes the weight of currency $i$, indicates the maximum percentage by which a currency's market Ecu rate may fluctuate against its Ecu central rate before the currency reaches its bilateral margin against any other ERM currency.[4] The divergence indicator is based on the notion of a divergence threshold, which is set at 75 per cent of the MDS.[5] By construction, a currency departing from its central rate should cross the divergence threshold and trigger the divergence indicator before it reaches any of the bilateral margins defined by the currency paid. The formal provision of the EMS provides that, when a currency triggers its divergence threshold, a presumption is created that the country in question should undertake appropriate adjustments, whether by intervention in the foreign-exchange market or by fiscal or monetary policy action perhaps including a realignment of its currency. Because the design of the divergence indicator was based on a currency's Ecu-rate divergence, the device was thought of as singling out that particular currency which stood out against 'the rest of the pack'. It was by intention even-handed, applying equally to a currency standing out on the 'strong' as to one on the 'weak' side. This was the sense in which the divergence-indicator appeared to underpin the desire for symmetry.

In order to finance their obligation to defend the bilateral currency bands, countries participating in the ERM may draw upon the credit facilities of the European Monetary Co-operation Fund (EMCF). The most important of these instruments is the Very Short Term Financing (VSTF) facility, which provides finance for intervention in the foreign-exchange markets which is undertaken when the currency reaches its limit—so-called marginal intervention. This facility takes the form of a line of mutual credit which extends among the central banks of the system. Since marginal intervention is compulsory and must be conducted in unlimited quantities by the two central banks whose currencies have reached their bilateral margin, this credit line is automatic and unlimited.[6]

In principle, the design of the VSTF facility has important implications for monetary conditions in countries that are pushed to their bilateral margins. The use of the credit lines in these circumstances results in an increase in the liabilities of the central bank managing the stronger currency and an increase in the assets of the central bank managing the weaker currency. As a result, marginal intervention should produce a monetary expansion in the country with the stronger currency and a monetary contraction in the country with the weaker currency. In practice, however, the extent to which ERM members have allowed their domestic monetary policy to be dictated by the needs of the ERM has varied considerably, with Germany, in particular, typically acting to sterilize the monetary effects of ERM intervention. We discuss this asymmetry of the operation of the system in Section 12.3.

## 12.3. THE OPERATION OF THE SYSTEM IN PRACTICE

Although the ERM was conceived of as providing a framework for monetary stability within Europe, exchange rates were not considered immutably fixed, at least not at first. Adjustments or realignments of the central parities were allowed, and the early years of the system, in particular, featured a number of realignments of these central rates.

In this respect, the design of the ERM benefited from the experience that policy-makers had gained previously in attempting to implement parity changes within otherwise fixed-rate systems. Under the institutional arrangements that characterized both the Bretton Woods system and the Snake, for example, countries generally resisted parity changes for as long as possible, with the result that, when adjustment did occur, it was typically brought about, or accompanied by, intense speculative pressure. Speculators were, in effect, able to benefit from what became known as a 'one-way bet' on the currency movement. With the direction of movement in the currency known with almost complete certainty, speculators could afford to adopt extreme positions in the foreign-exchange market by borrowing the weak currency in order to buy the strong one in anticipation of a devaluation. The potential gains from such speculative activity are enormous. The gross gains produced by correctly anticipating a 10 per cent devaluation on the day, for example, would be equivalent to an annual interest differential equal to (10 × 365) 3,650 per cent. By comparison, until the recent turbulence in the European foreign-exchange markets, realignments within the ERM have mostly been made without excessive speculative pressure developing. Realignments became less frequent within the system as time elapsed, and many exchange-rate adjustments occurred without disturbing the market rate, which remained within existing bands, thus eliminating the one-way speculative option that accompanies discrete exchange-rate movements.

Details of the realignments within the ERM, expressed in terms of the total number of adjustments *vis-à-vis* the Deutschmark over the period 1979–89, are presented in Table 12.2. Thirty-nine realignments, implemented in eleven discrete adjustments, have occurred in total. However, twenty-seven of these were made during the initial five-year period, 1979–83, when economic—notably inflationary—conditions of the participating countries still diverged significantly. In contrast, the period 1983–9 was characterized by relatively stable exchange rates within the ERM. Only twelve parity changes were recorded in this latter period and the average size of adjustment was considerably smaller than that experienced during 1979–83 (3.8 per cent compared to 5.3 per cent for the ERM as a whole).

A further feature of exchange-rate adjustments over the period was the increasing tendency for such realignments not to accommodate the differences in inflation among the ERM countries fully as the period progressed. The point may be easily seen by referring to the final row in each part of Table 12.2, which shows the degree of inflation offset provided by the nominal realignments within the period. For all countries except the Irish Republic and Italy, the earlier period was characterized by nominal adjustments that more than fully offset the inflation differential between Germany and the country concerned: for countries participating in the narrow band of the ERM, the inflation offset amounted to just over 100 per cent during this period. From 1983 onwards, however, the degree of inflation compensation fell considerably, with the offset to the inflation differential between Germany and other narrow-band currencies amounting to only 50 per cent during the latter period.

The apparent ability of the ERM to stabilize variations in exchange rates is typically accounted as one of the most successful aspects of the system. As indicated in Table 12.3, however, whilst this stabilizing effect seems clear for intra-EMS exchange rates, it is less clearly visible for movements in the exchange rates between ERM members and the rest of the world.

TABLE 12.2. *Realignments in the EMS 1979–1989*

| Realignments vis-à-vis the Deutschmark | Belgium/ Luxemburg | Denmark | France | Irish Republic | Italy | Netherlands | Narrow band | ERM |
|---|---|---|---|---|---|---|---|---|
| **1979–1983** | | | | | | | | |
| No. of realignments | 5 | 7 | 4 | 4 | 5 | 2 | 22 | 27 |
| Average size (%) | 4.9 | 4.4 | 7.1 | 5.2 | 6.3 | 2.0 | 5.1 | 5.3 |
| Average cumulative price differential (%) | 1.7 | 3.1 | 6.7 | 12.0 | 9.8 | 1.0 | 5.0 | 5.9 |
| Degree of offset (%) | 296.6 | 139.8 | 105.4 | 43.5 | 64.4 | 203.2 | 101.2 | 89.7 |
| **1984–1989** | | | | | | | | |
| No. of realignments | 2 | 2 | 2. | 3 | 3 | — | 9 | 12 |
| Average size (%) | 1.5 | 2.5 | 4.5 | 4.7 | 4.7 | — | 3.5 | 3.8 |
| Average cumulative price differential (%) | 5.3 | 6.8 | 8.3 | 6.1 | 9.3 | — | 6.6 | 7.3 |
| Degree of offset (%) | 28.5 | 36.5 | 54.5 | 77.2 | 50.7 | — | 52.7 | 52.1 |

*Source:* CEC (1990: table 2.4).

**TABLE 12.3.** *Variability of bilateral nominal exchange rates for the ERM countries, the EC non-ERM, and the United States and Japan 1979–1989*

| Countries | 1974–8 | 1979–83 | 1984–6 | 1987–9 |
|---|---|---|---|---|
| Against 20 industrialized countries | | | | |
| USA | 2.1 | 2.3 | 2.6 | 2.4 |
| Japan | 2.4 | 2.9 | 2.7 | 2.4 |
| ERM | 1.8 | 1.6 | 1.3 | 1.1 |
| Non-ERM countries | 2.4 | 2.4 | 2.2 | 1.7 |
| | | | | |
| Against ERM countries | | | | |
| USA | 2.2 | 2.6 | 3.0 | 2.8 |
| Japan | 2.3 | 2.7 | 2.1 | 1.9 |
| ERM | 1.6 | 0.9 | 0.6 | 0.4 |
| Non-ERM countries | 2.2 | 2.3 | 1.8 | 1.4 |

*Source*: CEC (1990: tables 3.4–3.6).

Here, exchange-rate variability is measured as the standard deviation of the monthly percentage change of the nominal bilateral exchange rate—these standard deviations being aggregated into single values through the use of the Ecu currency weights in the case of the ERM and EC non-ERM groups respectively.

High-frequency measures of this nature can be used to adduce evidence concerning the short-run volatility of the exchange rate but do not illuminate the question of whether exchange rates are misaligned or not. Misalignment in this context refers to the capacity for the real exchange rate, or competitiveness, to depart from its equilibrium value over particular periods of time.[7] Such departures, if left uncorrected, pose particular problems for the pattern of trade and, ultimately, for the spatial location of production among countries.

The welfare effects of a reduction in volatility, on the other hand, are probably not great; what counts is whether the volatility can be predicted and whether traders can hedge themselves with little cost against it. In conventional theory the forward markets afford hedging opportunities at low cost for short horizons. However, a finding that the EMS reduced short-run volatility in nominal exchange rates suggests that it may also have prevented misalignments from growing as quickly as they might otherwise have done, which might be recorded as a more substantial achievement. But it does seem clear that any such dampening effect was not enough to discourage some significant misalignment from eventually emerging (see, for example, the evidence in Table 12.2 relating to the propensity of nominal realignments within the ERM to offset inflation differentials between members and thereby protect a country's competitive position). Indeed, some observers (see below) attribute the crash of the EMS in part to perceptions that some currencies had become seriously misaligned.

Despite the original intention of making adjustment within the ERM symmetric, considerable evidence has accumulated which suggests that substantial asymmetries remained within the system. Two factors in particular are commonly identified as being illustrative of these operational asymmetries. The first relates to the fact that the Deutschmark is now widely acknowledged as providing the *de facto* nominal anchor and reserve currency of the system, with dollar interventions dominated by the actions of the Bundesbank. Secondly, the burden of intervention to support parities within the ERM has been disproportionately borne by the weaker, and generally non-German, currencies.[8] In addition, as Mastropasqua, Micossi, and Rinaldi (1988) find, the Bundesbank typically tends to offset the domestic monetary consequences of German involvement in supporting activities by buying or selling interest-bearing debt to the private sector—so-called sterilization operations. As a result, monetary policy in Germany is determined by domestic considerations alone, whilst the remaining, non-German, ERM members essentially accommodate the stance of German monetary policy. Moreover, the relevance of this result has become increasingly important as ERM members have placed greater reliance on their currency value *vis-à-vis* the Deutschmark rather than their Ecu parity.[9] As a consequence of this, ERM members have typically found themselves constrained by their bilateral limits relative to the strongest currency rather than the divergence thresholds of the system. These factors, together with the adoption of the ERM as a disinflationary framework by the non-German members of the system, led investigators to propose that, to all practical intents and purposes, the operations of the ERM had come to conform to a 'greater Deutschemark zone'. This proposition, usually ascribed to Giavazzi and Giovannini (1989) and Giavazzi and Pagano (1988), is considered in greater detail in Section 12.4.

## 12.4. THE GERMAN LEADERSHIP HYPOTHESIS

Whilst the relative performance of the German economy and the historical strength of the German balance of payments obviously suggest that Germany merits an important role within the ERM, the willingness of other countries to accept Germany as the dominant partner implies that these countries must anticipate benefits accruing from the arrangement. For non-German members of the ERM, these gains have usually been expressed in terms of the benefits they achieve by 'importing' Germany's reputation for counter-inflationary policy.

This proposition is based upon the notion of a 'reputational policy' of the form described by Barro and Gordon (1983). Here the costs to a country, in terms of the loss of output, associated with a policy of inflation reduction, depend crucially upon the ability of the authorities to convince the private sector that they mean to pursue an effective counter-inflationary policy and will not renege on this commitment. Within this framework, credible governments may make announcements concerning future disinflationary strategy and, because these announcements are believed by the private sector, they have the immediate effect of reducing inflationary expectations within the economy. As a consequence, the desired effects of policy may be achieved at lower unemployment cost than would have occurred had the reputation of the authorities been lower.

Within the ERM, the counter-inflationary stance of German monetary policy is generally well known. The decision of countries to pre-commit themselves to a fixed exchange rate with respect to Germany therefore constitutes a very visible commitment to low inflation, which is relatively straightforward for the private sector to monitor. The alternative, assuming that the fixed exchange-rate system is maintained, is a gradual erosion of competitiveness for the higher inflation country.[10] Of course, the decision by countries to pre-commit to the German standard implies that the operation of the ERM will be asymmetric in the way described previously: the Bundesbank independently chooses its monetary policy, whilst all remaining EMS members 'tie their hands' on monetary policy and simply target their exchange rates to the Deutschmark. The EMS is *de facto* a Deutschmark zone.[11]

Although the intuitive argument in favour of the German leadership hypothesis is compelling, the empirical evidence that may be adduced in its favour is less than fully supportive. Evidence relating to the interaction of monetary policy among ERM members, for example, suggests a rich structure of cross-country interactions: German monetary policy influences the other ERM members, but is itself affected by monetary developments that originate elsewhere in the system, especially in France. French monetary policy also influences policy developments among the non-German ERM members.

Strictly interpreted, this evidence would appear to run counter to the notion of German leadership, but does favour a view of the EMS operating in a symmetric, or bipolar, manner, with France and Germany representing the two poles of behaviour in the latter case. Weber (1991), in particular, argues that a bipolar interpretation of the EMS, with Germany offering a hard-currency option and France offering a soft-currency option to members, provides a convenient framework for analysing developments within the system prior to 1987. He suggests, however, that the system has become increasingly dominated by the Deutschmark from 1987 onwards, as the disinflationary stance of ERM members has hardened.

Direct tests of whether the EMS has facilitated a convergence on the inflation performance of Germany have also produced conflicting evidence. A casual inspection of the data relating to the inflation performance of ERM and non-ERM countries, for example, suggests that, overall, ERM countries have performed little, if at all, better than non-ERM countries in reducing inflation. However, more sophisticated exercises that investigate whether German inflation 'affects' wage and price developments in other ERM countries (see e.g. Artis and Nachane (1990)), find strong evidence of an 'EMS effect' in the sense that the predicted inflation in Germany is a significant determinant of price inflation in all EMS countries except the United Kingdom over the period 1979–85. This result is frequently inter-preted in an expectational context—in effect, ERM membership disciplines the economy by raising the cost of inflation.

A commonly used measure of disinflationary costs is expressed in terms of the sacrifice ratio. This measure calculates the cumulative change in unemployment (or lost output) over a period as a ratio of the change in the rate of inflation over the same period. Expressed in this way, the measure has the advantage of aggregating gains from credibility and changes in the expectations formation process; for this reason, countries subject to an EMS-effect of the credibility type might be expected to exhibit a lower sacrifice ratio than countries that do not. The key disadvantage of the measure is that it does not distinguish between the influence of policy and the influence of other non-policy factors.

Sacrifice ratios, based alternatively on unemployment or output measures, are presented in Table 12.4 for a number of prominent ERM and non-ERM countries. Unemployment-based measures cover the whole period 1979–89, whilst the output-based measures also report information relating to the sub-periods 1979–82 and 1979–85. Inspection of these results indicates that, for the majority of countries, the unemployment-based measures yield a more pessimistic picture of the transitory costs of disinflation than that obtained from the output-based measures. Only three countries (the United States, Canada, and Sweden) managed by the end of the period to reduce unemployment to, or below, its initial level and even here the success was only temporary, the 1991 level of unemployment exceeding the initial level in each case.[12]

Surprisingly, these results suggest that the sacrifice ratio for Germany is particularly unfavourable—a finding that might be related to a relatively high degree of real rigidity within the German economy. Moreover, countries with particularly close links to the Deutschmark also appear to rank poorly on the basis of this measure, despite the expectation that such a linkage would strengthen credibility and hence lower the transitory costs of disinflation for these countries. Combining these results with the evidence reported by Artis and Nachane (1990), it would appear that, while the link to the Deutschmark helped to dampen inflationary expectations within other ERM countries, the absence of changes to the wage-formation

TABLE **12.4.** *Sacrifice ratios*

| Country | Unemployment-based measures[a] 1979/81–1986/9 | Output-based measures[b] | | |
|---|---|---|---|---|
| | | 1979–82 | 1979–85 | 1979–88 |
| Belgium | 3.00 | 6.10 | 0.90 | 0.50 |
| Denmark | 1.25 | 0.90 | −0.15 | 0.15 |
| France | 2.15 | 0.50 | 0.50 | 0.20 |
| Germany | 6.40 | 2.20 | 1.20 | 1.60 |
| Irish Republic | 3.35 | 0.30 | 0.50 | 0.50 |
| Italy | 1.40 | 0.65 | 0.45 | 0.20 |
| Netherlands | 4.95 | 1.85 | 0.80 | 1.10 |
| UK | 3.40 | 0.90 | 0.60 | 0.20 |
| Canada | 2.75 | 1.50 | 0.80 | 0.15 |
| Japan | 0.70 | 0.50 | 0.10 | −0.30 |
| Norway | 1.05 | 2.00 | 0.00 | 0.50 |
| Sweden | 1.20 | 0.65 | 0.00 | −0.40 |
| USA | 0.85 | 1.35 | 0.40 | 0.30 |

[a] Calculated as the cumulative rise in the rate of unemployment between 1979–81 and 1986–9 divided by the change in the rate of consumer price inflation over the same period.
[b] Cumulative output losses between 1979 and 1982, 1985, and 1988 respectively divided by the change in the rate of consumer price inflation between 1979–81 and 1984, 1987, and 1990 respectively. In calculating the output losses, trend or capacity output has been approximated by a cubic trend.

*Source*: Schelde-Anderson (1992: table 5).

process and the natural rate of unemployment implied that those countries were forced to follow the rise in German unemployment in order to validate the lower rates of inflation.

### 12.5. CAPITAL CONTROLS

The maintenance of capital controls within a system of managed exchange rates is usually based upon two arguments. These arguments highlight the potential of capital controls to limit the extent of fluctuations in domestic interest rates in the period immediately prior to a discrete change of the exchange rate that is anticipated by the market, and suggest that, by adopting capital controls, the monetary authorities can avert speculative attacks against their foreign-exchange position. In each case, therefore, the role of the currency speculator is crucial.

The motivation behind speculative capital flows is one of making a capital gain from anticipated movements in spot rates or interest rates. A risk-neutral currency speculator would be indifferent between holding sterling- or Deutschmark-denominated assets, for example, if the interest rate on sterling assets equalled the interest rate on Deutschmarks plus the anticipated depreciation of sterling relative to the Deutschmark—the uncovered interest parity condition. If the anticipated sterling devaluation exceeds the sterling interest advantage, holders of sterling assets will switch their portfolio into Deutschmarks in the expectation of making a capital gain by repurchasing sterling at a lower value in the future. Moreover, irrespective of whether the interest differential offsets the expected currency movement or not, since the value of domestic currency falls with a devaluation, holders of domestic high-powered money have an incentive to avoid the loss by selling the domestic currency to the central bank in exchange for foreign currency prior to the devaluation, then buying domestic currency back once the devaluation has occurred. If foreign-exchange transactions were costless, the effect of such speculative activity would be to reduce the foreign-exchange reserves of the central bank to zero.

The difficulty is that, within a regime of controlled floating, the interest differential required to offset expected currency movements is typically very high. A simple example may be used to illustrate the point. Suppose that a discrete devaluation, equivalent to a fall of 5 per cent per annum, was expected next month within an otherwise fixed-rate regime. The interest differential required to offset this would be 5 per cent on comparable one-year bonds. For interest-bearing instruments of shorter maturity, however, the required interest differential would be correspondingly higher: 20 per cent on three-month assets, 60 per cent on one-month assets, and well in excess of 100 per cent on overnight deposits.[13] Capital controls can protect domestic interest rates from the need to assume such levels when discrete changes in the currency value are expected by the market. They do so by prohibiting domestic and foreign residents from borrowing at the domestic rate of interest in order to lend abroad in the expectation of capital gains from the currency movement. Of course, such a prohibition on currency transactions would also have the advantage of preventing speculative attacks on the foreign-reserve position of the central bank.

In investigating the effectiveness of capital controls, attention has focused on the size of the on-shore/off-shore interest differential. In the absence of capital controls, this differential should represent a pure arbitrage opportunity for agents operating in the foreign-exchange market. Evidence obtained by de Grauwe (1989) and Giavazzi and Giovannini (1989), however, suggests that capital controls enabled France and Italy in particular to violate the interest-parity condition, and, as a result, allowed ERM members to maintain a considerable degree of monetary autonomy, especially during the early days of ERM. The importance of capital controls has gradually been reduced within the ERM following the

Capital Liberalization Directive of 1988.[14] Controls were removed entirely from capital movements in and out of France and Italy, and the two-tier foreign-exchange market that allowed discrimination between commercial and capital account transactions in Belgium was eliminated. By 1990 controls remained in effect for Greece, the Irish Republic, Portugal, and Spain, and even in these countries the scope of control was very limited. As a consequence, the potential for capital movements among the ERM countries has increased substantially, and this feature has frequently been identified as a major contributory factor to the turbulence that occurred in the European foreign-exchange markets during September 1992 and August 1993. It is to these events that we now turn.

## 12.6. CRISIS IN THE ERM

The events in the foreign-exchange and financial markets associated with the crisis in the ERM during September 1992 and July–August 1993 have been among the most important since the EC began. Strain on the system had been mounting for some time. Although the underlying causes of the events have still not been fully resolved, it is apparent that the decision not to revalue the Deutschmark following German unification in 1989 must feature strongly. The immediate consequence of this decision was that incipient inflationary pressure within Germany was met by the Bundesbank with higher interest rates, and the relative freedom with which capital could move among the ERM countries meant that little impediment prevented these rates from being transmitted to other members of the system. As a result, severe deflationary pressure built up in the majority of countries. This pressure was further exacerbated by the decision of the UK government to use the ERM as the mainstay of its domestic disinflationary strategy and to join at a central parity that many commentators suggested was too high.[15]

In the event, the immediate trigger for the exchange-market crisis was the political uncertainty that surrounded the referenda on the Treaty on European Union (TEU). Denmark had rejected the Treaty in early June, and the resultant strengthening of the Deutschmark placed considerable pressure on the lira and sterling. For the lira, market concern over the country's high level of public debt and excessive budget deficit contributed to these pressures. In the United Kingdom the continued recession and weak current-account position influenced market perceptions that sterling might be devalued within the ERM, given the apparent constraints on interest rates in that country. Tension was partially eased by intervention, particularly in support of the lira during the summer. By the end of August, however, pressure again began to mount with the approach to the

French referendum concerning the TEU, fed especially by opinion polls that suggested a significant risk of rejection.

Currency speculation reached a peak in September. Massive intervention was required by the middle of the month in order to prevent the lira falling below its ERM floor, despite a sharp increase in short-term interest rates. The lira was devalued by 7 per cent on 12 September but remained under considerable pressure in the week that followed. At the same time the Spanish peseta fell from the top to the bottom of its ERM band. Comparable levels of intervention were required to prevent sterling falling below its ERM floor on 16 September, yet, despite this and a 2 per cent rise in official interest rates, sterling's membership of the ERM had to be suspended. Because intervention and higher interest rates had failed to keep the lira off its ERM floor, it, too, was suspended on 17 September. After the departure of the lira and sterling from the system, the French franc came under intense pressure, especially after the close (positive) result for the referendum. This was only beaten off by a combined defence operation mounted by the French and German central banks.

After the September crisis, significant pressure re-emerged among the ERM currencies in November. The Spanish peseta and Portuguese escudo were both devalued by 6 per cent on 23 November. By the end of the year sterling had depreciated by approximately 15 per cent, the Italian lira by 16 per cent, while the French franc and German mark were little changed.

Pressure on the ERM continued through much of 1993, and on 30 July the French and Belgian francs, the Danish krone, the Spanish peseta, and the Portuguese escudo all fell close to their floors against the Deutschmark, despite substantial intervention by central banks. Only the Netherlands guilder and Irish pound remained unscathed. As a consequence, finance ministers and central bankers decided on 2 August that operational changes were required to the structure of the ERM and announced that new margins of fluctuation, amounting to ±15 per cent of the central rate, would be permitted within the ERM. Only the Netherlands chose, by bilateral arrangement, to retain the original ±2.25 per cent band against the Deutschmark. The EMS had all but collapsed.

Reforming the EMS in the light of these events is obviously of paramount importance, especially given the key role that ERM has been given in the drive for European Monetary Union (EMU) (see Chapter 13 for details). Although the precise detail of these reforms remain uncertain, a number of candidates for reform have been identified in the literature. The most promising of these relates, in general terms, to the reimposition of capital controls within the EMS. Eichengreen and Wyplosz (1993), for example, propose that all institutions taking an open position in the foreign-exchange market be required to make non-interest-bearing deposits with their central bank. Such measures were previously utilized by countries like Spain and Italy in order to slow down adverse speculative pressure, the cost of the scheme being passed on to currency traders, thereby discouraging the 'one-way bet'. Of course, this type of policy would not provide permanent support for weak currencies, but would enable central banks to pursue orderly intervention or realignment unconstrained by the threat of a speculative attack.

## 12.7. CONCLUSIONS

From its introduction in 1979, the ERM has provided a framework for nominal exchange-rate stability within Europe. In the early period the ERM acted very much like a crawling peg with a number of realignments, often involving a devaluation of the franc against the Deutschmark. The ERM subsequently shifted away from this characterization and adopted the features of a semi-fixed regime. From 1987 onwards, as France pursued its *franc fort* policy, the franc maintained its position against the Deutschmark and the counter-inflationary stance of the ERM was strengthened, with a consequent rise in disinflationary pressures throughout Europe.

In addition to its impact on nominal exchange rates, the ERM is often credited with stabilizing real exchange rates via its effect on the inflation rates of the ERM members. The precise mechanism for achieving this end, however, is unclear, though the role of Germany as the low-inflation, dominant partner of the ERM appears to be important in this respect. The evidence obtained from measures such as the sacrifice ratio, however, suggests that lower inflation among the non-German ERM countries has been possible only by accepting a marked increase in unemployment.

From the point of view of events during 1992 and 1993, the ERM has demonstrated a clear weakness in its ability to weather speculative attack. While relaxation of capital controls throughout Europe may have contributed to this situation, the failure of Member States to adopt a flexible attitude with respect to realignments within the ERM must also bear some part of the blame. As originally designed, the ERM would have required a realignment of the Deutschmark following reunification, and the subsequent events in European foreign-exchange markets might have been substantially different had this course of action been adopted.

# NOTES

1. The original members of the EMS were Belgium, Denmark, France, Germany, the Irish Republic, Italy, Netherlands, and the United Kingdom. The United Kingdom, however, initially chose not to participate in the ERM.
2. Italy eventually adopted the narrower ±2.25 per cent band in Jan. 1990.

3. Asymmetric adjustment was characteristic of earlier attempts to manage the exchange rate. The loss of foreign-exchange reserves by deficit nations placed a greater obligation for countries with weaker currencies to adjust than reserve accumulation did for strong currencies under both the Bretton Woods system and the Snake.

4. The adjustment $(1-w_i)$ recognizes the fact that, when a currency moves away from its central rate, it pulls the value of the Ecu with it. The extent of the movement in the Ecu depends upon the weight of the particular currency in the composition of the Ecu, and adjusts the divergence threshold to reflect deviations of a currency from other currencies in the Ecu basket.

5. An adjustment was made in calculating the divergence threshold to account for the non-participation of the drachma, and the wider margins adopted within the ERM by Italy, Portugal, Spain, and the United Kingdom.

6. The repayment period for the VSTF facility was initially set at forty-five days following the month in which intervention occurred. However, this period was subsequently extended to seventy-five days by the Basle–Nyborg agreement signed in September 1987. The Basle–Nyborg accord also made the VSTF facility available on a voluntary basis for financing *intra-marginal* intervention (that is, foreign-exchange market intervention undertaken *before* a currency hits its ceiling or floor against any other).

7. The distinction between short-run volatility and long-run misalignment was drawn by Williamson (1983). For a discussion of the empirical evidence, see Artis and Taylor (1988).

8. An important point in this respect is that, 1992–3 aside, most of the intervention has been *intra-marginal*, which, by its very nature, has operated in an asymmetric manner; Germany never initiated much intra-marginal intervention itself.

9. A clear example of such behaviour is reflected in the fact that, when the United Kingdom joined the EMS, emphasis was placed almost entirely on the sterling–Deutschmark value rather than the central Ecu rate.

10. Of course, this erosion of competitiveness itself may be considered part of the adjustment mechanism. At the extreme, industries experiencing a loss of competitiveness will reduce output and thereby contribute to increased unemployment within the economy.

11. For an interesting comparison of the 'rules of the game' as contained within the original EMS and those implied by a greater Deutschmark area, see McKinnon (1993).

12. Of course, the difference between the unemployment-based and output-based measures may also indicate that the equilibrium rate of unemployment has increased relative to the level of potential output in the countries concerned.

13. On 18 Sept. 1992, for example, overnight interest rates in the Irish Republic were set at 300 per cent; on 26 Nov. the overnight rate was 100 per cent; on 3 Aug. 1993 Danish overnight rates reached 250 per cent.

14. Capital controls in the United Kingdom were removed by the Conservative government in 1979.

15. On the question of whether the United Kingdom joined the ERM at the right rate, see e.g. Williamson (1991) and Wren-Lewis *et al.* (1990).

# REFERENCES

Artis, M. J. (1986), 'The European Monetary System: An Evaluation', *Journal of Policy Modelling*, 9/1: 175–98.

―― and Nachane, D. (1990), 'Wages and Prices in Europe: A Test of the German Leadership Hypothesis', *Weltwirtschaftliches Archiv*, 126 (Mar.), 59–77.

―― and Taylor, M. P. (1988), 'Exchange Rates, Interest Rates, Capital Controls and the European Monetary System: Assessing the Track Record', in F. Giavazzi, S. Micossi, and M. H. Miller (eds.), *The European Monetary System* (Cambridge: Cambridge University Press), 185–206.

Barro, R., and Gordon, D. (1983), 'Rules, Discretion and Reputation in a Model of Monetary Policy', *Journal of Monetary Economics*, 12: 589–610.

CEC (1990): Commission of the European Communities, 'One Market, One Money: An Evaluation of the Potential Benefits and Costs of Forming an Economic and Monetary Union', *European Economy*, 44: 1–351.

de Grauwe, P. (1989), *Is the European Monetary System a DM-zone* (Discussion Paper No. 126; London: Centre of Economic Policy Research).

Eichengreen, B., and Wyplosz, C. (1993), 'The Unstable EMS', *Brookings Papers in Economic Activity*, 1: 51–143.

Giavazzi, F., and Giovannini, A. (1989), *Limiting Exchange Rate Flexibility: The European Monetary System* (Cambridge, Mass.: MIT Press).

―― and Pagano M. (1988), 'The Advantage of Tying one's Hands: EMS Discipline and Central Bank Credibility', *European Economic Review*, 32: 1055–82.

Haldane, A. G. (1991), 'The Exchange Rate Mechanism of the European Monetary System: A Review of the Literature', *Bank of England Quarterly Bulletin* (Feb.), 73–82.

McKinnon, R. I. (1993), 'The Rules of the Game: International Money in Historical Perspective', *Journal of Economic Literature*, 31 (Mar.), 1–44.

Mastropasqua, C., Micossi, S., and Rinaldi, R. (1988), 'Interventions, Sterilization and Monetary Policy in European Monetary System Countries 1979–87', in F. Giavazzi, S. Micosi, and M. H. Miller (eds.), *The European Monetary System* (Cambridge: Cambridge University Press) 252–87.

Schelde-Anderson, P. (1992), 'QECD Country Experiences with Disinflation', in A. Blundell-Wignall (ed.), *Inflation, Disinflation and Monetary Policy*, proceedings of a Reserve Bank of Australia Conference held at the H. C. Coombs Centre for Financial Studies, Kirribilli, 10–11 July 1992 (Sydney: Ambassador Press), 104–73.

Weber, A. A. (1991), 'Reputation and Credibility in the European Monetary System', *Economic Policy*, 12: 58–102.

Williamson, J. (1983), *The Exchange Rate System* (Policy Analyses in International Economics, 5; Washington DC: Institute for International Economics).

―― (1991), 'FEERs and the ERM', *National Institute Economic Review* (Aug.), 45–50.

Wren-Lewis, S., Westaway, P., Soteri, S., and Barrell, R. (1990), 'Evaluating the U.K.'s Choice of Entry Rate into the ERM', *Manchester School, Supplement*, 59: 1–22.

# 13

# European Monetary Union

MIKE ARTIS

## 13.1. INTRODUCTION

With the agreements reached at Maastricht at the end of 1991, the Member States of the European Community (EC) came to the end of an unparalleled effort to think through the implications of monetary union in Europe. The resultant Treaty on European Union (TEU) set out a constitution for the Central Bank of the Union, a timetable for the approach to full union, and a set of criteria or fitness conditions for membership which individual countries would have to satisfy. This was the culmination of a process of intergovernmental discussion and negotiation inaugurated by the setting-up of the Delors Committee in June 1988, which was charged with setting out the requirements for a move to full monetary union in Europe. Such a project had been mooted before (back in 1970, the Werner Committee (CEC 1970) had set a date for monetary union of 1980), but it had never before been so carefully analysed.

However, it soon became clear that the translation of the Maastricht Treaty into practical progress towards the ultimate target was fraught with difficulty. First, the Danish people failed to ratify the Treaty in a first referendum called for the purpose; then the French referendum of July 1992 produced only a small majority in favour (the so-called 'petit oui'); whilst the ratification process in the UK Parliament proved to be exceptionally long drawn out. But the tribulations attending the process which contributed to the confusion about the immediate prospects for monetary union also served to initiate the débâcle of the Exchange Rate Mechanism (ERM) of the European Monetary System (EMS) in 1992–93. In September 1992 the pound sterling and Italian lira were both forced to float against other European currencies; around the same time, the Spanish peseta and the Portuguese escudo were obliged to devalue. Later on the Irish pound was devalued. There were intermittent tensions and speculative raids throughout the following months, culminating in the crisis at the end of July 1993 which resulted in the decision early in August to widen the bands of the ERM to 15 per cent (for details, see Chapter 12). The abandonment of the narrow-bands ERM was perceived as a body blow to earlier hopes of achieving a move towards complete monetary union before the end of the century. Yet there remained in many countries an evident desire to realize this goal, and the Maastricht Treaty provides a formal framework for its realization.

At the end of 1993 these uncertainties still remained partially unresolved and for this reason it seemed wise to orient the bulk of the discussion in this chapter around an analysis of the *general* principles of monetary union.[1] This is in fact the task of the next section. After that the discussion returns to an account of the specific promptings behind the process of negotiation which led to Maastricht and the TEU. This too illustrates some general principles, for it will be argued that there is an ineluctable tendency towards exchange rate and monetary union in Europe; whilst European Monetary Union (EMU) in the near future may be in doubt, EMU in the long run is a more certain bet. Then we will examine the provisions of the TEU, some of which again—for example, the proposed constitution of the European Central Bank—illustrate general principles. Finally, we take a brief look at the short-run outlook for EMU, as it appeared towards the end of 1993.

## 13.2. MONETARY UNION: THE GENERAL PRINCIPLES

A monetary union between two or more countries means that those countries agree to maintain the same currency. In the European context, where before there were French and Belgian francs, Italian lire, Dutch guilders, German Deutschmarks etc., there would be after monetary union a single currency (which, it is usually supposed, will be called the Ecu). Thus the central point about a monetary union is that, when countries proceed to join one, they give up the possibility for their own currency to be separate from those in the other countries and *therefore give up the possibility of allowing the rate of exchange between their own currency and those of the other members of the union to vary.*

### A Cost-Benefit Analysis

The appraisal of the pros and cons of joining a monetary union can be thought of as a cost-benefit analysis.[2] Since the key feature of belonging to a monetary union is that it is no longer possible to allow the rate of exchange to vary between your own country's currency and those of the other members of the union, this cost-benefit analysis can be re-expressed as follows. The benefits of monetary union are the benefits of having a single currency to use over a wider area; the costs are the costs of not being able to let the exchange rate (against other member countries) vary.

The general view is that the costs and benefits so expressed fall and rise respectively with the degree of integration between the economies concerned. This is shown in Fig. 13.1 (drawn from Krugman (1990)). Costs and benefits are expressed as a percentage of GDP along the vertical axis, whilst integration—perhaps measured as the ratio of intra-union trade to GDP—is measured along the horizontal. The *CC* curve then shows the costs of union as falling with integration, whilst the *BB* curve shows the benefits of union as rising with integration. If this representation is correct (and the more detailed analysis below indicates that it may be subject to some qualification), and European integration is growing with time, then at some point in the future the representative European economy will have passed to the right of the point *t\**, where benefits begin to exceed costs. Indeed some European economies are probably already in this position.

We need now to discuss more generally the nature of the costs and benefits of monetary union and to verify the slopes of the *CC* and *BB* curves shown in Fig. 13.1.

### The Benefits of a Single Currency

The most obvious and clear-cut benefit of a single currency is that it is no longer necessary to incur the costs of exchange from one currency to another. Any traveller will know that these costs are not negligible: first of all, there will be a commission charge (usually a fixed amount); secondly, the price at which the traveller can purchase foreign currency for domestic currency will differ from (specifically will be lower than) the price at which he can exchange back his surplus foreign currency. This

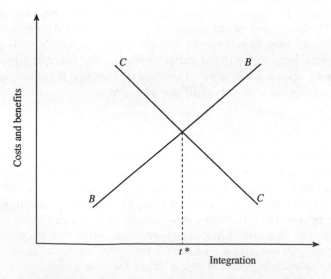

**FIG. 13.1.** The Krugman diagram: costs and benefits of monetary union
*Source*: Krugman (1990).

pricing schedule reflects the fact that the provision of foreign-exchange services uses up real resources. There are large economies of scale in foreign-exchange transactions, so that the position for big traders is in fact much less costly than it is for the average tourist. Nevertheless, these foreign-exchange transactions costs are not negligible and their removal constitutes a gain from monetary union. A moment's reflection suggests that this gain will indeed rise with integration—since the larger the ratio of trade to GDP, the greater the benefit from *not* having to change from one currency to another. This motivates the upward slope of the *BB* schedule in Fig. 13.1. The gain will also be bigger the less efficient (and thus the more costly) the *existing* foreign-exchange-transactions system, so countries with backward banking systems will gain more from monetary union (on this score, anyway) than those with more advanced systems. The Commission, in its analysis of EMU (CEC 1990), quantified this transactions-cost gain from the move to a single currency, for the EC as a whole, at 0.2 per cent of EC GDP.

Other gains have also been claimed for a single currency; unlike the expected benefit from the reduction in transactions costs, these other benefits cannot readily be quantified—though this does *not* necessarily mean that they are small. In particular, it seems likely that the removal of exchange-rate variations between the economies of the EC would provide much more assurance to corporate location decisions. At present, a company contemplating the location of a new plant within the European economy has to take account of the risk of exchange-rate variation, and this may lead it at the margin to 'scatter' its plants across the various economies, as this would be a way of hedging the risk of exchange-rate variation. Removing this source of uncertainty, the argument goes, would allow investors to locate according to economies of scale and would lead to more plants of the optimum size, bringing about a reduction in unit costs of production and a clear increase in efficiency. (It should be clear that what is required here is a reduction in *real* exchange-rate uncertainty, and the argument assumes that, in the absence of nominal exchange-rate jumps, countries' international competitiveness would be much more stable.) Clearly, this source of gain would take time to realize; indeed, it would only be realized as new investment decisions take place.

At a more general level it has also been argued (e.g. by the Commission (CEC 1990)) that removing exchange-rate uncertainty will reduce the risk premium in real interest rates; if so, it would encourage more investment and capital accumulation, leading to increases in output per head. However, it can be disputed how far removing one source of uncertainty will lead to a reduction in overall uncertainty in the economy: some economists argue that there is an irreducible 'lump of uncertainty' in an economy, which can only be shifted around, not reduced in size. On this argument, abolishing exchange-rate uncertainty will lead to greater uncertainty in some other respect: there might be more uncertainty about countries' tax regimes for example, as national governments turn to fiscal devices to offset their inability to allow exchange-rate variations to cushion the effects of adverse shocks on the economy.

Another source of benefit from establishing a single currency could arise from a reduction in the market discrimination that currently exists (with the prices of motor cars of the same specification, for example, standing higher in the United Kingdom than they do in France), as the quotation of prices in common currency encourages arbitrage activity and reduces the market segmentation on which such discrimination relies. A move to a single currency would also allow economies to be made in the holding of non-European currencies; there are economies of scale to be had from the holding of any reserve (a commonplace conclusion to be drawn from inventory theory), so the required holdings of foreign-exchange reserves in the new European Central Bank would be less than the sum of the holdings of the present individual national central banks. How far such a gain would be realized would depend on the evolution of a European exchange-rate policy. Finally, it can be argued that, with a single common currency, Europe would be represented as a single member with a strong voice in a world economy dominated by the 'Group of Three' (G3)—Japan, the United States, and Europe. Europe might have a stronger voice in such a milieu than in the present set-up, where the annual 'Summit Seven' (G7) meetings, though including no less than four European powers—France, Italy, Germany, and the United Kingdom—as well as Japan, the United States, and Canada, do so on the basis that each country represents itself and the pan-European interest is not necessarily expressed.[3]

### The Costs of Forgoing Exchange-Rate Variability

The point of having separate currencies with an exchange rate between them is to be able to let that exchange rate change. In classical economic analysis, the purpose of letting the exchange rate change is to have it act as a shock absorber for disturbances that impact on the partner economies in different ways—in the jargon, to absorb *asymmetric* shocks. Since going to monetary union involves giving up this shock absorber, the following questions need to be examined:

- How good is the exchange rate as a shock absorber? Does increasing integration make it less or more useful?
- How likely are asymmetric shocks to occur? Can we say whether integration makes them less or more likely?
- Are there alternative shock absorbers which could be made to function in a monetary union?

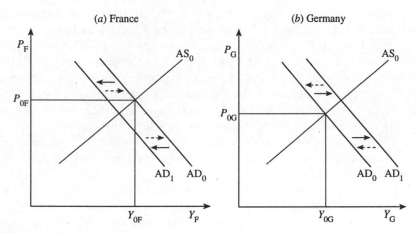

FIG. **13.2.** The exchange rate as a shock absorber

We examine first the way in which the exchange rate is supposed to act as a shock absorber in the framework of AD/AS analysis.

Fig. 13.2 presents the analysis diagrammatically. Fig. 13.2*a* refers to, say, France; Fig. 13.2*b* to, say, Germany. The exchange rate is taken to be fixed but adjustable. On the assumption, initially, that nominal wages are fixed, the aggregate-supply (AS) schedule slopes up from left to right in price–output space for both countries, because, as prices rise, real wage costs fall, leading employers to take on more labour and produce more output. The aggregate-demand (AD) schedule slopes down from left to right, because, with a lower price, the economy will be more competitive, with a higher demand for exports and a lower demand for imports; and because, with lower prices, the value of real money balances will rise. An increase in government expenditure or a shift in demand independent of price will cause a shift of the schedule. Suppose now that the exchange rate is changed—specifically, that the French franc is devalued in terms of the German Deutschmark. French output becomes cheaper relative to German output. This will mean that the aggregate demand for French output will rise and that for German output will fall. The AD schedule in the left-hand diagram will move to the right and that in the right-hand diagram will move to the left.

Now suppose that, from an initial position indicated by the $AD_0$ and $AS_0$ schedules with the corresponding price and output levels, a shock occurs which—because of the structure of the economies—is asymmetric between them. For example—the suggestion is fanciful, but the point is general— suppose that consumers' tastes change. It becomes unfashionable to drink champagne, whereas the consumption of sausages becomes the acme of good taste. The French economy is relatively intensive in champagne, whilst the German economy is intensive in the production of sausages. So the 'taste change' implies a leftward shift in the AD curve in France to $AD_1$ and a rightward shift of the AD curve in Germany to $AD_1$. Output will fall below equilibrium in France and rise above it in Germany; prices will rise in Germany and fall in France. However, it appears that a devaluation of the French franc in terms of the Deutschmark could provide exactly the right offset. A devaluation will shift the AD curve in France to the right and the AD curve in Germany to the left, as shown by the broken arrows. In fact, a depreciation of the right amount will restore the original position. This is the classic argument for the exchange rate as shock absorber for asymmetric shocks.[4]

There is, however, a catch. The price indicated by $P$ ($P_F$ or $P_G$) in Fig. 13.2 is the 'domestic' price level, the value-added or GDP deflator. However, in terms of what their money wages can buy, workers will be concerned with the consumer price index—that is, the price of the basket of goods consumed by the representative worker. The consumption basket of French workers will undoubtedly contain sausages imported from Germany—along with many other imported items, of course. A devaluation of the French franc will raise the franc price of all these items: the consumer price index will rise, even if domestic price levels (both in France and in Germany) stay the same. Algebraically, we can write the consumer price index in France, $P_{CF}$ in terms of the domestic price indices $P_F$ and $P_G$ and the exchange rate $e$ as $P_{CF} = aP_F + (1 - a)eP_G$. Here, $a$ and $(1 - a)$ are the shares of domestic and imported (German) goods in the French consumption basket. Clearly a rise in $e$ (a devaluation) will increase the value of $P_{CF}$ for given values of $P_F$ and $P_G$. This point is very important. If the French economy is quite integrated with Germany and $a$ is therefore quite small, a given rise in $e$ will raise $P_{CF}$ quite a lot. French workers' real wages ($W_F/P_{CF}$) will fall noticeably. This is likely to lead to a demand by French workers for a rise in nominal wages sufficient to compensate them for the loss of real wages, due, as they see it, to the devaluation. If so, then the AS schedule will shift to the left in the left-hand part of the diagram and the offset provided by devaluation will be imperfect. Prices will rise and output will not be restored to its previous level. It is not hard to see that, if the French government were to respond by promoting a fresh devaluation, this would only produce a further rise in nominal wages and so prices. 'Real wage resistance' (where workers attempt to protect real wages by nominal wage increases), if accompanied by repeated devaluations, will quickly produce a wage–price-devaluation spiral.

*The qualification to the usefulness of the nominal exchange rate as a shock absorber, then, is that wage–price reactions may undo the effect of the nominal exchange-rate adjustment.* The classical theory assumes in essence that a nominal exchange-rate change *is* a real exchange-rate change. Yet a good deal of experience suggests that nominal exchange-rate changes can excite wage–price reactions that undo the effect of the change before very long. Experience to this effect in the 1970s and 1980s is one of the reasons why the EMU project seemed acceptable to many countries. It is also a reason why the *CC* curve in Fig. 13.1 slopes down from left to right—for, the more integrated economies become, the larger the portion of the consumption basket which is imported and the faster and the more pronounced the negative wage–price reactions to nominal exchange-rate change are likely to be.

Whilst the shock-absorber role of the exchange rate is subject to qualification, it is by no means true that the qualification is absolute. Whilst exchange-rate depreciation does tend to excite offsetting wage–price reactions, these reactions are not necessarily immediate or immutable to policy actions. At the very least an exchange-rate depreciation can give a breathing space while other policies are brought into play.

But, of course, a shock absorber is needed only if there are shocks to absorb. Clearly, unexpected developments are frequent, yet it is important to note that it is *differences* in economic structure which make shocks asymmetric: in the taste shock example above, the shock was asymmetric only because of the different specializations of the French and German economies. Is it likely that the process of integration among the European economies will produce 'more similar' economic structures and thus make asymmetric shocks less likely? The answer to this question is difficult to determine. If integration means 'convergence', then by definition the European economies are set to become more homogeneous—perhaps in tastes as well as production structures; but if integration means more specialization according to comparative advantage, as classical trade theory would suggest, then the answer is the opposite. The evidence from the United States suggests that there is likely to be more specialization between regions of a monetary union than between countries (albeit neighbouring) which still have their own independent currencies. Indeed, when the benefits of EMU were discussed earlier in this chapter, one of those identified was precisely the likelihood of greater concentration of output in large-scale units with less scattering of plant across the European production area.

It is also as well to recall that, despite the impression that had been growing of a Europe of ever-more convergent economies, the experience of German unification has been precisely one of an asymmetric shock of an almost textbook quality. This shock clearly put insupportable strain on many of the exchange rates in the ERM (see Chapter 12); had those exchange rates been 'irrevocably locked', as in a monetary union, there clearly would have been a very big price to pay. Fortunately, it does seem possible to describe this particular shock as unique and unrepeatable.

It is also fortunate that the exchange rate, itself imperfect in this role, is not the only possible absorber of asymmetric shocks. There are several other mechanisms worth discussing in this context. Community regional policy (see Chapter 7); community budgetary policy (see Chapter 14); national fiscal policy; factor migration; and wage–price flexibility.

*Community regional policy* clearly provides a mechanism for offsetting the repercussions of asymmetric shocks between countries; but it is not easy to see this mechanism playing a major role in monetary union—to date, its scale has simply been too small. What about *community budgetary policy*? US economists, viewing the proposal for monetary union in Europe, emphasize that in the United States the federal budget offers an automatic stabilizing function between the various states.[5] Because of the federal income tax, a state which falls on bad times (say, Texas when oil prices are low) automatically has to pay less income tax; and various federal expenditures, including federal support of unemployment compensation payments, would expand in such a context. The combined effect is that, through reduced federal tax requirements and higher federal expenditure entitlements, a temporarily disadvantaged state obtains a substantial offset to any primary income fall. (Whilst the precise figures are the subject of dispute, a commonly quoted estimate is that '30c in the $' of primary income decline is buffered in this way.) However, the EC does not have a budget of anything like the scale of the US federal budget. Nevertheless some observers argue that it should be possible to obtain a stabilizing effect without the huge scale of tax revenues and expenditures of the US budget, or, relative to GDP, of any of the national European budgets for that matter. The major expenditure items—defence, education, welfare payments, and so on—could continue to remain the property of national budgets. What is needed is a mechanism which defines when a member country is faring badly, relative to its usual average, in relation to the other countries, and a transfer system that will provide a degree of corrective support (see Goodhart (1994) for further explanation). However, whilst something like this may be feasible in principle, no such provisions were contained in the Maastricht Treaty, nor have they yet been articulated at a practical (policy) level.

Alternatively, it may be argued that *national fiscal policies* can be relied upon to perform a stabilizing function with some efficiency. Recall that in terms of Fig. 13.2 it was argued that government spending would shift the AD schedules; so an active national fiscal policy could be used to offset asymmetric shocks. Within a monetary union the resultant budget deficits would be comparatively easy to finance. For temporary shocks, indeed, the solution is ideal. In the case of permanent shocks, however, a real adjustment, not a demand adjustment, is what is called for; from this point of view it could be argued that the use of fiscal policy serves only to delay and hinder the adjustment that is, in the end, the only real solution. Unfortunately, it is not always easy to tell, in practice, whether a given shock is permanent or temporary.

The final two alternative mechanisms under consideration do provide such a real adjustment. *Factor migration* removes the problem of unemployed (and symmetrically overstrained) resources in an obvious way. In terms of the earlier fanciful example, unemployed French champagne workers could migrate to work in German sausage factories. This simultaneously relieves the labour shortage in Germany and resolves the unemployment problem in France. Within national boundaries unemployed resources tend to move more freely than between countries, and at present labour mobility between the Member States of the EC is quite limited. Over the longer run, with the aid of measures like the mutual recognition of professional qualifications, this position may of course change.

The final mechanism referred to is *wage–price flexibility*. For any permanent shock, an adjustment of real wages and relative prices is in fact what is required to provide a complete solution to the problem, rather than simply a temporary buffer. Paradoxically, some of the buffer mechanisms suggested can work against the long-run solution. For example, lavish support of a depressed region is unlikely to assist in bringing about the adjustment to lower relative real wages that is needed. Hence, it can be argued, the relative absence of credible alternative absorbers to the exchange rate in a European monetary union may not be such a bad thing: for it will hasten, not hinder, the development of *more flexible wage–price responses*. What this means can be represented quite simply in terms of the AD/AS analysis presented before: but this time we concentrate only on the left-hand part of the diagram—the case of the country (in our example, France) suffering a deflationary demand shock. Fig. 13.3 shows a case where from the initial position (shown by $AD_0$, $AS_0$), a permanent adverse demand shock causes an initial deflation (shown by the distance $Y_{0F}$–$Y_F$). Underlying $AS_0$ is a particular nominal wage; should nominal wages fall, the AS schedule will move to the right. With wage–price flexibility the deflation in output (and accompanying unemployment) will produce precisely such a result. In the end AS moves to $AS_1$ and equilibrium output is restored. French wages and output prices will have fallen; French consumer prices will not have fallen as much (German prices will have stayed the same or risen, and the exchange rate is fixed), so French real wages will have fallen. But this is the nature of the shock: the swing of tastes against the product that France is 'good at' understandably reduces French living standards. Without devaluation, this adjustment has to be brought about by a deflationary response to the initial fall in output. Even with devaluation, this final result cannot be avoided if full employment is to be restored—but the path of adjustment will be different, involving some inflation as well as some unemployment. The first best adjustment, of course, would be for wages and prices to adjust instantly.

The analysis above covers the case for and against monetary union in

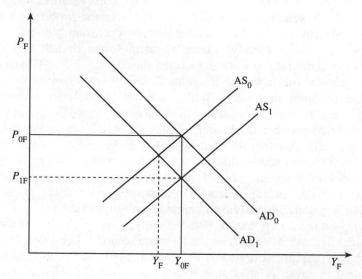

**FIG. 13.3.** Adjusting to a deflationary shock: The case of wage–price flexibility

Europe in general terms and provides an elaboration of the approach depicted by the Krugman diagram. The next question is to ask why the project of EMU became so important in the late 1980s. The general analysis can be drawn on to help us answer this question.

### 13.3. THE BACKGROUND TO THE MAASTRICHT NEGOTIATIONS

One answer to the question posed in this section—Why did the EMU project 'take off' in the late 1980s?—is that it was the success of the EMS which led countries to embrace the idea of full monetary union.

The operation and achievements of the EMS are discussed at length in Chapter 12 of this book and the reader is referred there for a detailed treatment. The central point for present purposes is that towards the end of the 1980s there was a widespread belief that the EMS had been successful beyond all expectations. It had not only been successful in its proximate objective—that of stabilizing nominal exchange rates between participating economies. It was also viewed as having provided a framework for counter-inflationary policies in Europe, through which other countries had, in effect, been able to import into their own systems the counter-inflationary success and reputation of the Bundesbank. By committing themselves to an exchange-rate peg against the Deutschmark, other countries were pledging to contain their own inflation to German levels. However, the dominance of Germany implied in such a description of the EMS was in practice diluted by the fact that countries could realign their central parities and could use the protection afforded by exchange controls over capital flows (so-called 'capital controls') to opt out of the requirement always to follow German policy in detail. This compromise was felt to have worked well, but by the late 1980s the continued maintenance of the compromise was undermined by the commitment, undertaken under the Single European ('1992') legislation, to phase out capital controls. This seemed liable to make realignments more difficult to engineer without inviting uncontrollable speculation. For this reason the dominance of Germany would be increased. Such a prospect was not welcome to the larger countries, like France, which began to press for a 'European' solution, with a European Central Bank (ECB) in which France might have a say and for which economic conditions in France would be as relevant as those in Germany.

This development can usefully be viewed in terms of Padoa-Schioppa's 'inconsistent quartet' (Padoa-Schioppa 1988), which comprises:

- free trade,
- free capital movements,
- fixed exchange rates, and
- national policy autonomy.

The Padoa-Schioppa proposition is that international monetary arrangements can never succeed in reconciling all four of these desirable conditions. Historically, all such arrangements have involved some compromise: thus, under the post-war Bretton Woods system there was a substantial compromise on the freedom of capital movements (at least to begin with); in the earlier stages of EMS there was a similar, though less drastic, compromise together with some compromise on fixed exchange rates (which were changed through realignments), as well as some compromise of national policy autonomy to the extent implied by acceptance of German dominance in the interest of curbing inflation. With a desire to maintain fixed exchange rates and free trade, the commitment to phase out capital controls pointed to a loss of national policy autonomy. The EMU solution can be thought of as the only way to retrieve a degree of autonomy, in the context of sharing in the common decisions of a ECB.

Of course, an alternative compromise in these circumstances would have been to abandon fixed exchange rates as a goal and instead to embrace the floating-rate solution. However, not only would that have appeared to throw away the prime achievement of the EMS; it would also have been seen as fundamentally contrary to the need for a customs union like the EC to maintain fairly stable competitive conditions and as contrary to the requirements of common EC policies. The argument is that, if countries engage in periodic devaluations, this will be seen as an attempt to steal a competitive march on partner economies, and will lead to an unravelling of the counter-protectionist achievements of the EC. As for the second point, this is amply illustrated by the difficulties posed for the operation of the Common Agricultural Policy (CAP) by changing exchange rates. Since the basis of the CAP is the setting of common prices across Europe, producing a given pattern of competitiveness, changes in intra-European exchange rates require detailed intervention to maintain the intention of the originally agreed set of prices. The more common European policies there are, the more fixed exchange rates are needed (see Giavazzi and Giovannini 1989).

However, it was not only economic considerations of the type mentioned above that sparked the recent interest in EMU. The unification of Germany also provided an important stimulus. The prospect of this event promoted a desire to involve Germany in West European institutions and arrangements. The belief was that this would be a constructive way of containing the interests of an even larger and more powerful Germany—as against the alternative in which a new Germany would dominate the rest of Europe by virtue of its sheer economic size and influence. EMU is a leading example of just such an institution.

With these important factors in the background, the first fruit of the newly awakened interest was the formation of a committee in 1988 (the so-called Delors Committee) to study the way in which progress might be made towards monetary union in Europe (the committee was *not* asked to conduct a cost-benefit analysis of the proposal). Reporting just one year later, the Delors Committee established a number of important features that were subsequently to influence the shape of the Treaty on European Union (TEU). As our interest is in the provisions of the Treaty itself rather than in the detail of the Delors Report, we can be brief in summarizing its main contributions. First, the Delors Report was *gradualist*, in that it specified an approach through three stages to full monetary union. In Stage One, all countries should be in the narrow fluctuation band of the ERM, with realignment still a feature of the adjustment process and all capital controls phased out. In Stage Two it was expected that resort to realignment would take place 'only in exceptional circumstances' and that convergence of the economies would be substantially realized. The European System of Central Banks (ESCB) would be set up, and the margins of fluctuation might be narrowed in preparation for the final stage. In Stage Three exchange rates would become 'irrevocably locked', and this would lead to monetary union. An ECB, at the head of the ESCB, would be ready to conduct policy on its own initiative in Stage Three. Substantiating the 'gradualist' image of the Report, these proposals for transitional stages contained no dates, save for the initiation of Stage One, suggested for 1 July 1990. Despite being gradualist in this sense, however, the Delors Report dismissed the possibility of gradualism in another sense: it rejected the idea that a common currency should be created which could circulate in parallel with national moneys before being adopted as the *single* currency in Stage Three.[6] Perhaps the most controversial aspect of the Report was that it introduced the idea that participating countries would have to agree to some constraints on their *fiscal* positions, as well as forgoing independence in monetary policy. (As this is also a feature of the TEU, we postpone consideration of the rationale for fiscal constraints to the next section). Finally, the Report indicated the necessity for a careful construction of the constitution of the ECB that it proposed and the need for an intergovernmental conference (IGC) to set out the amendments to the Treaty of Rome that would be required by a commitment to move to monetary union.

## 13.4. THE PROVISIONS OF THE TEU

The Treaty that emerged from the IGC and was agreed upon in Maastricht in December 1991 substantially followed the lead given by the Delors Report. It put flesh on the bones of the Delors Report's 'stages', by giving dates; it elaborated on the meaning of convergence and on the meaning of fiscal discipline by spelling out precise 'convergence criteria'; and it spelt out in detail a constitution for the ECB. The Treaty reflected the outcome of intensive diplomacy spaced over several weeks, in which the interests of the participating countries were expressed. From what is known of the negotiating process it is possible to attribute some of the key features of the Treaty to the intervention or insistence of particular countries, although, as already indicated, most of these are already to be found in the Report of the Delors Committee.[7] Thus, the stringency of the fiscal criteria is commonly attributed to the insistence of Germany, as is the institutional character of Stage Two in the Treaty provisions. On the other hand, the comparatively early dates proposed and the provision for a 'two-tier' approach to EMU are commonly attributed to the influence of France. It must be borne in mind that, although the Treaty was signed and agreed to (with some waivers) by all participants, the interests of the different countries are diverse. (We return to this issue in the last section).

### The Stages

The Treaty uses the same language of transitional stages as the Delors Report; but it is assumed that Stage One has already been reached. Stage Two starts on 1 January 1994. At this point the European Monetary Institute (EMI) will commence its work. The EMI is not envisaged as having executive power to conduct monetary policy or even to promote its co-ordination across the member countries, although it may make recommendations and form opinions in this regard; the EMI's main job is to study the requirements of the ECB, which will have executive power in Stage Three, when a single common currency will replace the individual national currencies of the participating countries. In terms of timing, the Treaty provides for Stage Three to commence at the earliest on 1 January 1997, on the basis of that majority of countries which satisfies the 'convergence criteria'. However, in the absence of such a majority, the Treaty provides for Stage Three to commence in any case not later than 1 January 1999 on the basis of that minority of countries which satisfies the criteria.

### The Convergence Criteria

The Treaty spells out criteria which a country must satisfy in order to be eligible for membership of the EMU. The point of these criteria, in general, is to ensure that the constraints on policy implied by participation in the EMU are likely to prove acceptable within the country concerned. This calculation cannot simply be left to the judgement of the government of that country because of the consequences implied for other members of the union of a bad judgement: a political crisis arising in one member country could spill over to others. For example, if a particular country found it too difficult to accept the unemployment implied by the policies of the ECB, political pressure would arise to modify those policies, perhaps with the consequence that inflationary pressures would be created for other members of the union.

The TEU criteria come under four heads and relate to: inflation convergence; interest-rate convergence (as explained below, these can be thought of as indirect inflation convergence criteria); a country's ERM conduct; and, finally, the fiscal criteria.

According to the *inflation-convergence criterion,* a country's inflation rate (measured by consumer prices) should be observed, over a period of a year before the examination, not to have exceeded by more than 1.5 per cent that of the three best performing countries. The *interest-rate-convergence criterion* requires that a country's average long-term nominal interest rate over the same period should not have exceeded that of the three best price performers by more than 2 per cent. This criterion can be thought of as relying on the forward-lookingness of financial markets to provide an assurance that inflation convergence, if observed, is not simply a 'flash in the pan'. If it were, then the country would be likely to fail the interest-rate criterion, because the expected future inflation would be built into a high-interest differential against the good performers. The position of each of the EMS countries in 1992 with respect to the inflation and interest-rate criteria is spelt out in detail in Chapter 2.

The *ERM criterion* requires that a country should have been in the 'normal' bands of the ERM, 'without tension' and without initiating a depreciation, for at least two years. The two *fiscal criteria* specify reference values for the ratio of the budget deficit to GDP (at 3 per cent) and for the ratio of the stock of outstanding government debt to GDP (at 60 per cent) and require that a country should not exceed these reference values, although there are escape clauses. A country may still be deemed to qualify under the fiscal-convergence criteria if the excess of actual over reference values is 'exceptional and temporary' or is declining continuously and substantially. The position of each of the Member States with respect to the fiscal criteria in 1990–3 is shown in Chapter 2.

The role of the fiscal criteria has been hotly debated. These criteria are designed to hold, not only as convergence criteria in the transition to EMU, but also after EMU has been established. The argument in their favour can take one of two (or both) forms. One argument is that what restrains a government of a country on a floating or adjustable-peg exchange rate from indulging in fiscal expansion is the apprehension that this would cause a depreciation leading to inflation. But inside a monetary union this restraint would be removed. The country's 'exchange rate' against other members is irrevocably fixed, and the country need fear no inflationary reprisal for its fiscal actions. But such actions could harm other countries—say, by inducing a depreciation of the exchange rate of the Ecu against the dollar and the yen. But there is an obvious difficulty with the premiss of this argument, much theory and some recent experience suggesting that fiscal expansion leads to exchange-rate appreciation, not depreciation.

In any event, a more prominent argument in defence of the fiscal criteria is that connected with the idea that excessive public debts result in resort to the printing press ('monetization').[8] Despite the fact that its constitution (see below) forbids the ECB to lend to any national government, which might be thought to provide a safeguard against resort to the printing press in this case, the fear is that a country with an unmanageable public debt problem (Italy is the country which observers have most in mind in this context) could constitute a political crisis of an order that could create strong pressure on the ECB to pursue an expansionary monetary policy. This might occur, either directly through pressure from the country concerned and from other governments wishing to demonstrate 'solidarity', or indirectly through the pressures arising from the threatened collapse of European banks and financial institutions holding the bonds of the problem country in their portfolios. As the crisis looms, the value of these bonds would plummet, putting the safety of deposits in doubt and creating the potential for a 'sauve qui peut' run on the financial system. Once again, the fact that the ECB is not burdened with responsibility for the financial system in the Maastricht constitution is not necessarily felt to be a sufficient safeguard.

It is possible to question the force of these arguments. It can be argued that, if a government over-borrows and precipitates a debt crisis, then that is its own affair, at least as long as there is no presumption of a bail-out by other governments: that all that was needed was to make this clear was always the UK government's (unavailing) line of argument in the negotiations that led to the TEU. And indeed, as already mentioned, the constitution of the ECB specifically forbids it from lending to a national government and assigns it no bank supervision duty. Moreover, it must be pointed out that placing limits on governments' room for fiscal manœuvre emasculates one of the adjustment tools that governments might need when exchange rates are fixed. It is not surprising that the fiscal criteria in the TEU turned out to be one of the most controversial parts of that Treaty. Countries expect participation in monetary union to involve the resignation of national monetary autonomy—this is what it is all about, after all; resigning a considerable degree of autonomy over fiscal policy both in the run-up to EMU and thereafter is a different matter. A partial resolution of this difficulty lies in the escape clauses that accompany the fiscal criteria and in the fact that the criteria will inevitably bite more deeply in the transition than afterwards.

## The ECB

None of the general analytical arguments concerning monetary unions which were reviewed earlier touched on the issue of inflation control. Yet, in the context of European monetary union this has been of the utmost importance, and a great deal of effort has been put into the design of a constitution for the ECB which, it is hoped, will secure the goal of price stability. The reasons for this emphasis are not far to seek. First of all, much of the success of the EMS (or, more strictly, the ERM) as it was perceived was identified with the fact that member countries used it as a counter-inflationary framework; in the move from ERM to EMU, countries necessarily lose the ability to use the Deutschmark as their counter-inflationary 'anchor', and a replacement is needed. Secondly, the dominant country involved—Germany—for good historical reasons places great store on a stable currency. EMU without Germany would be meaningless; but for Germany to contribute to EMU requires that the ECB should be oriented towards producing a stable level of prices.

The attention paid to the design of the constitution of the ECB, as a means of ensuring low-inflation outcomes, conforms to a comparatively recent economic literature which is concerned with the analysis of credibility in economic policy. The analysis in question takes for granted that the technical means exist to control inflation and concentrates instead on the question whether policy-makers will always *wish* to control inflation. It is a standard proposition in macroeconomic analysis to say that, whilst it is possible to reduce unemployment below the 'natural' or equilibrium rate by raising inflation, this is only a temporary trade-off; once agents become accustomed to the inflation rate, the trade-off disappears. The contribution of the modern analysis of credibility in economic policy is to take this point one step further. If governments are prone to take advantage of this temporary trade-off, then agents will come to expect them to do so and consequently will predict a high level of inflation. This means that in the long run unemployment will be at its natural rate (which it would be anyway), while inflation will be much higher than socially desirable. The analysis goes on to suggest that a way round this problem is to find a means for making commitments on low inflation credible. If they are credible, then the long-run solution will provide low inflation, as desired. One means of bringing this state of affairs about, it has been suggested, is to make the ECB independent of electoral pressure and to invite it to pursue the objective of price stability with no, or little, qualification. Empirical analysis shows an inverse correlation between independence in central banks and the rate of inflation: the more independent the central bank, the lower the inflation rate (Grilli, Masciandaro, and Tabellini 1991).

Independence in this context has several dimensions: it is not just that the ECB should be formally independent in the constitutional sense. It is necessary that the terms of office of the Governor and the Board of Directors should protect these individuals from pressure to deviate from the objective of price stability. The ECB should not be burdened with other duties and obligations that might oblige it to engage in an expansive monetary policy incompatible with the control of inflation. The Deutsche Bundesbank has many of these features and in the Maastricht constitution for the ECB we can see many of the same features—typically somewhat strengthened—repeated. To begin with, the ECB is independent of national governments and of the Commission. It is at the centre of the ESCB, a system comprised of central banks which are themselves required to be independent. The ESCB is given one principal goal of monetary policy— that of price stability. The Treaty says that 'the primary objective of the ESCB shall be to maintain price stability'. It goes on to add, 'Without prejudice to the objective of price stability, it shall support the general economic policies in the Community . . .' (Article 2). This qualification has not generally been seen as providing a significant dilution of the primary objective of the ESCB. The ECB is forbidden from lending to national governments or to Commission organizations; the responsibility for the supervision of banks and financial institutions is placed elsewhere. This is so, in order that its pursuit of price stability will not be compromised by actions taken in pursuit of these other possible obligations. Similarly, whilst exchange-rate policy is not the ECB's direct prerogative, it is afforded considerable influence over any such policy. In addition, the terms of office of the Governor and members of the Board are drawn up in such a way as to remove the possibility that ECB officials might act as if they were 'representatives' of their country under the influence of their country's government.

On the face of it, then, the statutes of the ECB seem to guarantee a very high degree of independence to that institution. Indeed, some observers have queried whether the provisions do not go too far in this direction. Thus, it is common (though not universal) practice for central banks to be assigned the duty of supervision of the banking and financial system. A central bank will almost certainly acquire relevant information for this task in the course of carrying out monetary policy operations and this information is wasted if the task of supervision is assigned to another institution. Another disadvantage of an 'excessively' independent central bank is that it makes difficult, if not impossible, the task of co-ordinating fiscal and monetary policy and, still more, of promoting such a co-ordination within the context of an international (G3) agreement to co-ordinate economic policy. Efforts towards concluding such agreements are a recurrent feature of international economic policy, the latest episode being the one inaugurated by the United States in 1985—the so-called 'Plaza Agreement'—an effort which foundered only some three years later. One of the reasons for its eventual demise is said to be the failure to co-ordinate fiscal with monetary actions.

One reason why the proposed constitution of the ESCB–ECB is so 'hard' is probably that there is an apprehension that a new institution with no accumulated reputation needs extra advantages to compensate for its lack of history. But this suggestion reveals a point of difficulty with the constitutional approach. Transplanting a constitution—even a strengthened one—is not the same as transplanting history: it may be that, in countries with low inflation and independent central banks, it is history that makes the actions of the central bank, which must often be harsh ones, acceptable to the public. Thus, the Bundesbank has latitude to make temporarily 'unpopular' decisions; similar actions undertaken by the ECB might not be well received in some of the countries in the EMU—say, in the inflation-prone economies of Italy, the United Kingdom, or Spain. This is another reason, of course, for the insistence on convergence criteria.

## 13.5. PROSPECTS FOR EMU

At the end of 1993 the prospects for EMU still remain uncertain. The Maastricht Treaty has been ratified, but, on the original interpretation of the ERM 'normal-bands' convergence criterion (i.e. ±2.25 per cent bands), the ERM crisis of July–August 1993 leaves all countries (except Germany and the Netherlands) in default. More importantly, there is a widespread apprehension that a return to the 'normal' narrow bands will not be feasible in the foreseeable future, because of the risk of exciting another speculative crisis, unless there is a significant change in the conduct of monetary policy in Europe in the direction of greater symmetry in policy stance. In practice this would mean that the EMI would have to be conceded more authority to co-ordinate policy during Stage Two than has hitherto been contemplated.

The ERM crisis has also underlined for many the importance of the reservations which the Bundesbank holds about EMU. Since the wording of the Treaty refers to 'normal', not 'narrow', bands, it would be technically open to countries to seek a different way forward by declaring the so-far 'temporary' ±15 per cent bands, adopted in the wake of the 1993 crisis, to be 'normal'. It would then be possible, in principle, to move from Stage Three without running the gauntlet of a narrow-bands phase at all.[9] Of course, the other convergence criteria would still need to be met; and here the main difficulties seem likely to be posed by the fiscal criteria. Whilst the position in late 1993 with respect to the inflation and interest-rate criteria appears quite favourable, the recession (and, in Germany's case, the cost of unification) has left all countries with increased deficits and higher debt/GDP ratios (see Chapter 2). Given this background, we might expect to see the various escape clauses invoked. But if any country prefers to go slowly, it will be easy to cite fiscal non-convergence as a reason for caution. From what is known of the interests of the countries concerned, it seems clear that the main issue will be whether Germany prefers caution. The other countries in the 'core group' (usually thought of as comprising Belgium, the Netherlands, Denmark, and France) have little or nothing to lose by forming a monetary union, especially one 'inside Maastricht', for this would not privilege Germany: in the alternative they have no scope for independent monetary policy anyway and are dependent on Germany. By the same token Germany does have something to lose—its independence of monetary policy action. It might prefer to go slowly, perhaps on the basis of forming monetary union with a small core group of adherents first, and then accepting other countries at a later stage. This could even possibly occur outside the Maastricht framework. But Germany cannot overlook the possibility that failure to progress towards a comprehensive EMU could result in an about-turn in favour of flexible exchange rates with unstable conditions of competitiveness emerging. For reasons recounted above, progress towards EMU seems ineluctable in the end; yet for some countries it is hard to envisage that the process will be complete before the end of the century.

# NOTES

1. Accessible book-length treatments appear in de Grauwe (1992) and Gros and Thygesen (1992). Emerson and Huhne (1990) provide a shorter, highly read-able, account.

2. More precisely, this is the economist's way of appraising such an option. It may be that the overriding imperatives are political, in which case the cost-benefit analysis tells us something about the economic cost (or possibly, additional benefit) of taking up an option which is overwhelmingly attractive on political grounds: Goodhart (1994) provides an account which explicitly confronts the issues of political economy as they arise in this context.

3. The President of the Commission has 'observer' status at G7 meetings.

4. Note that, if the shock were symmetric, the exchange rate would not be a helpful shock absorber. For example, if the taste change had been from champagne *and* sausages to (say) Stilton cheese, then it would be helpful for the sterling–French franc and sterling–DM exchange rates both to appreciate, but it would not be helpful for the French franc–DM rate to change.

5. The pioneering contribution in this vein was by Sala-i-Martin and Sachs (1992).

6. The Delors Report viewed a parallel currency as bringing with it the danger of inflation. During the negotiations in the intergovernmental conference which led to the TEU the UK government proposed a parallel currency—the so-called 'hard Ecu'—the chief feature of which was its counter-inflationary characteristic. However, the proposal was widely viewed as a diversionary tactic by a government not really committed to monetary union, and, perhaps for this reason, was not pursued beyond the stage of discussion.

7. The membership of the Delors Committee was not directly representative of governments. The core of the committee membership was constituted by the Governors of the central banks of the EMS; in addition, there were three independent persons, and two Commission members, including the Chairman, M. Delors.

8. For a techincal treatment of this issue, see e.g. Leslie (1993).

9. See Artis and Lewis (1993) for more extensive comment on this and other possible ways in which the European countries might seek to move forward.

# REFERENCES

Artis, M. J., and Lewis, M. K. (1993), 'Après le déluge: Exchange Rate and Monetary Policy in Britain and Europe', *Oxford Review of Economic Policy* (Sept.), 36–61.

CEC (1970): Commission for the European Communities: *Report to the Council and the Commission on the Realization by Stages of Economic and Monetary Union in the Community* (the Werner Report), Supplement to Bulletin II–1970 of the European Communities (Brussels: CEC).

———(1989), *Report on Economic and Monetary Union in the European Community* (the Delors Report) (Luxemburg: Office for Official Publications of the European Communities).

———(1990) 'One Market, One Money: An Evaluation of the Potential Benefits and Costs of Forming an Economic and Monetary Union', *European Economy* (Oct.), 44: 1–351.

De Grauwe, P. (1992), *The Economics of Monetary Integration* (Oxford: Oxford University Press).

Emerson, M., and Huhne, C. (1990), *The ECU Report* (London: Pan Books).

Giavazzi, F., and Giovannini, A. (1989), *Limiting Exchange Rate Flexibility: The European Monetary System* (Cambridge, Mass.: MIT Press).

Goodhart, C. A. E. (1994), 'The Political Economy of Monetary Union', in Peter B. Kenen (ed.), *Understanding Interdependence: The Macroeconomics of the Open Economy*, papers presented at a conference honouring the fiftieth anniversary of *Essays in International Finance* (Princeton, NJ: Princeton University Press).

Grilli, V., Masciandaro, D., and Tabellini, G. (1991), 'Political and Monetary Institutions and Public Financial Policies in the Industrial Countries', *Economic Policy*, 13 (Oct.), 341–92.

Gros, D., and Thygesen, N. (1992), *European Monetary Integration* (Harlow: Longman).

Krugman, P. (1990), 'Policy Problems of a Monetary Union', in P. de Grauwe and L. Papademos (eds.), *The European Monetary System in the 1990s* (Harlow: Longman).

Leslie, D. G. (1993), *Advanced Macroeconomics* (Maidenhead: McGraw-Hill).

Padoa-Schioppa, T. (1988), 'The European Monetary System: A Long Term View', in F. Giavazzi, S. Micossi, and M. Miller (eds.), *The European Monetary System* (Cambridge: Cambridge University Press), 369–84.

Sala-i-Martin, X., and Sachs, J. (1992), 'Fiscal Federalism and Optimum Currency Areas: Evidence for Europe from the United States', in M. B. Canzoneri, V. Grilli, and P. R. Masson (eds.), *Establishing a Central Bank: Issues in Europe and Lessons from the United States* (Cambridge: Cambridge University Press), 195–219.

# 14

# The EC Budget

ROBIN BLADEN-HOVELL AND ELIZABETH SYMONS

## 14.1. INTRODUCTION

Budgetary considerations have dominated the proceedings of the European Community (EC) for much of its thirty-six-year history. Disputes about whether the EC should have its own financial resources, rivalry among the EC institutions over which of them—the Commission, the Council of Ministers, or the European Parliament (EP)—should exercise control over the budget, together with the problem of budgetary imbalance, particularly with respect to the United Kingdom, have all contributed to periods of budgetary crisis. Moreover, unlike the budgets of national governments, the EC budget is circumscribed by a strict prohibition on borrowing. Budget balance was written into the Treaty of Rome, and subsequent amendments have only served to relax the restriction on borrowing for a limited range of specific purposes—to support the balance of payments and to promote investment within the EC. As a result, the financial resources available to the EC at any time have been of central importance in determining the scale of EC activities, and have effectively dictated the timing and pace at which EC policies have developed.

The purpose of this chapter is to describe the current structure and provisions of the EC budget and review the major developments that have given rise to these budgetary arrangements. The chapter contains six sections. The broad structure and the procedural arrangements for the budget are presented in section 14.2. A detailed analysis of the EC general budget is undertaken in subsequent sections of the chapter: revenue and the issue of 'own resources' for the EC, together with the question of budgetary imbalance for the United Kingdom, are covered in Section 14.3; EC expenditure is discussed in Section 14.4. The income and expenditure components of the budget are brought together in Section 14.5, where we outline the problems of trying to define the net budgetary balance for EC members, whilst policy options relating to possible future developments for the budget are presented in Section 14.6. A summary of the main issues and conclusions completes the chapter.

## 14.2. BACKGROUND

EC policies provided for by the 1957 Treaties of Rome (the European Economic Community and the European Atomic Energy Community) and the administrative expenditure of the EC institutions are financed by the general budget of the European Communities. EC operations provided for by the 1951 Treaty of Paris, and the promotion of trade with associated developing countries are financed by separate specific budgets—the European Coal and Steel Community budget, and the European Development Fund, respectively.

The general budget of the EC is small in relation to the national budgets of the Member States, accounting for some 1.1 per cent of EC GDP in 1992, compared with more than 30 per cent, on average, for the budgets of Member States' national governments. Many areas of EC policy are regulatory in nature and have little requirement for spending, except for administration. Thus, for example, the EC's role in policing the customs union, or in implementing competition policy, requires limited financial resources. As indicated by Fig. 14.1, the main area of EC expenditure is on agricultural policy and, in particular, on the agricultural guarantee that aims to maintain stable prices for farm output above the world level through intervention in the market for agricultural produce (see Chapter 4). Appropriations for the agricultural guarantee contained in the 1992 budget, for example, accounted for some 54 per cent of total EC spending—a proportion that has fallen significantly from the peak values obtained in the early and

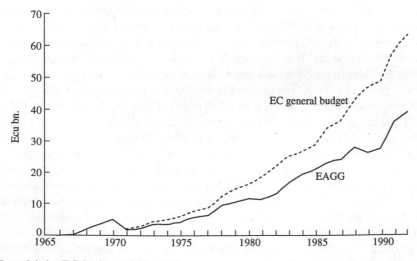

FIG. **14.1.** EC budget 1965–1992

mid-1980s, when agricultural spending frequently represented over 70 per cent of EC expenditure.

The Commission, the Council of Ministers, and the EP are all involved, to varying degrees, in the adoption and execution of the general budget. The budgetary procedure begins with the Commission preparing a 'preliminary draft budget' for the EC based upon estimates of expenditure proposed by the EC institutions.[1] The preliminary draft budget is initially submitted to the Council of Ministers, who establish, by means of a qualified majority, the form of the draft budget to be placed before the EP.

Since 1975 the EP has had the right to propose amendments to the draft budget, and, following the first reading of the document in the EP, the modified draft is returned to the Council for a second reading by that body. On its second reading, the Council must secure a qualified majority in order either to accept any of the modifications proposed by the EP that increase expenditure, or to reject amendments that do not. Unless the entire budget is subsequently rejected by the EP, the level of compulsory expenditure—spending that relates to commitments derived from the internal and external obligations of the EC which are established by the EC Treaties, or by secondary legislation adopted in accordance with the Treaties—is determined at this stage of the budgetary procedure.[2] The second reading of the budget by the EP is mainly concerned with the level of non-compulsory expenditure for which the EP may reject or accept the Council's proposals. Unless the EP rejects the budget entirely, the Parliamentary President then declares the budget to be adopted.

This balance of power between the Council and the EP in the budgetary decision-making process had been very slow to emerge, the period between 1975 and 1987, in particular, being especially difficult in this respect. Granting the EP the power to amend the draft budget proposed by Council effectively split the legislative and budgetary functions of the EC. Legislative power in the EC rests solely with the Council, while budgetary power has been shared by the EP and the Council since 1975. Disagreement between the institutions led to a series of incidents during the early 1980s that effectively paralysed the budgetary procedures of the EC. In December 1979, for example, the EP rejected the draft budget for 1980, with the result that the budgetary procedure was delayed by six months.[3] During this six-month period, the financing of the EC budget had to proceed month by month on the basis of the previously agreed budget— the so-called provisional-twelfths arrangement. This facility was utilized again in 1982 and 1985 when the EP once more rejected the draft budget, and yet again in 1988 when the Council was unable to establish a draft of the budget for that year because of the lack of political agreement concerning a new limit for EC resources.

Various attempts at improving the budgetary procedure have been made throughout the period from 1975 onwards and have met with varying degrees of success. The latest, and apparently one of the more success-ful, reforms was the Interinstitutional Agreement signed in 1988. This settlement, whilst not seeking to alter the respective budgetary powers of the various institutions, sets out the basis upon which the EP and the Council can achieve a joint agreement concerning the overall size of the budget and redirects budgetary discussion to the question of allocating resources within each of the ceilings of the financial perspective. Details of this framework are discussed further in Section 14.4.

### 14.3. THE EC GENERAL BUDGET: REVENUE

During the first twelve years of the EC's existence, the budget was funded entirely by direct contributions from the Member States. Since 1970, how-ever, the budget has been financed from the 'own resources' of the EC—that is, by revenues that the Member States have agreed should be the resources of the EC by right. As shown in Table 14.1, the own-resources system established in 1970 had three elements: customs duties on goods imported from outside the EC, agricultural levies, and a share of the VAT revenue raised in each country. Because the range of goods subject to VAT in different countries varied, the VAT base adopted by the EC for this purpose was standardized, with the EC being entitled to, at most, the revenue generated from a 1 per cent VAT rate applied to this 'harmonized' base.

As the 1970s progressed, it became apparent that the original system of own resources was inadequate in a number of important respects, the essential problem being twofold. First, the yield from traditional own resources, such as customs duties and agricultural levies,[4] fell gradually during the 1970s as progress was made world-wide in dismantling tariffs by means of the General Agreement on Trade and Tariffs (GATT) negotia-tions, and the EC itself became increasingly self-sufficient in the produc-tion of agricultural products. Secondly, VAT revenue effectively stagnated over the period, as the share of GNP accounted for by consumer expendi-ture declined in the economies of the EC countries. The combined effect of these two factors was to place considerable pressure on the own-resource system at precisely the time when the spending needs of the EC increased both because of new policies being adopted and the accession of new members.

An initial attempt at resolving the budgetary crisis was made at the European Council meeting at Fontainebleau in June 1984. The new sys-tem, based on the principle of raising the VAT ceiling to 1.4 per cent, was to take effect from January 1986, with transitional financing arrangements being applied to the budgets of 1984 and 1985. These temporary arrange-ments involved intergovernmental advances, which were repayable in the case of the 1984 budget, but were non-repayable for the 1985 budget. In

TABLE 14.1. The development of financial resources for the EC budget

| Agreement | Dates in force | Details of resources | UK rebate details |
|---|---|---|---|
| EEC and Euratom established by the Treaties of Rome, March 1957. | 1958–70 | 1. Revenue consists entirely of contributions by the Member States. | n.a. |
| Original 'own resources' system of funding EC general budget, established by the Luxemburg agreement, April 1970. | 1970–84 | 1. Customs levies and duties on imports from outside EC;<br>2. agricultural levies;<br>3. VAT-based contribution, calculated on a harmonized (i.e. hypothetical) base, subject to maximum rate of 1%. | 'Financial mechanism' to reduce VAT contribution of Member States meeting certain criteria: available 1976–80, but never triggered. From 1979 UK 'compensation' agreed in form of expenditure measures agreed at various dates. |
| Fontainebleau summit, June 1984. | 1984–7 | 1. As above;<br>2. as above;<br>3. maximum VAT rate raised to 1.4%. | UK rebate as reduction in VAT rate applied to UK (two-thirds of difference between UK percentage share of VAT and UK's share of allocable spending; German contribution to financing of UK rebate limited to two-thirds of full amount). |

| | | | |
|---|---|---|---|
| Brussels (Delors agreement), February 1988. | 1988–92 | 1. As above;<br>2. as above;<br>3. maximum VAT rate retained at 1.4%, but VAT base capped at 55% of GNP in all Member States;<br>4. 'fourth resource', calculated in relation to GNP of Member States;<br>5. aggregate revenues limited to 1.2% of EC GNP. | As under Fontainebleau system, adjusted to reflect capped VAT base and additional GNP-based resource. |
| Delors II proposal, 1992. | 1993–7 | 1. As above;<br>2. as above;<br>3. maximum VAT rate reduced to 1% and VAT base capped at 50% of GNP in all Member States;<br>4. 'fourth resource', calculated in relation to GNP of Member States;<br>5. aggregate revenues limited to 1.37% of EC GNP. | Unspecified. |

*Note:* n.a. = not applicable.
*Source:* Adapted from Smith (1992).

1986, however, the budget outturn was virtually at the limit of the 1.4 per cent VAT ceiling, with budget balance only being retained by means of deferring certain items of agricultural expenditure until 1987.[5] The Fontainebleau reform had effectively failed.

A solution to the EC's budgetary difficulties was eventually found in 1988. By then, the third enlargement of the EC to include Spain and Portugal on 1 January 1986, together with the successful conclusion of the Single European Act (SEA) in February 1986 setting out the medium-term goals of the EC, had established a sounder political base for a thorough reform of EC finances. In February 1987 the Commission presented comprehensive reform proposals (see CEC 1987*a*, 1987*b*), which together became known as the 'Delors package'. The broad outline of this package was subsequently adopted at the Brussels European Council meeting held on 11–12 February 1988, the proposal being finally accepted in June 1988.

The main thrust of the Delors package was to ensure that the EC be given suitable resources that would be sufficient to enable it to operate throughout the period 1988–92. The reform maintained the traditional own resources derived from customs duties and agricultural levies and, subject to minor modifications to the VAT base described in Table 14.1, proposed that the VAT resource continue with a ceiling of 1.4 per cent. To these traditional own resources, however, the Delors package proposed adding a new, 'fourth resource'. This new source of finance was to be a variable, 'topping-up', resource which would provide the revenue required to cover expenditure in excess of the traditional own-resources and VAT receipts, subject to an overall ceiling for the total of all own resources of 1.2 per cent of EC GNP.

The overall effect of introducing the GNP-based fourth resource is to make the EC tax system more progressive by tying each Member State's contribution more closely to actual levels of prosperity within the EC. The uniform rate of the fourth resource is determined by reference to the additional revenue needed during each budgetary procedure to cover the EC's requirements. During the financial year 1992, for example, the estimated revenue provided by this resource corresponded to a call-in rate of 0.17 per cent.

Complete details of the own resources of the EC in 1992, disaggregated by Member State, are shown in Table 14.2. In that year, 60 per cent of the total EC budget was derived from VAT receipts, a further 36 per cent coming from customs duties and the GNP-based fourth resource, with agricultural levies, including those from sugar and isoglucose, together contributing only 4 per cent of EC finance. In terms of the contributions from the individual Member States in 1992, Germany accounted for almost 29 per cent of the total own resources received by the EC, whilst four countries (Germany, France, Italy, and the United Kingdom) together accounted for some 75 per cent of the total funding.

TABLE **14.2.** *Own resources in 1992 by Member State (Ecu m.)*

| Member State | Type of resource | | | | | |
| --- | --- | --- | --- | --- | --- | --- |
| | Agricultural levies | Sugar and isoglucose | Customs duties | GNP-based own resource | VAT-based own resource | Total own resources |
| Belgium | 84.1 | 69.4 | 832.5 | 294.3 | 1,108.1 | 2,388.4 |
| Denmark | 6.3 | 39.1 | 222.3 | 189.3 | 618.0 | 1,074.9 |
| France | 74.7 | 321.8 | 1,548.9 | 1,719.0 | 7,505.7 | 11,170.2 |
| Germany | 142.0 | 333.0 | 3,546.0 | 2,413.3 | 10,162.2 | 16,596.5 |
| Greece | 16.2 | 16.9 | 178.1 | 111.5 | 508.5 | 831.2 |
| Ireland | 2.0 | 12.0 | 153.2 | 54.4 | 248.2 | 469.7 |
| Italy | 346.1 | 124.2 | 1,037.4 | 1,787.2 | 5,278.0 | 8,572.9 |
| Luxemburg | 0.1 | — | 11.5 | 17.4 | 79.2 | 108.2 |
| Netherlands | 108.4 | 78.2 | 1,160.7 | 400.1 | 1,700.4 | 3,447.8 |
| Portugal | 117.2 | 0.1 | 117.0 | 103.0 | 469.7 | 806.9 |
| Spain | 141.3 | 50.0 | 555.8 | 774.2 | 3,531.5 | 5,052.8 |
| UK | 177.9 | 67.7 | 2,236.5 | 1,459.3 | 3,456.6 | 7,398.0 |
| TOTAL | 1,216.2 | 1,112.4 | 11,599.9 | 9,323.1 | 34,666.0 | 57,917.6 |
| (% of total budget) | (2.1) | (1.9) | (20.0) | (16.1) | (60.0) | (100.0) |

*Source:* CEC (1992a: 21).

## The VAT own resource and compensation for the United Kingdom

The issue of budgetary imbalance was central to the financial difficulties experienced by the EC during the 1970s and early 1980s. The issue had two dimensions: a UK problem that dates from as early as 1974 and which underlay the renegotiation of the United Kingdom's terms of entry to the EC in that year; and a German problem, first expressed at the European Council meeting held in London in 1981, which highlighted the German position as main contributor to the EC and proposed a reduction in that country's share of financing the compensation for the United Kingdom.

For the United Kingdom, the problem of budgetary imbalance arose essentially as a result of two features characteristic of the UK economy. On the one hand, the United Kingdom represented a country with a small agricultural sector, importing a large proportion of farm produce from outside the EC, and as such it benefited very little from the EC's agricultural spending. On the other hand, the United Kingdom found itself a large contributor to the financing of the EC because a very large proportion of the country's GNP was accounted for by the EC's VAT base. Since 1974, the EC budget has contained various provisions for correcting the contribution made by the United Kingdom, bringing the UK contribution more closely in line with the expenditures of the EC within the United Kingdom.

The first correcting mechanism was agreed at the European Council meeting held in Dublin in March 1975. Under this arrangement, compensation, in the form of partial repayment of VAT contributions, was to be provided from the EC budget to any country that found itself satisfying three conditions: a per capita GDP less than 85 per cent of the EC average; a rate of growth less than 120 per cent of the EC average, and with a share in EC revenue at least 10 per cent higher than its share in EC GDP. At the time of the agreement it was expected that this arrangement would benefit Ireland and Italy in addition to the United Kingdom. In practice, however, the conditions governing the repayment of VAT contributions were never triggered by any of these countries during the period 1976–80 that the arrangement was in force. As a result, a second correcting mechanism, that took the form of increased Regional Fund expenditures in the United Kingdom, was agreed at the Dublin European Council meeting of November 1979. However, the criteria determining the size of these expenditures were never made clear, and the administration of these funds was marked by continual dispute. This situation continued until 1984, when the Fontainebleau agreement established a more systematic basis of compensation for the United Kingdom.

Under the Fontainebleau agreement, the United Kingdom received an abatement to its contribution to the EC budget, calculated as two-thirds of the difference between the United Kingdom's percentage share of VAT payments to the EC, and its percentage share of those parts of EC expenditure that can be allocated to Member States.[6] This reduction in the UK contribution was financed by additional payments made by all other Member States, except Germany, in accordance with their respective percentage share of VAT payments. For Germany, however, allowance was made, in recognition of that country's position as main contributor to the EC. Accordingly it was required to pay only two-thirds of its normal share of the compensation, the balance being divided among the remaining Members on the same scale.

The effect of incorporating compensatory payments to the United Kingdom in the determination of the VAT own resource in 1992 is shown in Table 14.3. Here the amount of VAT own resource, calculated at a uniform rate of 1.26 per cent, is shown for each country in column 1. The effect of capping the VAT base at 55 per cent of GNP at market prices benefits the Irish Republic, Luxemburg, Portugal, and the United Kingdom in this stage of the process. The gross amount of compensation for the United Kingdom is deducted from the total obtained and shared among the other members of the EC in accordance with the procedure described above; this is shown in column 2. New totals for each country, obtained by summing columns 1 and 2, are given in column 3. The maximum VAT contribution made by any country, set by the 1988 Brussels agreement at 1.4 per cent, is shown in column 4 of the table, the actual own-resource contribution for any country (shown in column 6) being the lesser of the amounts shown in columns 3 and 4. Where a country's potential contribution to the VAT own resource in any year exceeds the 1.4 per cent upper limit, as was the case for Belgium, Denmark, and Italy in 1992, the difference is carried across and paid by the Member under the heading of the GNP-based, 'fourth resource' (shown in column 5).

### 14.4. THE EC GENERAL BUDGET: EXPENDITURE

Expenditure by the EC may be broadly classified under two headings: compulsory expenditure and non-compulsory expenditure. The distinction is largely political and is closely tied to the division of budgetary power between the EP and the Council of Ministers, which together constitute the budgetary authority for the EC. Generally speaking, the division places expenditure made under the European Agricultural Guidance and Guarantee Fund (EAGGF) Guarantee Section and repayments and aid to Member States in the compulsory category, whilst classifying expenditure under the headings of structural funds and cohesion policies, appropriations for operations in the energy sector, and virtually all administrative expenditure as non-compulsory.

The importance of the distinction between these two categories of expenditure lies in the fact that, subject to certain constraints, the EP has

TABLE 14.3. *Determination of the VAT own resource 1992 (Ecu m.)*

| Member State | VAT own resource at uniform rate | Compensation for UK | Total | VAT at 1.4% | Compensation for UK to be added to fourth resource | VAT own resources to be paid |
|---|---|---|---|---|---|---|
| Belgium | 1,001.2 | 113.1 | 1,114.3 | 1,108.1 | 6.2 | 1,108.1 |
| Denmark | 558.4 | 70.1 | 628.5 | 618.0 | 10.6 | 618.0 |
| France | 6,830.9 | 674.8 | 7,505.7 | 7,560.0 | — | 7,505.7 |
| Germany | 9,613.9 | 548.3 | 10,162.2 | 10,640.0 | — | 10,162.2 |
| Greece | 464.8 | 43.8 | 508.6 | 514.4 | — | 508.6 |
| Irish Republic[a] | 226.8 | 21.4 | 248.2 | 251.0 | — | 248.2 |
| Italy | 4,769.0 | 647.3 | 5,416.3 | 5,278.0 | 138.3 | 5,278.0 |
| Luxemburg[a] | 72.4 | 6.8 | 79.2 | 80.2 | — | 79.2 |
| Netherlands | 1,543.3 | 157.1 | 1,700.4 | 1,708.0 | — | 1,700.4 |
| Portugal[a] | 429.3 | 40.4 | 469.7 | 475.1 | — | 469.7 |
| Spain | 3,227.5 | 303.9 | 3,531.4 | 3,572.0 | — | 3,531.4 |
| UK[a] | 6,083.6 | −2,627.0 | 3,456.6 | 6,732.9 | — | 3,456.6 |
| TOTAL | 34,821.1 | 0.0 | 34,821.1 | 38,537.6 | 155.1 | 34,666.0 |

[a] VAT base capped at 55%.

*Source*: CEC (1992a: 19).

the final say on non-compulsory spending. The limit to the EP's power in this respect was originally specified in Article 203(9) of the Treaty of Rome, as amended at Luxemburg in 1970. This agreement states that the rate of increase of non-compulsory expenditure is limited to a 'statistical maximum rate' derived from a formula based upon three factors: the rate of growth in the EC, the rate of inflation, and the size of Member States' budgets. There was, however, a provision for this ceiling to be exceeded by agreement between the Council of Ministers and the EP. If the Council approved a draft budget which increased non-compulsory expenditure by more than half the 'maximum' rate of increase, the EP had the power to add further expenditure of up to one half of the 'maximum' rate. The real maximum is therefore up to 50 per cent greater than the 'maximum' determined by the formula and, in effect, the Council of Ministers could restrain aggregate expenditure only by allowing the EP a significant say in deciding priorities for non-compulsory expenditure.[7]

Thus the budgetary system established by the Treaty of Rome had a strong bias towards increased spending. Between 1980 and 1989, for example, non-compulsory expenditure rose faster than the statistical maximum rate in each financial year except 1985.

In June 1988 the EC adopted the broad outlines of a financial reform— the Delors package—in order to ensure a more orderly increase in expenditure and a better balance of spending across the various expenditure categories. The essence of the reform was to promote budgetary discipline by placing the objectives of the general budget within the context of a medium-term programme. Initially, the agreement contained a financial perspective, shown as Table 14.4, for the first-year period 1988–92, which laid down annual ceilings for the main categories of expenditure. The perspective was subsequently updated annually by the Commission at the beginning of the budgetary process, ceilings being adjusted in line with movements in GNP and prices, adjusted to take account of the actual conditions of implementation in the previous year, or revised on the basis of a proposal by the Commission.[8]

The general effect of this reform was to limit the expansion of agricultural spending by the EC—to 74 per cent of the rate of growth of EC GNP in any period—whilst doubling in real terms the amount allocated to the Structural Funds over a period of five years.

Details of the expenditures made by the EC in 1991, classified by sector and recipient, are shown in Table 14.5 (1991 is the most recent year for which expenditure may be disaggregated by recipient country). Spending under each heading is assigned to Member States on the basis of the location of the relevant EC expenditure. The total allocated in this way accounts for some 91.9 per cent of the total budget, the remaining 8.1 per cent relating mainly to expenditure on overseas aid and administration.

The largest category of expenditure is listed under the heading of the

TABLE 14.4. *Expenditure commitments under the 1988 financial perspective (Ecu m. at 1988 prices)*

| Expenditure category | 1988 | 1989 | 1990 | 1991 | 1992 |
| --- | --- | --- | --- | --- | --- |
| EAGGF Guarantee | 27,500 | 27,700 | 28,400 | 29,000 | 29,000 |
| Structural operations | 7,790 | 9,200 | 10,600 | 12,100 | 13,450 |
| Policies with multi-annual | | | | | |
| allocation | 1,210 | 1,650 | 1,900 | 2,150 | 2,400 |
| Other policies | 2,103 | 2,385 | 2,500 | 2,700 | 2,800 |
| Repayments and | | | | | |
| administration | 5,700 | 4,950 | 4,500 | 4,000 | 3,550 |
| Monetary Reserve | 1,000 | 1,000 | 1,000 | 1,000 | 1,000 |
| TOTAL | 45,303 | 46,885 | 48,900 | 50,950 | 52,800 |
| of which | | | | | |
| compulsory | 33,698 | 32,607 | 32,810 | 32,890 | 33,400 |
| non-compulsory | 11,605 | 14,278 | 16,090 | 17,970 | 19,400 |
| Own resources required as | | | | | |
| % of EC GNP | 1.15 | 1.17 | 1.18 | 1.19 | 1.20 |

*Source*: CEC (1992*b*: 116).

EAGGF Guarantee, which occurs as a result of the operation of the CAP. This item of expenditure was introduced into the budget in April 1962 and is associated with the various types of intervention expenditure on agricultural markets, refunds on exports of agricultural products to non-member countries, and half of the expenditure connected with the set-aside programme. The next three columns reflect expenditure on structural operations conducted by the EC. These comprise the Guidance Section of the EAGGF (introduced in 1964), the European Regional Development Fund (introduced in 1975), and the European Social Fund (introduced in 1958). Together they account for 20 per cent of the total budget in 1991. The essential purpose of all three funds is to promote better economic and social cohesion within the EC. In each case the EC contribution must be accompanied by national funding and so involves co-operation between the Commission and the Member States' authorities. Use of the structural funds is determined by five objectives which were set out in 1986 under the SEA. These objectives state that the Funds should contribute to: the promotion of the development and structural adjustment of the regions whose development is lagging behind; the conversion of regions seriously affected by industrial decline; the fight against long-term unemployment; the occupational integration of young people; and, finally, the adjustment of agricultural structures and development of rural areas.

Alongside the Funds, the Community also finances a series of other

TABLE 14.5. *Expenditures made in 1991, by sector and recipient Member States (Ecu m.)*

| Member State | EAGGF Guarantee | EAGGF Guidance | Regional Fund | Social Fund | Repayment by Member States | Other | Total[a] |
|---|---|---|---|---|---|---|---|
| Belgium | 1,459.4 | 11.3 | 46.4 | 65.3 | 12.5 | 1,039.1 | 2,634.0 (4.9%) |
| Denmark | 1,215.6 | 14.1 | 11.3 | 45.8 | 4.2 | 88.8 | 1,379.8 (2.6%) |
| France | 6,332.7 | 362.9 | 323.2 | 513.5 | 63.2 | 556.0 | 8,152.5 (15.2%) |
| Germany | 4,990.5 | 181.0 | 94.8 | 239.7 | 252.9 | 838.5 | 6,597.4 (12.3%) |
| Greece | 2,211.8 | 223.4 | 537.2 | 349.1 | — | 367.0 | 3,688.5 (6.9%) |
| Irish Republic | 1,628.7 | 153.6 | 411.9 | 403.8 | 101.5 | 110.3 | 2,809.7 (5.2%) |
| Italy | 5,347.0 | 203.8 | 710.8 | 414.5 | 5.7 | 629.5 | 7,311.2 (13.6%) |
| Luxemburg | 2.8 | 5.5 | 18.3 | 1.8 | — | 240.2 | 268.5 (0.5%) |
| Netherlands | 2,469.8 | 15.2 | 34.6 | 122.5 | 211.6 | 146.0 | 2,999.8 (5.6%) |
| Portugal | 316.4 | 196.9 | 971.2 | 379.3 | 49.4 | 315.1 | 2,228.2 (4.1%) |
| Spain | 3,300.3 | 420.3 | 1,488.8 | 697.0 | 482.3 | 486.0 | 6,874.8 (12.8%) |
| UK | 2,252.7 | 98.5 | 530.1 | 636.9 | 137.6 | 413.6 | 4,069.5 (7.6%) |
| TOTAL | 31,527.8 | 1,886.4 | 5,178.6 | 3,869.3 | 1,320.8 | 5,231.0 | 49,008.5 (91.9%) |

[a] Figures in parentheses show the percentage of the total budget allocated. The remaining 8.9% unallocated includes payments for overseas aid and administration.

*Source:* CEC (1002c: 15).

**TABLE 14.6.** *EC support for the new* Länder *(Ecu m., 1990 prices)*

| Structural fund | 1991 | 1992 | 1993 | Total |
|---|---|---|---|---|
| EAGGF Guidance | 130 | 200 | 270 | 600 |
| European Regional Fund | 500 | 500 | 500 | 1,500 |
| European Social Fund | 270 | 300 | 330 | 900 |
| TOTAL | 900 | 1,000 | 1,100 | 3,000 |

*Source*: CEC (1991: 31).

structural operations which have far smaller budgets. These include the specific industrial development programme for Portugal (1988–92), the integrated Mediterranean programmes (1985–93), the common transport policy, and the common fisheries policy. These expenditures, together with spending on energy, technology, co-operation with development countries, and administration, are collected together in column 6 of the table.

The most recent development in the EC's structural policy concerns the five new German *Länder* and East Berlin. A breakdown of these funds is shown in Table 14.6. The restructuring of these regions is clearly an enormous task and the EC committed Ecu 3 billion of structural aid between 1991 and 1993 to support the efforts made by Germany itself. The emphasis for this aid has been placed on increasing productivity, creating jobs, retraining, and cleaning up the environment. These objectives are being pursued within the general framework of rebuilding the economy and, in particular, of integrating the regions fully and quickly into the internal market.

### 14.5. THE NET BALANCE

Information similar to that contained in Sections 14.3 and 14.4 provides a basis for calculating the 'net contributions' of the individual Member States and can thereby be used to identify, at least at one level, the cross-country distributional incidence of the EC budget. Official estimates of the net contribution begin by identifying those items of EC expenditure which may be allocated to the individual Member States. As indicated by Table 14.5, these comprise some 90 per cent of the total budget. On the revenue side, Member States are assumed to contribute to this spending in proportion to the own-resource contributions that they make to the EC budget as a whole (see Table 14.2). The difference between the two values, expressed as a proportion of per capita GDP for the individual Member States, then corresponds to a notion of formal incidence commonly adopted in the public finance literature. The effect of using this calculation to rank EC

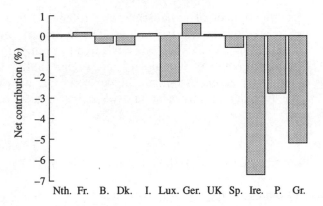

FIG. **14.2.** Net contributions as a proportion of GDP

members by their 'net contribution' in 1991 is shown in Fig. 14.2: on this basis, the Irish Republic, Portugal, and Greece appear as the main beneficiaries of the EC budget; Germany is the main contributor.

As is well known, however, calculations of cross-country distributive incidence of this form are subject to a variety of theoretical and practical problems (see e.g. Ardy (1988)). At a practical level, for example, the assignment of EC revenue or expenditure may not be a particularly good guide to the location of where either the benefits of spending or the burden of taxes will be felt. This argument is most commonly made in the context of the 'Rotterdam effect' in recording revenues received from customs duties. Good imported through major ports in the EC will pay duties at the point of entry, even if they are subsequently consumed elsewhere in the EC. Similarly, agricultural export subsidies may be recorded in a different Member State from the residence of the farmer who produced the goods being exported.

The second objection is, in many respects, even more fundamental. A number of EC measures have economic effects which are more far-reaching than simply the impact of expenditure. EC-intervention purchases of agricultural goods, for example, reduce supply generally and hence increase prices throughout the EC, irrespective of where the intervention takes place. Where these EC-produced goods are traded between Member States, at prices higher than would otherwise prevail, real income transfers take place. Resource transfers arising through unbalanced agricultural trade within the EC, for instance, represent a significant component of the overall economic gains and losses to Member States of the CAP and should, therefore, be considered at the same time as the resource flows associated with the formal incidence of the budget.

Whether the finances of the EC should take any formal account of the pattern of net contributions revealed by these calculations is a question which has been the subject of exhaustive, and often highly politicized, discussion during previous budgetary rounds. The budgetary problems of the United Kingdom in the 1980s may be considered to exemplify precisely this type of disagreement. As has been made clear in the discussion concerning many of the items of budget, however, it may be a deliberate objective of the EC that resources should be redistributed between the Member States.

## 14.6. FUTURE BUDGETARY DEVELOPMENTS

As indicated in Section 14.4, existing arrangements for financing the EC budget were due to come up for review in 1992. Accordingly, in the February of that year the Commission published a general assessment of the expenditure requirements of the EC over the next five years and made proposals for revising the financial resources of the EC (see CEC (1992*d*)). This document, commonly referred to as the 'Delors II' package, proposed raising the real value (in 1992 prices) of EC expenditure from Ecu 67 billion in 1992 to Ecu 87.5 billion in 1997, with priority being given to additional expenditure on economic and social cohesion, promotion of 'a favourable environment for competitiveness', and foreign aid. Although agricultural spending was to increase in real terms, it was scheduled to continue falling as a proportion of the total budget. In order to finance this general increase in expenditure, the Commission proposed a number of changes to the EC's own resources which are summarized in the final row of Table 14.1. The principal effect of these changes would be to raise the ceiling on own resources from 1.2 to 1.37 per cent of EC GNP by 1997, achieved mainly by extending the role played by GNP-based contributions in financing the budget, whilst reducing the role of VAT-based finance. Although subsequent events, notably the uncertainty surrounding ratification of the Maastricht Treaty, led to the Delor II proposals being shelved, the problem of EC finance remains high on the political agenda.

The priority given to economic and social cohesion in the Delors II proposals was made in recognition of the continuing need for the EC to address regional disparities. Such disparities can arise for a variety of reasons and may reflect either the transitional impact of adjustment to the single market, or longer-term structural problems that require a more sustained redistributive policy response. Indeed both of these factors were considered important when, at Maastrict, four low-income countries, led by Spain, insisted on and received assurances that the structural funds of the EC would in the future be increased.

However, a further argument in favour of increasing the level of EC expenditure may be based upon the potential use of the budget as an instrument of economic stabilization. This role for the EC budget was originally proposed by the MacDougall Committee in 1977 (see CEC (1977)). The committee's argument was based on the view that fiscal transfers would be necessary in order to stabilize income divergences between nations, once measures designed to promote exchange-rate stability had removed the scope for less prosperous Member States to devalue relative to the more prosperous countries. The MacDougall Report considered that, in order to fulfil this stabilizing role, the EC budget would need to increase to at least 5 per cent of EC GNP, with spending being assigned in line with regional income disparities within the EC.

More recent evidence, however, suggests that a stabilization role could be fulfilled at much lower levels of budgetary expenditure. What is at issue here is the use of the budget to buffer temporary asymmetric shocks between Member States, not its use to promote long-term redistribution between countries. Discussion of the effects of moving to full European Monetary Union (EMU) has focused the likely need for such a mechanism (see Chapter 13), many economists pointing to the existence of fiscal buffering mechanisms within existing large-scale monetary unions (the United States, for example) to underline the point. In fact, according to Commission calculations, a dedicated stabilization mechanism based on the national levels of GNP and relative unemployment rates within the EC could function effectively without the need for a large increase in budgetary expenditures. On the assumption that income support would be triggered once unemployment differentials reach 2 per cent, the programme would be able to offset approximately 20 per cent of a decline in a region's relative income at a cost to the EC budget of only 0.25 per cent of EC GDP.[9] As a result, effective regional stabilization would be available to the EC without a fundamental modification to European finances.

## 14.7. CONCLUSIONS

Despite its relatively small size, the budget has dominated debate within the EC for much of its thirty-six-year history. Disputes over the control of EC expenditure and rivalry between the various institutions have frequently resulted in budgetary negotiations being conducted in an atmosphere of political crisis. Financial reforms which establish budgetary procedures that avoid such difficulties have therefore been a characteristic feature of EC development for much of the period.

Existing budgetary arrangements were established in 1988 as a means of overcoming many of these problems. By establishing a medium-term framework of financial perspectives and adding the fourth resource, the Delors package was able to stabilize expenditure and guarantee adequate finance for the budget. These arrangements were due for review in 1992, but, because of the uncertainty caused by the delays in the ratification of the Maastricht Treaty, little practical progress has been made in agreeing a replacement financial structure; the main proposal—the Delors II package—has been shelved until current levels of uncertainty concerning the future direction of the EC have been resolved.

# NOTES

1. The preliminary draft budget is also subject to the limits set by the financial perspectives. These limits are discussed in Section 14.4.
2. Conversely, all other expenditure is non-compulsory. This definition was agreed in the joint declaration signed by the EP, the Council of Ministers, and the Commission on 30 June 1982.
3. The EP has rejected the draft budget on just three occasions. These rejections relate to the budgets of 1980, 1982, and 1985.
4. Agricultural levies in this context actually cover three sources of revenue. Agricultural levies in the strict sense, relate to variable taxes charged within the framework of the Common Agricultural Policy (CAP) on imports of agricultural products from non-member countries. In addition, however, sugar levies are imposed on sugar companies which pay them either to cover expenditure on market support (production levies) or to regulate disposal (storage levies). A final category, isoglucose production levies, was introduced in May 1977 and serves the same purpose as the sugar levy, even though isoglucose is not an agricultural product.
5. In practice, the effective VAT rate was less than 1.4 per cent, because of the UK refund.
6. Obviously the formula meant that the scale of the UK's abatement would vary from year to year as the pattern of revenue and expenditure varied across the EC.
7. Even the 'real maximum' is not a figure that the Treaty makes binding on the budgetary authority. By agreement, the Council and the EP (acting by a super-majority) may agree whatever rate of increase they wish, though this ability is now subject to an 'Inter-Institutional Agreement on budgetary discipline'.
8. The financial perspective for 1991, for example, was revised in 1990 in order to provide aid to Central and Eastern Europe and to take account of the financial consequences of German unification and the Gulf crisis.
9. This calculation was based on the historical movements in unemployment within the EC and is referred to by Eichengreen (1993).

# REFERENCES

Ardy, B. (1988), 'The National Incidence of the European Community Budget', *Journal of Common Market Studies*, 26/4: 401–29.

CEC (1977): Commission of the European Communities, *Report of the Study Group on the Role of Public Finance in European Integration*, i. *General Report*, ii. *Individual Contributions and Working Papers* (the MacDougall Report) (Economic and Financial Series, Nos. A13 and B13; Brussels: CEC).

—— (1987a), *The Single Act: A New Frontier for Europe*, COM (87) 100 (Brussels: CEC).

—— (1987b), *Report on the Financing of the European Communities Budget*, COM (87) 101 (Brussels: CEC).

—— (1991), *Financial Report of the European Community* (Brussels: CEC).

—— (1992a), 'Final Adoption of Amending and Supplementary Budget No. 3 of the European Communities for the Financial Year 1992', *Official Journal of the European Communities*, L349 (Nov.), 1–121).

—— (1992b), *Community Public Finance: The European Budget after the 1988 Reform* (Brussels: CEC).

—— (1992c), 'Annual Report of the Court of Auditors Concerning the Financial Year 1991', *Official Journal of the European Communities*, C330 (Dec.), 1–496.

—— (1992d), *From the Single Act to Maastricht and Beyond: The Means to Match our Ambitions*, COM (92) 2000 (Brussels: CEC).

Eichengreen, B. (1993), 'European Monetary Union', *Journal of Economic Literature*, 31 (Sept.), 1321–57.

Smith, S. (1992), 'The European Budget after 1992', working paper (London: Institute of Fiscal Studies).

Strasser, D. (1992), *The Finances of Europe: The Budgetary and Financial Law of the European Communities*, 7th edn. (Luxemburg).

# 15

# Foreign Aid and External Assistance

FREDERICK NIXSON

## 15.1. INTRODUCTION

Foreign aid or economic assistance consists of transfers of real resources to less developed countries (LDCs) on concessional terms. It excludes, by definition, purely commercial transactions, and should also exclude military aid, which, although it is non-commercial and concessional, does not have as its main objective the promotion of economic development. Aid raises a number of fundamental questions about development and under-development and the relationship between rich and poor countries (although not all donor countries are rich: China has made substantial sums of aid available in the past to countries such as Tanzania). These include the following:

- Why do donors give aid?
- Why do poor countries accept aid?
- How should aid be given?
  loans versus grants
  tied aid versus untied aid
  bilateral versus multilateral aid
  project versus programme aid
- Which countries should be given aid?
- What is the impact of aid on the process of growth and development?
- What is the nature of the aid relationship?

Clearly, simple and straightforward answers cannot be given to these questions, and, even after fifty years of experience of aid, the debate continues (recent contributions to the debate include Cassen *et al.* (1986); Mosley (1987); Riddell (1987)). Donors give aid for a number of reasons. Humanitarian motives may dominate, but more usually there are economic, political, and strategic factors that determine the amounts given and the countries selected by donors for assistance.

Equally, poor countries may accept aid for a variety of reasons—the urgency of the problems facing them, the domestic absence or shortage of the resources that aid can provide, the building-up of a relationship with a donor or group of donor countries for political reasons, and the role that aid can play in maintaining a particular regime in power and/or consolidating and extending its power.

Aid can be given in various forms—as grants or loans, technical assistance, or commodity (largely food) aid—and with various forms of conditionality attached. Aid may be given for a project (to build a road, for example) or be made available for a programme (e.g. in the transport sector). Bilateral aid is given by the aid agency of one country (the UK Overseas Development Administration, for example) to recipients in another. Multilateral aid (through the EC, the World Bank, or various UN agencies, for example) is usually considered to be superior to bilateral aid, as it avoids the problems that can arise in bilateral one-to-one relationships. Bilateral aid is normally tied (either to a particular project or programme and must be spent in the donor country); multilateral aid may be project- or programme-tied, but, by definition, it cannot be tied to a particular country.

Aid can be tied in various ways (Bhagwati 1967) through formal and informal restrictions, the use of export and import credits, and aid provided in the form of technical services and goods. There is general agreement that tied aid reduces its value to the recipient (lower cost sources of supply in non-donor countries will not be allowed to bid for aid projects). Tied aid benefits donor-country enterprises and its extensive use has led in the past to allegations that aid policy is subservient to a donor country's commercial interests.

When we consider the effectiveness of aid, it is useful to refer to what Mosley (1987: ch. 5) has called the 'macro-micro paradox'. This refers to the apparent paradox that, whereas the microeconomic evaluation of aid projects is usually positive, there appears to be no statistically significant correlation, either positive or negative, between inflows of aid and the rate of growth of the recipient economy. Mosley (1987: 139–40) and White (1992) suggest various reasons why this situation exists—inaccurate measurement and fungibility within the public sector (that is, if certain conditions are satisfied, aid can never be completely tied to a specific project— see Singer (1965)), and backwash effects from aid-financed activities that affect adversely the private sector.

Our knowledge of the impact of aid on development—so defined as to include economic growth, structural change, and the move towards certain socio-economic goods (less poverty, more employment, greater life expectancy, etc.)—is thus piecemeal and incomplete. We cannot prove that aid is either necessary or sufficient for economic and social development or that the relationship between donor and recipient countries is either advantageous or disadvantageous to the latter. Despite their policy statements, the aid programmes of most bilateral donors are dominated by political and geo-strategic considerations. If humanitarian factors are not of the highest priority, it should not surprise us if we find it difficult to establish a positive causal connection between aid and development.


## 15.2. EC DEVELOPMENT POLICY

The development policy of the EC has a number of distinct components which have evolved separately over time. The Lomé Conventions represent the oldest and most fully developed area and are the main focus of attention of this chapter (see Section 15.5). But the EC has also developed (i) a Mediterranean policy, based on a series of bilateral agreements, (ii) a series of co-operation instruments linked to common policies (generalized trade preferences, participation in commodity agreements, food aid), and (iii) an aid system set up by the EC on a unilateral basis. This includes emergency aid given in the event of natural or other disasters, aid to non-governmental organizations (NGOs) working on development projects in the Third World, financial and technical contributions to development projects, and industrial co-operation by means of financial aid to enterprises.

The EC emphasizes the 'fundamental characteristics' of its development policy (Frisch 1992). These include:

- contractual arrangements freely negotiated by the EC and African, Caribbean, and Pacific (ACP) economies;
- the creation of joint institutions to allow continuing dialogue; and
- the global approach to co-operation involving a wide range of instruments in the fields of both trade and aid.

In 1989 EC Development Co-operation commitments and payments accounted for less than 3 per cent of the EC budget (a fall of almost 50 per cent over the 1980s) (CEC 1990), and, as has been noted by a number of observers, development aid is only one, and perhaps not the most important, way in which the EC influences the development of both ACP economies in particular and Third World economies in general. The EC's commercial policy (the generalized system of preferences) and its Common Agricultural Policy (CAP), as well as the bilateral aid programmes of individual Member States, all exert powerful influences, and, even though we focus on aid in this chapter, these other influences should not be forgotten.

Although, as noted above, the focus of this chapter is on the Lomé Conventions, it should be noted that the EC gives significant amounts of aid to a number of non-ACP states, a point we return to in the discussion of Table 15.8 below.

With respect to the Lomé Conventions, the EC emphasizes the notions of equality and partnership (Lister 1992), although the notion of 'partnership' has been challenged by a number of commentators, and the aid relationship is a complex one, more in the realm of political economy than economics more narrowly defined. We note here the historical, cultural, commercial, and strategic factors which underlie relationships between rich and poor countries in general and the EC and ACP states in particular, and focus on only one aspect of those relationships: aid.

## 15.3. A NOTE ON AID STATISTICS: TERMS AND DEFINITIONS

All members of the EC are members of the Organization for Economic Co-operation and Development (OECD). One of the specialized committees of the OECD is the Development Assistance Committee (DAC), the members of which have agreed 'to secure an expansion of aggregate volume of resources made available to developing countries and to improve their effectiveness'.

The Commission of the European Communities takes part in the work of the OECD and is a member of the DAC. Greece and Luxemburg are not members of the DAC and they are therefore not included in the DAC aid tables. Greece does contribute, however, to EC aid programmes and multilateral institutions, and Luxemburg has indicated its intention to become a member of the DAC.

'Aid' or 'assistance' refers only to items which qualify as 'Official Development Assistance' (ODA)—that is, grants or loans:

- undertaken by the official sector;
- with promotion of economic development or welfare as main objectives;
- at concessional financial terms (if a loan, at least 25 per cent grant element).

Technical co-operation is included in aid. It consists almost entirely of grants to nationals of developing countries receiving education or training at home or abroad and payments to defray the costs of teachers, administrators, advisers, etc., serving in developing countries.

## 15.4. THE ODA RECORD OF EC MEMBER STATES

Total ODA from DAC countries to developing countries and multilateral institutions increased in 1991 to US$57 billion from US$53 billion in 1990. Allowing for price changes and changes in exchange rates *vis-à-vis* the US dollar, this represented an increase of 3.3 per cent in real terms.

Of the total of US$57 billion, the United States and Japan accounted for US$11.3 billion and US$11.0 billion respectively (all figures are rounded). The ten EC members of the DAC accounted for US$27 billion, that is

TABLE 15.1. *Comparative ODA Performance of EC countries 1980/1–1990/1*

| Member State | ODA at 1990 prices and exchange rates (US$m.) | | | Annual average % change in volume | | ODA as % of GNP | | |
|---|---|---|---|---|---|---|---|---|
| | 1980/1 | 1985/6 | 1990/1 | 1980/1–1990/1 | 1985/6–1990/1 | 1980/1 | 1985/6 | 1990/1 |
| Belgium | 868 | 856 | 857 | −0.1 | 0.0 | 0.54 | 0.51 | 0.44 |
| Denmark[a] | 761 | 991 | 1,188 | 4.6 | 3.7 | 0.74 | 0.85 | 0.95 |
| France[ab] | 6,339 | 7,496 | 7,360 | 1.5 | −0.4 | 0.52 | 0.59 | 0.61 |
| Germany | 5,513 | 5,866 | 6,549 | 1.7 | 2.2 | 0.45 | 0.44 | 0.41 |
| Irish Republic | 48 | 78 | 65 | 3.1 | −3.5 | 0.16 | 0.27 | 0.18 |
| Italy | 1,347 | 3,099 | 3,314 | 9.4 | 1.4 | 0.16 | 0.34 | 0.30 |
| Netherlands[a] | 2,344 | 2,303 | 2,520 | 0.7 | 1.8 | 1.01 | 0.97 | 0.90 |
| Portugal | 74 | 30 | 169 | 8.7 | 41.0 | 0.02 | 0.06 | 0.28 |
| Spain | 777 | 227 | 1,041 | 3.0 | 35.7 | 0.10 | 0.09 | 0.21 |
| UK[a] | 3,027 | 2,864 | 2,849 | −0.6 | −0.1 | 0.39 | 0.32 | 0.32 |
| EC Members (total) | 21,107 | 23,811 | 25,912 | 2.1 | 1.7 | 0.45 | 0.48 | 0.43 |

[a] Includes forgiveness of non-ODA debt in 1990 and 1991.
[b] Including TOMs (overseas territories) but not DOMs (overseas departments).

*Source:* OECD (1992: table V-3, p. 89).

TABLE **15.2.** *Burden-sharing indicators*

| Member State | ODA per capita of donor country (1990 US$) | | Grant equivalent of total ODA[a] as % of GNP (1990–1 average) | Aid apportions as % of central government budget[b] (1990–1 average) |
|---|---|---|---|---|
| | 1980/1 | 1990/1 | | |
| Belgium | 88 | 86 | 0.45 | [1.15] |
| Denmark | 149 | 231 | 0.97 | 3.20 |
| France | 118 | 130 | 0.61 | 2.30 |
| Germany | 89 | 92 | 0.45 | [2.40] |
| Ireland | — | 37 | 0.16 | 0.60 |
| Italy | 24 | 58 | 0.28 | 0.69 |
| Netherlands | 165 | 168 | 0.96 | [2.68] |
| Portugal | — | 16 | 0.28 | — |
| Spain | — | 27 | 0.20 | 0.59 |
| UK | 54 | 99 | 0.31 | 1.15 |

*Note*: Includes forgiveness of non-ODA debt in 1990 and 1991.

Dash = nil or negligible.
[a] Calculated on gross disbursement basis.
[b] [ ] = secretariat estimate.

*Source*: OECD (1992: table 3, p. A-12; table 4, p. A-13).

approximately 47 per cent of the total (note that these figures are in current prices and dollar exchange rates and differ slightly from those given in Table 15.1).

For DAC members as a whole, ODA as a proportion of GNP was 0.33 per cent in 1991. For the ten EC members, the equivalent figure was 0.43 per cent, ranging from 0.97 per cent for Denmark to 0.16 per cent for the Irish Republic (Table 15.2). This ratio has remained remarkably stable over recent years, although Denmark, Italy, Portugal, and Spain have registered increases throughout the 1980s and the Netherlands, Belgium, the United Kingdom, and Germany have registered falls.

The annual average change in the real value (at 1990 prices) of ODA over the period 1980/1–1990/1 was 2.4 per cent for all DAC members and 2.1 per cent for the ten EC members. Only Belgium and the United Kingdom registered negative growth over this period. The higher DAC average growth figure was largely the result of the rapid growth of ODA from a number of non-EC countries—Finland, Japan, Switzerland— although two EC members—Italy and Portugal—achieved high growth rates, albeit starting from low bases, especially in the case of Portugal.

Table 15.2 also indicates the proportion of the central government budget that is devoted to ODA (column 3). The unweighted average for all DAC countries in 1990 was 1.8 per cent. In a period of general budgetary constraint, aid budgets are often vulnerable and aid expenditures are amongst the first items to be cut. Over the period 1980–90, ODA as a proportion of the central government budget has fallen in Belgium, Germany, the Netherlands, and the United Kingdom. Only in the case of France and Italy has there been a slight rise over the whole decade (although this masks a fall between 1985 and 1990) (OECD 1992: table V-4, p. 90).

Although it is recognized that multilateral institutions have a key role to play in the development process, most donor countries, for the reasons outlined above, prefer to maintain direct control over their aid programmes through bilateral relationships. The early to mid-1970s saw a significant expansion in the role of multilateral aid, including a major expansion of aid from EC members through EC programmes. In the later half of the 1970s, the proportion of ODA channelled through multilateral institutions levelled off, and in the 1980s the proportion, expressed as a percentage of GNP, actually declined (OECD 1992: table V-5, p. 42).

Table 15.3 gives details of EC Member States' contributions to multilateral bodies. Excluding contributions to the EC (of which more below), most EC members of the DAC contribute less than 25 per cent of their total ODA to multilateral institutions (Denmark is the exception in this respect). Relatively large donors (France and Germany) contribute less than 20 per cent multilaterally. The United Kingdom (at 22 per cent) is on a par with Japan (23 per cent) and slightly above the United States (19 per cent).

TABLE 15.3. *Trends in contributions to multilateral institutions by EC countries 1969/71–1989/91*

| Member State | % total ODA | | Multilateral ODA as % GNP 1990–1 |
|---|---|---|---|
| | 1969–71 | 1989–91 | |
| Belgium | 13 (25) | 25 (42) | 0.09 (0.17) |
| Denmark | 44 (44) | 36 (42) | 0.34 (0.40) |
| France | 5 (11) | 11 (22) | 0.06 (0.13) |
| Germany | 15 (24) | 18 (33) | 0.07 (0.13) |
| Irish Republic | n.a. (n.a.) | 18 (60) | 0.03 (0.10) |
| Italy | 17 (34) | 23 (37) | 0.06 (0.10) |
| Netherlands | 19 (26) | 20 (29) | 0.18 (0.26) |
| Portugal | 1 (n.a.) | 6 (26) | 0.02 (0.07) |
| Spain | — — | 16 (38) | 0.03 (0.07) |
| UK | 23 (23) | 22 (44) | 0.06 (0.13) |

*Notes*: Figures in parentheses include contributions to the EC.
n.a. = not available.
Dash = nil or negligible.
*Source*: OECD (1992: table V-5, p. 92; table 3, p. A-12).

TABLE 15.4. *Contributions of Member States to EC aid 1991 (net disbursements)*

| Member State | Total (US$m.) | Share of total EC aid (%) | Of which EDF (US$m.) | Total net disbursements as % of ODA |
|---|---|---|---|---|
| Belgium | 178 | 4.1 | 74 | 21.4 |
| Denmark | 83 | 1.9 | 39 | 7.0 |
| France | 951 | 21.7 | 440 | 12.7 |
| Germany | 1,225 | 28.0 | 412 | 17.8 |
| Ireland | 31 | 0.7 | 9 | 43.1 |
| Italy | 632 | 14.4 | 236 | 18.9 |
| Netherlands | 248 | 5.7 | 106 | 9.9 |
| Portugal | 38 | 0.9 | 17 | 17.8 |
| Spain | 245 | 5.6 | 106 | 20.8 |
| UK | 743 | 17.0 | 309 | 22.9 |
| TOTAL | 4,374 | 100.0 | 1,748 | |

*Source*: OECD (1992: table 26, p. A-36).

When we take contributions to the EC into account, the share of ODA going through multilateral channels obviously rises, quite dramatically in some cases—the Irish Repubic, Spain, and Portugal—and doubling in the case of France and the United Kingdom.

Table 15.4 gives details of contributions to the EC in 1991. Germany was the largest contributor (28 per cent of the total) followed by France, the United Kingdom, and Italy. The Irish Republic is the smallest donor in absolute terms and channels the largest proportion of its ODA through the EC. Portugal, on the other hand, is the second smallest donor in absolute terms but channels a below-average proportion through the EC. The European Development Fund (EDF) absorbed 40 per cent of Member States contributions in 1991.

Table 15.5 gives an indication as to the relative global importance of the EC as a multilateral institution. In 1991 it provided US$3.5 billion of concessional finance, an increase of approximately US$630 million over 1990. As a proportion of total concessional finance available, the EC accounted in 1990 for 20 per cent, representing a fall from 1988 but a rise over the entire period covered. Non-concessional lending has tended to stagnate in the late 1980s, as problem countries cut back on investment projects as a consequence of the implementation of structural adjustment programmes (OECD 1991: 119). The EC is thus a multilateral institution of some importance in terms of its provision of ODA.

As noted above, aid can be either tied or untied. The tying of aid has always been a controversial topic, with critics arguing that tying reduces the value of aid and lowers its 'quality'. The other determinant of the 'quality' of aid is its grant element. This reflects the financial terms of a commitment: interest rate, maturity (interval to final repayment), and grace period (interval to first repayment of capital). The grant element measures

TABLE 15.5. *Net disbursements of concessional and non-concessional flows by EC*

| Year | Disbursements (US$m.) | | As % of total flows of multilateral organizations | |
| --- | --- | --- | --- | --- |
| | Concessional | Non-concessional | Concessional | Non-concessional |
| 1970–1 | 208 | 34 | 17.6 | 4.1 |
| 1975–6 | 611 | 42 | 15.7 | 1.6 |
| 1980 | 1,061 | 257 | 13.6 | 5.3 |
| 1985 | 1,287 | 152 | 16.0 | 1.9 |
| 1986 | 1,407 | 190 | 16.2 | 2.4 |
| 1987 | 1,659 | 140 | 16.9 | 2.1 |
| 1988 | 2,508 | 56 | 22.5 | 0.9 |
| 1989 | 2,473 | 121 | 19.9 | 1.7 |
| 1990 | 2,843 | 299 | 20.1 | 2.9 |
| 1991 | 3,478 | 154 | n.a. | n.a. |

*Note*: n.a. = not available.
*Source*: OECD (1992: table 28, p. A-38).

TABLE **15.6.** *Financial terms of ODA commitments 1981–2 and 1990–1 averages and tying status 1990*

| Member State | Grant element of total ODA (norm 86%) (%) | | % bilateral ODA untied 1990[a] |
|---|---|---|---|
| | 1981–2 average | 1990–1 average | |
| Belgium | 97.7 | 94.8 | 0.0 |
| Denmark | 95.1 | 100.0 | 0.0 |
| France | 88.8 | 86.2 | 39.5 |
| Germany | 83.1 | 85.3 | 19.5 |
| Irish Republic | 100.0 | 100.0 | 0.0 |
| Italy | 90.1 | 89.0 | 9.4 |
| Netherlands | 94.1 | 94.1 | 34.7 |
| Portugal | n.a. | 77.1 | 0.0 |
| Spain | n.a. | n.a. | 0.0 |
| UK | 98.4 | 98.9 | 0.0 |

*Note*: n.a. = not available.

[a] Fully and freely available for essentially world-wide procurement.

*Source*: OECD (1992: table 5, p. A-14; table 6, p. A-15).

the concessionality—that is, the softness—of a loan. The market rate of interest is conventionally taken to be 10 per cent. The grant element of a loan is thus nil for a loan with an interest rate of 10 per cent or higher and, by definition, the grant element of a grant is 100 per cent. The grant element will lie in between these two limits for a soft loan. Although maturity and grace periods are important, it is the interest rate that is the major determinant of the softness of a loan (OECD 1992: pp. A-99–100).

The data in Table 15.6 show that EC Member States score highly with respect to the concessionality of their aid, with high grant elements in all cases. They do less well, however, with respect to the tying of aid, with only France and the Netherlands untying more than one-third of their bilateral aid in 1990 (multilateral aid, by definition, cannot be tied to individual donor countries).

The final point to be considered in this general overview relates to the distribution of EC aid. The regional distribution is given in Table 15.7. The Sub-Saharan region is the major recipient of EC aid, although its relative importance has fallen over the period 1985/6–1990/1.

Concern has been expressed in the Third World that the changes that have occurred in Eastern Europe and the former Soviet Union will cause a diversion of aid from developing countries conventionally defined. Some of the countries of the former Soviet Union, such as the Central Asian

TABLE **15.7.** *Regional distribution of EC ODA 1980/1–1990/1* (% of total gross disbursements)

| Region | 1980/1 | 1985/6 | 1990/1 |
|---|---|---|---|
| Sub-Saharan Africa | 60.4 | 65.2 | 58.2 |
| South Asia | 17.2 | 9.3 | 7.2 |
| Other Asia and Oceania | 5.0 | 5.5 | 4.9 |
| Middle East and North Africa[a] | 12.0 | 12.6 | 19.7 |
| Latin America and Caribbean | 5.4 | 7.4 | 10.1 |

[a] Includes small amounts to Southern Europe.

Republics, have similar characteristics to developing countries, and consideration is being given to adding them to the DAC list of Developing Countries (OECD 1992: 94). In general, however, DAC members have argued that so far there has been very limited aid diversion and it is difficult to predict how important an issue this will become in the future.

Table 15.8 gives a more detailed breakdown of aid recipients. The 'top twenty-five' aid recipients in 1990/1 accounted for about 54 per cent of total EC aid, but it can be seen that this percentage is significantly lower than those for 1980/1 and 1970/1. Of the twenty-five countries listed in Table 15.8 for 1990/1, seven of them (Egypt, Turkey, Jordan, Bangladesh, India, Tunisia, and China) are not ACP member states, yet together they account for almost 20 per cent of EC economic aid. Egypt is the largest individual recipient of EC aid (and, indeed, it is the largest recipient of total DAC aid (see OECD 1992: table 43, p. A-65). This re-emphasizes the point made above (Section 15.2) that, although most attention is given to ACP member states, the EC has wider interests which encompass South Asia, the Middle East, and (to a much more limited extent) Latin America.

The distribution of aid thus reflects a mixture of historical relationships (colonialism) and contemporary geo-political realities, although the latter are less evident in the case of a multilateral institution like the EC than they are in the case of major bilateral donors. In the case of the United States in 1990/1, for example, over 40 per cent of ODA went to Egypt and Israel (OECD 1992: table 43, p. A-64).

## 15.5. THE LOMÉ CONVENTIONS

### Historical Background

The Lomé Convention between the twelve Member States of the EC and the sixty-nine African, Caribbean, and Pacific (ACP) states represents the

TABLE **15.8.** *Major recipients of EC aid 1970/1–1990/1 (% of total ODA)*

| 1970–1 Country | Aid | 1980–1 Country | Aid | 1990–1 Country | Aid |
|---|---|---|---|---|---|
| Cameroon | 9.0 | India | 9.6 | Egypt | 5.5 |
| Zaire | 8.4 | Sudan | 4.1 | Côte d'Ivoire | 4.3 |
| Senegal | 8.2 | Egypt | 3.6 | Cameroon | 4.2 |
| Madagascar | 6.1 | Bangladesh | 3.5 | Turkey | 3.6 |
| Côte d'Ivoire | 4.9 | Senegal | 3.4 | Ethiopia | 3.4 |
| Burkina Faso | 4.2 | Somalia | 3.1 | Sudan | 3.3 |
| India | 3.7 | Ethiopia | 3.0 | Jordan | 3.1 |
| Niger | 3.5 | Zaire | 2.8 | Mozambique | 3.0 |
| Mali | 3.3 | Mali | 2.7 | Bangladesh | 2.6 |
| Gabon | 3.0 | Tanzania | 2.6 | India | 2.3 |
| Chad | 2.9 | Kenya | 2.4 | Tanzania | 1.5 |
| Turkey | 2.8 | Zambia | 1.9 | Mali | 1.5 |
| Togo | 2.7 | Madagascar | 1.9 | Burundi | 1.5 |
| Algeria | 2.2 | Guinea | 1.7 | Malawi | 1.4 |
| Benin | 2.2 | Rwanda | 1.6 | Guinea | 1.3 |
| Mexico | 2.0 | Morocco | 1.6 | Kenya | 1.3 |
| Pakistan | 2.0 | Côte d'Ivoire | 1.6 | Tunisia | 1.2 |
| Congo | 1.9 | Turkey | 1.5 | Namibia | 1.2 |
| Egypt | 1.9 | Burundi | 1.5 | Zaire | 1.2 |
| Burundi | 1.8 | Pakistan | 1.5 | Angola | 1.2 |
| Somalia | 1.8 | Uganda | 1.4 | Mauritania | 1.1 |
| Netherlands Antilles | 1.8 | Malawi | 1.4 | Somalia | 1.1 |
| Rwanda | 1.5 | Indonesia | 1.3 | Niger | 1.1 |
| Bangladesh | 1.5 | Burkina Faso | 1.2 | China | 1.1 |
| Central African Rep. | 1.4 | Mauritania | 1.2 | Zambia | 1.0 |
| Total above | 84.5 | Total above | 62.1 | Total above | 53.9 |
| Unallocated | 3.6 | Unallocated | 10.3 | Unallocated | 20.1 |
| Total ODA (US$m.) | 203 | Total ODA (US$m.) | 1,244 | Total ODA (US$m.) | 3,213 |

main framework within which co-operation between the EC and the Third World takes place.

Of the sixty-nine ACP states (sixty-eight original members with Namibia joining at independence in April 1990), forty-six are from Africa, fifteen are from the Caribbean, and eight are from the Pacific. A number of overseas countries and territories (OCTs) (particularly those of the United Kingdom and France) remain a part of the system.

When the Treaty of Rome was signed in 1957, most of the countries that now constitute the ACP were still colonies. The Treaty of Rome provided for an element of aid to these colonies, however, in the form of an implementing Convention added to the Treaty. It provided for a form of unilateral association between the EC and its Member States and OCTs through which trade and aid links could be maintained.

The first EDF was established in 1958 and gave grants for economic and social infrastructure projects largely in French-speaking OCTs. The 1960s was a decade of decolonization, and in 1963 the Yaoundé (Cameroon) Convention was signed between the EC6 and eighteen now-independent African countries (including Madagascar). A second EDF was established to give loans as well as grants, and the Convention included provisions for preferential trade arrangements and for the provision of financial and technical assistance. The Second Yaoundé Convention was signed in 1969, with a third EDF.

In January 1973 the United Kingdom joined the EC and some twenty Commonwealth countries were included in the protocol to the Act of Accession, opening the way to the negotiation of some form of special relationship with the EC, an opportunity also offered to those independent states in Africa that were neither members of the Commonwealth nor members of the AASM grouping (Association of African States and Madagascar) which had negotiated the Yaoundé Conventions.

After a period of some uncertainty as to how newly independent ACP countries would view their position *vis-à-vis* Europe, the first Lomé Convention was signed in February 1975 in Togo and, in June 1975, forty-six ACP countries institutionalized themselves as a group with a permanent structure.

Lomé I has been described as a 'partnership of equals' and a number of joint institutions were created to administer the Convention. It introduced Stabex—a system designed to stabilize commodity earnings (see below)— and, at a time of stalemate in the global negotiations aimed at the creation of a New International Economic Order (NIEO), it 'appeared to offer an opportunity for a group of industrialised and developing countries to break out of the impasse . . . to establish a regional arrangement that would incorporate a number of items on the NIEO agenda' (Stevens 1990: 77).

The optimism that characterized Lomé I was shown to be premature by events that followed the first oil-price shock of 1973–4. A brief boom in some primary commodity prices was followed by the second oil-price shock of 1979–80. The Sub-Saharan economies in particular were hard hit by global economic instability and began a period of stagnant or falling per capita incomes from which the majority of African economies have not yet recovered.

Lomé II was signed in 1980, with a larger EDF and a Sysmin facility (see below), but was regarded as disappointing by the ACP. Lomé III was signed in 1985, as the 'decade of structural adjustment' (see below) was beginning to emerge. Lomé III made a commitment to 'self-reliant development' on the basis of food security and self-sufficiency, enhanced by a broad-ranging 'policy dialogue' between EC Member States and the ACP states. Stabex conditionality was tightened up (see below), however, and policy dialogue increasingly encompassed involvement in macroeconomic policy-making through the provision of resources through programmes of structural adjustment.

Stevens (1990: 84) argues that the first three Lomé Conventions did not lead to a radical transformation in the economies of the ACP. Lomé aid has been widely criticized on two counts: (i) it has been poorly used, financing projects either poorly designed or whose possibilities of success have been weakened by a hostile policy environment, and (ii) aid has been badly administered by the donor, with slow rates of disbursement. Donor procedures are allegedly slow and cumbersome, with duplicated appraisal procedures, over-centralization, and 'meddling' by Member States (Stevens 1990: 85).

In addition, it is argued that the 'aid relationship' has changed over time, with the EC attempting to impose a more orthodox donor–recipient relationship than was initially felt either necessary or desirable. 'Policy dialogue' has increasingly come to mean a shift in the balance of power for aid decision-making towards the EC to give it a greater voice in the selection of aid-financed projects and sectoral policies relevant to the success of those projects (Stevens 1990: 84).

### Lomé IV

The fourth Lomé Convention was signed in December 1989. For the first time it covers a period of ten years, although the Financial Protocol covers the first five years only and is negotiable thereafter.

The Convention is a lengthy document (the full text is published in the *Courier* (1990), which highlights new areas of development aid policy which had been somewhat neglected in the previous conventions:

(a) *protection of the environment*: the control of desertification and a commitment to ensure that economic and social development is based on a sustainable balance between economic objectives, management of natural resources, and improvement of human resources;

(b) *agricultural co-operation and food security*: the emphasis is on the regional dimension of food security policies and the role of women in rural development;

(c) *industry and services*: industrial co-operation and the promotion of services that support economic development are given new prominence. Such services include support for external trade, promotion of tourism, and development of transport and communications and information technology;

(d) *cultural and social co-operation*: this is extended to new issues such as population, nutrition, and women in development;

(e) *other provisions* in Lomé IV include a special programme of aid to the countries of Sub-Saharan Africa which have low incomes and large debts and specific measures to assist the least-developed landlocked and island ACP states. As in previous conventions, there are provisions for emergency aid for the victims of natural disasters, refugees and repatriated persons.

## Finance

Details of the Financial Protocol are given in Table 15.9.

Total funding is Ecu 12 billion for the first five years. Apart from the funds managed by the European Investment Bank (EIB), all financing is in the form of grants. The main innovation in the development financial protocol is the commitment to structural adjustment support which is allocated Ecu 1,150 million.

## Structural Adjustment

In very broad terms, structural adjustment is a set of policies designed to reduce internal and external imbalances in an economy. Whereas stabilization policies are largely concerned with the reduction in aggregate demand, structural adjustment focuses on the increase in aggregate supply. Both sets of policies complement each other and both share many common elements—more liberal trade policy (removal of quantitative restrictions, reduction in tariffs), improved resource mobilization and allocation (through fiscal and monetary reform, removal of subsidies, reform of public enterprises, reform of agricultural sector pricing policies), and institutional reforms.

The Lomé IV provisions that cover structural adjustment (Articles 243–50) emphasize that these policies are intended to promote long-term development in the ACP states, accelerate the growth of output and employment, and be consistent with the political and economic model of

TABLE **15.9.** *Convention of Lomé IV: Financial protocol 1990–1995* (Ecu m.)

| | | | |
|---|---|---|---|
| EDF Funding | | | 10,800 |
| of which: | | | |
| *Stabex | | 1,500 | |
| *Sysmin | | 480 | |
| *Grants | | 7,995 | |
| of which: | | | |
| Emergency refugee assistance | 350 | | |
| Interest rate subsidies | 280 | | |
| Structural adjustment | 1,150 | | |
| Other grants | 6,215 | | |
| *Risk capital | | 825 | |
| EIB Funding | | | 1,200 |
| Total Funding | | | 12,000 |

*Note*: Additional to the Ecu 12,000m. for the ACP states, there is provision for Ecu 165m. assistance for the OCTs (Ecu 140m. from EDF, Ecu 25m. from EIB).
*Source*: *Courier* (1990: 15).

the ACP state in question. Adjustment has to be economically viable and socially and politically bearable. These are ambitious objectives, the achievement of which cannot be taken for granted. The record of structural adjustment programmes is mixed, to say the least, and, although the EC argues that it will be pragmatic and realistic in its approach, only time will tell whether this will ensure success.

### Trade and Commodities

It is important to keep in mind that trade policy, though not of direct concern in this chapter, probably has a greater economic impact on the ACP states than development co-operation policy *per se* ('Trade not Aid' has been a slogan popular in the Third World for many years). The ACP states enjoy free access to the EC market for the majority of their agricultural and manufactured products. These agreements have been extended and strengthened in Lomé IV and there is also increased support for processing, marketing, distribution, and transport activities.

### Stabex

An important element in the Lomé Conventions has been Stabex (System for the Stabilization of Export Earnings). The basic aim of Stabex has not changed over the four Conventions. That aim is to remedy: 'the harmful effects of the instability of export earnings and to help the ACP states overcome one of the main obstacles to the stability, profitability and sustained growth of their economies, to support their development efforts and to enable them in this way to ensure economic and social progress for their peoples by helping to safeguard their purchasing power'(Article 186(1)). When it was introduced in 1975, the Stabex system was welcomed for its innovatory approach, its simplicity of operation, and the relatively rapid transfers that it provided. The ACP states supported Stabex, seeing it as providing them with soft (untied) aid inflows which were less troublesome than project aid and which, for the smaller ACP states, often provided quite significant amounts of foreign exchange.

Stabex under Lomé I and II was virtually unique as a scheme of development assistance. It had no specifically prescribed end-use, there was no formal conditionality, and it was not procurement-tied. Hewitt (1983) evaluated a sample of Stabex transfers over its first five-year period of operation (Lomé I) and during the first two years of Lomé II. His conclusions were in general positive, although only a relatively small proportion of the US$200 million disbursed had been used directly in favour of the export crop or commodity that had triggered the claim.

Lomé III saw a change with respect to conditionality and specified that transfers were to be devoted to maintaining financial flows in affected sectors or 'for the purpose of promoting diversification, directed towards other appropriate sectors and used for economic and social development' (Article 147(2)). These changes were in part a reflection of the EC's concern with policy dialogue and structural adjustment referred to above.

Lomé IV has seen a further tightening of conditionality, with respect to the uses to which transfers can be put, although it has been extended to include new products, and there are a number of other changes to make it more flexible and fairer to recipients.

Stabex can be drawn upon by any ACP states. It applies to the earnings from an ACP state's exports of the products covered by Stabex if, during the year preceding the year of application, earnings from the export of each product to all destinations represent at least 5 per cent of total export earnings (this is the so-called 'dependency threshold'). For the least developed, landlocked, and island states, the figure is 1 per cent. The reference level against which the shortfall in export earnings is measured is taken to be the average of export earnings during the previous six years (less the two years with the highest and lowest figures). The transfer basis (that is the amount to be reimbursed to the ACP state) is the difference between the reference level and the actual earnings in the year of application, minus an amount corresponding to 4.5 per cent of the reference level (in the case of the least-developed ACP states, this figure is 1 per cent).

There are other changes in the technical details of Stabex under Lomé IV as compared to Lomé III, but for the purposes of the present discussion what is important are the changes in conditionality. The sector that records the loss of export earnings must be given priority, although the concept of

**TABLE 15.10.** *Stabex transfers by product 1975–1989*

| Product/Group products | Lomé III (1985–1989) | | Lomé I–III (1975–1989) | |
|---|---|---|---|---|
| | Allocated amounts (Ecu) | % of the total | Allocated amounts (Ecu) | % of the total |
| Coffee | 589,494,410 | 40.40 | 850,571,356 | 33.78 |
| Groundnuts | 168,023,123 | 11.52 | 440,641,445 | 17.50 |
| Cocoa/cocoa products | 203,908,818 | 13.92 | 353,456,761 | 14.04 |
| Cotton | 84,611,974 | 5.80 | 164,505,748 | 6.53 |
| Timber | 107,111,119 | 7.34 | 147,493,817 | 5.86 |
| Coco/copra products | 101,336,328 | 6.95 | 143,532,914 | 5.70 |
| Palm-oil products | 77,727,124 | 5.33 | 92,239,282 | 3.66 |
| Iron ore | | | 61,789,536 | 2.45 |
| Tea | 45,905,104 | 3.15 | 56,531,537 | 2.24 |
| Oil cakes | 20,848,292 | 1.43 | 52,434,242 | 2.08 |
| Others | 60,894,295 | 4.16 | 156,927,537 | 6.16 |
| TOTAL | 1,459,050,587 | 100.00 | 2,518,224,175 | 100.00 |

*Source: Courier (1992a).*

'sector' is a wide one and includes production, processing, marketing, distribution, and transport activities within it. Diversification into other productive activities within the agricultural sector is permitted once difficulties in the sector that triggered the claim are overcome. Stabex transfers by product are detailed in Table 15.10. It can be clearly seen that coffee has been the majority beneficiary of the system, taking 34 per cent of Stabex transfers over Lomé I–III.

## Sysmin

This is a special facility set up for those ACP states whose mining sectors occupy an important place in their economies and which are facing difficulties—technical, economic, or political—beyond the control of the state or the undertaking concerned. When such difficulties threaten the viability of the undertaking, leading to a significant fall in revenue for the ACP state, financial assistance will be made available, either to re-establish or rationalize, at a viable level, production and export capacity, or to be used to encourage conversion or diversification of projects or programmes (full details are given in Lomé IV, chapter 3, Articles 214–19, reprinted in *Courier* (1990)).

It covers copper, phosphates, manganese, bauxite and alumina, tin, iron ore, and uranium (and, in certain circumstances, gold). The record of Sysmin under Lomé III was disappointing and steps have been taken in Lomé IV to simplify and improve its functioning. Its key concerns are viability and diversification. Sysmin operations will also be possible where an ACP state's export earnings suffer as a result of disruption but without the viability of the mining sector necessarily being affected.

## The European Development Fund (EDF)

The financial resources which the EC makes available for development projects in the ACP states are channelled through the EDF. As can be seen in Table 15.9, the EDF has Ecu 10,800 million to disburse over the period 1990–5.

All EDF financial transfers are now in the form of grants so as not to add to their burden of debt. Table 15.11 gives details of the sectoral distribution of EDF aid for Lomé II and III. It can be seen that high priority has been attached to rural development under Lomé III, with an almost doubling of the absolute amount of aid made available, and an increase in its share of total aid from just under 25 per cent to approximately 30 per cent. The aid share allocated to transport and communications has fallen, explained in part by a deliberate shift away from this sector (especially aid assistance for roads and bridges). The decline in the share of the industrial sector is in part a reflection of the difficulties experienced with Sysmin.

TABLE **15.11.** *Sectoral breakdown of EDF aid approved up to 30 June 1991*

| Sectors | Lomé II | | Lomé III | |
|---|---|---|---|---|
| | Ecu m. | % | Ecu m. | % |
| Rural production | 1,133 | 24.7 | 2,092 | 29.8 |
| Transport and communication | 833 | 18.2 | 1,092 | 15.4 |
| Industry | 916 | 20.0 | 798 | 11.4 |
| Health, social development, and water engineering | 677 | 14.8 | 521 | 7.5 |
| Stabex | 630 | 13.7 | 1,436 | 20.5 |
| Others[a] | 393 | 8.6 | 1,089 | 15.5 |
| TOTAL | 4,582 | 100.0 | 7,028 | 100.0 |

[a] Includes emergency aid, aid to refugees, trade promotion, and various smaller sectors.
*Source*: *Courier* (1992*a*).

Health, social development, and water engineering have also experienced both an absolute fall and a fall in their share of total aid. In health, there has been a greater emphasis on operational expenditure (technical assistance, training, and operational costs) and on health campaigns, and less on the financing of infrastructure (construction and equipment). The social sector and water engineering have in part received less because large multi-component programmes in the rural sector now include both the social dimension and water-engineering sector expenditures.

Stabex transfers have increased as a proportion of the total (from 14 to 21 per cent approximately) and there are a number of new instruments classified under 'others'. These include quick disbursing import programmes, so-called 'thematic actions'—especially against desertification, drought, and natural disasters, aid to refugees, and increased support for trade promotion.

The financial provisions for development aid assistance by the EIB are shown separately in Table 15.9. The EIB's contribution to aid takes the form of loans at market rates, which are reduced by means of EDF aid (amounting to Ecu 1,200 million under Lomé IV) to between 3 and 6 per cent per annum. EIB lending has gone mainly to help in financing infrastructure development, although there has been a decline in that sector's share, with a corresponding increase in lending to the energy sector. In the industrial sector, there has been a shift in lending away from large industrial projects towards support for small and medium-sized projects, reflecting the EIB's commitment to promoting the small and medium-sized private enterprise sector, through local financial intermediaries (investment corporations, development banks, etc.).

TABLE **15.12.** *Total European development funds: Breakdown of cumulative payments by beneficiary country 1960–1986*

| Country | Total (Ecu m.) | % of total |
| --- | --- | --- |
| Senegal | 471.7 | 6.0 |
| Zaire | 401.6 | 5.1 |
| Côte d'Ivoire | 342.5 | 4.4 |
| Madagascar | 337.8 | 4.3 |
| Sudan | 322.1 | 4.1 |
| Cameroon | 309.8 | 3.9 |
| Ethiopia | 300.7 | 3.8 |
| Mali | 283.9 | 3.6 |
| Niger | 278.2 | 3.5 |
| Tanzania | 224.8 | 2.9 |
| Sub-total | 3,273.1 | 41.7 |
| TOTAL ACP | 7,850.9 | 100.0 |

*Source*: Eurostat (1988: 208).

## The Geographical Distribution of EC Aid

Tables 15.12 and 15.13 give an indication of which ACP states receive the most EC aid through the EDF and Stabex.

With respect to the distribution of payments by the EDF, it can be seen that the 'top ten' recipients, all from Sub-Saharan Africa, received over 41 per cent of the total over the period 1960–88. Francophone countries received approximately three-quarters of the total funding accounted for by the 'top ten'.

The EC agrees upon a 'National Indicative Programme' with each ACP state, but the allocation of aid between the ACP states is decided upon by the EC unilaterally and according to its own, unpublished criteria. Recent statistical analysis (Anyadike-Danes and Anyadike-Danes 1992) suggests that, although population and per capita income are important criteria, as too is the special status accorded to the 'least developed' ACP states, African ACP states on average have benefited more than non-African members, and Lomé aid allocations have been influenced by pre-Lomé associations with the EC (the AASM members).

The geographical distribution of Stabex transfers, shown in Table 15.13, is 'easier' to explain, depending as it does on the export performance of the commodities covered by the scheme. However, African economies are the major beneficiaries (Senegal and Côte d'Ivoire accounted for over one-quarter of total transfers over the period 1975–85) and Papua New Guinea is the only non-African recipient in the 'top ten'.

The French commitment to Africa, in particular, is very strong, and reflects the notion of 'Eurafricanism'—the idea that Europe and Africa

TABLE 15.13. *Geographical distribution of Stabex transfers 1975–1985*

| Country | Total (Ecu m.) | % of total |
|---|---|---|
| Senegal | 237.8 | 16.0 |
| Côte d'Ivoire | 158.3 | 10.6 |
| Sudan | 142.5 | 9.6 |
| Papua New Guinea | 97.1 | 6.5 |
| Ghana | 90.6 | 6.1 |
| Ethiopia | 60.2 | 4.0 |
| Tanzania | 50.5 | 3.4 |
| Kenya | 44.9 | 3.0 |
| Togo | 42.2 | 2.8 |
| Mauritania | 37.0 | 2.5 |
| Sub-total | 961.1 | 64.5 |
| TOTAL TRANSFERS | 1,487.8 | 100.0 |

*Source*: Eurostat (1988: 210).

are organic complements for one another (Lister 1992). Others might interpret the relationship as one of dependency and domination.

## 15.6. CONCLUSIONS

As Panić (1992) has noted, few countries have had as much experience with foreign aid as the Member States of the EC. They were large recipients of aid during and after the Second World War (both relief aid and assistance under the Marshall Plan). With post-war reconstruction complete, they have become the most important donors of ODA, along with the United States and Japan.

As we have argued above, all aid, and the aid relationship itself, is open to criticism, and EC aid is no exception in this respect. The size, nature, and the effectiveness of EC ODA have been subject to criticism, not least because of the long lags between commitment and actual disbursement. The EC aid programme, in addition, has been attacked 'for its failure to carry out adequate preliminary studies and to adapt projects to local conditions' (Panić 1992: 12).

These criticisms are not unique to EC ODA and by international standards the EC is not a 'bad' donor. In the Lomé IV Convention, there are provisions for the more systematic and independent assessment of projects and for greater preference to be given to local enterprises in carrying out those projects. There is a desire to increase aid co-ordination between Member States (see below) and to give greater attention to the longer-term viability of EC ODA-funded projects.

## The Impact of 1992 on Development Co-operation

The Single European Market (SEM) is likely to have a profound impact on Third World countries in general and the ACP states in particular. LDCs will be affected by growth and trade policy changes implied by the EC's internal-market programme, and there are implications too for issues such as direct foreign investment and international migration (Koekkoek, Kuyvenhoven, and Molle 1990).

There are, however, no direct references to development aid in the plan to complete the SEM. Stevens (1992) nevertheless outlines four main reasons why '1992' could have an effect both on the absolute amount of aid and its distribution:

1. *Procurement*: it would be logical to extend current moves to open government procurement so that all Member States can tender for aid contracts from any individual Member State (that is, the abolition of tying aid by source within the EC). Greater competition between Member States for aid contracts would, other things being equal, increase the value of aid.
2. *Aid volume*: if procurement-tying was abolished, aid volumes might fall (Member States could no longer use aid programmes to support domestic industries, for example).
3. *Aid channels*: more open procurement could lead to a greater proportion of Member States' ODA being channelled through multilateral institutions, including EC institutions (although there is no guarantee that multilateral aid will always avoid the drawbacks of bilateral ODA (Panić 1992: 17)).
4. *Aid diversion*: this has both intra- and extra-EC dimensions; intra-EC in that there may be a diversion of budgetary expenditures towards Member States adversely affected by the creation of the SEM (that is, away from ODA); extra-EC in that there may be a tendency to offer additional ODA to those LDCs most adversely affected by other consequences of the SEM (towards the Caribbean and the Mediterranean states, for example).

As yet, there has not been a diversion of aid from the LDCs towards Eastern Europe and Russia, and financial aid to those areas is additional to conventional development aid (Stevens 1992: 30). In the medium term, however, Stevens suggests that the boundary between middle-income LDCs and Eastern Europe states may become blurred, and there is certainly concern amongst Third World aid recipients that such diversion will occur increasingly in the future.

Panić (1992) concludes that only if the SEM succeeds in raising and in equalizing the efficiency and income levels of Member States will it have a significant effect on ODA, but that 'whether individual Governments like it or not, the successful creation of the SEM would represent the first step towards much greater political as well as economic unification in Western Europe; and this would bring about a major shift in the Community's ODA in favour of centralised development assistance policies' (1992: 16).

## Towards the Year 2000

The Commission itself has highlighted some of these issues in its own development policy statements (see *Courier*, (1992*b*)).

It points to the lack of co-ordination between national and EC development co-operation policies, the lack of consistency between the latter and other EC policies, and the lack of a 'European expression and stimulus' in international bodies.

Article 130X (Title XVII) of the Treaty on European Union (TEU), provides for the co-ordination of development co-operation policies and for consultation between Member States and the EC on aid programmes.

The objectives of development co-operation policy are to 'encourage the consolidation of democracy within the developing countries, within the framework of a return to political stability'. The aims of Article 130U(1) of the TEU are to ensure that:

- the developing countries, especially the least developed, have lasting economic and social development;
- the developing countries gradually and harmoniously fit into the international economy; and
- poverty in the developing countries is combated.

With respect to regional variations in policy:

- *Sub-Saharan Africa*: EC priority support will go to policies aimed at economic restructuring and the democratic reform of the administration of those countries.
- *The Mediterranean*: emphasis will be placed on technical assistance to strengthen institutional reform and regional and economic co-operation.
- *Latin America*: emphasis will be on policy dialogue and the promotion of investment and the private sector.
- *Asia*: emphasis will be on boosting the EC's presence in the region (through trade and investment) and on increasing awareness of environmental issues. The least developed countries will continue to receive conventional development aid.

Pious exhortation and vague policy statements do not, of course, make for good development co-operation policies. The creation of the SEM and the coming into force of the TEU will bring about changes which will affect the different regions and countries of the Third World in different, and unpredictable, ways. The move to more aid being made available through multilateral channels is not unambiguously beneficial to recipients if at the same time it is accompanied by greater (and perhaps inappropriate or unacceptable) conditionality. The bilateral aid programmes of EC Member States will continue to be of importance, and it would be foolish to predict likely future changes in those programmes. Much will continue to depend on the quality of the aid relationship between donors and recipients and, more widely, on the overall development relationship, which will include issues of trade policy, market access, non-concessional resource transfers, and broader questions such as environmental concerns and international migration.

# REFERENCES

Anyadike-Danes, M. K., and Anyadike-Danes, M. N. (1992), 'The Geographic Allocation of the European Development Fund under the Lomé Conventions', *World Development*, 20/11 (Nov.), 1647–61.

Bhagwati, J. (1967), 'The Tying of Aid', UNCTAD Secretariat, TD/7/Supp.4, United Nations; repr. in J. Bhagwati and R. S. Eckaus (eds.), *Foreign Aid* (Harmondsworth: Penguin, 1970), 235–93.

Cassen, R. *et al.* (1986), *Does Aid Work?* (Oxford: Clarendon Press).

CEC (1990): Commission of the European Communities, *The Community Budget: The Facts in Figures*, 3rd edn. (Luxemburg: CEC).

—— Directorate-General for Development (1992), *The Role of the Commission in Supporting Structural Adjustment in ACP States* (Luxemburg: CEC).

*Courier* (1990), 120 (Mar.–Apr., Brussels).

—— (1992*a*), 132 (Mar.–Apr., Brussels).

—— (1992*b*), 134 (July–Aug., Brussels).

Eurostat (1988), *ACP Basic Statistics* (Luxemburg).

Frisch, D. (1992), 'The European Community's Development Policy in a Changing World', the Second Bradford Development Lecture, Oct., mimeo.

Glaser, T. (1990), 'EEC–ACP Cooperation: The Historical Perspective', *Courier*, 120 (Mar.–Apr.), 24–8.

Hewitt, A. (1983), 'Stabex: An Evaluation of the Economic Impact over the First Five Years', *World Development*, 11/2 (Dec.), 1005–27.

Koekkoek, A., Kuyvenhoven, A., and Molle, W. (1990), 'Europe 1992 and the Developing Countries: An Overview', *Journal of Common Market Studies*, 29/2 (Dec.), 111–31.

Lister, M. R. P. (1992), 'The European Community and Africa: A Development Regime', paper presented to Annual Conference, Development Studies Association, Nottingham, mimeo.

Mosley, P. (1987), *Overseas Aid: Its Defence and Reform* (Brighton: Wheatsheaf).

—— (1991), 'Structural Adjustment: A General Overview, 1980–9', in V. N. Balasubramanyam and S. Lall (eds.), *Current Issues in Development Economics* (Basingstoke: Macmillan), 223–42.

OECD (1991): Organization for Economic Co-operation and Development, *Development Co-operation: 1991 Report* (Paris: OECD).

—— (1992), *Development Co-operation: 1992 Report* (Paris: OECD).

Panić, M. (1992), 'The Single Market and Official Development Assistance: The Potential for Multilateralising and Raising EC Assistance', *Journal of Development Planning*, 22 (New York: United Nations), 3–17.

Riddell, R. (1987), *Foreign Aid Reconsidered* (London: James Curry).

Singer, H. (1965), 'External Aid: For Plans or Projects?', *Economic Journal*, 75: 539–45; repr. in J. Bhagwati and R. S. Eckaus (eds.), *Foreign Aid* (Harmondsworth: Penguin, 1970), 294–302.

Stevens, C. (1990), 'The Lomé Convention', in K. Kiljunen (ed.), *Region-to-Region Cooperation between Developed and Developing Countries: The Potential for Mini NIEO* (Aldershot: Avebury, Gower Publishing Co.), 77–88.

—— (1992), 'The Single Market, All-European Integration and the Developing Countries: The Potential for Aid Diversion', *Journal of Development Planning*, 22: 19–35.

White, H. (1992), 'The Macroeconomic Impact of Development Aid: A Critical Survey', *Journal of Development Studies*, 28/2 (Jan.), 163–240.

# Discussion Questions

1. How far has economic integration within the EU been subordinated to the achievement of political objectives?
2. How far has the ceding of sovereignty to supranational institutions influenced the course of economic integration within Europe?
3. 'The shape of the EU's institutions reflects the need to harness national and common interests to the pursuit of specific policy goals'. Do you agree?

CHAPTER 2

1. What are the main problems involved in making international comparisons of countries' GDP? Illustrate with respect to the Member States of the EU.
2. Outline the Maastricht 'convergence criteria'. How closely do the EU countries appear to be meeting these?
3. Describe how you would assess the level of development and the economic strength of an economy. Illustrate your answer by reference to the Member States of the EU.

CHAPTER 3

1. Define a customs union and a free trading area. With the aid of diagrams explain how their formation results in trade creation and trade diversion, and the effect of these on the welfare of member countries.
2. Under what circumstances is a country likely to benefit from the greater exploitation of economies of scale by joining a customs union?

CHAPTER 4

1. Analyse and compare the effects of marketing quotas and reductions in support prices to control production within the EC.
2. Explain the 'reform' measures which the EC has taken to restrict the trade distorting effects of the CAP. To what extent can these be explained by pressure exerted on the EC in the Uruguay Round of GATT negotiations?
3. What factors determine the participation of farmers in the voluntary

arable land set-aside scheme of the CAP? What groups will be the main beneficiaries of the reform of the cereals policy?

## CHAPTER 5

1. Outline the main objectives of EU competition policy? What are the main problems facing the EU in developing a more effective competition policy?

2. What is meant by a 'dominant market position'? What are the main economic problems likely to arise from the exercise of market power by dominant firms within the EU? How might these problems be best resolved?

## CHAPTER 6

1. What sorts of activities in science and technology do you think national governments should support and why? Illustrate, using specific examples.

2. Why have industrial policies for supporting 'national champions' proved disappointing in Europe? What lessons can be drawn from such experiences?

3. What do you consider to be the major problems facing the EU in the construction and implementation of its policy towards science and technology?

## CHAPTER 7

1. The UK has had various forms of regional policy for many decades, yet spatial disparities in the unemployment rate have failed to narrow. Does this mean that regional policy has been a failure?

2. Compare and contrast the different approaches to regional policy adopted by the larger Member States of the EU.

3. Individual Member States of the EU have their own regional policies. Is there any need, therefore, to have a regional policy for the EU as a whole?

## CHAPTER 8

1. Explain why the pace of change in the Common Transport Policy was much slower prior to the mid-1980s than it has been subsequently.

2. What have been the main economic consequences which have resulted from the harmonization measures within the Common Transport Policy? To what extent are such measures consistent with the achievement of efficiency and equity objectives?

3. What are the main problems which remain to be addressed through a Common Transport Policy and by what means should their solution be sought?

## CHAPTER 9

1. What are the respective advantages and disadvantages of regulatory instruments and economic instruments when used to achieve environmental policy objectives within the EU?

2. Explain why monetary measures of environmental benefits and dis-benefits could be useful in environmental policy formulation within the EU. Why is it so difficult to obtain reliable measures in practice?

3. How might future EU environmental policies best contribute to the attainment of sustainable development?

## CHAPTER 10

1. Why has the process of economic integration within the European Union not been matched by any comparable convergence in the sphere of social policy?

2. For what reasons, in what ways and with what success did the EC seek to enhance the role of social policy during the period from the mid-1980s to the ratification of the Maastricht Treaty?

3. Outline and assess the main alternative views about the 'proper' aims and methods of European Union social policy.

## CHAPTER 11

1. What problems has the Commission of the European Communities encountered in trying to ensure 'fair play' between Member States and to prevent them from surreptitiously subsidising their indigenous firms? Give examples.

2. How has the EC employed the provisions of the Multi-Fibre Arrangements to protect its textile and clothing industries? Explain with the aid of diagrams who has benefited and who has lost as a consequence. What problems are involved in moving to a more liberal system as required by the GATT Uruguay round?

3. Why has the EC negotiated 'Voluntary Export Restraints' and imposed anti-dumping duties on imports of consumer electronic products? Has it employed any other non-tariff barriers? Illustrate your answer with examples.

CHAPTER 12

1. The operation of the ERM prior to the 1992 crisis is often considered to have been a major success. Outline how this success might be measured. Do the findings justify this view?

2. The ERM was initially conceived as providing symmetric adjustment for all participants. What is meant by symmetry in this context? How was this property built into the ERM? To what extent has the system operated symmetrically in practice?

3. Outline the sequence of events leading up to the 1992–3 crisis in the ERM. To what extent do you think the crisis was avoidable?

CHAPTER 13

1. Describe the nature of the costs and benefits of European Monetary Union.

2. What are the key features of the statutes of the European Central Bank? What is their economic significance?

3. Why do the Maastricht criteria for membership of a European Monetary Union specify conditions pertaining to fiscal policy? How compelling do you find these arguments?

CHAPTER 14

1. Outline the main features of the 'own resource' system of funding the European Community. To what extent would this system have changed under the proposals of the Delors' II reform?

2. What are the main arguments for and against a continuing budgetary rebate for the UK? To what extent has the EC's response in this respect been a success?

3. Outline the difficulties encountered in constructing measures of budgetary incidence for Member States of the EC. To what extent do net contributions of the individual Member States reflect the distribution of net benefits across the Community?

CHAPTER 15

1. Compare and contrast the record of the major EC aid donors during the 1980s.

2. What are the main factors which influence the 'aid relationship' between EU donors and ACP recipients?

3. Discuss the main changes that have occurred over time in the Lomé Conventions.

# INDEX

432          *Index*